100 YEARS IN CELEBRATION OF
THE AMERICAN DREAM

THE NATIONAL ASSOCIATION OF REALTORS®

100 YEARS IN CELEBRATION OF
THE AMERICAN DREAM

Edited by Stacey Moncrieff

Published by Wiley Publishing, Inc.

For information about the NATIONAL ASSOCIATION OF REALTORS®, visit REALTOR.org or call 800-874-6500.

ISBN-13: 9780470178171
ISBN-10: 0470178175

Manufactured and printed in the United States of America

NATIONAL ASSOCIATION OF REALTORS®

The Voice for Real Estate

Foreword

REALTORS® occupy a unique place in American society.

As businesspeople whose livelihoods are tied to the health of our local markets, we're deeply engaged in our communities. As mostly self-employed entrepreneurs, we're firm believers in the American spirit of free enterprise. As sales practitioners, appraisers, and managers of real estate assets, we're unabashed optimists about the long-term value of real property. We're also dedicated to the principle that property ownership is critical to a free and democratic society and committed to promoting and maintaining the highest level of professionalism in our industry.

These core beliefs have guided the evolution of the NATIONAL ASSOCIATION OF REALTORS® from its very start in May 1908. Through two World Wars, the Great Depression, the Civil Rights Movement, the fall of communism in Eastern Europe, and the advance of technology, REALTORS® have stood as standard bearers for our profession and champions of the American dream, in the United States and around the world.

Today, NAR represents a diverse mix of more than 1.3 million men and women. As we embark on our second century, we recall the words of Daniel H. Burnham, the renowned architect and city planner who was a contemporary of NAR's founders: "Make no little plans. They have no magic to stir men's blood."

Perhaps those words served as inspiration to the early leaders of NAR. Burnham went on to say, "Remember that our sons and grandsons [and today he might add daughters and granddaughters] are going to do things that would stagger us." Looking toward the future of the NATIONAL ASSOCIATION OF REALTORS®, we're confident that's so.

Pat V. Combs
2007 NAR President

Richard F. Gaylord
2008 NAR President

Table of Contents

Preface. ix

Introduction xiii

Chapter 1
The Start of Something Big I

Chapter 2
Home Ownership in America 35

Chapter 3
Walking the Walk 79

Chapter 4
Evolving Conscience IO7

Chapter 5
City Sculptors I47

Chapter 6
March of Progress I93

Presidents of NAR and Timeline 280

Notes 297

Bibliography 305

Index 323

Preface

When we set out to commemorate the first 100 years of the NATIONAL ASSOCIATION OF REALTORS®, we knew it would be no easy task. Rather than compiling a chronological history, we identified themes to highlight NAR's most significant contributions. Writing the history was complicated by the fact that the Association has had two name changes in its 100-year history. It started in 1908 as the National Association of Real Estate Exchanges. From 1916 to 1972, it was named the National Association of Real Estate Boards and was commonly known by its acronym, NAREB. However, another real estate organization, the National Association of Real Estate Brokers, also uses the acronym NAREB. To avoid confusion, the book uses NAR, or Association, throughout. The term REALTOR® was adopted by NAR in 1916 as a designation signifying Association membership. However, the term wasn't registered with the United States Patent and Trademark Office until 1949 (for REALTORS®) and 1950 (for REALTOR®). For consistency and out of respect for the trademark, we have used the term with the registration symbol in most places.

We received copyright permission from a variety of sources for photographs and other images. In all cases—except for photos in the public domain—the copyrights remain in force. Anyone seeking to reuse an image from the book should contact the copyright holder for permission.

The development of this book has spanned three years, and numerous individuals contributed to its completion.

CONTRIBUTORS

Elizabeth Arthur is a research analyst at Threshold Information, a research firm based in Evanston, Illinois. She wrote about the origin and defense of the REALTOR® trademark and contributed profiles of the Association's long-time general counsel Nathan William MacChesney and the coiner of *Realtor*, Charles Chadbourn. Elizabeth has a master's degree in Library and Information Science from the University of Illinois Urbana–Champaign. She is the former archives manager for NAR and provided needed inspiration at the start of this project.

Barbara Ballinger resides in St. Louis where she frequently writes about real estate, interior design, and family business for Harris Publications, the *Chicago Tribune, i4 Design* magazine, *Robb Report, Developer,* and *REALTOR® Magazine*. She was a major contributor to the book, writing about the Association's advocacy of home ownership, as well as a good portion of the final chapter, which covers NAR's role in the evolution of the business. She also profiled J.C. Nichols, a remarkable pioneer in the development of planned communities. Barbara is the author and co-author of a dozen books, including *Successful Home Building and Remodeling* (Kaplan, 1998). She has a bachelor's degree from Barnard College/Columbia University and a master's degree from Hunter College. She has two grown daughters.

Brad Broberg is a free-lance writer specializing in business, real estate, and health care. He's a regular contributor to *On Common Ground,* a magazine published by NAR that focuses on smart growth. For this book, Brad wrote about NAR's role as a pioneer in community planning and its more recent leadership in smart growth. Before he became a free-lance writer, Brad worked for more than 20 years as a newspaper reporter and editor in South King County, Washington. He lives in Federal Way, Washington, with his 13-year-old daughter.

Damian Da Costa specializes in writing about community development issues and was the principal writer of the chapter on fair housing and NAR's changing role—from antagonist to advocate. He holds degrees from Yale University and the Graduate Center of the City University of New York and lives in Brooklyn. Damian worked on this project in collaboration with Magnificent Publications, a Washington, D.C.–based company that organizes teams of writers, editors, designers, and other communications professionals to assist clients on complex communications projects.

Robert Freedman is a senior editor of *REALTOR® Magazine* and edited *Broker to Broker* (John Wiley & Sons, 2005), a compilation of residential real estate brokerage best practices drawn from the magazine. He is a specialist in federal legislative and regulatory affairs; for this book, he documented NAR's growing influence on Capitol Hill. Rob is also a past president of the American Society of Business Publication Editors and author of the book *Second Life Business Strategies* (McGraw-Hill, 2007), a look at how organizations are leveraging virtual reality technology for marketing and business development. Rob holds a master's degree in humanities from Marymount University in Arlington, Virginia. He lives in Alexandria, Virginia, with his wife, Sandy, and their daughter.

Jim Hatfield has written magazines articles, speeches, video scripts, and Web copy for businesses and organizations, including Allstate, Motorola, Microsoft, NAR, and Sara Lee. For this book, he wrote on the technology revolution and profiled the Association's 11 chief executives. Jim has written for television in Los Angeles, San Francisco, and Chicago, where he received 16 local Emmys as executive producer of public affairs and magazine programming at WBBM-TV. He served as a public information officer in the U.S. Air Force in Los Angeles and at Cape Kennedy (today Cape Canaveral) in Florida. He holds a bachelor's degree from Grinnell College and a master's degree in journalism from Columbia University. He and his wife, Jane—a REALTOR®—live in Glen Ellyn, Illinois. They have two grown sons.

Frederik Heller is manager of the NAR archives and virtual library and is based in Chicago. He wrote about the founding of the Association, work that expanded on his *History of NAR,* written for the archives at *REALTOR.org.* He has been with the Association since 1990 and spent several years managing its Washington, D.C., resource center. Frederik has a bachelor's degree from Bates College and a master's in Library & Information Science from the Catholic University of America. Frederik has written extensively for both NAR and library professionals. He lives in Chicago with his wife and young son.

Benjamin Kende, a Chicago photographer, produced the photo collages that open each chapter. He is highly regarded for creating poetic and narrative still-life photographs for his clients, including national advertising agencies, graphic design firms, corporations, and professional associations. See more of his work at *www.kendephotography.com.*

Cliff Niersbach joined the NAR staff in 1975. He is currently vice president of Board Policy and Programs. Among his other responsibilities, Cliff has served as staff executive to the Association's Professional Standards Committee since 1978. For the book, Cliff wrote about the history of the NAR Code of Ethics. Cliff is a graduate of Northwestern University and the John Marshall Law School. He lives in Chicago with his wife, Diane, and their daughters Sarah and Suzanne.

Robert Sharoff writes about architecture and real estate for the *New York Times, Chicago Magazine,* and other publications. He contributed the portion of Chapter 5 covering the evolution of commercial real estate. He is the co-author—with architectural photographer William Zbaren—of the award-winning *American City: Detroit Architecture 1845–2005,* (Wayne State University Press), the first book published in more than 30 years on that city's historic architecture. He holds a master's degree from Northwestern University. In the late 1990s, Robert was an associate editor at *REALTOR® Magazine.* Robert lives in Chicago with Mr. Zbaren and their daughter, Ella.

ACKNOWLEDGMENTS

The NAR Information Central/Library staff provided invaluable assistance on the research for this book. Special thanks go to Russell Carlson for his enthusiastic research; Victoria Broady for her work scanning and organizing images; and Dionne Winchester for cataloging images. The timeline at the end of this book was based on one developed in 2005 by the Information Central/Library staff, and I thank them for their painstaking effort. In addition to Russell, Victoria, and Dionne, they are: Kerrie Walsh Bartlett, Catherine Dodge, Denise Foligno, Mary Glick, Frederik Heller, Karen Janisch, John Krukoff, Marion Leon, Mary Martinez, Donna McCormick, David Shumaker, Anne-Marie Siudzinsky, and Karen Swanson. Thanks also to former library staff member Jennifer Hazen.

The staff of *REALTOR® Magazine* has my undying gratitude for the patience they showed over the course of this project and for the assistance they provided along the way. I'm particularly grateful to Julie Fournier and Kathy Marusarz and former staffers Christina Hoffmann Spira and Ingar Quist. Karin Albright-Coleman, Isabella Mathews, and Jennifer Reihl also lent an organizational hand. To the magazine's publisher, Frank J. Sibley, and editorial director, Pamela Geurds Kabati, thank you for stepping forward to seek funding for this project and for entrusting it to me.

Members of the NAR Centennial Team and other NAR staff cheered me on and provided great ideas and insights. Among them was Nancy Wilson Smith, who shared the knowledge and wisdom she gained in 34 years on the NAR staff. Len Tovar helped connect me with many past NAR presidents, who provided oral histories to my friend and colleague, Gabriella Filisko. Jeffrey Hornstein's outstanding book, *A Nation of REALTORS®* (Duke University Press, 2005) provided inspiration and direction to all the writers of this book; I'm grateful to him for his diligent scholarship and his review of a portion of this book. Fred Underwood provided important direction for our discussion of fair housing. Miriam Lowe, Jack Howley, and Carol Weinrich documented NAR's international impact. Their work was the basis for the international history found in Chapter 6. This book also owes much to the late Pearl Janet Davies, author of the 1958 book *Real Estate in American History.*

Thanks to those who contributed imagery, including Amy Baird of the Greater Baltimore Board of REALTORS®; Doug Damerst of the Florida Association of REALTORS®; Rachel Dobbins of the Seattle-King County Association of REALTORS®; REALTOR® Paul Everson of Cleveland; Belton Jennings of the Orlando Association of REALTORS®; Gary Krysler and Dianna Dearen of the Women's Council of REALTORS®; Diane G. Scherer of the Phoenix Association of REALTORS®; the Plymouth & South Shore Association of REALTORS® and former NAR presidents Norm Flynn and Cathy Whatley. I'm deeply grateful.

Finally, thanks to my husband, Bruce, for his good advice and encouragement and my children, Nathan, Celeste, and Adam, for their love and support during this project.

Stacey Moncrieff
Editor-in-Chief, REALTOR® Magazine
August 2007

Introduction

"Under all is the land. Upon its wise utilization and widely allocated ownership depend the survival and growth of free institutions and of our civilization."
—from the preamble of *the NATIONAL ASSOCIATION OF REALTORS® Code of Ethics*

Could the founding fathers of the NATIONAL ASSOCIATION OF REALTORS®, who first gathered in Chicago in 1908, possibly have foreseen the tremendous impact an organized real estate industry would have on the evolution of the United States of America? The opening lines of the preamble to the REALTORS® Code of Ethics—added in 1924, about a decade after the original Code was adopted—seem to demonstrate a visionary understanding by these early real estate practitioners that their work would have a profound impact on shaping our society and its values.

And, indeed, over the last 100 years, the National Association and its members have had just such an impact, helping to establish home ownership as a cornerstone of the American Dream and advocacy of private property rights as one of the fundamental principles that unite us as Americans. Thanks in part to NAR and its members, the home ownership rate in the United States reached nearly 70 percent in 2006, up from 46.5 percent in 1900, and consumers today have more choices then ever in terms of property styles and locations. Real estate has emerged as a key driver in the nation's economy, with residential and commercial real estate accounting for 19.3 percent of the gross domestic product in 2006. NAR and its members now serve as the collective "Voice for Real Estate" for industry professionals and property owners nationwide. Research connected with the Association's Public Awareness Campaign—a national advertising program launched in 1998—shows that public trust of REALTORS® is at an all-time high.

This book—published to commemorate the organization's centennial in 2008—details the contributions NAR has made within U.S. borders and beyond over the past century. From these details, five contributions emerge as REALTORS®' most significant to date:

1. **Professionalization of the Real Estate Industry.** When they gathered in Chicago in 1908, the founders of the National Association of Real Estate Exchanges, as it was then called, wanted to bring professionalism to their ranks and differentiate themselves from the "sharks" and "curbstoners" who called themselves real estate professionals.

Page Carter of Kansas City, Missouri, chaired the committee that created the first Code of Ethics, adopted in 1913, as guidelines for how to conduct business in an upright manner. At the 1913 convention in Winnepeg, Canada, Carter said the Code could never tell people specifically what to do in a given situation. The word ethics, he pointed out, derives from a Greek word meaning character, and the Code could only guide ethical real estate men to operate in keeping with their own character and their own sense of right. Carter quoted former President Theodore Roosevelt, who in a speech at Harvard University in 1910, said, "It is the practical work of realizing the ethical principle in action that finally counts."

Today, REALTORS® are required to have regular ethics training, and adherence to NAR's Code of Ethics is one of the things that sets them apart from other real estate practitioners. The Code has been through many revisions since its adoption in 1913; the current Code is available at the Association's Web site, REALTOR.org.

2. **Promotion of Home Ownership and Private Property Rights.** Although the founding fathers of organized real estate first came together to promote professionalism in their business, another of the group's early aims, and just as important, was to educate the public about the many benefits of real estate ownership. Early in the 20th century, the association began collaborating with governmental agencies, other associations, civic groups, and private businesses to spread the concept that home ownership represented financial security and social stability, it invested people in the quality of life in their communities, and it created a reason for people to become involved in those communities—in short, it was a privilege worth sacrificing for.

To make the ideal of home ownership a reality for more Americans, NAR has worked closely with the federal government over the years. The Association was a key player in the creation of the Federal Housing Administration in 1934, which helped opened the doors of homeownership to moderate-income families. NAR also influenced the development of the Federal National Mortgage Association (Fannie Mae) in 1938 and, in 1970, the Federal Home Loan Mortgage Corp., government-sponsored enterprises that created a secondary market for mortgages, ensuring a steady, low-cost supply of financing for home purchases. Later, NAR championed tools such a mortgage revenue bonds to make lower-cost funding available to first-time buyers. Today, through its Housing Opportunity Program, NAR is bringing its considerable influence to bear on local governments and employers, advocating for affordable workforce housing.

As the preamble to the Code of Ethics makes clear, the Association strongly believes that property ownership is not only good for people and communities but essential to a free society. The Association's 2003 president, Catherine Whatley of Jacksonville, Fla., explained REALTORS®' passionate commitment to private property rights, including favorable tax treatment for property owners, in a column she wrote for REALTOR® Magazine, NAR's membership publication, during her presidency. "NAR's efforts to protect property rights are an extension of our country's highest ideals," she said. "Historians tell us that colonists came to the 'New World' seeking not just religious liberty. Many also sought to improve their lot through ownership of land. Pre-Revolutionary philosophers and scholars, such as John Locke and William Blackstone, regarded private property rights as fundamental to individual liberty. Their writings helped influence the migration to the New World and shape the thinking of the revolutionary movement, with its motto 'Liberty and property.' And their beliefs gained the weight of constitutional protection with ratification of the Fifth Amendment in 1791 and the 14th Amendment in 1868."

REALTORS®' support of property rights doesn't end at America's borders. Over the years, NAR and its members have reached around the globe, playing a key role in fostering an organized system of private property ownership in other countries through the International Consortium of Real Estate Associations (ICREA), founded in 2001, and the International Real Property Foundation, which NAR established in 1992 as the Eastern European Real Property Foundation to help create orderly real estate markets within the former Soviet Union and its sphere of influence. Later, the foundation expanded its work into other developing countries and, so, broadened its name.

3. **Creation of an Organized System for the Purchase and Exchange of Real Estate.** As the original name of NAR—the National Association of Real Estate Exchanges—suggests, one of the ways the early pioneers of real estate were striving to bring order to real estate markets was through the creation of listing exchanges. By organizing nationally, these leaders evolved the practice and policies of sharing listings among competitors in a system known as the

Multiple Listing Service. Ultimately, the MLS became the vehicle through which real estate could be bought and sold with order, ease, and an assurance of honesty—and the MLS of today still fundamentally serves this purpose.

Exactly when and where the first MLS was founded is a matter of debate: some sources identify the first system as having been created as early as 1887 in San Diego, while others claim it was in 1907 in Cincinnati. Regardless of the timing, the idea behind the MLS was clear from the start, as expressed by one of its possible originators, William A. Keadin of Cincinnati: "I conceived the idea of establishing more friendly and honorable methods in the business between brokers by interchanging their listings through a central bureau, or clearinghouse, thereby creating more confidence between owners, agents, as well as the courts, and assuring owners under exclusive contracts the concerted action of the members of the bureau."

In 1956, the national association convened its first Committee on Multiple Listing Policy at its convention in St. Louis. Ten years later, NAR conducted its first MLS survey, with the published information about practices viewed as a boon to real estate professionals. At the time, 44 percent of the real estate boards who responded to the survey had an MLS. In 1972, the Association wrote its first *Handbook on Multiple Listing Policy*, which was intended to guide member local boards of REALTORS® in how to operate an MLS for optimum service and efficiency.

Today, more than 200,000 locally owned real-estate offices and branches of real estate firms use the nation's more than 900 MLSs, most of which remain local. And while there is no national MLS serving the real estate industry, the NAR Web site REALTOR.com provides the public with a single source of information about homes listed for sale around the country.

4. **Promotion of Equal Opportunity for All.** In the 39 years since the passage of the Fair Housing Act, NAR has evolved into a true leader in the promotion of equal housing opportunity—developing landmark education for its members, seeding programs for minority home buyers, seeking out a more diverse membership, and building bridges with minority real estate associations.

In 1975, NAR joined the U.S. Department of Housing and Urban Development and the U.S. Department of Justice to formulate the Voluntary Affirmative Marketing Agreement (VAMA), a set of guidelines that clarified REALTORS®' rights and responsibilities under the original Fair Housing Act of 1968. The VAMA, designed to help strengthen the act, marked a turning point in NAR's relationship with the federal government, creating a sense of teamwork between the two entities that continues to this day. In 1996, the HUD/NAR Fair Housing Partnership replaced the VAMA, refocusing joint efforts toward identifying and eradicating the causes of housing discrimination.

In 2001, NAR joined with several other real estate organizations to create the HOPE (Home Ownership Participation for Everyone) Awards, the first of their kind. Every two years, the HOPE Awards—presented in partnership with the Asian Real Estate Association of America, Chinese American Real Estate Professionals Association, Chinese Real Estate Association of America, National Association of Hispanic Real Estate Professionals, and National Association of Real Estate Brokers Inc.—gives $10,000 apiece to individuals or organizations whose programs have demonstrated a benefit to minority home ownership.

NAR also now offers a certification course to help REALTORS® understand and embrace racial and ethnic diversity in the marketplace, called "At Home with Diversity," as well as a Diversity Tool Kit and an active Equal Opportunity and Cultural Diversity Committee that has among its missions to make REALTORS® leaders in a real estate environment that is rich with cultural diversity. NAR today celebrates the country's racial and ethnic diversity and strives to make the benefits of real property ownership available to all.

5. **Building Community.** Organized real estate has long placed an emphasis on the importance of building community, through its members' roles in the early development of planned communities, NAR's founding role in the Urban Land

Institute, its influence in the Smart Growth and land-use planning debates of today, and its establishment of recognition programs to spotlight extraordinary REALTOR® community service.

Speaking at the 1924 NAR convention in Washington, D.C., J.C. Nichols of Kansas City, a father of community planning and an inspiration to today's new urbanists, said, "Cities are handmade. Whether they are physically bad or physically good, is the responsibility of the REALTOR®... Laboratories of research are needed in the real estate profession. *Realology* should be as much an established science as geology and zoology." From the early days of their organization, REALTORS® have felt a responsibility to build good communities—both in the physical and relationship sense.

In 2000, REALTOR® Magazine launched its Good Neighbor Awards program, to highlight the many leadership roles REALTORS® play in quality of life issues in their communities. Since then, winners of this award have been involved in service work around the country and around the world, from sheltering the homeless, to putting a class of low-income grade school children through college, to starting orphanages in Mexico and Romania. The award program gives grants of $10,000 each to the charities of five winners every year, and past winners form an active "Society of Good Neighbors" that seeks to promote and inspire community service nationwide.

The list of just some of the National Association's accomplishments over the last 100 years is impressive, to be sure. But NAR is a dynamic organization that continues to shape new aspects of its legacy every day, in its offices in Chicago, Illinois, and Washington, D.C., and in every city and town around the country where its members do business and make vibrant contributions to their communities and their industry.

Over the next 100 years, what will be REALTORS®' most significant contributions to our society? As the population of our country grows increasingly diverse, NAR and its members will most certainly continue to play a key role in helping new immigrants find their piece of the American Dream. And we expect NAR and its members to play a lead role in harnessing new technologies to further smooth and speed the real estate transaction for all involved parties. According to NAR's latest strategic plan, the organization in the coming years also seeks to strengthen its relationship with consumers—serving home owners and property investors through the entire lifecycle of ownership, instead of just primarily the transaction—and more fully realizing NAR's role as The Voice for Real Estate®.

It's hard to predict in any detail what a picture of organized real estate might look like in 2108. With history as our teacher, we know that REALTORS® and the REALTOR® organization will face the future with bold ideas and bright, pioneering spirits. Former NAR Executive Vice President Almon R. "Bud" Smith once called REALTORS® some of the country's last, great pioneers, earning their living as business entrepreneurs and seeing land, homes, buildings, and communities not so much for what's there, but for what's possible. Clearly, these pioneers helped ground the values of our country over the last century, and they will undoubtedly help shape those values in the 100 years ahead. It's to these people—the nation's REALTORS®—that this book is warmly dedicated.

Pamela Geurds Kabati
Vice President and Editorial Director, Publications, NAR

Frank J. Sibley
Senior Vice President, Communications, NAR

100 YEARS IN CELEBRATION OF

THE AMERICAN
DREAM

CHAPTER ONE

The Start of Something Big

The strength of the NATIONAL ASSOCIATION OF REALTORS® today reflects the ambitious vision of its founders: the 120 men who gathered in May 1908 at a Young Men's Christian Association hall in Chicago. Their stated goal was "to unite the real estate men of America for the purpose of exerting effectively a combined influence upon matters affecting real estate interests."

It wasn't the first attempt to organize a national association for the real estate industry, but the visionary players involved and the timing of the meeting made this an effort that was destined to succeed. The country had recovered from a major depression, and the population—aided by a big influx of immigrants, mostly from Europe—was shifting from rural to urban. Real estate was becoming a complex business, one that required the assistance of someone in the know.

The founders sought to bring professionalism to an enterprise that had evolved more or less without rules. They understood that to earn the trust of a skeptical public, they needed to bring form and standards to the business of real estate. The foundation they built has proved enduring. What emerged from that meeting in 1908 was the National Association of Real Estate Exchanges, which 100 years later thrives as the NATIONAL ASSOCIATION OF REALTORS®.

"The most natural privilege of man, next to the right of acting for himself, is that of combining his exertions with those of his fellow creatures and of acting in common with them."

ALEXIS DE TOQUEVILLE, *Democracy in America*

Two million dollars. It was a shocking, unbelievable sum of money at the time, representing the hard work and hopes of dozens of unsuspecting people who had put their trust in the respected businessman.

Peter van Vlissingen had been known as one of Chicago's most reputable businessmen and a generous philanthropist before his arrest on November 16, 1908. Charged with forging mortgage documents and title deeds, he confessed to swindling 25 people out of $700,000 over the course of 18 years. Fearing for his own safety once the news of his arrest became public, he asked the court for a speedy trial, which he received: Arrested at 1:30 p.m., van Vlissingen was brought before the court, sentenced, and in prison by 5:15 that same afternoon. A few days later, the Illinois state's attorney discovered that van Vlissingen had, in fact, defrauded more than 100 people through forgeries totaling nearly $2 million. Outrage spread rapidly as news of the scandal was publicized in front-page headlines across the country.[1]

SEEDS OF A PROFESSION

Van Vlissingen's case brings into sharp focus the challenges facing honest real estate prac-titioners at the beginning of the twentieth century. Land had become a major commodity as the rapidly growing middle class began to aspire to home ownership. Although real estate was full of trustworthy, respectable men who truly wanted to help their fellow citizens, sharks like van Vlissingen were difficult to avoid. Almost anyone could declare himself a dealer in real estate, there were few effective laws to regulate them, and too many opportunities existed for fraud to take place.

The National Association of Realtors®'s first organizing meeting took place just a few months before van Vlissingen's arrest—and five blocks from where he had his offices. The need for an organized body of practitioners had surfaced gradually. From the colonial era through much of the nineteenth century, the buying and selling of real estate was a relatively simple process, with land usually sold at auction, given away by the government, or transferred through some agreement between owner and buyer.[2] As the population grew, so did demand for land. Larger tracts were divided into smaller parcels by investors and speculators, and land granted by the government to settlers or as compensation to former soldiers eventually needed to be resold. The transfer of land from one owner to another became more complex, creating a need for someone familiar with local real estate practices and available properties in the area.

Ed von Hosen Mervin Aferr Mr. Putnam · Phil Moessinger
Sam Thorne Brose Douglass R.S. Taylor Joseph P. Day W.H. Hannan Irving Hiett Nate Upham

Early members of the Association's Executive Committee kept the fledging association going, often ponying up funds beyond their dues. They were committed to the idea of a national association that would differentiate them from the cheats and "curbstoners" who called themselves real estate men.

People genuinely interested in providing a service and facilitating transactions stepped in to fill that need, but others more interested in their own financial gain also came along to offer their so-called assistance. Buyers and sellers were just as likely to encounter an unscrupulous real estate dealer as an honest one.[3] In cities where real estate activity was high, real estate practitioners began to form local organizations as a means of sharing information about properties for sale and becoming acquainted with other practitioners in the area who could be trusted.

The first such organization was the New York Real Estate Exchange, which was formed in 1847 and dissolved a year later.[4] It was followed more than a decade later by the Baltimore Board of Real Estate Brokers and Property Agents, formed in 1858 and still in existence today as the Greater Baltimore Board of REALTORS®. The

Baltimore board was formed for the purpose of "regulating the business of the real estate broker," according to its constitution. Members were obliged to respect their fellow brokers and follow the board's rules of ethics and were able to enjoy a convenient central marketplace for properties. Those who violated the rules were expelled from the board and had their name and reason for expulsion publicized in local newspapers. Recognizing the advantages a local exchange could offer both to real estate brokers and to the public, other rapidly growing cities followed in Baltimore's footsteps, forming boards and exchanges that would later become founding members of the NAR.

Practitioners who saw the value of organizing locally soon recognized the need to do so on a national level. Architects, bankers, doctors, educators, lawyers, and other professionals already had national organizations in place, but the real estate business remained unorganized beyond the local level.

EARLY ORGANIZING EFFORTS RUN AGROUND

Several early attempts were made to establish a national organization for real estate. The most successful of these was the short-lived National Real Estate Association, formed in Birmingham, Alabama, in 1891. At its initial meeting at the end of March that year, 31 delegates met with the intentions of improving conditions in the real estate business, creating uniform laws and regulations governing real estate transactions, and making real estate titles more secure. Thomas T. Wright of the Nashville (Tennessee) Real Estate Board was credited with the idea behind the new organization, and his city was selected as the location of the delegates' next meeting.

The Industrial Revolution brought tremendous growth to U.S. cities in the latter half of the 19th century, leading to the need for honest, knowledgeable real estate practitioners. Baltimore, pictured here in 1876, is the site of the oldest still-existing exchange. It was founded in 1858.

MARYLAND HISTORICAL SOCIETY

In Birmingham the members of the National Real Estate Association did little more than proclaim their objectives and set up the new organization. At the Nashville meeting in 1892, however, a stronger association began to take shape. Word of the effort to unite the business had spread. More than 800 real estate practitioners from 19 states assembled in the Senate Chamber of the Tennessee State Capitol. The meeting was proclaimed in news reports as "one of the largest assemblies of business men ever seen south of the Ohio River."[5] The delegates adopted a constitution and created an ambitious agenda that included establishing simplified, uniform laws to regulate real estate in each state; establishing uniform business principles and practices; gathering information and educating members about the business; encouraging greater understanding between agents, property owners, and buyers; discouraging "wild speculation and fictitious booms"; and building a "high standard of ethics among real estate men."

By March 1892 the National Real Estate

Association had 266 dues-paying members, primarily from Atlanta, Chicago, Duluth (Minnesota), and other fast-growing cities. At its next meeting, held from October 4 to October 6, 1892, in Buffalo, New York, 1,500 real estate men from almost every state and Canada attended. Speeches were

THE NATIONAL REAL ESTATE ASSOCIATION HAD NO MEANS OF COLLECTING DUES AND NO PAID EXECUTIVE OR STAFF.

Three years after its founding, the National Real Estate Association was gone, a victim of the economic crisis of 1893.

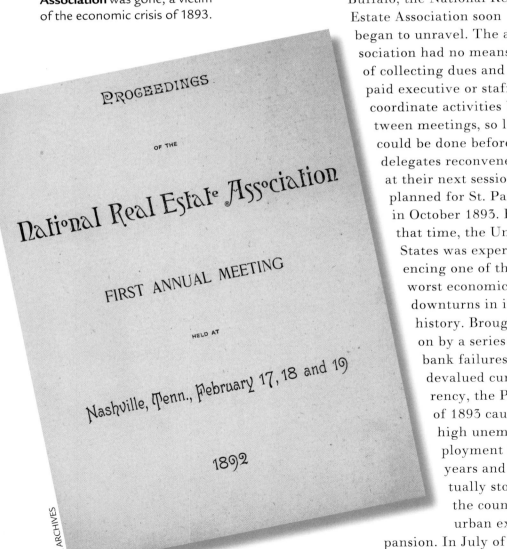

PROCEEDINGS

OF THE

National Real Estate Association

FIRST ANNUAL MEETING

HELD AT

Nashville, Tenn., February 17, 18 and 19

1892

given, committees were formed, and roundtables were held on such topics as property taxes, model appraisal forms, and the importance of ethics.

Although much was accomplished in Buffalo, the National Real Estate Association soon began to unravel. The association had no means of collecting dues and no paid executive or staff to coordinate activities between meetings, so little could be done before the delegates reconvened at their next session, planned for St. Paul in October 1893. By that time, the United States was experiencing one of the worst economic downturns in its history. Brought on by a series of bank failures and devalued currency, the Panic of 1893 caused high unemployment for years and virtually stopped the country's urban expansion. In July of that year, the National Real Estate

Association sponsored an international real estate congress in Chicago at the World's Columbian Exposition. By October, however, the association's membership was dwindling. The St. Paul meeting was abruptly canceled for lack of financing, and efforts to revive the association at a gathering in Milwaukee in early 1894 failed. The NREA was gone.

What began in Birmingham, though unsuccessful in its goal of creating a permanent national association, firmly planted the idea that such an organization was necessary for the future of the real estate business. The desire to unite nationally was not forgotten, even though it would not be attempted again until several years later. In the summer of 1904, a local exchange in Upstate New York called for a meeting in St. Louis to form a national association. The 100 delegates organized a new organization, also called the National Real Estate Association, with the objective of providing business services such as a national listing exchange and a low-interest loan bureau. Officers were elected and dues were set at $6 per year. The delegates met again in February and formed one of the oldest state associations still in existence today, the Real Estate Association of New York State. But after February 1905 the second national association went no further and, like its predecessor, disappeared from view.

PLEASE COME TO CHICAGO

What did not disappear, however, was the enthusiasm of real estate men from across the country for the idea of uniting their efforts in the form of a national organization. In July 1907 the Portland (Maine) Real Estate Association issued an invitation to all other local boards to gather in Maine for the purpose of forming a national real estate board. Most boards declined because Maine was too far for many of the delegates to travel, but the desire to form a national union wasn't going to be squelched. At a meeting of seven Midwestern real estate boards hosted in Duluth, Minnesota, on August 3, 1907, Edward Sanderson Judd of Chicago made the statement that ultimately launched the NATIONAL ASSOCIATION OF REALTORS®:

> *I wish to call to your attention the possible desirability of the formation of state, interstate, and national organizations of real estate men. If the idea of a national organization—or even a Central West organization—should meet with the approval of the seven associations here represented and of other such organizations as might care to join the movement, it may be possible to have a gathering at, say, Chicago [in] another year.*

Chicago, besides being centrally located, was already of considerable importance in the real estate world. The city had risen from the ashes of the Great Fire of 1871, establishing itself as a center for architecture. In 1885 Chicago became home to the world's first skyscraper, the nine-story Home Insurance Building. For the World's Columbian Exposition of 1893, organizer Daniel Burnham brought together a team of renowned architects. The resulting exposition complex—dubbed "The White City"—brought national attention to the city and

CHICAGO HISTORY MUSEUM

ushered in a wave of beaux arts style building. Furthermore, the real estate practitioners of the city were already well organized. The Chicago Real Estate Board, today the Chicago Association of REALTORS®, was founded in 1883. It's thought to have been the first board in the country whose primary mission was to set a bar for membership.

In short, Judd had selected the perfect location. His proposal was immediately accepted by the other six boards in attendance at the Duluth meeting. On March 15, 1908, the Chicago board sent invitations to the 45 real estate boards known to be active at the time.

One of the most popular stories after the Great Chicago Fire of 1871 was that of William D. Kerfoot, a real estate practitioner who would go on to become a leader in the Chicago Real Estate Board. The day after the fire ended, he opened for business in this shanty, posting a crude sign that said, "All gone but WIFE, CHILDREN, and ENERGY." The sign "made him seem the embodiment of the undaunted determination of Chicago entrepreneurs," according to the Chicago History Museum's online exhibition on the fire.

Recognizing that organizing nationally meant rethinking and reshaping the real estate business, the 120 delegates who came to Chicago in May 1908 set out to build an organization that would achieve that end. "An outcome of the gathering is to be a national organization of real estate men," explained an editorial in the *Chicago Tribune* shortly before the meeting began. "Such an association has been contemplated for a long time. It is strongly urged in the general interest of a business whose importance and influence have steadily increased during recent years."[6]

At the onset of the meeting, Edward A. Halsey, chair of the national organization committee, told those assembled that the primary duties of the new organization would be to adopt a uniform method of doing business and to make every effort to establish a unified system of real estate laws throughout the country. The Association must also find a way to eliminate the poorly qualified "curbstoners" and untrustworthy sharks who were injuring the real estate business. "In other words," Halsey said, "we propose, if we can, to wipe out the riffraff that brings this business into disrepute." It would become standard rhetoric at Association meetings as the organizers worked to establish themselves as the standard-bearers of the "square deal."

Most of the first day and night of the meeting were occupied with writing the Association's constitution and bylaws.

The 1893 World's Columbian Exposition helped make Chicago a center for architecture and a natural location for the first national real estate association.

Born Optimist

He was the man with the vision: Edward Sanderson Judd, the Association's fifth president, is credited with planting the seed that would grow into the NATIONAL ASSOCIATION OF REALTORS®. At a 1907 meeting in Duluth, Minnesota, Judd proposed a gathering of boards for the purpose of forming a national association.

"The real estate association of Portland, Maine, began the agitation for a national association," he once said, but Portland had been deemed too long a journey for many people. In truth, Judd himself had been thinking of the benefits of such an association for some time, according to the late NAR historian Pearl Janet Davies, who wrote in her unpublished 1957 book on the Association, *Real Estate Achievement in the United States:* "To him goes the honor of launching the idea successfully and of carrying it to fruition."

As Judd saw it, a national association would be a forum for discussing state legislative issues, comparing business strategies, and cultivating good fellowship. Notably, he never mentioned involvement in national legislative policy, though by the time of his presidency in 1912, the association was involved in debates over the national income tax, which became law in 1913.

Judd was a native New Englander and a graduate of Williams College in Massachusetts. He had worked as a reporter for the *St. Louis Globe-Democrat* before settling in Chicago, where he studied law at Union College of Law. After practicing law for three years, he entered the real estate business. In 1888 he became manager of the loan department of E. A. Cummings and Company, and in 1903 he founded his own real estate company, Edward S. Judd & Company. By the time the 1908 organizing meeting rolled around, he was serving as president of the Chicago Real Estate Board.

Active in Chicago civic life, Judd was a member of the Chicago City Plan Commission, a group of 328 men appointed in 1909 by Chicago Mayor Fred A. Busse to champion a new city plan. The plan had been developed by Daniel Hudson Burnham, the charismatic architect

Edward Sanderson Judd

NAR ARCHIVES

who had served as director of works for the 1893 World's Columbian Exposition in Chicago and who had designed such landmark buildings as the Flatiron Building in New York and Union Station in Washington, D.C. Burnham's plan called for beautification of the city, reclamation of the lakefront for public use, establishment of the city's forest preserves, and better living conditions for the people. It reflected the principles of the City Beautiful movement, which advocated for grandeur as a means of reversing urban decay.

It's no fluke that Judd was part of Burnham's effort. He and other members of the Chicago Board were strong supporters of the City Beautiful movement and took seriously their role as stewards of their communities.

"The successful real estate man is a born optimist," Judd told his hosts at the 1907 Duluth meeting, "and it is that spirit of belief in better things to come which encourages effort and which has contributed so much to the splendid growth of your city and all the urban communities of the United States."

National Convention

OF THE

Real Estate Exchanges

OF THE

UNITED STATES

HELD IN

CHICAGO

th, thirteenth *and* fourteenth
Nineteen hundred and eight

IN THE

Men's Christian Association
Auditorium

The NATIONAL ASSOCIATION OF REALTORS® was first incorporated as the National Association of Real Estate Exchanges.

The delegates adopted the name National Association of Real Estate Exchanges. The membership base was made up of state and local real estate boards, but individual real estate brokers from areas not covered by local boards were also allowed to become members. The word *national* in the Association's name referred to both the United States and Canada (the Canadian boards went on to create their own national body, the Canadian Real Estate Association, in March 1943). Dues were set at $1 per year, with an initial membership fee of $50.

The new association was to be run by an Executive Committee made up of one representative from each member board, a board of managers that would act between meetings of the Executive Committee, and a paid executive. Among other provisions outlined in the constitution were the formation of standing committees on financing and auditing, taxation, state and municipal legislation, organization of new local boards, and a code of ethics.

Edward Halsey was selected as the National Association's first executive secretary and given a stipend of $200 for the first four months to cover expenses, and August H. Frederick of St. Louis was elected presi-

Boards Participating in the 1908 Organizing Meeting

REAL ESTATE EXCHANGE OF BALTIMORE

REAL ESTATE ASSOCIATION OF BELLINGHAM, WASHINGTON

CHICAGO REAL ESTATE BOARD

CINCINNATI REAL ESTATE EXCHANGE

CLEVELAND REAL ESTATE BOARD

DETROIT REAL ESTATE BOARD

DULUTH (MINNESOTA) REAL ESTATE EXCHANGE

GARY (INDIANA) REAL ESTATE BOARD

KANSAS CITY REAL ESTATE EXCHANGE

LOS ANGELES REALTY BOARD

MILWAUKEE REAL ESTATE ASSOCIATION

MINNESOTA REAL ESTATE BOARD

OMAHA REAL ESTATE EXCHANGE

PHILADELPHIA REAL ESTATE BROKERS ASSOCIATION

ST. LOUIS REAL ESTATE EXCHANGE

ST. PAUL REAL ESTATE EXCHANGE

SEATTLE REAL ESTATE EXCHANGE

SIOUX CITY (IOWA) REAL ESTATE EXCHANGE

TACOMA (WASHINGTON) REAL ESTATE ASSOCIATION

CALIFORNIA STATE REALTY FEDERATION

Note: The Boston exchange sent a last-minute notice that its delegate was unable to attend. The Portland, Oregon, board learned of the meeting too late but asked to be considered a charter member.

dent of the Association for the duration of its organizing year. Other sessions of the organization meeting were spent discussing such issues as the burdens of taxation and the concept of municipal bonds, conservation of the nation's natural resources, liberalizing immigration laws, and ways to show the benefits of the organization to real estate brokers and the public.

EARLY PRIORITIES

The National Association of Real Estate Exchanges was officially incorporated on July 2, 1908, making its first home in the offices of the Chicago Real Estate Board at 57 Dearborn Street. With an initial association membership of 1,646, Halsey undertook a campaign to recruit new members. During his tenure as executive secretary, which ended in June 1909, he also worked on a list of goals that the Association might accomplish in the future, a list that included such ideas as the widespread use of exclusive agency and making available a sign that could be displayed on members' office walls showing their membership in the National Association.

For the first few years after its founding, the work of the National Association consisted mainly of learning how to operate nationally and exploring the various facets of the evolving business of real estate. The Association's annual conventions became one of its most important vehicles, since it was at the major meetings that real estate men from around the country could meet and exchange ideas. While the meetings of 1908 and earlier focused on how to organize a national association to represent them, the annual conventions after 1908 marked

CHICAGO HISTORY MUSEUM, 1907

LIBRARY OF CONGRESS

An auditorium of the YMCA building in Chicago served as the site of the National Association's first meeting in 1908. Among the actions taken by the National Association on its first day of existence was the sending of a telegram to President Theodore Roosevelt expressing support for his conservation initiatives. In the same month the National Association was founded, Roosevelt (right, with naturalist John Muir in Yosemite Valley, California) held a meeting with the Conference of Governors to discuss conservation.

the first time that real estate businessmen from around the country could gather to discuss topics of interest to their profession. Discussions of city planning, building restrictions, and subdivision layout dominated the first convention after the founding, held in Detroit in June 1909. Taxation was the major issue discussed in 1910, and uniform state property laws and model housing codes were on the minds of attendees of the 1911 convention. In a tradition that continues with the Association's annual meetings today, the early conventions allowed those involved in the real estate business to explore common issues and trends and identify areas where action was needed.

As early as 1911, the foundation was being laid for the Association's federated

STATE OF ILLINOIS

Department of State.

James A. Rose, Secretary of State.

• • •

To All to Whom These Presents Shall Come≈Greeting:

WHEREAS, *a* CERTIFICATE, *duly signed and acknowledged, having been filed in the office of the Secretary of State, on the* **2nd** *day of* **July** *A. D.* **1908**

for the organization of the

NATIONAL ASSOCIATION OF REAL ESTATE EXCHANGES,

under and in accordance with the provisions of "*AN ACT CONCERNING CORPORATIONS,*" *approved April 18, 1872, and in force July 1, 1872, a copy of which certificate is hereto attached.*

Now, Therefore, I, JAMES A. ROSE, Secretary of State of the State of Illinois, by virtue of the powers and duties vested in me by law, do hereby certify that the said

NATIONAL ASSOCIATION OF REAL ESTATE EXCHANGES,

is a legally organized Corporation, under the laws of this State.

In Testimony Whereof, I hereto set my hand and cause to be affixed the Great Seal of State.

Done at the City of Springfield, this **2nd**

day of **July** *A. D.* **1908**

and of the independence of the United States the one hundred and **32nd**.

JAMES A. ROSE,

Secretary of State.

> **The founders' stated purpose was "to unite the real estate men** of America for the purpose of exerting effectively a combined influence upon matters affecting real estate interests."

The National Association of Real Estate Exchanges was incorporated in Cook County, Illinois—still the headquarters location. Edward Judd, who was serving as president of the Chicago board in 1908; Edward Halsey, the Association's first executive secretary; and Nathan William MacChesney, the Association's legal counsel, were the signatories on the articles of incorporation.

4M.–10–'06.   DS457–Illinois Printing Co., Danville, Ill.

STATE OF ILLINOIS, } SS.

Cook **County,**

FEE $10

JUN 3 0 1908

To **JAMES A. ROSE,** *Secretary of State:*

We, the Undersigned,   Edward S. Judd, Edward A. Halsey and
Nathan William MacChesney

citizens of the United States, propose to form a corporation under an Act of the General Assembly of the State of Illinois, entitled "An Act concerning Corporations," approved April 18, 1872, and all acts amendatory thereof; and for the purpose of such organization we hereby state as follows, to-wit:

1. *The name of such corporation is*

   NATIONAL ASSOCIATION OF REAL ESTATE EXCHANGES.

2. *The object for which it is formed is* to unite the real estate men of America
   for the purpose of exerting effectively a combined influence
   upon matters affecting real estate interests.

3. *The management of the aforesaid*   Association   an Executive Committee
   shall be vested in a board members of at least 9 Directors, *who are to be elected* annually
4. *The following persons are hereby selected as the* Directors *to control and manage said corporation for the first year of its corporate existence, viz:*

   Persons named on attached sheet marked "Exhibit A"

5. *The location is in the city of*   Chicago   *in the County of*   Cook
   in the State of Illinois, and the postoffice address of its business office is at No.   57
   Dearborn   *Street, in the said city of*   Chicago.

SIGNED.

Edward Judd
Edward A. Halsey
Nathan William MacChesney

(005)

structure. Executive Committee members, meeting in July, considered the subject of "a proper basis upon which to admit state organizations and the question of accepting individual members from cities which had a local board. . . ." It was the first step in forming what is known today as the three-way agreement.

By 1912 the National Association had begun in earnest to tackle the problems that faced the real estate profession. Under the leadership of Samuel Skidmore Thorpe, the Association's president in 1911, the organization took steps to strengthen itself. Thomas Ingersoll, who, like Thorpe, hailed from Minneapolis, was hired as the first full-time executive secretary of the Association in 1912, and the headquarters was moved from its temporary quarters at the Chicago Real Estate Board to a space at Thorpe's office in Minneapolis. With Ingersoll working full-time to coordinate the Association's activi-

ties, the organizers were in a better position to act between meetings. The Association began to issue news statements to the press and could communicate more frequently with members through *The National Real Estate Journal,* the Association's magazine, which began publishing in 1910.

Over the course of the next few years, the National Association took several steps in developing the real estate profession and becoming the organization we see today. In addition to educating members through annual meetings and the *National Real Estate Journal,* it began making its positions known to the nation's lawmakers. Of more direct importance to

In 1916, the Association was renamed the National Association of Real Estate Boards. Convention badges remained eleaborate works of art.

individual real estate practitioners was the adoption of the Association's Code of Ethics in 1913. In 1916 the Association changed its name to the National Association of Real Estate Boards, reflecting the changing nature of the local member organizations from simple exchanges of listing information to more service-oriented professional boards.

The year 1916 also saw the introduction of a new name for the Association's individual members, the term REALTOR®. Coined by Charles Chadbourn, a past president of the Minneapolis Real Estate Board, the word quickly became a vital and enduring tool in conveying the benefits of membership in the Association to both real estate brokers and the general public.

In recounting the tale of how he came up with the term, Chadbourn explained that the idea came to him in 1915 after seeing a news headline that read "Real Estate Man Swindles a Poor Widow." He assured his fellow members that the scoundrel had nothing to do with the National Association or one of its local exchanges but was an "obscure speculator."

However, recently discovered information suggests that the real estate man referred to in the headline was not an obscure speculator at all, but more likely was the National Association's former president, August H. Frederick, who, mirroring Chadbourn's story, was convicted of swindling a poor widow in 1915. Real estate fraud unfortunately was still a common occurrence in 1915, and the transgressions of an "obscure speculator" would not have been the subject of screaming headlines. The downfall of A. H. Frederick, however, a well-known businessman, active church official, and aspiring politician who had been elected president of the St. Louis Board of Aldermen the day before his arrest,

Early National Association conventions—vigorously sought by local exchanges—were occasions for merrymaking, including mayoral welcomes, speech contests, and songs.

NAR ARCHIVES, THE NATIONAL REAL ESTATE JOURNAL

PLYMOUTH AND SOUTH SHORE ASSOCIATION OF REALTORS®

Members of the National Association and their spouses prepare to board a train in Chicago for the 1911 convention in Denver. The train was said to be the finest equipment owned by the North Western Railway and the Pullman Company. The practice of chartering trains to the meetings continued into the 1960s, though by the 1950s, some members—like this group from Massachusetts—were traveling to the meetings by air.

The Three-Way Agreement

In April 2004 the National Association surpassed 1 million members for the first time in its history—and the growth spurt didn't stop there. By early 2007 membership stood at more than 1.3 million.

Three factors contributed to the astounding gain, 45 percent between 1999 and 2004 alone: booming home sales, the growing recognition of REALTORS® as real estate professionals, and a concept known as the three-way agreement that has been part of the Association's structure for at least 70 years.

The agreement gives state and local associations the right to use the term REALTORS® in their name. It also allows state and local associations to grant use of the terms REALTOR® and REALTOR-ASSOCIATE® to individual members. In exchange, state and local associations agree to accept the charge of properly granting the membership terms and to subscribe to and uphold the Code of Ethics. Each local association also agrees to maintain membership in good standing in its state association. Put simply, through the three-way agreement, the National Association is part of a federation in which membership in one organization is tied to membership in all.

There's a synergy, stability, and strength in the system, wrote 2004 NAR President Walt McDonald of California in his May 2004 REALTOR® Magazine column. "The [national, state, and local associations] work together to provide member benefits in a way that none of the segments could provide on their own."

Symbolic of the agreement's power are the organization's disaster-relief efforts in the first decade of the new millennium. Using nothing more than e-mail communication to members and state and local associations, the National Association raised a total of $15 million to help families affected by the September 11, 2001, terrorist attacks, survivors of the South Asian Tsunami in 2004, and survivors of Hurricanes Katrina, Rita, and Wilma in 2005.

It's in the political sphere where the power of the three-way agreement is evident every day. By joining forces, the national, state, and local associations raise millions of dollars each year for the REALTORS® Political Action Committee and generate thousands of letters to Congress on issues that matter to the nation's real estate practitioners and property owners. *Fortune* magazine for several years ranked the top 25 lobbying organizations in the nation's capital. NAR consistently made the list, ranking number 9 in 2001.

The "REALTOR® confederacy" is a model other national groups would like to emulate. President of the NAR in 2002, Martin Edwards of Memphis, Tennessee, remembers a 2001 meeting with Bill Frist, the Tennessee senator who would go on to serve as Senate Majority Leader from 2003 to 2007. Edwards was briefing Frist on the Association's staunch opposition to banks entering real estate. Afterward, Frist asked for a few more minutes of his time.

Frist, who is also a surgeon, told Edwards that he'd been involved in advocating for doctors on a national level and was amazed at the level of cooperation within organized real estate. "How did the REALTORS® put it together? How, if I do something in Washington, do I hear about it in Memphis or in Nashville so quickly?" Edwards recalls him asking. "I told him about the three-way agreement."

WHOSE IDEA WAS IT?

The question of how local, state, and national associations related to one another was discussed in the earliest days of the Association, when it was still known as the National Association of Real Estate Exchanges. In 1911, a San Antonio practitioner, H. C. King, submitted an application for associate membership. King already belonged to the San Antonio Real Estate Exchange, however, and the Association's founders hadn't contemplated individual members applying from cities in which a local exchange existed.

To consider the questions raised by King's application, the Association's Executive Committee appointed a special committee chaired by incoming president Samuel Skidmore Thorpe of Minneapolis. Other members of the special committee were W. W. Hannan of Detroit, 1909 president; N. J. Upham of Duluth, Minnesota; and Nathan William MacChesney of Chicago, the association's general counsel. The special committee was also asked to consider the basis on which to admit state associations.

Meeting at the Brown Palace Hotel in Denver, Colorado, on July 19, 1911, the Executive Committee approved Thorpe's recommendation—that King's application be returned; he was already a member by virtue of his membership in the San Antonio exchange. The committee also approved Thorpe's recommendation that the constitution and bylaws be amended "in order to provide a means for admitting State Organizations."

Within a decade, leaders of the National Association were beginning to talk about a three-way agreement. At the 1948 convention in New York, the Association's executive secretary, Herbert U. Nelson, talked about the progress of the three-way agreement and credited Glenn Willaman, executive secretary of the California association, with presenting the initial concept to NAR's board of directors. Privately, Walter Rose of Orlando, Florida the Association's 1936 president, claimed to be "grand poppy" of the movement, and, indeed, Florida was the first state to qualify under the three-way proposal.

"FIRMING THE FOUNDATION"

In 1978 the three-way agreement was strengthened with an amendment to the bylaws that required National Association dues to flow through the local association. From that point, no individual member's dues would be paid directly to NAR.

In a 1980 article titled "Firming the Foundation," Bill North, then NAR general counsel, said the change ensured that all the services NAR provided to local boards would be equally shared. He called local boards "the foundation of the REALTOR® family and the keystone of the confederation."

The bylaw change simplified dues collection for NAR while making the Association a more potent force, not just in Washington but throughout the country and the world.

In July 2000 NAR Managing Director of Member Policy Kevin Milligan neatly summed up the value of the three-way agreement. "The federated structure allows the REALTOR® organization to use its combined resources and influence to have a unified, powerful voice in shaping public policy, setting recognized standards for ethical real estate practice, and contributing to the betterment of the industry."

President
A. H. FREDERICK.
St. Louis

was reported prominently in newspapers across the country. It is highly probable that his story inspired Chadbourn's invention. A. H. Frederick went on to serve ten years in prison for forging deeds of trust and was expelled from the local real estate board. His conviction was such an embarrassment to the National Association that his name was virtually expunged from official records.

The number of people who chose to accept the Association's Code of Ethics and become known as REALTORS® grew rapidly. William W. Hannan, president in 1909, had declared at the founding meeting that the ultimate membership goal of the Association should be 4,000 to 5,000 members. That goal was surpassed in 1912, but for several years thereafter the Association membership remained fairly stagnant at around 6,000. With the conclusion of World War I and the nation's economic expansion, demand for real estate services grew, along with the desire of many brokers to align themselves with the professional organization, and NAR's membership expanded from 6,700 in 1918 to more than 24,000 in 1926.

THE PROFESSION EVOLVES

During that time, NAR and its members took several more steps in the evolution of the real estate industry. Today, real estate brokerage is a well-defined business, with a wide range of specialties and allied professions, but that wasn't the case when the Association was founded in 1908. Real estate at the beginning of the twentieth century encompassed land development, appraisals, mortgage lending, and other activities now recognized as separate but essential to real estate. Still, the need for specialization in real estate was recognized early on, and in

1909 Hannan suggested creating divisions within the Association to cater to different fields.

In 1923 the Association revisited the idea and set up several divisions, many of which live on as organizations affiliated with the NAR. NATIONAL ASSOCIATION OF REALTORS®. Over the years other organizations also had their beginnings as specialized arms of the National Association. The Urban Land Institute, for example, was founded as an independent research agency by NAR in 1939; the Appraisal Institute, now an independent association based in Chicago, started as NAR's Appraisal Division in 1928. (A chart of organizations that have spun off from NAR appears in Chapter 6.)

Another association operating today also had its start with the NAR, but not as a specialized division or agency. The National Association of License Law Officials (now the Association of Real Estate License Law Officials) was founded at the NAR annual convention in Toronto in 1930. The group, representing the state government officials who administer licensing laws for real estate professionals, arose out of work begun by National Association members several years earlier as part of their effort to professionalize the industry and weed out unqualified practitioners.

In his 1907 speech suggesting the creation of a national organization, Edward S. Judd promoted the notion of a uniform system of licensing laws. The pros and cons of real estate licenses were hotly debated at the National Association's annual meetings beginning in 1912. Proponents of license laws put forth their value in protecting the public and honest brokers alike through the licensing process, educational exams, and a system of penalties for license violations. Those opposed to the idea believed the laws would be ineffective in excluding dishonest brokers and were simply unnecessary. "To have real estate men come out openly and demand they be licensed on these grounds is an admission of their own weakness," wrote St. Paul Real Estate Board vice president J. J. Kenna in *The National Real Estate Journal* in early 1915, going on to suggest that peer pressure would be sufficient to keep incompetent brokers from joining the Association.

With those who favored license laws in the majority, the National Association's Licensing Committee prepared a model license law for the annual meeting in 1913. Known as the MacChesney Act, in honor of Nathan William MacChesney, the association's general counsel from its founding until 1947, the model law eventually became the foundation of many of the first state licensing laws. In 1916—the same year its name was changed to the National Association of Real Estate Boards—the Association officially endorsed the licensing of real estate brokers, recommending that local boards actively pursue them in their respective legislatures. After several attempts, by the end of 1919 license laws were successfully enacted in California, Michigan, Oregon, and Wisconsin.

Membership in the National Association peaked in 1926. By then the housing boom that began after World War I was starting to lose steam. Increasingly unaffordable homes and the instability of the mortgage market contributed to declines in the ranks of REALTORS® for the first time since 1908. By the time the Great Depression was in full swing in the 1930s, membership in the National Association of Real Estate Boards had dropped significantly, hovering near 10,000 to 12,000.

NAR worked closely with the federal government in formulating a series of measures that would help revive and strengthen

By the second decade of the twentieth century, practitioners were organized enough to have both internal and external communication. NAR began publishing *The National Real Estate Journal* in March 1910. In 1915, a Seattle newspaper forecast "cordial, intelligent cooperation" among practitioners in the city.

Weekly Bulletin of the Minneapolis Real Estate Board

DEFINITION OF REALTOR—AN ACTIVE MEMBER OF THE NATIONAL ASSOCIATION OF REAL ESTATE BOARDS

Tuesday, August 8, 1939   Board Rooms, 324 Hodgson Bldg.   Vol. 23, No. 33

← WHEN COINING "REALTOR"

Happy Birthday *to* Father Realtor C.N.CHADBOURN

on His EIGHTIETH Birthday,
Thursday, Aug. 10, 1939

from all Minneapolis Realtors

C. N. Chadbourn, 1912, as Board President

CHARLES N. CHADBOURN has a justifiable right to feel proud on the occasion of his eightieth birthday. He has contributed to the real estate profession its most honored possession, the word *Realtor*. He continuously renders to his own Minneapolis Real Estate Board and to the National Association of Real Estate Boards every service which is asked of him and many, many more which are never requested. He maintains a keen and active interest in civic affairs and has been, and is, a major bulwark in the fight for economy in government and property tax reduction. Yes, Charlie, you can rightly "give yourself a pat on the back" and all your Realtor friends are happy and proud on this occasion that they have the privilege and good fortune to associate through the years with America's No. 1 Realtor—CHARLES N. CHADBOURN.

on EIGHTIETH BIRTHDAY →

C. N. CHADBOURN. 1939, as BOARD DIRECTOR

BOTH IMAGES: NAR ARCHIVES

Charles Nathanial Chadbourn, 1859–1942

Father REALTOR®

Like many of the National Association's early leaders, Charles Nathaniel Chadbourn (1859–1942) was concerned that the public was unaware of the distinction between "the responsible, expert real estate man" and "the curbstoner who possesses no such qualifications."

Chadbourn had a simple solution—a term that would distinguish the members of the National Association from the "alleged 'Real Estate Man' . . . some unknown individual, not a member of our local board, and of no standing in the community." The term was *REALTOR®,* and for more than 90 years, NAR members have set themselves apart by using *REALTOR®* as part of their business identity.

Chadbourn was born August 10, 1859, in Columbus, Wisconsin, and attended Oberlin College in Ohio. After graduating, he moved to Minnesota, settling in 1880 in Minneapolis, where he worked in the grain business as a cashier. In 1887, he and his father, Charles H. Chadbourn, founded an investment brokerage. Eventually Chadbourn's brother Rodney joined the firm, and it was incorporated in 1893 as Chadbourn Finance Co. Chadbourn was prominent in the commercial and civic life of Minneapolis. He was one of the founders of the Minneapolis Symphony Orchestra and served as treasurer of the Minneapolis Taxpayers Association for many years. He also served for eight years on the municipal Board of Estimate and Taxation.

As one of the organizers of Minnesota's state real estate association, Chadbourn was also involved with the movement to start a national real estate organization. At the National Association of Real Estate Exchanges' first annual convention in Detroit in 1909, he was appointed to the Resolutions Committee. In 1917, he was made chairman of the REALTOR® Committee, as well as a vice president. For several years, he also served on the Association's Executive Committee.

LASTING LEGACY

In 1925 at the annual convention in Detroit, the board of directors passed a resolution of appreciation for Chadbourn's service to NAR and presented him with a watch bearing the following inscription:

Charles N. Chadbourn
Coiner of the word Realtor
From the Past Presidents of the
National Association of
Real Estate Boards
June 1925

Throughout his career, Chadbourn continued to track the use of the term he'd coined. In the NAR archives are two letters he sent to writer H. L. Mencken regarding Mencken's use of the term in the August 31, 1935, issue of *The New Yorker.*

The Minneapolis board honored Chadbourn on his eightieth birthday, calling him "Father REALTOR®" and "America's No. 1 REALTOR®." Chadbourn died in 1942 at age 83.

An Association of Realtors

By C. N. CHADBOURN

(Ex-President Minneapolis Real Estate Board.)

A FEW days since a news-urchin on the street thrust a paper under my nose bearing the flaming headlines, "Real Estate Man An Embezzler," and importuned me to buy and read "All about the Big Scandal in a Real Estate Office!" A hasty perusal disclosed the fact that the alleged "Real Estate Man" was some unknown individual, not a member of our local board, and of no standing in the community. But for lack of other visible means of support, he posed as a "Real Estate Man."

The incident set me to thinking. Every member of the Minneapolis Real Estate Board was to some extent besmirched by the actions of a man with whom none of them had ever dealt, and all merely because he bore the same business title as themselves. One very cogent reason why Real Estate is not classed among the professions is that anyone, even though his credit may not even be good for the leasing of an office may nevertheless proclaim himself a "Real Estate Agent."

What is the standard of admission into any of the three principal professions? The man who is a graduate of a medical school is a doctor, he who has been admitted to the bar is a lawyer, while he who has been duly ordained, may call himself a minister. Each one of these has adopted the code of ethics approved by his profession and those who have dealings with him place a certain reliance upon the code which he has accepted.

The National Association has achieved such a standing in all the states of the Union that there is now imposed upon it the duty of informing the public in some very definite manner that these irresponsible adventurers are not included among its membership. That its members are governed by a code of ethics which gives a high moral standard to their business dealings. That as such members they are entitled to and do receive the protection of the National Association.

As a practical method of securing such a result I propose that the National Association adopt a professional title to be conferred upon its members which they shall use to distinguish them from outsiders. That this title be copyrighted and defended by the National Association

Charles Nathaniel Chadbourn, in this 1915 article in *The National Real Estate Journal,* explains the headline that inspired him to invent the term REALTOR®. In later tellings, the headline was "Real Estate Man Swindles Poor Widow."

From the start, NAR viewed service to state and local associations as essential to its mission. Meanwhile, state and local groups participated in promotion of the REALTOR® brand.

the real estate market, including promoting the use of long-term amortized mortgages, better use of available land, and more efficient use of materials to lower the costs of building and owning a home. As the nation began to climb toward economic recovery in the late 1930s, the numbers of new members

also started to increase, albeit slowly. NAR would not see the levels of membership enjoyed in 1926 until the end of World War II. By that time, the Association was well-established on its path to becoming the nation's largest professional association and a strong advocate for home ownership in America.

NAR ARCHIVES

The NATIONAL ASSOCIATION of REAL ESTATE BOARDS

• WHAT IT DOES •

• HOW IT FUNCTIONS •

A HANDBOOK — to assist secretaries of local Real Estate Boards and State Real Estate Associations. Published as a supplement to the weekly Secretaries' Confidential Letter. May 26, 1934.

PHOENIX ASSOCIATION OF REALTORS®

Deal with a REALTOR ..it pays
LOOK FOR THIS EMBLEM
to be sure
ARIZONA ASSOCIATION OF REALTORS

NATIONAL ASSOCIATION REALTORS ARE ACTIVE MEMBERS OF CONSTITUENT BOARDS OF REAL ESTATE BOARDS

GREATER BALTIMORE BOARD OF REALTORS®

PHOENIX ASSOCIATION OF REALTORS®

Thirteenth Annual Banquet
Real Estate Board of Baltimore
Saturday, March Ninth
Nineteen Twenty-Nine
Lord Baltimore Hotel

Wise Counsel

For nearly 40 years, from 1908 to 1947, Nathan William MacChesney served as general counsel for NAR. As counsel to the Chicago Real Estate Board, MacChesney attended the 1908 convention and was one of the principal architects of the Association. He worked with the founders to draft NAR's original charter, constitution, and bylaws; he published an early book on real estate law; and he wrote the first model real estate license act.

In 1922, MacChesney won the U.S. Supreme Court decision establishing the constitutionality of real estate license legislation. He also won, in the courts of many states, the Association's exclusive right to the term REALTOR®. MacChesney wrote two books on real estate law—*The Law of Real Estate Brokerage* and *Principles of Real Estate Law*—that were long considered standard texts. At the time of his resignation from NAR in July 1947, the Board of Directors made him an honorary director for life.

For five decades MacChesney was a senior partner at MacChesney and Becker, one of Chicago's oldest law firms. Over the course of his legal career, he served as Judge Advocate General of Illinois, president of the American Institute of Criminal Law & Criminology, president of the American Society of Military Law, and president of the Illinois State Bar Association.

Colleagues and friends referred to MacChesney as "General MacChesney" in honor of his distinguished military career. He served in the Spanish-American War, World War I, and World War II and was awarded the Purple Heart. He was deeply involved in social issues, serving as advisor to the Salvation Army and several local Chicago charities and arguing before the Supreme Court on the constitutionality of child labor legislation.

MacChesney was also a statesman. He served as

NATHAN WILLIAM MACCHESNEY, 1878–1954

NAR ARCHIVES

minister to Canada and as consul general for Thailand. A trustee for Northwestern University for many years, he headed the university's alumni association and was known as the father of its downtown campus.

REALTOR®: Term of Distinction

The history of the REALTOR® trademark is long and storied. In 1916, the same year it became known as the National Association of Real Estate Boards, the Association adopted the term *REALTOR®* as a mark to be used exclusively by its members to set themselves apart from "irresponsible curbstoners"—the term used to describe fly-by-night practitioners who operated from the curb rather than an office.

For the ensuing 90 years, Association attorneys have fought numerous threats to water down its meaning. NAR's perpetual policing of references to the term; the establishment of trademark status in 1950; and successful programs to educate editors, journalists, and even REALTORS® of its meaning and use have combined to give the term a resiliency and strength associated with only the most recognized brands in the world today. A brand study conducted for NAR in 2005 postulated that the REALTOR® brand generates $32,000 in incremental income for each member over the course of his or her membership (see "A $32,000 Word" on page 33).

The term was coined in 1915 by Charles N. Chadbourn, a member and past president of the Minneapolis Real Estate Board. In April 1916, on Chadbourn Bros. & Co. letterhead, Chadbourn addressed Nathan William MacChesney, the National Association's general counsel, regarding the history of the word. In his history, Chadbourn said:

> This is an artificial new word I constructed from the root of the word "realty," with the purpose of having it used as a title by members of local Real Estate Boards, which are constituent members of the National Association of Real Estate Boards, to distinguish them from persons who do not possess such membership.

A few weeks earlier, Chadbourn had addressed the Executive Committee at the 1916 annual convention in New Orleans:

> We have taken up at the national meetings—at every meeting, I think—the question of real estate as a profession. Now, we want all of us to raise the standard of real estate men throughout the country and to raise the standard of the business, and I have given this matter some thought. One day, while I was walking up the street, a news urchin forced a sheet under my nose and asked me to read all about a scandal in a real estate office. I didn't buy that paper, but I afterwards learned that the scandal was of some unknown individual who was not a member of our board, and who nevertheless, because he was called a real estate man, had brought disgrace on the whole profession to some extent, and it occurred to me that we ought to go into the question of having some distinctive title.
>
> The adoption of a distinctive title would soon create in the public mind a sharp line of demarcation between the irresponsible curbstoner and the reliable expert and would add substantial value to membership in the National Association. I therefore submit a resolution that this board adopt this, and that this Executive Committee be empowered to carry out this idea of conferring this title of REALTOR® upon the individual members of the National Association.[7]

On March 27, 1916, eight years after the founding of the National Association and three years after the establishment of a Code of Ethics, the Executive Committee passed Chadbourn's resolution.

A document compiled in March 1948 by the Association's Department of Research and Surveys tells the most cited version of Chadbourn's story, and it is this colorful version that Pearl Janet Davies featured in her 1958 book *Real Estate in American History*. The story is told in Chadbourn's own voice:

I was on my way to a meeting of our board in 1915. A street newsboy was peddling a sensational sheet which bore the headline "Real Estate Man Swindles a Poor Widow." A casual examination of the article showed that the "real estate man" in question was not a member of our local real estate board but was only an obscure speculator with desk room in some back office. Nevertheless, by his dishonor he had besmirched every "real estate man" in Minneapolis, including all the members of the board.

Then the thought occurred to me, "Why should not real estate board members adopt some name to call themselves which would distinguish them from such rascals?" [8]

A VIGILANT DEFENSE

The term REALTOR® gained acceptance quickly, according to Jeffrey Hornstein, author of *A Nation of Realtors®: A Cultural History of the Twentieth-Century American Middle Class* (Duke University Press, 2006). It wasn't long, however, before people began using the term generically to refer to any practitioner, as they might use *doctor* or *lawyer*. Inevitably, practitio-

C. N. Chadbourn   R. W. Chadbourn   Thos. L. Cooley

Chadbourn Bros. & Co.
REAL ESTATE AND INSURANCE
825-827 Palace Building
Telephones: { N. W. Main 2716
              T. S. Center 3716

REALTORS

MEMBERS OF
THE MINNEAPOLIS REAL ESTATE BOARD
THE NATIONAL ASSOCIATION OF REAL ESTATE EXCHANGES

MINNEAPOLIS, MINN., April 18, 1916.

Mr. Nathan William MacChesney,

Chicago, Ill.

My dear Mr. MacChesney:

I am enclosing a history of the word "Realtor," which I think you will find quite complete. If anything is lacking, please let me know and I will endeavor to supply. *it*.

Would it not be well at this time to have the Minneapolis Real Estate Board pass some resolution like the following?

"Resolved, that the Minneapolis Real Estate Board hereby adopts the title "Realtor" to be used to designate active membership in this Board; that it recommends to all active members that they use this title to signify their membership in this Board and that the privilege of using said title be cancelled and terminated whenever such member shall cease to be an active member of this Board."

I am having Mr. Nelson, Executive Secretary of our Board, investigate the laws and ordinances regarding the restricted residence districts here and will forward them to you in a few days.

With kind regards to Mrs. MacChesney, I remain,

Yours very truly,

C. N. Chadbourn

NAR ARCHIVES

Charles Chadbourn's letter to Nathan William MacChesney is on the first letterhead known to depict the word REALTORS®.

The National Association of Real Estate Exchanges

Hereby confers upon _____

by virtue of his membership in _____
(Name of local board printed here)
which is a constituent member of this Association, he having assented to
the Code of Ethics adopted by this Association, the title of

Realtor
(Copyrighted)

granting him the right to use said title both personally and in connection
with the Real Estate business of the firm or corporation with which he is
connected, until ....191, when this license ex-
pires by limitation.

The National Association of Real Estate Exchanges

By Walter C. Piper, President,
By H. R. Ennis, Secretary.

Certified _____
(Name of local board here)

by ....President
.... Secretary

Attest

Chadbourn proposed that certificates be sent out to NAR members each year confer-
ring upon them the title of REALTOR®. "As people get used to the new word," he said,
"it loses any awkwardness which it may seem to have on first acquaintance."

ners who weren't members sought access to the term. As a result, local committees formed to ensure the word was being used correctly.[9]

Chadbourn realized that the newly coined word needed to have lasting significance in the eyes of the public. He expressed this intention in the March 15, 1916, issue of *The National Real Estate Journal* by publishing a sample certificate along with his plan to have the Association adopt the REALTOR® term. On the draft certificate, "copyrighted" appears immediately beneath the word REALTOR®.

Even paperwork filed with the Secretary of State of Illinois on May 18, 1917, shows the Association's intention to copyright the word REALTOR. The Certificate of Change of Name reprints the language of the entire resolution, passed almost one year earlier:

> . . . RESOLVED, That we recommend to the Executive Committee the adoption of the title "REALTOR®" to be used exclusively by members of this Association.
> That the Executive Committee be and is hereby empowered to investigate the feasibility of copyrighting said title . . .

The man who led this effort was Nathan William MacChesney, who served as general counsel for the National Association from its founding in 1908 until his retirement in 1947. At the time of the word's adoption, federal law did not allow for it to be registered as a trademark. Many states did allow the registration of the term, however, and by the time he retired, MacChesney had successfully registered the trademark in 46 states.[10] With the passage of the 1946 Trademark Act, known as the Lanham Act, the National Association was able to register the term as a collective membership mark. In a letter written in 1965 to the editor in chief of *Webster's Third New International Dictionary*,

Thomas Scully, then NAR's general counsel, explains:

> *Prior to the enactment of the Lanham Act in 1946, only marks affixed to physical objects could be registered and protected under the laws of the United States. The Lanham Act added provisions for the registration and protection of "services" under the Trade Mark Act.*[11]

The collective marks REALTORS® and REALTOR® were registered with the United States Patent and Trademark Office on September 13, 1949, and January 10, 1950, respectively, under Registration Numbers 515200 and 519789.

William D. North, in the 1980s when he was serving as general counsel for the Association, called the REALTOR® name "an inherently intangible asset" that "must be defended at all times against all comers in all forums in all circumstances. Moreover, it must be defended not merely from those who would destroy or downgrade it, but also from those who would usurp it for themselves."[12]

Again, it was MacChesney who began that vigilant defense in the courts. The first case decided in court arose in 1920. Together with the Minneapolis Real Estate Board, the National Association sued the Northwestern Telephone Exchange Company for inappropriately printing *REALTOR* in its telephone directory. The District Court in Hennepin County, Minnesota, ruled that the defendant be enjoined from using the term in connection with nonmembers.[13] By the time MacChesney retired in 1947, NAR had racked up 20 legal cases establishing its exclusive right to the term.

In 1957 the first federal court decision upheld NAR's ownership rights to the term. In *NAREB v. the Peninsula Real Estate Association,* Federal Judge Michael J. Roche permanently

NAR ARCHIVES

Over time, Chadbourn's invention evolved into a sacred story, widely circulated at such National Association rituals as local board charter presentations. The Chadbourn story was retold in countless educational campaigns, including this pamphlet.

enjoined a nonmember board, the Peninsula Association in San Mateo, California, from using the words "Realter" and "Realters" and an emblem similar to that of NAR in its advertising. Ten local boards joined NAR in the suit, which was filed in the United States District Court in San Francisco. The Peninsula association was ordered to destroy all literature containing these words and to pay the costs and attorney fees in the court action.[14]

The past decade brought two major court challenges to the membership marks, both wins for NAR. In 2002 a former REALTOR® sought to continue using the term. As a former member, the judge ruled, the plaintiff had to offer evidence of the marks becoming generic after her membership ended. Laurie Janik, NAR's general counsel, said at the time of

For Immediate Release   **For Immediate Release**

Sixth in the series distributed by:

Department of Public Relations
National Association of Real Estate Boards
1300 Connecticut Avenue, N. W.
Washington 6, D. C.

HEARTH and HISTORY

NOT EVERY REAL ESTATE MAN IS A *REALTOR!*

ONLY AN ACTIVE MEMBER OF THE *NATIONAL ASSOCIATION OF REAL ESTATE BOARDS* AND ITS AFFILIATED BOARDS MAY DESIGNATE HIMSELF AS A **REALTOR,** WHICH IS A COLLECTIVE MARK (SIMILAR TO A TRADEMARK) REGISTERED IN THE U.S. PATENT OFFICE.

REALTOR WAS COINED TO DISTINGUISH ETHICAL PRACTITIONERS.

IN 1915, CHARLES N. CHADBOURN, PAST PRESIDENT OF THE MINNEAPOLIS REAL ESTATE BOARD, WAS DISTRESSED TO READ A NEWSPAPER HEADLINE: "REAL ESTATE MAN SWINDLES POOR WIDOW." REALIZING THAT THIS REFLECTED ON THE BOARD MEMBERS, HE COINED THE TERM **REALTOR** TO INDICATE THOSE OF REPUTE IN THE BUSINESS. THE TERM WAS ADOPTED BY NAREB IN 1916.

SOMETHING MUST BE DONE ABOUT THIS!

After the Association successfully registered the term *REALTOR®*, it continued to vigilantly police use of the term.

the ruling, "The decision is clear that she had failed to do so."

The second decisive victory for NAR came in 2004 when the U.S. Patent and Trademark Office issued a 39-page ruling in *Zimmerman v. NAR.* Jacob Zimmerman was a recent graduate of Cornell University who had registered about 1,900 Internet domain names containing "realtor." His plan was to bundle the names with Web design services targeted for real estate practitioners. When NAR objected, Zimmerman brought suit asking that NAR's registrations be canceled. He argued that since the 1922 publication of Sinclair Lewis's novel *Babbitt,* numerous news articles and court decisions had used REALTOR® and REALTORS® generically to refer to real estate practitioners.

After examining the evidence, the Patent Office's Trademark Trial and Appeal Board denied Zimmerman's request. The court ruled that the record showed no evidence of generic use of REALTOR® or REALTORS® by competitors, by the trademark holder (NAR), or by at least 11 dictionaries (including the *Oxford English Dictionary*).[15] The fact that the Association publishes "hundreds of pages of marketing and promotional materials" and "issues guidance containing specific rules" for use of the REALTOR® marks, name, and logo "in print, in advertisements, and on the Internet" illustrates the extent of its policing efforts.

NAR'S WORK IS NEVER DONE

Indeed, the Association regularly issues letters of warning to those who misuse the REALTOR® marks. In a 1961 case that foreshadowed NAR's battle over Web domain names, REALTOR® Durand "Duke" Taylor relinquished the cable address REALTORS, which his company and its predecessor, the Charles G. Edwards Company, had used since 1925 when Edwards was NAR president.

Even fictional characters aren't safe from the Association's watchful eye. In 1962, Herbert A. Carlborg, director of program practices for CBS, heard from Edwin L. Stoll, director of public relations for NAR, after the culprit of a *Perry Mason* episode had the REALTOR® seal shown on his office door. Forty years later, CBS was again in the Association spotlight. The network issued an apology after attaching the term REALTOR® to someone who acted unethically in a 2002 episode of *CSI: Crime Scene Investigation*.[16]

Today, the Association posts lengthy guidance at its Web site, *REALTOR.org*, specifying how

In 1957, NAR advised the Salt Lake City Board that a practitioner's use of the term Realtrix was an improper variation of the service mark REALTOR®. Since "-rix" is normally indicative of the feminine gender and "-or" of the masculine, NAR reasoned, the natural inference would be that Realtrix is a variation of a generic word and thus would weaken the service mark.

After Durand "Duke" Taylor gave up the cable address REALTORS, the Western Union Telegraph Company registered it as the abbreviated cable address for NAR.

They laughed when she sat down at the typewriter

. . . and capitalized the R in Realtor. But their laughter changed to editorial amazement when they learned that every leading U. S. dictionary now shows (or will show in its next printing) Realtor spelled with a capital R.

That's because Realtor® is registered as a service mark in the U. S. Patent Office. And when correctly used to designate only a member of the National Association of Real Estate Boards, is quite properly entitled to a capital R.

So we'll appreciate it if you, too, will make a mental note to capitalize the R each time you sit down at the typewriter and use the term Realtor.

Realtor—a professional in real estate who subscribes to a strict Code of Ethics as a member of the local and state boards and of the National Association of Real Estate Boards.
Realtors' National Foundation, Inc., 1300 Connecticut Ave., N.W., Washington, D.C. 20036

NAR ARCHIVES

Now all dictionaries agree

Every leading dictionary distributed in the United States now carries (or will carry in its next printing) a proper definition of the term Realtor®.

A Realtor is a person engaged professionally in real estate who is a member of the local and state boards and of the National Association of Real Estate Boards. Realtor is registered as a service mark in the U.S. Patent Office.

We love to see you put Realtor in print. We like the look of it even better when it's used correctly—to apply only to members of NAREB. *And, of course, with a capital R.* We hope you'll use it that way. Every time.

REALTORS' NATIONAL FOUNDATION, INC., 1300 CONNECTICUT AVE., N. W., WASHINGTON, D. C. 20036

members and member boards can and can't use the terms. The manual also includes usage rules for the REALTOR® logo and for REALTOR-ASSOCIATE®, a term the Association adopted in 1974 when it began admitting sales associates.[17]

A reporter covering the 2004 *Zimmerman* case for *The Daily Oklahoman* expressed admiration at the Association's resolve in defending its marks: "It's fascinating for REALTORS® and anyone interested in how some words can bob along in the national lexicon without ever being anchored in the language. Such defini-tional sway is why the NATIONAL ASSOCIATION OF REALTORS® fights so doggedly."

LOOK, MA, WE'RE IN THE DICTIONARY!

Correct use of the term REALTOR® in diction-aries played a role in the *Zimmerman* vic-tory—and those dictionary entries didn't come about by happenstance. The Association has maintained an active dialogue over the years with dictionary editors. The term made its first dictionary appearance just one year after its adoption by NAR. While serving as chairman of the REALTOR® Committee in 1922, Chadbourn wrote an article for the *Chicago Realtor* in which he noted, "It is established as an English word of good usage and is so recognized in [the addendum to] the recent edition of *Webster's International Dictionary.*"

At the Association's January 1961 meeting in Philadelphia, NAR's Public Relations Committee adopted a resolution requesting "publishers of dictionaries using incorrect definitions of the term REALTOR® to correctly define the terms at the next printing."[18] Because of the deference paid to dictionaries by newspaper editors—especially to *Webster's Third,* which was published in 1961—the National Association engaged in a letter-writing campaign to all dictionary publishers.

Most publishers responded favorably to NAR's plea, but Philip Babcock Gove, editor in chief at the G. C. Merriam Company, which published *Webster's,* refused to capitalize the term. More than two years of voluminous correspondence between NAR Executive Vice President Eugene P. Conser, General Counsel Thomas Scully, and Director of Public Relations Edwin Stoll documents the arduous process to convince Gove. Finally, on March 1, 1967, Gove wrote a letter to Scully offering to print the phrase "usually capitalized" after the lowercase listing. On April 17, 1967, NAR President Richard B. Morris of Buffalo closed the file on the subject by writing to the president of G. C. Merriam Company to communicate NAR's approval. Later that year, Morris announced the good news that "all principal dictionaries" in the country had agreed to define a REALTOR® as "an individual engaged in the real estate business who is a member of the National Association of Real Estate Boards."

Today, the term *REALTOR®* has entered the realm of Internet social networking sites. It ap-

One's a REALTOR®. One isn't.

©1983 NATIONAL ASSOCIATION OF REALTORS®

Not every cola is a Coke®. Not every copier is a Xerox®. Not every tissue is a Kleenex®. And not every real estate broker is a REALTOR®.

You in the news media can help us by following the *Associated Press Stylebook*, which states: "Use *Realtor* only if there is a reason to indicate that the individual is a member of the National Association of Realtors."

Although our preferred style is use of all caps followed by the registration symbol "®", REALTOR®, we recognize the typographical appearance problem of all-caps words. So, when use of our membership mark is appropriate and accurate, we ask only that the initial letter of "Realtor" be capitalized.

We thank you for your help.

REALTOR® is a registered collective membership mark that identifies a real estate professional who is a member of the NATIONAL ASSOCIATION OF REALTORS® and subscribes to its strict Code of Ethics.

NATIONAL ASSOCIATION OF REALTORS®

NAR ARCHIVES

This ad was included in a *Membership Marks Manual* NAR produced in the 1980s to aid local boards in protecting the term REALTOR®.

pears in *Wiktionary.org,* a Web site that defines itself as a multilingual free dictionary and thesaurus, being written collaboratively. The site mentions the word as having been coined by Chadbourn as a mark of membership and includes a usage note saying, "REALTOR® and REALTORS® are registered collective membership marks that identify a real estate professional who is a member of the NATIONAL ASSOCIATION OF REALTORS®." Ironically, however, Wiktionary offers several examples of generic use in books and other sources.

NO MATTER HOW YOU SAY IT . . .

Father REALTOR® himself, Charles N. Chadbourn, specified that the term REALTOR® should be pronounced with two syllables, accented on the first. The 1925 pamphlet *REALTOR: Its Meaning and Use* even included a phonetic spelling: Reel'-tor. But that hasn't stopped people from trying to turn REALTOR® into a three-syllable word. In 1940 past president Hugh Robert Ennis of Kansas City notified the National Association that the *Kansas City Star* had published an editorial that was "at variance with the Association's approved or recommended pronunciation." Ennis quotes the *Star* as saying:

The word REALTOR® . . . was coined by the National Association of Real Estate Boards as a name by which to designate its members. Few REALTORS®, however, pronounce the name correctly. It is more often heard as a two-syllable word, "REEL-tore," the second syllable rhyming with core, more, pore. *But according to three American dictionaries in which the name appears, the* New Webster's, Winston's, *and* Funk & Wagnall's, REALTOR® *is a three-syllable word, and the preferred pronunciation rhymes* tor *with* her, per. *(Note: the* or *of such words as factor, ambassador, legislator, conductor, director, etc., also should rhyme with* her, per, *and not with* core, pore.*) The correct pronunciations, then, are first choice, "ree-ul-ter;" second choice, "ree-ul-tawr."*

It turns out Nathan William MacChesney, the man who had defended use of the term for decades, didn't disagree with the *Star.* He once revealed to an Association colleague that he preferred the three-syllable pronunciation. "We have sufficient job on hand to control its meaning," he wrote, "without attempting to control its pronunciation."[19]

However you say it, the term was imbued from the beginning with an importance far beyond its basic meaning. In his 1922 article for *Chicago Realtor,* Chadbourn wrote:

The word REALTOR® signifies more than merely board and National Association membership. The true REALTOR® is a man of high ideals. He has made the Code of Ethics of the National Association a part of his personal code of honor. He would rather lose a record-breaking commission than violate his own conscience. He appreciates the heavy obligations which he owes his community, his clients, his profession, and himself. He realizes, as few laymen do, the intimate nature of the confidential relationship which exists between the REALTOR® and his client, who may be obliged at times to reveal to his REALTOR® embarrassing details of family differences and financial distress. In a recent editorial the Saturday Evening Post *called attention to the fact that there is [a] nationwide movement in full swing for the betterment of American business and for the framing and enforcing of an ethical code that will insure correct standards of fair dealing. "The Real Estate Men," the Post said, "have hit upon an exceedingly clever and ingenious device to assist them in the achievement of their aims."*

A $32,000 WORD

In commending National Association members who had volunteered to provide appraisal and negotiation assistance to the U.S. government during World War I, President William M. Garland in 1919 said: "In tendering your services during the war . . . I offered them from the REALTORS®. . . . The name REALTOR® therefore means something essential to our government; it thereby becomes a great and more practical asset to ourselves."

By 1967 the Association was working to make the value of the trademark explicit. Executive officers of state and local associations that year received a typewritten, three-ring binder known as the Real Estate Board Operation Manual. The section marked "REALTOR® Proper Use & Promotion" suggested that they "translate REALTOR® into terms of the marketplace and [show that] it means more profit for the people who have earned the right to use it."

Thirty-eight years later, in 2005, NAR commissioned a firm to do just that, quantify the dollar value of the term REALTOR®. According to AbsoluteBRAND, a brand valuation firm based in Milwaukee, the REALTOR® brand generates $32,000 in incremental income for a REALTOR® during an average membership length of ten years in the National Association. The study notes that a member who has six to ten years of real estate experience derives $4,500 in annual incremental income.

Had Charles N. Chadbourn known the power of his invention on December 31, 1927, the day he signed the legal document assigning the word to the National Association of Real Estate Boards, he may have had second thoughts. He was paid the sum of $1.

"IN TENDERING YOUR SERVICES DURING THE WAR . . . I OFFERED THEM FROM THE REALTORS® . . . . THE NAME REALTOR® THEREFORE MEANS SOMETHING ESSENTIAL TO OUR GOVERNMENT; IT THEREBY BECOMES A GREAT AND MORE PRACTICAL ASSET TO OURSELVES."

CHAPTER TWO

Home Ownership in America

Home ownership benefits not only the owners themselves but also the community and society at large. Is there an ideal more deeply ingrained in American culture? Probably not. In 1900 fewer than half of U.S. households owned their own home. Today the number approaches 70 percent. Perhaps no group has done more to promote the ideal of a home-owning nation than the NATIONAL ASSOCIATION OF REALTORS®.

"Widespread home ownership is the bulwark of democracy," declared the Association journal in 1934, in a resolution thanking President Franklin Roosevelt and the Congress for creating the Federal Housing Administration, legislation in which NAR played a key role.

Ten years earlier, the Association—then known as the National Association of Real Estate Boards—had added a preamble to its Code of Ethics, opening with the words: "Under all is the land. Upon its wise utilization and widely allocated ownership depend the survival and growth of free institutions and of our civilization."

That phrase lives on today as a touchstone for the Association's mission of expanding home ownership opportunities. In 2003, NAR President Cathy Whatley said in her REALTOR® *Magazine* column, "Ownership brings about a sense of belonging, an emotional connection, not just to the home itself but also to the neighborhood and community in which home owners live and work."

As early as the 1940s, most Americans identified themselves as middle class—and owning a home was one of the key ways they defined their status, said Jeffrey Hornstein in his 2005 book *A Nation of REALTORS®* (Duke University Press). "The cultural and political work of the REALTORS® and their allies in Washington and elsewhere definitively associated the American dream with home ownership," Hornstein wrote. "Today it is virtually redundant to speak of the 'American Dream of home ownership.' "

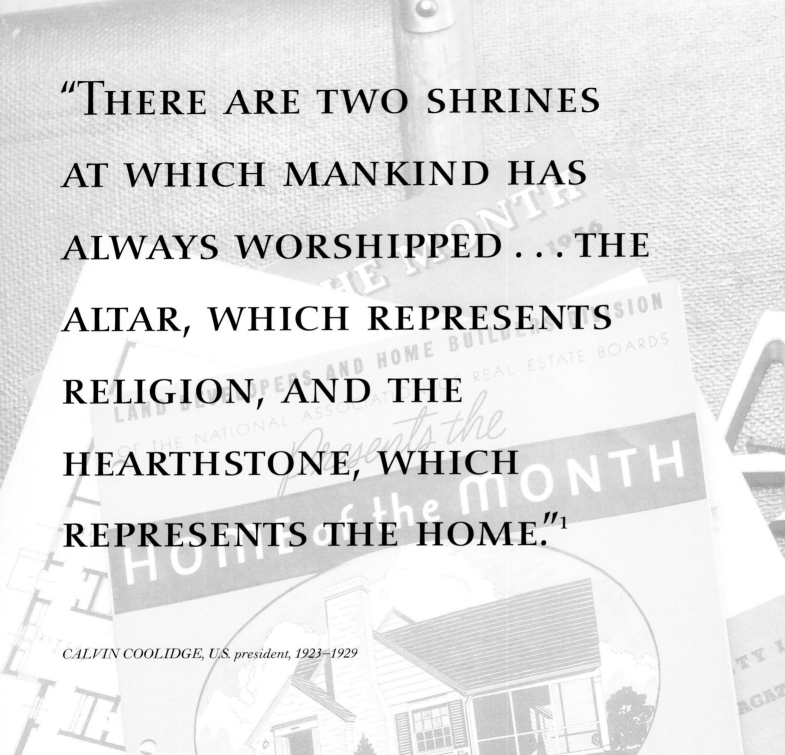

"THERE ARE TWO SHRINES AT WHICH MANKIND HAS ALWAYS WORSHIPPED . . . THE ALTAR, WHICH REPRESENTS RELIGION, AND THE HEARTHSTONE, WHICH REPRESENTS THE HOME."[1]

CALVIN COOLIDGE, U.S. president, 1923–1929

Today's quintessential American dream of owning land was one of the reasons that Europeans journeyed to America four centuries ago and later fought the American Revolution. It was as significant as the pursuit of religious liberty and freedom from unfair taxes.[2]

In the early days of this country, there was no single, systematic way for buyers to purchase property. In New York and Virginia, primogeniture survived until shortly before the American Revolution. In Florida, Spanish law—and in Louisiana, French law—dictated the rules of ownership.[3] Yet, despite the different approaches among states, ownership continued to be the goal of small tenants and farmers in the country's early agrarian economy.[4] The seeds of change toward a more organized landownership system were planted in the late 1700s when the Continental Congress passed a series of ordinances to replace the existing system of metes and bounds, in which rocks, streams, and trees determined property lines.

The Ordinance of 1785 created the framework of the country's national land policy in states west of the original 13 colonies. The ordinance enabled Congress to control the settling and sale of land through a system, devised by Thomas Jefferson, of rectilinear land surveys. The system created townships—six-square-mile areas divided into 36 sections, each one measuring one square mile, or 640 acres.

Through the survey process, the federal government set aside land to award to Revolutionary War soldiers. Most sections would be available to the public at auction, with one central section reserved for a school. The 1785 law—and the Northwest Ordinance of 1787, which created a path for the establishment of new states—remained the foundation of U.S. public land policy until the Homestead Act of 1862.

Landowners learned a valuable lesson in the Panic of 1837, when crop failure and a drop in English demand for cotton sent land prices plummeting. After a depression lasting four years, ownership again became a goal. Settlers were moving west and wanted a means to buy land that had not yet been surveyed by the government. The Preemption Act of 1841 legalized the rights of squatters to purchase 160 acres—for as little as $1.25 an acre—as long as they had occupied their plot for at least 14 months.

Twenty-one years later, President Abraham Lincoln signed the Homestead Act, making land even more affordable. Any head of a household who was at least 21 years old—including single women and freed slaves—could stake a claim to 160 acres. Over a five-year period, homesteaders had to build a home, make improvements, and farm the land, at which point they completed a

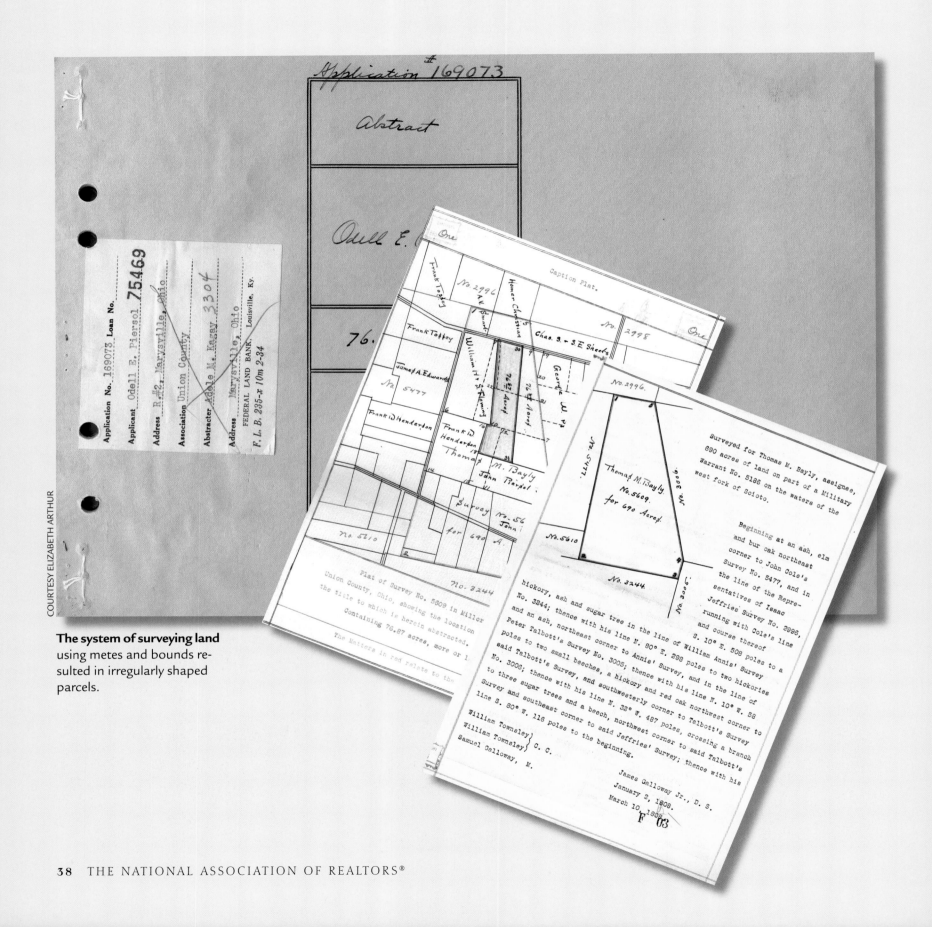

The system of surveying land using metes and bounds resulted in irregularly shaped parcels.

REALTOR'S
HEADLINES

See P. 4 for New Market Indicators

Washington, D.C.

Volume 29, Number 22   May 28, 1962

Realtors Find Oldest Pioneer, Receive Praise

Selection of the nation's oldest homesteader in terms of continuous ownership and the prime of Realtor standards of professional service featured the 1962 Realtor Week which closed on May 26. Attention now shifts to NAREB's Realtor Week award contest in which all boards are invited to compete for the designation of having held the best Week in the nation. Illustrating board activities in the form of a scrapbook, must be carried by the Realtor-Public Relations Committee, 1300 Connecticut Avenue, N.W., Washington 6, D.C., no later than June 27. Contest will appear on the back cover of the Realtor Week kit.

The oldest homesteader was found to be Mrs. Bertha W. Ingalls, of Colorado Springs, Colo. Her (title) was dated Mar. 3, 1887. She was honored last week at special functions of the Colorado Association of Real Estate Boards and the Logan County Board of Realtors and the Colorado Springs Board of Realtors. The homestead

Older Office Units Pressed By Competition

Older office buildings—particularly those in secondary downtown locations—are being forced to either modernize or lower rents to avoid losing tenants to new buildings in prime urban locations and suburbs, according to a NAREB survey released last week.

Conducted by the Department of Research, the market survey reflects the findings of reports submitted by Realtors. It was released by Louie Reese, Birmingham, Ala., president of the Institute of Real Estate Management.

The survey found that vacancy levels have not changed significantly in the past year for office units in prime location urban areas, while vacancies rose slightly in secondary location urban units and in sub-urban structures.

While the majority of survey reporters said rentals for downtown or suburban office buildings have held firm over the past year, a rise in rents for prime location, urban buildings was noted in 28 per cent of the areas, and lower rents were reported in 37 per cent of the areas for secondary location buildings.

The building of new office units equipped with the latest conveniences and situated in the middle of the downtown area has provided real competition for older buildings, which must either modernize, lower rents, or incur vacancies.

Mrs. Bertha W. Ingalls
Photo by courtesy of Colorado Springs Gazette-Telegraph

contest drew 200 inquiries and 65 entrants.

In the course of the dinners, luncheons, and other gatherings held by more than 650 real estate boards during the Week, Realtors were cited for their competence and ethics in meeting the real estate needs of the nation by civic leaders from all walks of life (see p. 3 for picture).

This year's Realtor Week was notable for special sections of news papers and increased TV attention.

National Ad Program Backed

NAREB's new national advertising (see REALTOR 21 for de-

plan "something Realtors have needed all along.

"We need to get back of a program like this," he said.

presidents have been asked ... Arthur P.

REALTOR'S
HEADLINES

See Section Two for Ad Plans

Two Sections—Section One

Washington, D.C.

Volume 29, Number 21   May 21, 1962

Record Realtor Week Gets Started; Boards Urged to Act on Ad Program

Subscription Call Issued

With one or more meetings or ports from local boards scheduled to be held during Realtor Week, present NAREB's new national advertising program to members this week.

Two sets of materials have been sent to all presidents to enable them to explain the program.

The first contained a "call to action" letter from Arthur P. Wilcox, NAREB president, and an advance copy of the supplement to this issue of REALTOR'S HEADLINES, setting forth full details. In his letter Mr. Wilcox provided each board and state with a subscription blank. It was explained that this can be somewhat high in view of the fact that it was computed on the basis of $25 for each plus $5 for each salesman. Therefore, the board of directors computed a program in which salesmen alone. Therefore, asked to refigure their ... on the basis of $25 per Realtor principal in a firm.

A mailing to board chairmen—in the case of Realtors materials for use by them in a speech explaining the program to members and—boards—a $1

FHA Will Set Up Own Credit Report System on July 1

Because "70 per cent of the reports from lenders (on the credit status of mortgage borrowers) were deficient," FHA will set up its own credit reporting system on July 1, the agency said last week.

Each local FHA insuring office is asking for bids from area credit reporting agencies on contracts with FHA under the terms of which the agencies selec...

Event Marked In All States

Realtor Week (May 20-26) is in full swing across the country with more than 625 real estate boards participating in the celebration intended to familiarize the public with the professional standards of service provided by Realtors.

Interest has been heightened on state and local levels by the signing of Realtor Week proclamations by many state governors, including Michael V. DeSalle, Ohio, and Farris Bryant, Florida.

National interest has been aroused by NAREB's search for the oldest homesteader in terms of land ownership in conjunction with the centennial of the Homestead Act which falls during Realtor Week and will be observed by boards.

Throughout the Week, real estate boards will be promoting home ownership and will urge inauguration of urban rehabilitation and conservation measures.

Typical examples of special board activities are:

A billboard advertising campaign in Minneapolis; a Realtor speakers' panel organized in Tulsa, Okla....

Marshall McCully, 94, Aline, Okla., shown above ready to defend his sod house built in 1893, is one of 200 persons interested in NAREB's search to find the home steader who has continually owned or held title to his land for the longest time. The winner will be announced this week.

NAR ARCHIVES

Through the Homestead Act of 1862, hundreds of thousands of Americans staked their claim to a piece of land. In a contest honoring the centennial of the Homestead Act, the National Association searched for the person who had held title to a homestead the longest. The winner was Bertha W. Ingalls, age 94, of Colorado. Ingalls and her husband, Charles, built a sod house on their land in Colorado Springs in 1887. Another participant, Marshall McCully, sent a photo of himself standing ready to defend his sod house, built in 1893. The contest took place during REALTOR® Week in May 1962.

NATIONAL ARCHIVES

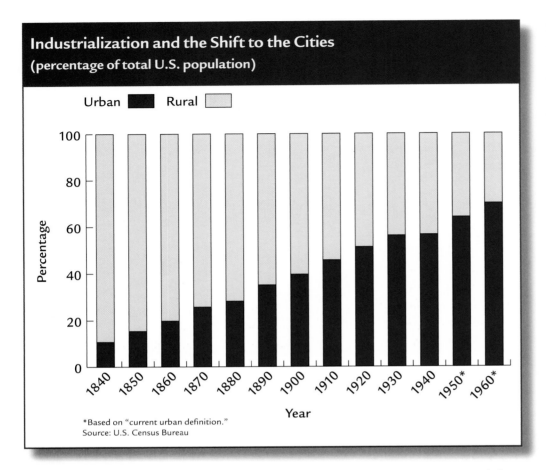

Industrialization and the Shift to the Cities
(percentage of total U.S. population)

Urban ■ Rural ▨

*Based on "current urban definition."
Source: U.S. Census Bureau

Year

Percentage

a book tracing the forces affecting real estate ownership in the 170 years between 1787 and 1957. Interest in housing conditions led to the first census statistics in 1890. The World's Columbian Exposition in Chicago in 1893 revealed a broad national interest in new building forms, advances in technology, and optimism for the country's future.

By 1900, nearly 40 percent of Americans were living in urban areas, double the percentage from 40 years earlier. But the age of industrialization had hardly ushered in a society of home owners. Seventy-five percent of those urban dwellers were renters. No doubt, many dreamed of owning a home but didn't see it as a realistic possibility.

It didn't help that the country was in the midst of a depression. By the time President Grover Cleveland opened the World's Columbian Exposition to the public on May 1, 1893, cracks in the economy were already beginning to show. The Panic of 1893 led to the failure of about 15,000 companies—including several railroads— and 500 banks. Unemployment remained high for years, and strikes—including the famous Pullman Strike of 1894—were rampant. Urban and suburban expansion came to a standstill throughout the country.[6]

Another bank panic in 1907 shook the country, but by 1908, the economy had largely recovered and a wave of immigrants from Europe was swelling the ranks of U.S. households. Still, people's confidence in real estate and other investments was badly shaken. The emergence of a single, unified real estate organization—working with various governmental bodies to espouse the benefits of buying—set the stage for growth in home ownership. The percentage of U.S. households that owned would climb from 46.5 percent in 1900 to more than 60 percent in 1960 and to almost 70 percent in 2006.[7] As home prices escalated, making the home not just a place of residence but also

"proving up" application signed by two neighbors. For a total of $18 in fees, the land was theirs. Widely available, affordable land gave farmers and workers in the West a chance to own, which they would not have been able to do as readily if they had stayed in more established eastern regions.[5] The Homestead Act remained in effect until 1976, though by 1910 there was little land left to claim; in Alaska, homesteading provisions were left intact until 1986.

In the mid-1800s, the economy began its transition from being primarily rural and agricultural to being dominated by cities and manufacturing. "The great surge to the cities beginning in the 1860s was sustained in the 1870s and intensified in the 1880s and 1890s," said the late NAR historian Pearl Janet Davies in her *Real Estate in American History* (1958), a good investment, the desire to buy a home intensified. By the 1980s, it was clear the home was no longer the exclusive domain of the married set. Singles were buying, too. Eventually, the home became the primary venue by which most Americans accumulated wealth—far ahead of their stock, bond, and mutual fund investments.[8] Not only did the numbers of owners increase, but so did the styles and locations of homes. And the NATIONAL ASSOCIATION OF REALTORS® emerged as a key driver in the nation's economy and as the collective voice for property owners nationwide.

HOW ATTAINING THE AMERICAN DREAM BECAME EASIER

When they gathered in Chicago in 1908, the founders of the National Association of Real Estate Exchanges sought to professionalize their ranks. But another aim, just as important, was to educate the public about the benefits of real estate ownership. Early in the twentieth century, the Association began collaborating with governmental agencies, other associations, civic groups, and private businesses to spread the concept that a home represented a privileged consumer durable worth sacrificing for.[9]

Several banking and tax law changes were needed, however, to make home ownership more attainable, ideas the National Association actively supported. Under President William Howard Taft, who served from 1909 to 1913, the idea of a national mortgage bank system gained momentum. In 1912 Taft asked the country's ambassador to France to gather information on how the successful European land mortgage discount banks operated. NAR founder Edward S. Judd advocated adopting Germany's land credit system, which would have made it possible for farmers to borrow money at rates lower than previously available.[10]

During Woodrow Wilson's presidency, the Federal Reserve Act of 1913 passed, allowing farm lending by national banks located outside central reserve cities. It was another three years, however, before national banks were authorized to make direct mortgage loans on urban real estate, and even those mortgages could be for a term of no more than one year and an amount no larger than 50 percent of the property's value.[11] It was also 1913 when Congress established the income tax system, making all interest, including home mortgage interest, deductible. Today, although individual taxpayers can no longer deduct consumer interest, the mortgage interest deduction lives on, thanks in large part to the Association's fight for its preservation. (See Chapter 3, "Walking the Walk" for more on the Association's legislative advocacy.)

In the Association's first decade, millions of European immigrants were entering the country through Ellis Island. The new immigrants swelled the ranks of U.S. households and hastened the growth of cities.

NEW YORK PUBLIC LIBRARY, 1907

With interest in real estate growing, the National Association recognized the importance of providing professionals and potential home owners with an accurate analysis of the value of homes, leading to more professional decisions. In 1914, appraisal committees of local realty boards began to compile appraisal information, the beginning of a specialization.

Local boards also put their energy into a new home ownership campaign that had been launched by the U.S. Department of Labor. The "Buy a Home" campaign—a reaction to socialist stirrings in Europe—told the American public that home ownership was in the national interest.

When the United States entered World War I in 1917, private building was banned and the campaign temporarily shelved.[12] After the war, the United States found itself in the throes of an influenza epidemic that, by 1919, would kill a half-million Americans. But for lovers of free enterprise, including REALTORS®, a bigger threat loomed: the growing presence of socialism. The Bolsheviks had taken control of Russia and, in 1919, formed an international communist party in Moscow with the goal of spreading communism worldwide. American business leaders responded in force. Motion picture industry executives devised propaganda campaigns to aid the government in its efforts to thwart communism.[13] REALTORS® cooperated with the Labor Department in renewing its home ownership campaign. NAR President William May Garland of Los Angeles said the Labor Department was acting on the premise that "ownership of the soil is the greatest insurance against Bolshevism." (Learn more about Garland, the Association's only two-term president, on page 84.)

Despite the drive, rentals continued to outpace home ownership throughout the 1920s, and housing shortages brought on by the wartime construction freeze remained acute.[14] A Senate Select Committee on Reconstruction and Production reported that there were 121 families for every 100 homes.[15] One reason was the difficulty of obtaining construction funding. At its convention in Kansas City, Missouri, in 1920, NAR issued a statement: "A national emergency exists in housing conditions in all centers of population, largely aggravated by the drainage of mortgage money from construction." Association leaders blamed three federal tax policies—the income tax on real estate mortgages, the excess profits tax on real estate sales, and the tax exemption that was given to municipal, state, and federal securities—for driving investment funds away from real estate at a time when cities desperately needed more housing.[16]

NAR called on the government to rectify the problem by, among other things, exempting the interest on real estate mortgages for an emergency period of six years and repealing the excess profits tax. NAR also called for an end to rent controls as a way to encourage more real estate investment. After the convention, NAR called a joint meeting of its committees on taxation, housing, home ownership, and legislation. The unanimous decision was to support a position against "all unjust exemptions."[17]

When Herbert S. Hoover was appointed

The U.S. Department of Labor under Secretary William B. Wilson rolled out its "Buy a Home" campaign in 1914, urging Americans to become home owners.

BE AN AMERICAN; OWN YOUR OWN HOME

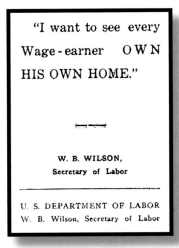

"I want to see every Wage-earner OWN HIS OWN HOME."

W. B. WILSON,
Secretary of Labor

U. S. DEPARTMENT OF LABOR
W. B. Wilson, Secretary of Labor

secretary of commerce by President Warren Harding in 1921, NAR gained an ally in the administration. Hoover strongly believed in home ownership and renewed the federal government campaign not only to encourage it but to improve the conditions of the nation's housing supply. "When I came to the Department, I was convinced that a great contribution to reconstruction and a large expansion in employment could be achieved by supplying the greatest social need of the country—more and better housing," he said in his 1952 memoir.[18] "Fully 30 percent of our housing was below American ideals of decent family life. The cost of construction was excessive, the designs were wretched, and the sentiment ["Own Your Home"] was losing force."

Hoover set up a Division of Building and Housing to coordinate housing policy. He called for a national conference to develop a standard building code and promoted zoning as a means to keep businesses and factories from encroaching into residential areas.[19] The commerce secretary also surveyed members of the Association, by then known as the National Association of Real Estate Boards, asking such questions as, "Is there a shortage of secondary mortgage money?" and "What percentage of the selling price of the house is usually required as a cash down payment?" NAR's Committee on Federal Cooperation sent the survey to member boards requesting a prompt reply.[20]

Hoover may have been aware of the Association's early leadership in mortgage lending. In 1923 the Association formed a mortgage finance division and undertook a landmark study of mortgage practices to look at the methods and risks of mortgage lending. The study helped establish the low risk of making mortgage loans on small homes and exposed the painfully high costs to consumers of the existing mortgage system. The research helped lay the groundwork for the development of the Home

REALTORS® in Birmingham, Alabama, supported the "Buy a Home" campaign with this 1916 trolley advertisement.

BUY A HOME MOVEMENT.
Carried on by Birmingham, Ala., Realty Men.

THE NATIONAL REAL ESTATE JOURNAL, NAR ARCHIVES

The New Orleans Real Estate Board—today the New Orleans Metropolitan Association of REALTORS®—kicked off its home ownership campaign in February 1918 with a banner across Canal Street. One lender said the campaign quickly put six mortgage applications on its books, with more applications coming in steadily.

OWN A HOME

MAKE NEW ORLEANS A CITY OF HOMES!

Own a Home and fight for it

BE A BOOSTER!

Headquarters 413 Carondelet St.

OWN YOUR HOME

To increase home ownership after World War I, the U.S. government appealed to Americans' sense of patriotism. The Buy a Home campaign was renamed "Own Your Home," and the Labor Department and the real estate and building industries advertised it aggressively.

Build NOW

During the War it Was PATRIOTIC Not to Build

Now we can best show our patriotism by building

U. S. Department of Labor W. B. Wilson, Sec. of Labor

Barr Lumber Co.

"Barr's Bureau of Building Information"
Building Service and Material

119 North Milton Avenue   Telephone 47

OWN·YOUR·OWN·HOME

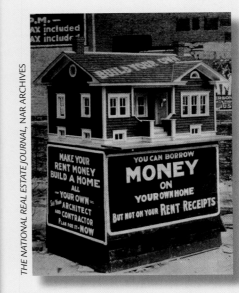

In 1919 REALTORS® and builders in Waterloo, Iowa, put a scale model house, produced by the Southern Pine Association, on a visible street corner, informing passersby about the benefits of building a home.

REALTORS® around the country organized home shows in support of the federal government's "Own Your Home" campaign. NAR's executive secretary, in a letter to Franklin Roosevelt, then head of the American Construction Council, suggested the two groups cooperate on the shows. One member of the Chicago committee was George R. Hemingway, uncle of writer Ernest Hemingway.

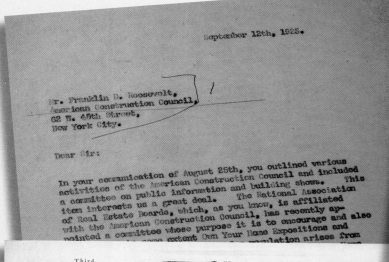

NAR ARCHIVES

After Secretary of Commerce Hoover finished his address he posed for this picture with ex-President Fred E. Taylor. The resemblance between these two is quite remarkable

As secretary of commerce in the Harding administration, Herbert Hoover spoke at the REALTORS®' 1921 convention in Chicago—expressing his alignment with NAR leaders on the goal of increasing home ownership. Afterward he was photographed with 1920 President Frederick Earle Taylor of Portland, Oregon.

Loan Bank system and the Federal Housing Administration.

Also in 1923, the Association appointed a committee to encourage and regulate home-building expositions throughout the country. Local real estate boards sponsored most of the shows, which displayed architectural plans, building materials, and household equipment to convince consumers to purchase houses. A letter on September 12, 1923, from NAR to the head of the American Construction Council discussed efforts to standardize those shows. The head of that council was none other than Franklin Delano Roosevelt, who would go on to promote home ownership once he became president.[21]

Attendance and reaction to the home shows proved the public's eagerness to be educated about the economic value, joy, and comfort of owning a home. Subsequent sales helped revive the construction industry and home building and worked toward easing the serious housing shortage that had developed during World War I.

Meanwhile, Hoover had put the government back in the business of promoting home ownership, and REALTORS® were among his partners in that effort. Hoover's focus wasn't just on increasing home ownership but on improving the quality of homes. For years, he headed an organization, Better Homes in America Inc., to educate homeowners about quality design and construction. Promoted by *The Delineator,* a popular Butterick women's publication, the organization formed a national network of 9,000 local committees, whose members came from a wide range of business groups, including local real estate boards.[22]

Annual contests were held for the best small houses erected in thousands of communities annually. Detailed specifications were provided so that contractors could build the houses without seeking further assistance from architects, and catalogs were also available throughout the country. As part of "Better Homes Week" in 1923, a demonstration home was built on the National Mall, and activities and competitions were held around the country. That year, more than 1,000 demonstration homes went up around the country; by 1926, the number had increased to 3,000.[23] Expositions continued for many years, even throughout the Great Depression.

But there were factors working against national efforts to expand home ownership. By 1920 more people were living in cities than in rural areas—and many city dwellers preferred the more modern heating, lighting, and plumbing typically found in rentals.[24] As the NAR mortgage study had shown, lack of mortgage financing also deterred would-be home owners. Families were expected to buy their houses outright.[25] Those who didn't have the funds might be able to secure a mortgage, but usually for only up to 50 percent of the cost of the house. The amount had to be repaid upon maturation, typically within one to five years, or the loan had to be refinanced at an additional cost. Interest rates ran as high as 25 percent.

Hoover interested Julius Rosenwald of Chicago—an early executive and owner of Sears, Roebuck & Company—in lending second-mortgage money to steadily employed people at 6 percent. Rosenwald showed he could make a profit by lending at reasonable rates, and a number of financial institutions followed his example. Construction of housing units soared from 449,000 in 1921 to 937,000 in 1925, but dropped to 509,000 in 1929 with the onset of the Great Depression.

CHICAGO HISTORY MUSEUM

MAGAZINEART.ORG

A 1924 model home demonstration, sponsored by the *Chicago Daily News,* was one of the thousands around the country promoted by *Delineator* magazine. *Delineator* also developed a plan booklet to help women launch local committees. The book suggested getting business leaders, including the president of the local real estate board, involved.

ADDRESSING A NATIONAL CRISIS

During the Great Depression, Americans were standing in bread lines and home sales were on ice. The real estate downturn preceded the 1929 stock market crash. NAR records show that membership declined 56 percent in the nine years between 1926 and 1935, when it began a slow climb.

The Depression left many homeowners unable to renew their mortgages at reasonable rates. Between 1930 and 1940, about 1,000 homes were foreclosed daily, and home ownership plummeted more than 25 percent.[26] By 1940 the home ownership rate was at 43.6 percent, below the 47.9 percent it had been 20 years earlier. The ranks of practitioners fell, too.

REALTORS® strongly believed any federal intervention in the economic crisis should come in the form of credit relief rather than government-built housing.[27] Historians have called NAR "the most influential of the anti–public housing lobbies."[28] Indeed, the Association consistently opposed reformers' visions of government-developed and government-owned housing, arguing that the private market could do the job better and more efficiently. But the Association wasn't just fighting for its members' business interests.

Reflecting on the Association's battles with public-housing advocates, NAR Executive Secretary Herbert U. Nelson wrote in 1942 that NAR "has always believed [public housing] has been sold to Congress and the public on an unsound basis. Housing ought not to be looked upon as basic therapy for all the ills that afflict mankind, but, realistically, as a public subsidy of those who cannot afford to pay economic rent."[29]

In 1931, Nelson and NAR President Harry S. Kissell of Springfield, Ohio, wrote an article for the *Magazine of Wall Street* with their idea for helping relieve the country's financial crisis. They suggested creation of a mortgage discount bank system that would facilitate amortized, long-term installment-style mortgage payments at interest rates of 4 percent or less.[30]

Hoover, by then president, liked the idea. In December 1931, he held a White House Conference on Home Building and Home Ownership. Among the participants was 1930 NAR President Leonard Reaume, who reiterated the Association's support for a federal mortgage discount bank. In his State of the Union address, delivered just days after the conference, Hoover called for creation of a home loan discount bank.

The resulting Federal Home Loan Bank Act of 1932 was a whittled-down version of the initial idea. For instance, Hoover had recommended to Congress that the plan be available to a wide range of lenders, including savings institutions, insurance companies, and farm loan banks. When the act was enacted, however, the plan could be used only by savings and loan associations and a few savings banks. Hoover also complained that the act was "tragically delayed." Nevertheless, the act set in motion a mortgage revolution that would widen home ownership by creating a network of mortgage lenders with a common credit pool and uniform lending standards.[31]

When Franklin Delano Roosevelt suc-

THE NATIONAL REAL ESTATE JOURNAL, NAR ARCHIVES

December, 1932   THE NAREB NEWS SECTION   Page 9

BUFFALO BOARD'S 4th HOME SHOW SETS NEW RECORDS

Attendance Tops 1931 Record by Over 20,000

From virtually every standpoint—attendance, number of exhibitors, new business obtained by exhibitors and interest evidenced in home ownership and home modernization—the fourth annual Better Homes and Building Exposition conducted by the Real Estate Board at Buffalo, N. Y., the week of Oct. 24, was the most successful and productive of any of the shows thus far sponsored by the Board.

It was a show of records, according to a report from the Buffalo Board, despite conviction in the field of exposition promotion that "the fourth show never goes over."

Attendance for the week exceeded 95,000 persons as compared with last year's record of 75,000—and it rained three of the six nights. Old employes at the city auditorium where the show was held said the Friday attendance of approximately 25,000 persons was the largest Friday crowd in their recollection in the building.

Aside from the remarkable jump in attendance, the number of exhibitors increased to 97 from a total of 85 in 1931.

Exhibitors reported new business in volumes that exceeded their most hopeful expectations. One reported a sale of 107 refrigerators for an apartment building. Another said he sold 22 fireplaces. A Realtor exhibitor sold two houses. An exhibitor of furniture ordered double the amount of space for next year, and so on.

A feature of the exposition that did much to swell the attendance, particularly of women, was a fashion show staged by the city's largest department store. This attraction was said to have been the most complete and elaborate ever offered at a similar event in Western New York. It was given by 12 living models who displayed 52 creations for women's sports wear to bridal gowns.

Another attractive part of the exposition was the refrigeration and radio section which occupied 9,000 square feet of floor space.

Two of the nation's largest makers of bathroom and kitchen equipment displayed complete bathrooms that required two full days to set up. Nothing was missing from tiled walls and running water to soap and towels.

Lumber and building supply

New State Presidents

HAYDEN F. JONES   **JOSEPH LARONGE**

Mr. Jones is the new president of the California Association; Mr. Laronge, the president-elect of the Ohio Association

dealers of the Niagara Frontier constructed an elaborate joint exhibit showing almost every product in the building trades from concrete blocks to expensive interior woodwork.

New products at the show included a porcelained steel tile through the use of which old-fashioned baths and bathrooms may be converted into the "built-in" type, a ball-bearing faucet said to eliminate washer trouble and leaks, a drain cleaner that operates from a faucet, fume consuming pipeless gas heaters, ready-mixed cement, portable fireplaces, entry-proof nursery windows, many new gadgets in the electrical field and an all-electric kitchen.

Admission to the show was by complimentary ticket, 300,000 of which were supplied by the

exposition and distributed by the exhibitors. Visitors without these tickets paid a 25-cent admission charge.

An important factor in creating interest in the exposition was a poster contest conducted among pupils of the public and parochial schools by the *Buffalo Evening News*. Cash prizes totaling $200 were awarded.

A flood lighting system of nearly 1,000,000 candle power was employed in addition to the regular hall illumination. The ceiling of the hall was completely covered by a vast canopy of blue and gold cloth.

Gordon J. Kingdon, executive secretary of the Board, was manager of the exposition. Joseph M. Boehm was chairman of the Realtors' exposition committee.

Officers Elected by Long Island Chapters

Jamaica, L. I.—Following are the 1933 officers elected by chapters of the Long Island Real Estate Board, as reported in the Long Island Realty Magazine:

Garden City
President . . . . Oliver Chichester
Vice-President . . . Frances Mantel
Secretary-Treasurer . . P. J. Fleming

Long Island City
President . . . . Rudolph E. Motl
Vice-President . . . . George Seidel
Secretary . . . . Herbert E. Bode
Treasurer . . . . Frank Capek
Board of Trustees—Edward F. Hosinger, chairman; Philip W. Abatelli, John F. Klein, William A. Krahe, Royal Gensmere, Charles R. Hughes, William H. Murphy.

Queens Second Ward
President . . . . James B. Thompson
Vice-President . . . Carl Fredman
Secretary . . . . Samuel Smirlock
Treasurer . . . . Arthur G. Jaeger
Board of Trustees—George Johnston, Carl Skog, Lewis H. Woodburn.

Ridgewood, Glendale, Maspeth
President . . . Ferdinand Stehle
Vice-President . . C. W. Schreiber
Treasurer . . . Victor Maillard
Secretary . . . Joseph A. Schneider
Board of Trustees—Paul Bernsen, Herman Ringe, Jr., Henry A. Giesler.

Queens North Shore
President . . . . R. B. Guest
Vice-President . . Meyer Gladstone
Secretary . . . . Walter M. Johnson
Treasurer . . . . Nicholas Marg
Board of Trustees—Douglas Van Riper, chairman; Ira L. Terry, Edward J. Hughes, F. H. Reeve, J. Hart Welch, Clarence M. Lowes, Valentine Gray, J. Wilson Dayton, Samuel S. Toback, Robert W. Dasey, Frank J. Gannon, John J. Halleran.

Floral Park
President . . . Edmund D. Purcell
Vice-President . . . Edward Fava
Secretary . . . . William B. Joyce
Treasurer . . . . Edward O'Connor

BUFFALO BOARD'S HOME SHOW

Over 95,000 people visited the Buffalo Board's 4th annual Home Show in City Auditorium the week of Oct. 24, a new record

A national economic slump didn't stop consumers from wanting a home of their own. The Real Estate Board at Buffalo (New York) attracted 95,000 visitors to its fourth annual Better Homes and Building Exposition in 1932.

Harry S. Kissell, past president of NAR, was invited to the White House in 1933 to hand President Franklin Roosevelt a $95,000 check. The check represented the first dividend from the Federal Home Loan Bank System.

ceeded Hoover as president in 1933, the Depression was at its height. The president recognized that immediate credit relief for home owners was needed to prevent the mortgage system's collapse. In a radio broadcast outlining the New Deal program on May 7, 1933, he said, ". . . Congress is about to pass legislation that will greatly ease the mortgage distress among the farmers and the home owners of the nation, by providing for the easing of the burden of debt now bearing so heavily upon millions of our people."[32]

The Home Owners' Loan Corporation (HOLC), which Congress authorized in 1933, helped save thousands of distressed home owners from losing their houses. NAR was a key player in its creation. According to unpublished manuscripts in the Association's archives, Cordell Hull, chairman of the Senate Banking Committee (and later Roosevelt's secretary of state), invited NAR's Nelson to help draft the bill. It called for the federal government to issue bonds that owners could exchange for home mortgages of up

to $14,000—or 80 percent of the current appraised value, whichever was smaller—on one- to four-family houses valued at not more than $20,000. HOLC mortgages would be amortized over a period of 15 years at a rate of 5 percent. Amendments in 1939 extended the term up to 25 years.[33]

The HOLC, which ceased operation in 1951, pioneered the use of long-term amortized mortgages and did so at a slight profit to the government. Some historians have said the agency's appraisal techniques—which involved color-coded maps of neighborhoods—led to the practice of redlining by mortgage lenders and real estate practitioners. However, recent research suggests that HOLC's influence on lenders was limited and that the agency itself showed little evidence of racial bias. (See Chapter 4 for more on National Association and government policy with regard to race.)

As unemployment in the construction trades continued, Congress passed the National Housing Act in 1934, establishing the Federal Housing Administration (FHA). It provided mortgage insurance for one- to four-family homes and multifamily projects, permitted long-term amortized mortgages of up to 20 years (later extended to 30 years), and allowed buyers to put down as little as 20 percent and pay 6 percent interest. Once again, NAR's leadership was directly involved in the legislation, as well as in drafting FHA insurance provisions. Within eight years, FHA was insuring 24.7 percent of the nation's home mortgages.[34]

More readily available and affordable mortgages helped spur home building and buying, and NAR wanted to ensure that the country stayed on the right path. Paul E. Stark, 1937 NAR president, called for a central mortgage bank to ensure a steady supply of mortgage funds at low interest rates. If interest rates were dropped 2 percent and the

period of amortization increased to 30 years, he said, 5 million more American families could own their own homes.[35]

With the 1938 Housing Act, NAR got its wish in the form of the Federal National Mortgage Association, now known as Fannie Mae. Its original purpose was to purchase and hold or sell FHA-insured mortgages, thus replenishing the supply of funds to mortgage lenders. Over the years, it expanded to buy first mortgages backed by the Veterans Administration and later conventional mortgages. A 1968 law made Fannie Mae a private, shareholder-owned corporation and paved the way for the creation of mortgage-backed securities, which would further expand the supply of mortgage funds. In 1970 the government chartered the Federal Home Loan Mortgage Corporation, or Freddie Mac, to ensure competition in the secondary mortgage market. NAR consulted on the formation of both groups.[36]

In the 1930s, with housing starts on the rise, NAR continued to promote the joys of home ownership. The Association's Land Developers and Home Builders Division—which would later split off from NAR to form the National Association of Home Builders—teamed up with *McCall's* magazine to pick a "Home of the Month." Any REALTOR®-Builder erecting the house would have his name and the address of the house published in that month's issue of *McCall's*. It was a huge advertising opportunity, with 2.6 million copies of *McCall's* sold every month.

The country's entry into World War II again curtailed home building, but even before the war's end, the Association was talking with government officials about how to meet the pent-up demand. And demand there was. Household formation—which many people delayed during the Depression and war years—was on the rise. Two factors encour-

After passage of the 1934 National Housing Act, the new Federal Housing Administration put out promotional materials for REALTORS®, communities, and consumers under the Better Housing Program banner.

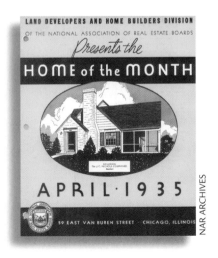

The April 1935 "Home of the Month," featured in *McCall's* magazine, was a modest design built by J.C. Nichols Companies, REALTORS®.

The President's Page

THE biggest thing now going on affecting the future of our business is undoubtedly the framing of regulations for Title II of the National Housing Act, the key provision, for mortgage insurance. We are much pleased that a real estate man active in our Association's work has been given a responsible part in respect to the drafting of these regulations. Your National Association has been given an opportunity to make suggestions directly as to workable and practicable regulations. Through our committee on real estate finance, of which Walter S. Schmidt, our president-elect, is chairman, and through every resource of our Association, we are giving FHA all the help we can.

●

Foreclosures are rapidly declining. Average monthly totals for the first seven months of 1934 as compared with the first seven months of 1933, show a drop of 12.2%. This is for all types of properties. Figures for the year 1926 show foreclosures then running an annual total of 66,672 in communities representing 53.6% of the country's total population. Our most recent monthly total is less than three times the 1926 average.

●

The Federal Real Property Inventory shows some fascinating facts that should be helpful. As yet everybody must do his own pencilwork in totaling data from individual cities. However, as so far reported, average residential vacancy is 7.6%. Vacancies run 5% or under in more than one fourth of all cities yet reported. In some cities vacancies are as low as 1.8%. The number of "doubled" families averages 9.5% of all families enumerated.

It is very important, for sound thinking, to realize, and help other people to realize, that vacancy percentages so far released in this Inventory are of the *total* number of residential units in the city. Reports so far published *do not give the vacancy figure for single-family dwellings* as apart from other residential vacancies. Neither do they segregate the unfit vacant units. Unfit structures account for 4% or more of all units in many cities reported. We earnestly hope that as soon as possible the Department of Commerce will give us separated data for single family dwellings. Local surveys made by real estate boards have for a long time shown single-family vacancies as low as 2%.

The single-family vacancy figure is the key figure for any new home building.

●

A leading Detroit Realtor reports residential rents there substantially higher, particularly for better-class single-family residences. He adds that practically every habitable single-family dwelling is taken. St. Louis reports rents rising recently, in both single-family residences and apartments. Stiffening is indicated in Baltimore, Orlando, Florida, Toronto, to quote a few very recent unofficial reports. We shall all watch with interest the fall renting season as it gets into swing.

●

A significant current development is the broad-gauged display advertising of local real estate as an investment now being carried on by a number of leading banks and trust companies. Also worth comment is the active interest which newspapers themselves are taking in the changing outlook for real estate. Our Association's recent survey of the real estate market, for example, showing an up trend in 70% of the cities reporting, was the best news we have been able to give out for some time. In newspaper use of this story, editorial comment makes up more than one out of four, and wire dispatches sent out by the great press association makes up almost one out of ten of all clippings so far received. This indicates a public interest measurably growing.

We have before us much need of further fact-finding, much need of study, much to adjust, much that needs planning, much that needs genuine creative thinking. But we may indeed take heart for the new work.

Hugh Potter

HUGH POTTER, *President*
National Association of Real Estate Boards

THE NATIONAL REAL ESTATE JOURNAL, NAR ARCHIVES

The National Real Estate Journal in 1946 provided guidance to practitioners on the new GI bill and working with servicemen. Government guarantees allowed veterans to buy houses priced up to $10,000 without having to put down any of their own money.

aged returning troops to buy rather than rent: First, federal subsidies for rental dwellings were scaled back. Second, the Servicemen's Readjustment Act of 1944, popularly known as the GI bill, made low-interest home, farm, and business loans readily available with 100 percent loan-to-value ratios.[37]

"The home purchase provisions, in the opinion of responsible Washington officials, will be one of the greatest stimulants to home-ownership this nation has experienced," Nelson wrote in the June 19, 1944, issue of

NAR's weekly *Headlines* newsletter. "Every responsible service man or woman with 90 days' service will have a chance to acquire a home." Nelson estimated the number of eligible servicemen and -women at 15 million. The loans and construction boom offered an opportunity—and responsibility—for practitioners, he said. "You will have unprecedented opportunity to sell houses and to create a vast new wave of home ownership." But he cautioned readers that they had a responsibility to offer "sound guidance, constructive advice,

Through Good Times and Bad

Looked at decade by decade, both home ownership and NAR membership have increased dramatically since 1900, with a big surge in both following World War II. National Association efforts to bring favorable tax treatment to real estate, rejuvenate home building, and make it easier for buyers to finance their homes played a big part in the postwar increase.

Looked at decade by decade the home ownership rate has also gone down three times over the past century. There was a slight but steady decline from 1900 to 1920, a time when mortgage options were scarce and many Americans were moving from farms to rental housing in cities. Meanwhile, the Association, whose members were just as likely to be involved in commercial real estate as residential, almost quintupled from its second year—1910—to 1920. By contrast, the 4.2 percentage point drop in home ownership during the Great Depression, accompanied by double-digit unemployment, led to a significant drop-off in NAR membership. Despite a small drop in home ownership between 1980 and 1990—most likely the result of high interest rates—NAR membership increased by almost 50,000. However, membership declined over the decade between 1990 and 2000 before shooting up again.

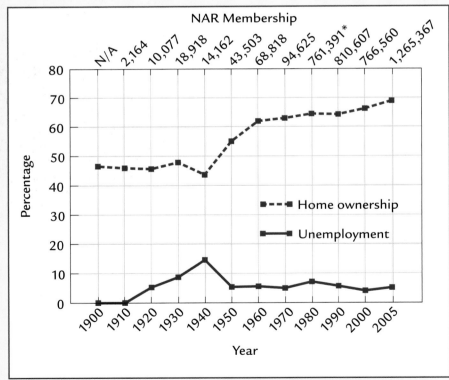

*The 705 percent increase from 1970 to 1980 reflects a decision in the early 1970s to welcome salespeople into the ranks of membership.
Sources: U.S. Census Bureau, Housing Vacancies and Homeownership; the Bureau of Labor Statistics; and NAR.

and wise counsel. Nothing short of that can be expected from REALTORS®."[38]

Before they could take advantage of those opportunities, REALTORS® and builders had to address the serious housing shortage that existed. "By 1947, you [had] millions of husbands and wives and children living . . . bunched up, crunched in with their in-laws. People would take any kind of a place that had a roof over it and a wall around it," recalled Kenneth T. Jackson of Columbia University in "The First Measured Century," a 2000 PBS special. "I think that we have never experienced in American history the kind of pent-up demand for housing that existed about 1947 [and] 1948."

OPPORTUNITY AND TURMOIL

The housing boom that followed the war is one of the defining times in the nation's housing history. Home ownership increased more than 11 percentage points from 1940 to 1950 and jumped another 7 percentage points by 1960. Couples and their baby-boom children were flocking to the fast-sprouting suburbs. According to a 1999 report by the U.S. Government Accounting Office, by 1950, the rate of growth nationally was 10 times higher in the suburbs than in the central cities.[39] At least for white, middle-class Americans, "Happy Days" were here, and NAR benefited with steady membership growth. Between 1940 and 1960, the number of NAR members grew nearly fivefold.

Although the American Dream of home ownership was firmly established, NAR leaders were actively concerned about the decline of urban centers (see profile of 1935 NAR President Walter S. Schmidt on page 55). NAR's 1952 President Joseph Lund of Boston appointed a Build America Better Committee

Turning the Tide

In 1935, Americans were caught in the grip of the Great Depression. The economy had hit rock bottom in 1933, and unemployment topped 20 percent.[*] The stock market's precipitous drop and resulting bank failures spelled misery for millions of Americans—including many real estate practitioners. More than a million homeowners faced foreclosure, new construction ground to a near standstill, and mortgage funds dried up.[†]

Among the most influential voices in solving the nation's housing woes was Walter Seaton Schmidt, 1935 NAR president. Schmidt, who headed a large real estate company in Cincinnati, spearheaded NAR's push to bring liquidity back to the mortgage banking system.

Earlier, in 1927, he had headed NAR's study on building obsolescence at the request of the U.S. Treasury Department. That study became the basis for income tax depreciation of real estate. It also helped demonstrate to Schmidt how little empirical data was available about real estate. After his presidency, he helped organize a research foundation that would become the Urban Land Institute.

REFUELING THE HOUSING MARKET

During his year as president, Schmidt was already beginning to see recovery in the national economy. He established the National Home Show Advisory Bureau to help local real estate boards organize home shows, which were considered a way to revive the flagging industry. Schmidt also actively encouraged private-public partnership to increase housing construction.

But his contribution to the turnaround had begun much earlier, when he headed NAR discussions about improving the flow of low-cost mortgage funds through a federal mortgage discount bank. In *The National Real Estate Journal* in June 1935, he wrote of his efforts, which started during his tenure as chairman of NAR's Committee on Real Estate Finance: "In the six years in which REALTORS® have worked consistently for a federal mortgage agency as the one central need of the mortgage system, we have tested out our proposal in discussion with every affected group in the mortgage and construction field."[‡] Schmidt's work helped bring about important changes in mortgage finance—including the creation of the Federal Housing Administration and Fannie Mae—that widely increased home ownership opportunities in the United States.

By the time Schmidt's term as NAR president neared its end, he was optimistic about the future of real estate. In December 1935, he wrote that "the finance problem has passed and the public has confidence in real estate. Potential mortgage money exists, and can be drawn on, today in amount greater than we have ever known it, and at the lowest interest rates ever prevalent in this country."[§]

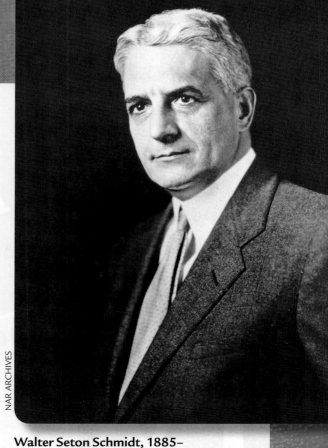

NAR ARCHIVES

Walter Seton Schmidt, 1885–1957 Walter Seaton Schmidt, 1935 president of NAR, helped bring about needed mortgage finance reforms during the Great Depression. Schmidt was also cofounder and first president of the Urban Land Institute.

[*]VanGiezen, Robert and Albert E. Schwenk, "Compensation from before World War I through the Great Depression," *Compensation and Working Conditions,* Bureau of Labor Statistics, Fall 2001.

[†]Schmidt, Walter S., "The President's Page," *National Real Estate Journal,* May 1935, p. 21.

[‡]*Ibid.*

[§]Schmidt, Walter S., "The President's Page," *National Real Estate Journal,* December 1935, p. 23.

VOL · 76 NUMBER 5

19 **11** 34

NOVEMBER

THE ARCHITECTURAL RECORD

COMPLETE RECOVERY OF BUILDING INDUSTRY REQUIRES PROPOSED DISCOUNT FACILITIES OF NATIONAL MORTGAGE ASSOCIATIONS

By WALTER S. SCHMIDT

Mr. Schmidt, President-elect of the National Association of Real Estate Boards, spoke in favor of the National Housing Bill before the Senate Committee on Banking and Currency. However, as chairman of the Mortgage Finance Committee of the National Association of Real Estate Boards, he advocated that the discount facilities provided by the Home Loan Bank and the insurance contemplated by the Housing Bill for mortgages on homes of $20,000 or less be extended in principle to mortgages on other types of real estate, and submitted a draft for a Federal mortgage discount corporation to be added as a separate title to the Housing Bill. The proposed title was not accepted, but the National Housing Bill as enacted permits the formation of National Mortgage Associations, which are authorized to provide discount facilities for all types of mortgages. Since Mr. Schmidt's article was written, announcement has been made that the RFC is ready to participate in furnishing capital for such associations.

In his final letter to members, published in *The National Real Estate Journal* in January 1936, Schmidt advocated for more building through lowered production costs and neighborhood planning.* It was in the area of urban planning, in fact, that Schmidt made his most enduring mark.

*Walter S. Schmidt, "The President's Page," *National Real Estate Journal,* January 1936, p. 23.

"THE GREAT MAN"

Schmidt was born in Cincinnati on July 4, 1885. When he was 26, his father died, leaving him the logical heir apparent to the Frederick A. Schmidt Realty Company. Schmidt's father had founded the company in 1878. His brother was a Jesuit priest and theologian, and "Walter wanted to become a priest, too," according to a nephew, Walter S. Bunker, who was named for Schmidt and followed him into the real estate profession. "But he felt he had to care for his sisters."

A lifelong bachelor, Schmidt embraced the real estate profession enthusiastically, becoming active in the Cincinnati Real Estate Board and serving as its president in 1919. By 1935, he'd built the family business into one of the largest real estate companies in the country. Along the way, he founded several companies in the building and insurance industries, employing family and friends.

While president of his family firm, Schmidt handled a large estate that included an entire downtown Cincinnati block with several big buildings. He conceptualized the idea to turn the block into the Carew Tower (named for a department-store magnate who was the building's first tenant). Work commenced one month before the 1929 stock market crash and was completed two years later.

Well known in Cincinnati, Schmidt chaired the Citizen's Committee on

In 1934, the year the FHA was established, Walter Schmidt argued in an article for *The Architectural Record* that additional steps were needed to ensure the flow of mortgage capital. His writings and testimony before Congress helped spur the 1938 law that led to the creation of Fannie Mae.

Replanning Cincinnati. He was also director of Cincinnati's Community Chest, chairman of its public recreation program, and active at his alma mater, Xavier University, which named a residence hall and field house for him.* According to Schmidt's nephew, his uncle was known among his college peers as "The Great Man" since he was thought to know everything. In 1934, he was honored as one of Cincinnati's 12 civic patriots.

LAND–USE PIONEER

In the year following his NAR presidency, Schmidt and six other leaders recommended to the NAR board of directors the idea of starting a research and educational organization. They envisioned an organization that would catalog significant data about the real estate industry so that important planning decisions could be made intelligently.

At the time, for instance, there were no statistics on how many residential buildings were fit only for destruction, how many could be salvaged, or what it would cost to provide each family with decent quarters. "Figures quoted are but wild hazards," said Schmidt. "The actual status of American real estate never has been determined. . . ."‡

The National Real Estate Foundation for Practical Research and Education was incorporated in Chicago as a separate research institute within NAR in December 1936. Among the trustees were Schmidt; William May Garland,

The Carew Tower in Cincinnati, brainchild of Walter S. Schmidt, became the nation's first multi-use development.† At the time, it represented the largest single real estate transaction in the country.

CINCINNATI MUSEUM CENTER

1917–1918 NAR president; Edward A. MacDougall; J. C. Nichols; and Hugh Potter, 1934 NAR president.

Three years later, the trustees voted to change the foundation's name to the Urban Land Institute (ULI) and to expand its mission. The organization also was changed to an independent nonprofit institute to avoid the perception that it benefited the business interests of REALTORS® or its trustees. Schmidt served as the organization's first president from 1940 to 1941. ULI, now headquartered in Washington, D.C., has more than 30,000 members in 50 states and 88 countries. Its mission is to provide leadership for the responsible use of land and to create and sustain thriving communities worldwide.

Schmidt died at age 72 in 1957, leaving a legacy of real estate and civic contributions and a favorite expression, "Under all is the land." Bunker headed his uncle's company before selling it in 1983. Schmidt, he said, "believed that everyone should own a piece of land."

*Eskew, Garnett Laidlaw, assisted by John R. MacDonald, *Of Land and Men: The Birth and Growth of an Idea,* Urban Land Institute, 1959, p. 11, and Xavier University phone call, November 5, 2006.

†Horstman, Barry M., "Golden Age of Architecture," *Cincinnati Post,* November 21, 1998.

‡Eskew, pp. 30–31.

to develop ideas for revitalizing run-down neighborhoods. Other pressing issues also came along—including the fight for fair housing and federal government accusations of price-fixing by local real estate boards and NAR. (The role of REALTORS® in fair housing and community building is discussed in Chapter 4 and Chapter 5, respectively. Price-fixing allegations are discussed in Chapter 6.)

The decade of the 1970s marked an era of intense political activity and increased visibility for the Association. In 1973, the Association officially changed its name from the National Association of Real Estate Boards to the NATIONAL ASSOCIATION OF REALTORS®, welcoming sales associates into its ranks and dramatically increasing its membership. The Association positioned itself as spokesman for the nation's property owners. A campaign known as REALTOR® Week—which since 1956

The construction of a home from ammunition boxes is emblematic of the acute housing shortage that followed World War II.

In the years following World War II, suburban development was on fire with REALTORS® showing the way for war veterans and other aspiring owners. Top: Levittown, N.Y. Bottom: Chicago.

BOTH PHOTOS: NATIONAL ARCHIVES

How To Buy Your Home

NAR ARCHIVES, 1960

Benchmarking the Nation's Housing Sales

The NATIONAL ASSOCIATION OF REALTORS® Research Department conducts a wide range of studies for and about the nation's REALTORS®. It also produces key economic data for use by government and housing industry economists, including the Existing-home Sales, or EHS, series. Before EHS started in the late 1960s, the National Association of Real Estate Boards, as the Association was then known, compiled annual data on the residential market.

EHS's predecessor dates back to May 1923, when NAR's Research Department created an index to help track the market. The original real estate market index was started as part of the Association's efforts to promote professionalism and academic research in various aspects of the industry. For a few years up until 1965, NAR also conducted survey panels in which it interviewed REALTORS® to gather details on market conditions. The federal government collected data on the housing market, too, but not on a monthly or even annual basis: The Census Bureau included housing data in the decennial census, and the Federal Reserve Board collected some information in its Survey of Consumer Finances in the early 1960s.

In the 1950s and 1960s, the residential market grew exponentially. The Association recognized a need for detailed statistics on the housing market that would be available more frequently than once each year.

Plans were drawn up in the spring of 1965 for an existing-home sales series, based on monthly reports from local multiple listing service bureaus. Members of the Executive Officers Council designed a standard data collection form to help gather the necessary information, and the series officially began in January 1966 with 120 local boards participating. By 1968, NAR had collected enough information to create a databank that could be analyzed and interpreted for a national audience.

The EHS methodology underwent changes in 1980 and again in the 1990s. In 2005, the Research Department began incorporating condominiums and cooperatives into the EHS number. That same year, the Association developed a leading economic indicator, the Pending Home Sales Index, to help its members and forecasters see the direction of housing sales.

Median Home Price

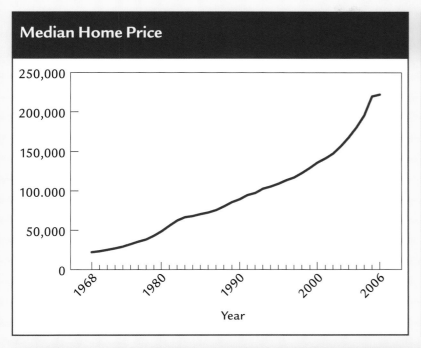

Existing Condo and Co-Op Sales (in thousands)

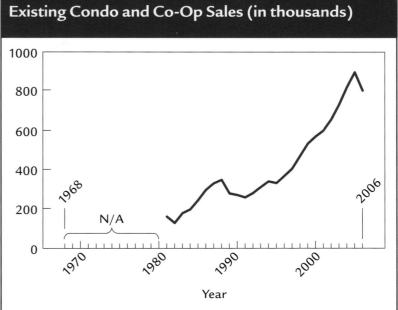

Existing Single-Family Home Sales (in millions)

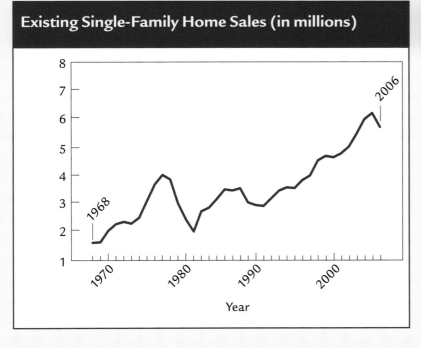

Interest Rates* (%)

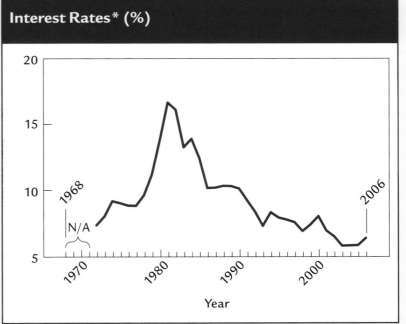

*Contract rate on 30-year fixed-rate conventional home mortgage commitment.
Sources: NAR and Freddie Mac.

RIGHT NOW, THE CONGRESS HAS A UNIQUE OPPORTUNITY TO HELP MAKE THE AMERICAN DREAM COME TRUE.

Today, the American dream of home ownership is a nightmare for millions of Americans.

With mortgage rates continuing to soar, 90% of first-time home seekers simply cannot afford the home they need.

Savings are grossly inadequate to provide housing. Many thrifts and small banks are in deep trouble. So are the millions of Americans dependent on them for their home mortgage money.

Depending on how Congress votes, a solution is at hand.

A break for savers and buyers.

Part of the tax bill currently being debated in Congress would allow savings and loan associations, mutual savings banks, commercial banks and credit unions to issue Tax-Exempt Savings Certificates for one year.

By keeping interest free of income taxes (limited to $1,000 for individuals and $2,000 for couples), these certificates would obviously benefit savers. By helping attract more money at lower cost, they would also strengthen depository institutions.

And, if Congress acts wisely, these certificates would also help make home ownership affordable for as many as 5 million American families.

Lower mortgage interest rates for home buyers.

The House Ways and Means Committee is recommending that funds from these Tax-Exempt Savings Certificates be tied to home mortgages.

And that would make mortgage money more available and less expensive. These certificates lower the cost of money for financial institutions by as much as three percentage points. And on a $75,000 home, that means monthly payments would fall from $807 to $664, a difference of $1,716 a year—equivalent to the average family's food bill for four months.

Now it's time for the House and Senate to act.

If the House and Senate follow the lead of the House Ways and Means Committee, financial institutions and home buyers will be helped during the next year (and could be helped more when permanent tax relief is provided).

Clearly, the House Ways and Means Committee is out front for housing.

And now it's time for the full House and the Senate to get moving.

Unless the savings from these certificates are earmarked for mortgages, as many as 5 million home seeking families may be denied their own home.

And that's no way to help Americans realize the American Dream.

NATIONAL ASSOCIATION OF REALTORS®
and
National Association of Home Builders

In the early 1980s, NAR and the National Association of Home Builders **teamed up** to spur congressional action on high interest rates.

had encouraged community involvement by members—was changed in 1975 to Private Property Week to emphasize Americans' constitutional right to own and transfer real property.

Meanwhile, the housing market was headed into bumpy times. An expansive monetary policy at the Federal Reserve raised concerns about inflation. Under Fed Chairmen Arthur Burns and G. William Miller, interest rates hovered in the 8 percent to 10 percent range, with inflation generally kept in check, and by 1978, existing-home sales had hit a record high of 3.986 million units. But inflation became a more urgent concern under Paul Volcker, who was appointed Fed chairman by President Jimmy Carter in 1979. By October 1981, rates hit 18.45 percent, and although they would come down in the following months, it would be five years before rates fell back into single digits and 10 years before single-digit interest rates would become the norm.

Home sales took a major hit—existing-home sales fell to 1.99 million units by 1982—and the home ownership rate was in decline.[40] To spotlight the affordability problem that resulted, NAR created the Housing Affordability Index, measuring whether a family earning the median income could qualify for a mortgage loan on the national median-priced, existing single-family home. (In 1982 a median-income family couldn't qualify, according to the index.) Several state associations, like the CALIFORNIA ASSOCIATION OF REALTORS®, also began measuring housing affordability. Ravi Kamath, professor of finance at Cleveland State University, called the affordability index a crude measure; nonetheless, Kamath said, it was "a successful prognosticator."[41]

Association leaders also advocated solutions for getting first-time buyers on to the "housing ladder." One such solution came in the form of a federal tax credit: in 1984, the federal government gave state and local governments the au-

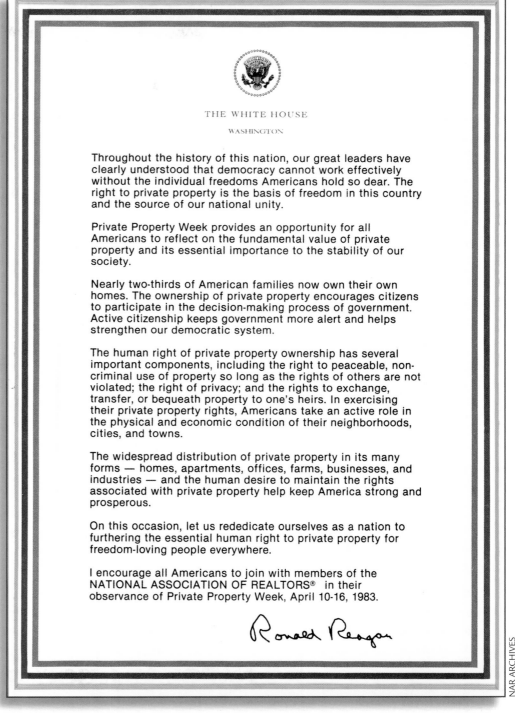

THE WHITE HOUSE
WASHINGTON

Throughout the history of this nation, our great leaders have clearly understood that democracy cannot work effectively without the individual freedoms Americans hold so dear. The right to private property is the basis of freedom in this country and the source of our national unity.

Private Property Week provides an opportunity for all Americans to reflect on the fundamental value of private property and its essential importance to the stability of our society.

Nearly two-thirds of American families now own their own homes. The ownership of private property encourages citizens to participate in the decision-making process of government. Active citizenship keeps government more alert and helps strengthen our democratic system.

The human right of private property ownership has several important components, including the right to peaceable, non-criminal use of property so long as the rights of others are not violated; the right of privacy; and the rights to exchange, transfer, or bequeath property to one's heirs. In exercising their private property rights, Americans take an active role in the physical and economic condition of their neighborhoods, cities, and towns.

The widespread distribution of private property in its many forms — homes, apartments, offices, farms, businesses, and industries — and the human desire to maintain the rights associated with private property help keep America strong and prosperous.

On this occasion, let us rededicate ourselves as a nation to furthering the essential human right to private property for freedom-loving people everywhere.

I encourage all Americans to join with members of the NATIONAL ASSOCIATION OF REALTORS® in their observance of Private Property Week, April 10-16, 1983.

Ronald Reagan

NAR ARCHIVES

In this 1983 proclamation, President Ronald Reagan called private property ownership "the basis of freedom in this country and the source of national unity" and encouraged Americans to join with NAR in its observance of Private Property Week.

This week, America will attend a homecoming.

APRIL 13-19, 1986
AMERICAN HOME WEEK

R
REALTOR

A National Celebration of Homes for People, Business and Industry

In 1986, Private Property Week was changed to American Home Week. REALTORS® were underscoring, as they had in the past, the importance of the home in America.

In 2001, NAR and five minority real estate associations founded the HOPE Awards to honor individuals and organizations that are lowering the barriers to home ownership for the nation's minority population. At the first HOPE Awards gala, NAR President Richard Mendenhall, center, said, "Our HOPE Award winners show that the innovation and passion are there to make home ownership equality finally happen."

thority to issue mortgage credit certificates that allowed first-time buyers to deduct a certain percentage of the mortgage interest they paid, dollar for dollar, from their federal income tax. Another solution, advocated by NAR and the National Association of Home Builders, was the use of mortgage revenue bonds by state and local housing finance agencies. Sales of the bonds helped finance below-market-rate mortgages for first-time buyers of single-family homes.

An early 1990s recession, spurred in part by Iraq's invasion of Kuwait, affected many markets, particularly California. But with interest rates dropping, affordability increased and home sales came back with a vengeance,

by 1992 once again topping 3 million per year. Between 1997 and 2005, existing-home sales hit records in all but one year, dipping slightly in 2000.

THE DREAM CONTINUES

By 2000 homeownership stood at 66 percent. Although it would climb slightly, the housing boom that followed 2000 had less to do with new home owners than with second-home and investment sales. The real estate brokerage community benefited from the gains. NAR's membership began a dramatic rise, surpassing 1 million in 2004. However, REALTORS® were

NAR

REALTORS® around the country participate in expanding home ownership through programs such as home buyer fairs, counseling, and education. NAR funds many local programs through its Housing Opportunity Program. In Fort Collins, Colorado, for example, REALTORS® helped dispel negative connotations of affordable housing with a campaign that highlighted the needs of the community's workforce. Pictured: Chris McElroy at the Fort Collins Association of REALTORS® Sensible Housing Summit in 2004.

concerned about people in their community who were left out of the housing boom.

In 2001, under President Richard Mendenhall of Columbia, Missouri, the Association teamed up with a group of minority real estate organizations to develop the HOPE (Home Ownership Participation for Everyone) Awards. The awards are given every two years to individuals and organizations that are working to close the gap in home ownership rates between whites and minorities. President George W. Bush threw his support behind the Association's efforts, in 2002 kicking off the White House Minority Homeownership Initiative. Bush vowed, through improved buyer education and mortgage financing options, to increase minority home ownership by 5.5 million within the next eight years.

Still, double-digit price appreciation in many areas was shutting out many would-be buyers—whites and minorities alike. In a speech to local and state association presidents in August 2001, Martin Edwards Jr. of Memphis, Tennessee, talked about making affordability the centerpiece of his NAR presidency in 2002. Many local and state associations were already actively involved in bringing affordable housing options to their communities. Edwards wanted to showcase those efforts and start a national dialogue about how lack of affordable housing affected core members of a community's workforce, including teachers, nurses, and firefighters. The result was the Housing Opportunity Program.

One of Edwards's overarching goals was to erase the bad association some people had with affordable housing. NAR produced a video, "The New Face of Affordable Housing," and began funding state and local REALTOR® association programs designed to increase the affordability and availability of housing in their communities. With the Housing Opportunity Program, "we turned a corner as an organization," Edwards later said. "We reinvolved ourselves in the issue of affordability."

Edwards's successor, Cathy Whatley of Jacksonville, Florida, recognized 12 "Hometown Heroes" who were bringing affordable housing solutions to their communities. And in 2006, the Housing Opportunity Program pioneered "Home at Work," a program to help employers make homeownership assistance a benefit for employees wanting to buy their first home.

The prolonged housing boom brought an enormous amount of media attention to the real estate industry, with many pundits forecasting doom for overheated markets. To better predict home sales activity in the near term, the Association's Research Department released a new leading indicator, the Pending Home Sales index. The index, first released in 2005, uses actual pending sales data to see the direction sales will take in the next two to three months.

By 2006, sales had slowed in many regions and cities. With media talk of a bubble bursting, the Association ran national advertising in early 2007 assuring Americans that the housing market was far from dead. Indeed, despite the slump, 2006 turned out to be the third-strongest year on record for existing-home sales. The ads pointed out that lower prices and higher inventories, combined with historically low interest rates, made it a great time for buyers to jump into the market. With NAR as its most visible proponent, home ownership remained an essential part of the American dream.

Our REALTOR® didn't think the market would change. He knew it would.

If you're thinking about selling your home, but you're unsure of the timing, there are some things your REALTOR® wants you to know. Today's current real estate market conditions—low rates and an abundant inventory—are offering buyers once-in-a-lifetime opportunities. Which means there will be more buyers in the market, looking for a home like yours.

Every market's different, call a REALTOR today.

Ask if your agent is a REALTOR,® a member of the National Association of REALTORS®

©2007 National Association of REALTORS!

NAR

NAR launched a national advertising campaign in 1998—dubbed the Public Awareness Campaign—to reinforce the value of working with a REALTOR®. In 2007, the campaign included ads designed to address changing market conditions.

NAR's Gift to America

The National Museum of American History developed the Web site www.americanhistory.si.edu/house to accompany "Within These Walls. . . ."

At the start of the new millennium, NAR teamed up with the Smithsonian Institution to showcase the central role of home in the American experience. "Within These Walls . . . ," an exhibition at the National Museum of American History Behring Center in Washington, D.C., opened May 16, 2001, and continues through 2017. The exhibition tells the story of one U.S. home and its inhabitants, including a real estate practitioner, whose lives intersected with American history at different crossroads.

"Our homes create the backdrop against which all of us become a part of American history," 2001 NAR President Richard A. Mendenhall said before the exhibition opened in May 2001. "This exhibition is a wonderful vehicle for REALTORS® to celebrate that."

"Within These Walls . . ." is built around a 240-year-old house from Ipswich, Massachusetts. In the early 1960s, the Ipswich House was saved from the wrecker's ball by a handful of local citizens just hours before it was to be razed. Smithsonian staff took the house apart piece by piece, transported it, and reassembled it inside the National Museum of American History on the National Mall. Throughout the 1970s the house was displayed to showcase its timber framing. Later, it was sealed off as historians dug deeper into its construction and tracked down the stories of the people who lived in it. Exhibition curators choose to highlight five families because of their role in the country's unfolding history.

1. *American colonists.* Abraham and Sarah Choate, a prosperous merchant couple, built the house in the 1760s. To them, its stately architecture signaled their place in Colonial American society, says Shelley Nickles, exhibition cocurator.

2. *Revolutionaries.* To Abraham and Bethiah Dodge, who owned the house in the 1770s and 1780s, the house was in the eye of the storm. Like other towns throughout the Colonies, Ipswich was roiled by Revolutionary fervor. Dodge, a young merchant, fought as a captain at the Battle of Bunker Hill in 1775.

COURTESY OF IPSWICH HISTORICAL SOCIETY

Birdseye view of Ipswich, Massachusetts, by George E. Norris, 1893, with Ipswich house highlighted.

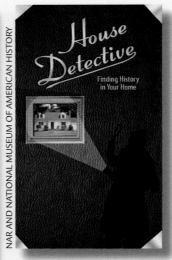

NAR AND NATIONAL MUSEUM OF AMERICAN HISTORY

Smithsonian curators developed *House Detective: Finding History in Your Home,* a booklet telling museum visitors how to piece together the history of their home.

COURTESY NATIONAL MUSEUM OF AMERICAN HISTORY

COURTESY RICHARD S. LYNCH

COURTESY RICHARD S. LYNCH

Among the inhabitants of the Ipswich house were real estate practitioner Josiah Caldwell and family (pictured here in a rendering of what they might have looked like) and widow Mary Scott, whose son Roy served in the Navy during World War II.

3. *Reformers.* In the 1800s, the antislavery movement was growing, and the new owners, Lucy and Josiah Caldwell and their adopted daughter, Margaret, opened their parlor to the crusade. Caldwell, a prosperous businessman and real estate dealer, was the first president of the Ipswich Anti Slavery Society. His wife hosted meetings of the women's counterpart organization and produced antislavery materials, says Nickles.

4. *Immigrant workers.* By the time the industrial revolution rolled in, the house had lost its place in the fashion center of Ipswich. It was purchased as an investment property and turned into rental apartments. Among its renters were Catherine Lynch, a widow from Ireland, and her daughter, Mary. Mary worked in a nearby hosiery mill, and Catherine took in laundry to pay the rent and make ends meet.

5. *World War II "home fronter."* From the Great Depression through the war, the house was home to hardship. After weathering the economic turmoil of the 1930s, the last resident of the house, Mary Scott, helped the country's war effort, planting a victory garden, preserving vegetables in her kitchen, and saving tin cans, foil, and leftover fats for recycling into war material.

"This house and NAR's affiliation as the exhibition's sole sponsor will reinforce for millions of people the importance of the home to the family, the community, and the nation," said Spencer R. Crew, director of the museum, in 2001.

How the Houses Have Changed

The Baltimore home of Reverdy Johnson, a U.S. senator and attorney general under President Zachary Taylor—pictured in 1893, 17 years after Johnson's death—was typical of the elegant nineteenth-century townhomes that became obsolete as affluent citizens moved out of central cities. What replaced them were apartment buildings to house migrants escaping rural poverty, as well as immigrants flocking to the United States.

As the home ownership rate has grown, the nature of the homes Americans own has changed, too.

At the start of the twentieth century, there were country homes and there were town-homes. Houses in town were often elegant structures with servants' quarters.

But with the growth of cities, streetcars, and automobiles, single-family-home owners began escaping the central business districts. The old, elegant town houses became obsolete, according to John Burchard and Albert Bush-Brown, authors of *The Architecture of America—A Social and Cultural History*.[42] Commercial businesses valued the land on which the town houses sat more than the houses themselves, which doomed them to demolition. Meanwhile, immigrants were flowing in from Europe and the number of servantless households was increasing. Demand for apartments soared.

Apartments that were owned rather than rented took one of two legal forms. Cooperative, or co-op, apartments, date back to 1883 in New York's Gramercy Park neighborhood. In 1916 Finnish immigrants established Sunset Park in Brooklyn, New York, which remains the oldest existing co-op in this country. With a co-op, the building represents a nonprofit corporation that holds the mortgage; individual owners hold shares in the corporation, with their number of shares determined by the size of their unit and its floor level. The corporation also owns the common areas, and it pays the property taxes and passes along the cost to the tenant-shareholder, usually through monthly maintenance fees.[43]

Unlike co-ops, condominiums offer ownership in "real property"—individual units as well as common areas of the building such as the exterior walls, roof, and lobby.[44] Owner-occupants can deduct payments made for mortgage interest and property taxes. Condos

MARYLAND HISTORICAL SOCIETY

NATIONAL ARCHIVES, C. 1940

NATIONAL ARCHIVES, C. 1940

NATIONAL ARCHIVES

are said to have ancient origins. They existed in Europe as early as the 1920s: According to *The Encyclopedia of Housing,* Belgium passed its first Condominium Act in 1924.[45] The concept spread from Europe to Latin America. U.S. developers became acquainted with the concept in Puerto Rico, and in 1961, President Kennedy signed a law authorizing the FHA to insure condo mortgages.[46] While condos initially appealed as a recreational housing alternative in Florida and California, interest increased

among a wider population and the number of condos in this country went from 60,000 in 1970 to more than 2 million in 1980[47] and to 4 million by 1990.[48] Town houses also regained popularity as an alternative for buyers who wanted a single-family detached or attached home on less land than a single-family home.

As part of its Existing-home Sales Series, the NATIONAL ASSOCIATION OF REALTORS® began tracking condo and co-op sales in 1981. In recent years, because of the high concentration

Thomas Jefferson's Monticello helped establish the notion of the home as a portrait of its owner.

CYNTHIA HOWE

Frank Lloyd Wright's influence is seen in the Prairie-style homes and low-slung bungalows in Oak Park, Illinois, where the architect had his first studio.

CYNTHIA HOWE

of condos in the most expensive metropolitan regions, the median condo price has surpassed the median single-family home price.

SINGLE-FAMILY STYLE

Meanwhile, the nature of single-family homes was changing. Well before the start of the twentieth century, American architecture had begun to emerge from the European tradition. American home styles were often indigenous to a locale's topography or climate and reflected the owner's individual style and budget. Dell Upton, a professor of architectural history at the University of Virginia and author of *Architecture in the United States,* pegged the start of this greater individuality to Monticello, the home that Thomas Jefferson designed and completed for himself in Charlottesville, Virginia, in 1809. At Monticello, Jefferson assembled a collection of familiar ideas from such sources as ancient Rome and sixteenth-century Italian architect Andrea Palladio into a new kind of house appropriate for the American landscape.[49] Jefferson synthesized the traditional elements in a new way and incorporated native materials, according to Leland M. Roth, an architectural historian at the University of Oregon. He thus helped establish the American notion of a home as an "individualized portrait" of its owners.[50]

Once Henry Ford's motorcars rolled off assembly lines beginning in about 1913, buyers could see distinct housing styles firsthand in suburbs that flourished beyond every large city—Beverly outside Boston; Tuxedo Park and Rye outside New York; Chestnut Hill and the Main Line towns near Philadelphia; and Winnetka, Glencoe, and Lake Forest north of Chicago.[51] Most houses built in the years between World War I and World War II reflected one of two distinct directions—a yearning for historic nostalgia or a modern look forward.[52]

Regional variations flourished. Frank Lloyd Wright's two-story Prairie-style home became a popular Midwestern genre, with its horizontal lines, hipped or gabled roofs, wide eaves, porches, and casement windows. The first ranch homes were built in Pasadena, California, in the early 1900s, and, a few years later, the bungalow emerged both in Chicago and Southern California with slight variations after a number of design books and articles on the style were published. Because of their affordability and popularity, bungalows were dubbed by many as the all-American family house.[53]

Publications helped democratize home building by publishing illustrations and even providing mail-order plans. As early as 1838, there were pattern books, such as Alexander Jackson Davis's *Rural Residences.* Magazines such as *Godey's Lady's Book, Ladies' Home Journal,* and *Craftsman* also published home plans, as did companies such as Sears, Roebuck. Even the federal government issued designs in its FHA publication *Principals of Planning Small Houses* in 1936. The "FHA Minimum House" featured a one-story, two-bedroom plan within a compact 534 square feet. A slightly larger version included 624 square feet. A later version of *Planning Small Houses* featured the option to expand the square footage and add such amenities as chimneys, fireplaces, and basements, and even group houses along streets and in cul-de-sacs. Beginning in the 1930s, *McCall's* magazine published its "Home of the Month" in conjunction with the Land Developers and Home Builders Division of the National Association of Real Estate Boards. One such example, in 1937, a California Colonial, featured efficient one-level living through photos, floor plans, and landscaping designs.

The suburban ranch of the 1940s and 1950s reflected the country's fascination with the informal lifestyle and natural materials

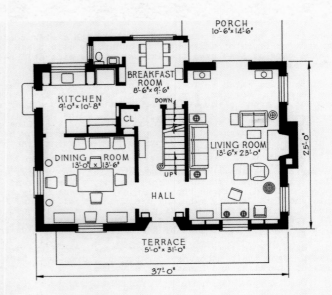

The first floor provides a unit composed of a living room for formal or general entertainment, a porch with French doors leading from the living room for outdoor living, and a third room in this unit usable as a card room, study or breakfast room, or for informal dining. This third room and the porch are connected.

A central hall separates, and connects with, unusually well-arranged units of rooms. The main dining room and kitchen are entirely separated from the living room, making a unit for formal dining. The kitchen and breakfast room make a separate unit that can be shut off from the rest of the house. An extra large view window in the rear of the breakfast room overlooks the garden. Children in the garden can be seen from the kitchen.

The first floor lavatory has a ___ious location. It is comfortably away from the living room, ___dy for use from any part of the first floor. It has two ___ direct ventilation. Its location is also ide___ who can enter the house through the br___

favored on the West Coast. A later variation, the split-level house, provided greater privacy between public and private spaces—an important consideration once families bought noise-producing TVs and phonographs.[54]

So many different styles gradually led to a smorgasbord of choices in neighborhoods, with each home owner or builder trying to express individuality. American-style Colonials sat cheek by jowl with Spanish-style, French country, and split-level homes. This lack of homogeneity led to the emergence of new, carefully designed planned communities such as Robert E. Simon's Reston, Virginia, in 1961, and James Rouse's Columbia, Maryland, in 1963. The management of these new towns typically set regulations regarding individual house styles, sizes, materials, and colors, as well as how shared open land would be maintained.

Beginning in 1960, older home buyers gained their own distinct housing option when real estate developer Del Webb built his first Sun City active adult retirement community 20 miles northwest of Phoenix on land that had once been cotton field. It contained five models, a shopping center, a recreation center, and a golf course and caused a stir when 100,000 visitors showed up, 10 times more than expected. Pulte Homes Inc. in Detroit bought Del Webb Corporation in 2001 to create one of the largest home-building companies nationwide.

Historic homes became a separate category in 1966 with passage of the National Historic Preservation Act. The act established the National Register of Historic Places to encourage preserving older homes through grants and tax credits. Some practitioners specialized in listing and selling these historic homes.

In the 1980s, the modest homes of earlier decades gave way to greater opulence. The concept of gated communities sparked interest as a way to add upper-class cachet. Lofts also made their mark. The loft, a wide-open

The 1940s and 1950s brought a new informality into the home, as families began spending their time gathered around television sets. Ranch and split-level-style homes gained popularity.

There was no shortage of buyers when Del Webb built his first affordable paradise for seniors—Sun City, near Phoenix. Webb had planned to build 400 homes in the first year, 1960, but all 400 sold in the first month.

COURTESY PULTE HOMES

COURTESY PULTE HOMES

space with exposed ceilings and walls, first appeared as a residential option in New York in the late 1950s. Initially, lofts were created in former manufacturing facilities and appealed to artists who needed inexpensive housing and sufficient square footage in which to work and live.[55] Gradually, a new "softer" version—with finished floors, ceilings, and walls—evolved to entice a wider spectrum of buyers. By the 1980s, even single-family suburban homes were designed with loftlike open plans.

In the latter part of the twentieth century, land prices soared. Land became more valuable than the houses built upon it, leading to a teardown trend that started in the 1980s and accelerated in the 1990s. "The rapid increase became a concern for preservationists in 2001, and more of a concern in recent years as it has spread into more middle-class neighborhoods," said Adrian Scott Fine, director of the National Trust for Historic Preservation's Philadelphia office. Homeowners demolished houses and sometimes trees they didn't think worth saving to build more modern, grander homes. The average size of a new home grew to 2,433 square feet in 2005 from 983 in 1950, according to the National Association of Home Builders. Owners were arraying their homes with large kitchens and baths, master bedroom suites, and new kinds of social spaces, such as hearth rooms off kitchens and media rooms. The changes reflected what architectural historian Leland Roth terms "the desirable norm of creeping affluence."

The New Urbanism movement unofficially got off the ground in 1981 at Seaside, Florida, where the Miami architectural firm of Duany Plater-Zybeck & Company introduced an alternative to sprawling, automobile-dependent suburbs. Also referred to as Traditional Neighborhood Design, or TND, New Urbanism strives to blend the best of both urban and suburban living with a hefty dose of nostalgia for what

connoted the all-American home with a front porch, picket fence, and small yard. Like other housing styles, TND has continued to evolve, most notably to reflect the growing popularity of outdoor living spaces. Meanwhile, by 2006, the green movement—already a factor in commercial development—had taken hold in home building.

Although the homes change, the need for knowledgeable professionals to market them continues.

The 1960s and 1970s brought planned communities—such as this development in Columbia, Maryland—with uniformity of housing style.

COURTESY COLUMBIA ASSOCIATION

By the 1980s, young professionals were flocking to loft spaces.

COURTESY MICHAEL TAPSON

Meanwhile, new urban architects Andres Duany and Elizabeth Plater-Zyberk were creating suburban environments with a traditional feel. Their Kentlands in Gaithersburg, Maryland, was begun in 1988.

COURTESY KENTLANDS CITIZENS ASSEMBLY

CHAPTER THREE

Walking the Walk

The United States' entry into World War I, besides turning the tide for the country's allies in Europe, marked the beginning of a long and often symbiotic relationship between REALTORS® and the federal government. President Woodrow Wilson signed this country's first selective service law in 1917, compelling men ages 18 to 25 to register for the draft. But the nation's businessmen wanted to do their part for the war effort, too, and REALTORS® were no exception. Their volunteer work during the war drew the personal praise of Wilson.

Since then, REALTORS® have continued to make their presence felt in Washington, advocating on behalf of the real estate industry and the nation's property owners. Among other things, REALTORS® have fought to gain favorable tax treatment for real estate, eliminate postwar rent controls, and increase home-ownership opportunities. Over time, the NATIONAL ASSOCIATION OF REALTORS® has built one of the largest political action committees in the country and deployed state-of-the-art technology to marshal its grassroots forces. But its strength still comes down to the shoe leather its members wear out maintaining personal contact with federal lawmakers.

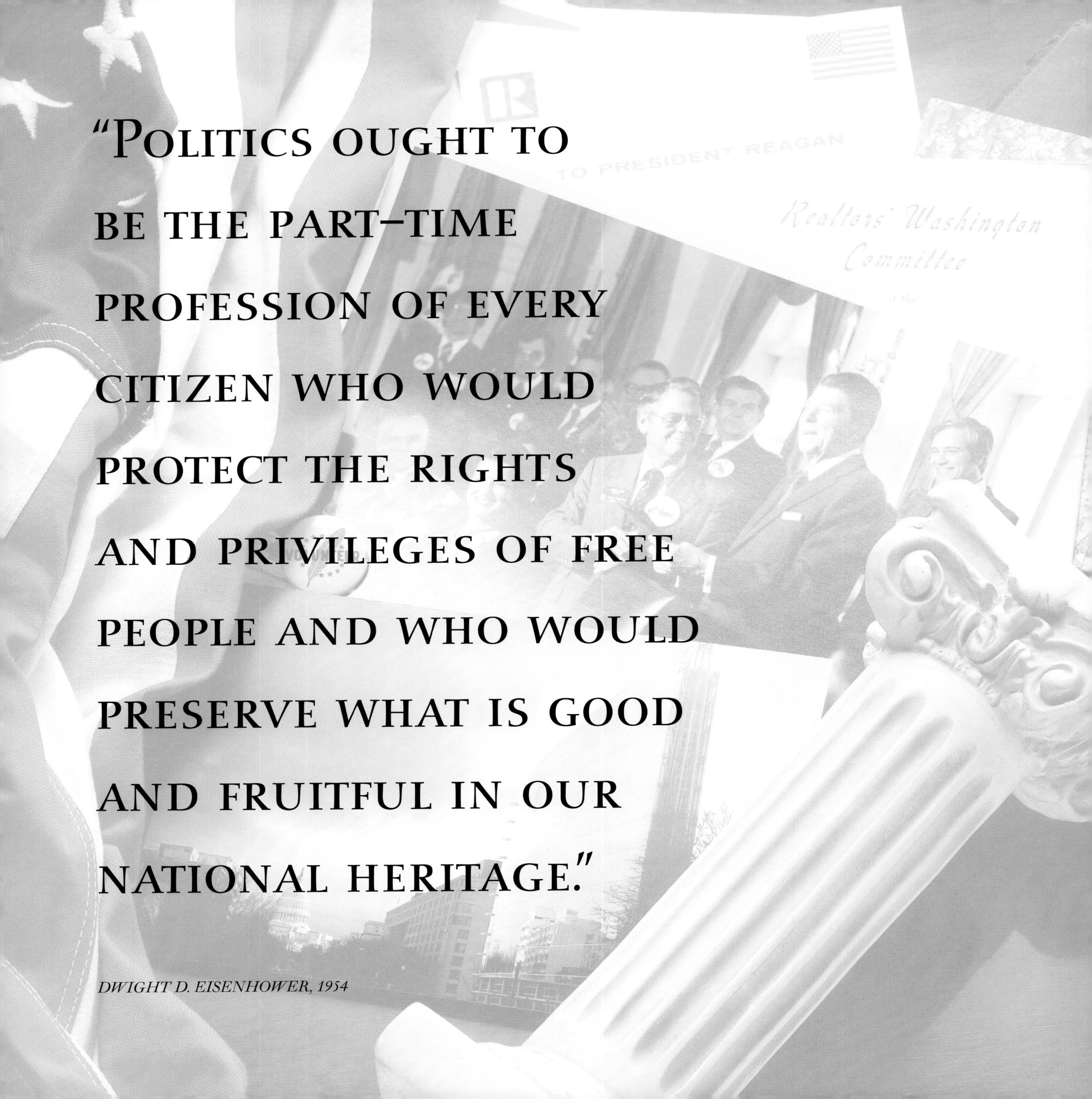

"POLITICS OUGHT TO
BE THE PART–TIME
PROFESSION OF EVERY
CITIZEN WHO WOULD
PROTECT THE RIGHTS
AND PRIVILEGES OF FREE
PEOPLE AND WHO WOULD
PRESERVE WHAT IS GOOD
AND FRUITFUL IN OUR
NATIONAL HERITAGE."

DWIGHT D. EISENHOWER, 1954

When Steve Forbes was traveling around the country in 1995 and 1996 as a U.S. presidential candidate touting a flat tax as the centerpiece of his candidacy, plenty of commentators thought he had hit on something big.

The flat tax wasn't a new concept. Federal lawmakers had begun a decade earlier introducing reform bills centered on a version of the tax. But in Forbes's hands, the proposal seemed to have found its moment in the sun. Then consumers started looking deeper into what it would mean to them should everyone start paying taxes at a flat 17 percent rate, with no deductions and credits, as Forbes had proposed. And they didn't like what they saw.

Among other things, without the mortgage interest deduction (MID) that had been in place since 1913, home values on a nationwide basis were expected to drop by 15 percent in two years. That would have eviscerated some $1.7 trillion in equity that owners had amassed in their homes, according to a study by DRI/McGraw-Hill, which NAR commissioned in 1995. Home sales would drop by 19 percent annually, and new-home starts would fall by 22 percent.

What's more, the amount of revenue to the government that the 17 percent tax rate was expected to generate would be nowhere near what was needed to fund the federal budget. That meant Congress would either have to embark on massive, politically painful spending cuts or replace the 17 percent rate with something far less politically attractive, such as a 23 percent or 24 percent rate.

"The idea of having everyone pay the same rate sounded great to a lot of people at first, including plenty of REALTORS®," said Art Godi, a REALTOR® from Stockton, California, who along with Edmund ("Gill") Woods Jr. of Holyoke, Massachusetts, was on the front line of efforts by REALTORS® to preserve MID against the flat-tax momentum. Godi was NAR president in 1996 and Woods in 1995.

"REALTORS® as much as anyone favored simplifying our federal tax code," Godi explained a decade after the battle. "We didn't have anything against that, and we took no position on the flat tax itself or any particular presidential candidate—as long as the mortgage interest deduction was preserved. But as the Association whose mission is to fight for preserving the American Dream of home ownership, we had to educate people that the attractiveness of the flat tax masked a devastating threat to their lifeblood—the value of their home."

And educate people is what the Association did.

In an unprecedented multifront campaign, REALTORS® at the national, state, and local levels worked together with assistance from NAR government affairs, research, and communications staff to turn the tide of public opinion away from a flat tax that did away with the MID. The centerpiece of the campaign was the NAR-commissioned research from DRI/McGraw-Hill.

"The research really helped bring home to people how much they stood to lose," Godi said.

On Capitol Hill, REALTORS® testified before congressional committees, and both Woods and Godi kept REALTORS®' concerns about the deduction front and center whenever they met with members of Congress. "We were always afraid someone in Congress was going to put the flat tax into a bill," said Godi. "Informally, when we had lunch with senators or congressmen, we tried to make them aware of the pitfalls."

The Importance of the Mortgage Interest Deduction

Unfortunately, the flat tax would have a devastating impact on real estate and the national economy. Eliminating, or even limiting, home mortgage deductions, has the potential to depress home values and preclude home ownership for millions of Americans. Tampering with this deduction would leave the American public uncertain about our government's commitment to home ownership.

This impact would far outweigh the benefits of implementing a simpler income tax system. A recent study undertaken by DRI-McGraw Hill outlines a number of important implications for the nation's housing industry if the United States adopts a flat tax that eliminates the mortgage interest deduction.

The major findings of this report include the following:

■ Nationwide, home owners will experience an estimated $1.7 trillion loss in the value of their homes. This loss would occur as home values dropped an average of 15 percent within the first two years of the flat tax. This translates into an average decline of $26,000 in every homeowner's net worth. Expensive homes would be even more harshly affected. Markets with high housing costs, including the Northeast and California, would also be more harshly affected.

■ Existing home sales would decline by 19 percent in the first year of the flat tax. Housing starts will be an estimated 22 percent lower than they would be under the current tax structure.

■ A substantial reduction in home values would make it more difficult for some owners to continue their mortgage payments. In fact, home values could sink below outstanding home mortgages. Financial institutions would require larger down payments, but individuals and families would find it more difficult to meet down payment requirements. Mortgage defaults will increase. Bank failures and a national credit crunch not only become possibilities, but probabilities.

■ Commercial real estate would also be adversely affected by the flat tax. As with residential real estate, neither interest nor tax expense would be deductible. Thus, all investors would experience an increase in carrying costs, with no deduction for taxes paid. Double taxation would be in effect.

■ The flat tax would create an uneven playing field for real estate in the investment arena. Capital gains for real estate would be taxed at the flat rate. However, capital gains for other investments, such as securities and stock, would not be taxable.

■ The flat tax would risk a national recession tied to trauma in the nation's housing industry. DRI/McGraw Hill estimated that the nation's Gross National Product would decline by 1.2 percent in the first year of flat tax enactment, and 1.6 percent in the second year.

Does a Flat Tax Really Promote Fairness Without the MID?

The flat tax is being promoted as a more rational, fair system of taxation that will level the playing field for Americans of all income levels. But in reality, the flat tax will hit the middle class the hardest, by increasing the cost of home ownership, and by placing home ownership out of the reach of millions of Americans. Even older home owners, many of whom see their homes as investment instruments to pay for college education or save for retirement, will be adversely affected.

The ability to deduct home mortgage interest is important to middle class Americans — those individuals and families with incomes between $25,000 and $75,000 per year. More than 43 percent of total mortgage deduction is claimed by tax payers with incomes of less than $50,000, and nearly 70 percent is returned to itemizers with incomes of less than $75,000.

Some proponents of the flat tax argue that only the wealthiest home owners in America would be affected by their proposals. This is untrue. Reducing, or even eliminating, the mortgage interest deduction will hit middle class taxpayers the hardest.

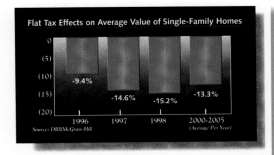

Flat Tax Effects on Average Value of Single-Family Homes

0
(5)
(10) -9.4%
(15) -14.6% -15.2% -13.3%
(20)
1996 1997 1998 2000-2005
Source: DRI/McGraw-Hill (Average Per Year)

Home Ownership: Part of the American Dream

The federal government has actively encouraged home ownership since the founding of our nation. As a result, more than 65 percent of all American families own homes, and the vast majority of the rest hope to do so one day. The mortgage interest deduction is not a temporary investment enhancement provision recently adopted to spur economic growth. It has been an essential element of U.S. tax law since the federal income tax code was adopted in 1913.

Eliminating or reducing the mortgage interest deduction violates a commitment forged more than 80 years ago between the American people and their government. It predates Social Security, Medicare, and nearly every other federal commitment between taxpayers and Washington.

We Must All Participate in the National Debate Over Tax Reform

To be sure, filing your income tax on a post card sounds appealing. All Americans paying the same percentage of their income in taxes seems fair. But amidst the simplicity of flat tax proposals lie complex and hidden dangers. These need a full and complete discussion in Washington and around the country. History makes clear that even the most carefully considered laws have unintended consequences. Even a short-term dislocation of America's housing market due to the elimination of home ownership tax incentives could have a negative and lasting impact.

America's home owners must participate in this debate. The stakes for our families, our nation and our future are too great.

We can support genuine tax reform that maintains incentives for the greatest source of stability and wealth creation the world has ever known — owning a home in America.

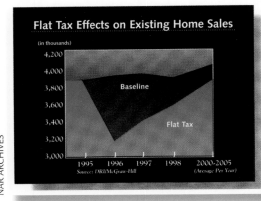

Flat Tax Effects on Existing Home Sales

(in thousands)
4,200
4,000
3,800 Baseline
3,600
3,400 Flat Tax
3,200
3,000
1995 1996 1997 1998 2000-2005
Source: DRI/McGraw-Hill (Average Per Year)

NAR government affairs staff, with Stephen Driesler at the helm, entered into coalitions with other groups concerned about the loss of the mortgage interest deduction, including the National Association of Home Builders and the Mortgage Bankers Association.

To arm REALTORS® at the state and local level, NAR librarians developed information tool kits on tax issues. The Association also formed cross-divisional "strike forces" composed of specialists in tax, research, government affairs, grassroots activities, and communications. The groups met regularly to discuss advocacy tactics and to devise responses whenever articles favoring the flat tax appeared in local or national publications.

"It was gratifying how all the different levels—local, state, and national—worked together," said Godi.

And it was effective. By mid-1996, the flat-tax campaign was faltering. Forbes fared poorly in spring primaries, and by the fall he was out of the race. With his exit, the flat tax lost one of its chief advocates and, for all intents and purposes, disappeared from the discussion.

For NAR, the victory provided a model it would turn to again and again in pursuit of its top federal priorities, including, most recently, keeping banking conglomerates out of real estate brokerage and management and winning support for small business health plans. To many lawmakers on Capitol Hill, the show of force NAR mustered during the flat-tax debate is emblematic of the political clout held by REALTORS®.

"WE ARE AT ATTENTION"

NAR's Washington presence began taking shape in the early 1900s when the Association formed a committee to weigh in on—appropri-

NAR ARCHIVES

ately enough—another tax issue. Lawmakers were mulling over plans for what would then be the new federal income tax. Among other things, the Association pressed Congress to exempt rents from taxation and then later to make mortgage interest deductible.

But REALTORS® didn't make their Washington debut until 1917. Following German submarine attacks on American merchant ships, the federal government was preparing for the country's entry into World War I. The leadership of the National Association, then known as the National Association of Real Estate Boards, volunteered its members to help the effort.

The government was expected to need a great deal of property in a short amount of time for mobilization camps, defense worker housing, and other facilities. The NAR board of directors passed a resolution to extend what help they could to the government. "If you desire to obtain leases, purchase property now under lease or option, or to obtain intelligent appraisals . . . or have us assist in obtaining

NAR's 1995 president, Edmund ("Gil") Woods, seated at table, right, testifies before Congress as part of an epic battle to preserve the mortgage interest deduction. The Association's victory cemented its reputation as one of the most influential lobbies on Capitol Hill.

The War President

Los Angelenos with a sense of history may remember William May Garland as the real estate man who brought the Olympics to their city at the height of the Great Depression in 1932. The X Olympiad was a huge success from both a competitive and a financial perspective. Among the American victors was Mildred "Babe" Didrikson, who took the gold medal and set new world records for both the 80-meter hurdles and the javelin throw. For his effort, Garland earned the International Olympic Committee's Olympic Cup, an honor usually granted to a committee, municipality, or country.* He was celebrated citywide, serving as Grand Marshal of the 1932 Pasadena Tournament of Roses Parade. (His home team, the University of Southern California, defeated Tulane 21–12 in the Rose Bowl that year.) Garland's enduring contribution to international sports—he served on the IOC from 1922 to 1948—earned him numerous awards, including the French Legion d'Honneur and the Belgian Order of Leopold.

To the NATIONAL ASSOCIATION OF REALTORS®, however, Garland's biggest contribution came 15 years before the 1932 games, when he served during World War I as the Association's only two-term president. With the nation preparing for war with Germany, Garland's predecessor, Henry P. Haas of Pittsburgh, had offered his services and those of his fellow REALTORS® to the federal government. Garland picked up on Haas's lead, rallying his fellow NAR members to the cause and even setting up an office in Washington, D.C., to coordinate volunteer efforts. His work earned the commendation of President Woodrow Wilson.

On his death in 1948 at age 82, Garland was hailed as the "dean of California real estate" by 1948 California Real Estate Association President Fred B. Mitchell. "His desire to serve his business associates, his community, and the world of sports made him a peer among REALTORS®

---

*Dwyre, Bill. "L.A. and the Olympics Were a Golden Match," *Los Angeles Times,* March 30, 2006.

for nearly a half century," Mitchell said.

In mid-1917, when Garland became president, NAR was still a fledgling organization. Garland saw the war as a potential threat to NAR's continued viability. "I know that adverse conditions exist throughout our land—conditions that overshadow the business we have in hand," he said in his inaugural address in Milwaukee in July (two months after the United States had entered World War I), "but we must present a cheerful smile. We must do everything we can to create business and help our fellow men. We must hold this organization together, and it is your cooperation individually . . . that will do this."

William May Garland, 1866–1948

A CALL FOR SACRIFICE

Being a loyal NAR member meant more than just paying dues and attending conventions. To Garland, NAR membership and civic duty went hand in hand. "The National Association no longer meets to simply learn how to sell real estate," Garland said at a 1917 luncheon in his honor before his hometown realty board in Los Angeles, "but to find out what it can best do for its country, its state, its county, and the community in which its individual members live."

Real estate leaders from around the country responded to Garland's call for wartime volunteers. In a letter published in the August 1918 *National Real Estate Journal,* Garland reported that every board had set up a

Government Appraisal Committee and that "most faithful, effective work has been done, and is now being done, throughout the country."

By that time, the Association's Nominating Committee—"realizing the extraordinary and peculiar conditions confronting our country at present, and further realizing that the first duty of every REALTOR® is to help win the war"—had asked Garland to stay in office another year.

In his letter, Garland urged REALTORS® who could afford the time to join him in the nation's capital, where he'd been working four months. "I want the name of every REALTOR® who is willing and anxious to do his part, who can afford to sacrifice his time, even if it hurts, so I can count on his presence here if I call on him, and who will, without excuse or delay, come direct to Washington."

In a line foreshadowing U.S. President John F. Kennedy's inaugural appeal for civic involvement, Garland said, "This war offers patriotic REALTORS® a chance not to get more but to do more for their country."

Yet Garland was also looking ahead to how the war effort could serve the Association in its future dealings with the government: "I feel that the group of men [that] does the most toward winning the war will have the greatest influence after this war is over. . . . Let us conduct this labor of love for our country that the greatest glory may be reflected on every REALTOR®."

Both before and after his NAR presidency, Garland was active in politics. He served as a "colonel" on the staff of California Governor James Norris Gillette (1907 to 1911) and was a delegate to the Republican National Conventions in 1900, 1924, 1928, 1936, and 1940. One of his great gifts to NAR was his ability to convey to his fellow REALTORS® the importance of working together to achieve their political objectives. "Nothing of a progressive nature can be accomplished by a great body of men unless those men are organized for action with a clear and distinct understanding of their rights and determined to obtain them," he once said.

Among the priorities discussed at the 1917 and 1918 NAR conventions were the need for standard education, the emerging field of real estate valuation, the importance of zoning laws, and the excessive tax burden that saddled real estate owners. "From the work [REALTORS®] are accomplishing," Garland told his Los Angeles colleagues in 1917, "they have every right to be considered one of the most useful and nationally influential organizations in the United States."

THINKING AHEAD

At the Association's 1919 convention in Atlantic City, Garland passed the torch to John Lowrie Weaver of Washington, D.C. With the war over, Garland urged REALTORS® to concentrate on priorities closer to home. He laid out an ambitious vision that included the creation of licensing laws in all states, cooperation in the national "Own a Home" campaign, formation of a rediscount bank that would increase the availability of mortgage money, creation of a transcontinental highway that would "knit the United States into one great family of neighborhoods," and formation of more state associations.

He also recommended a name change for the Association:

On tendering your services during the war to the different departments of the United States government, I offered them from the "REALTORS®"; as such they were accepted. Your identity is thus established in Washington. The name REALTOR®, therefore, means something essential to our government; it thereby becomes a great and more practical asset to ourselves. . . . Why should not this association be known as the National Association of Realtors? I certainly most sincerely recommend this change.

Garland's wish came true 56 years after his presidency. In 1973, the Association officially became the NATIONAL ASSOCIATION OF REALTORS®.

or financed by non-U.S. entities for federal acquisition.

Within a year, officials throughout the government, including President Wilson, were praising REALTORS® not just for their patriotism but for saving the government money it otherwise would have lost to property owners trying to cash in on the government's appetite for property. By some estimates, the savings to the government was in the millions of dollars. "Convey to [your members] my thanks for the spirit of service which they have shown," President Wilson wrote to the Association's 1918 president, William May Garland of Los Angeles.[2]

Throughout the war, the volunteer effort of REALTORS® grew. Federal officials sought the counsel of NAR leaders as the government launched a war property effort that ranged widely, from acquiring land for the merchant marine to developing housing for defense workers, and then later tapped prominent REALTORS®, among them Garland, to head up many of its newly created offices. By mid-1918, NAR had become an integral partner to the federal government, prompting the Association to create a permanent body to oversee its Washington operations. It was called the War Services Board and was headed up by Robert Armstrong, another Los Angeles REALTOR® and a former U.S. Treasury official.

To solidify this new federal focus and to keep its partnership with the government vital once the war ended, NAR moved its information bureau—up to that point headquartered in Minneapolis—to Washington. Three years later, the Association sent Armstrong to Washington to oversee it. Despite the Washington address of his office, Armstrong kept the Association's focus on providing information, not lobbying, a move that set NAR apart from other business organizations at the time. Indeed, more than 200 organizations

NATIONAL ARCHIVES

In 1916, as the nation geared up to enter the war in Europe, REALTORS® offered their services to Washington on the home front.

housing facilities . . . we are at attention in your service," the Association's president at the time, Henry Haas, said in a telegram to war secretary Newton Baker.[1]

Within months, REALTORS®—known as "dollar men" for providing their services for free or for token amounts—were working deals on behalf of the government. One long-term job involved appraising properties owned were by then maintaining lobbying offices in the Capitol. The trend likely helped nurture the environment that led to the notorious Teapot Dome oil reserve scandal in 1923, when Warren Harding was president.

SHAPING A FEDERAL PRESENCE IN HOUSING

REALTORS®' reputation for service helped ensure their views received serious attention by the government. Thus, through the 1920s and into World War II, they played a major role in shaping the look of the country's housing markets. That look—single-family, suburban housing financed by long-term fixed-rate loans—continues to characterize markets today.

It might have been otherwise.

Although few people within the industry or government wanted to see the introduction of European-styled "modern housing"—high-density, government-subsidized rentals—a struggling housing sector in the aftermath of World War I made it increasingly clear that some form of federal role was needed to boost housing production.

REALTORS® wanted a system of home loan discount banks to help ensure a steady flow of capital to their industry, much like the Federal Reserve provided to the commercial sector. With financing available, the private sector would have the fuel to meet the country's growing housing needs, a far better way to provide housing than adopting what REALTORS® feared would be a socialist-style alternative: housing built, owned, and managed by the government.

Herbert Hoover, first as secretary of commerce in the Harding and Calvin Coolidge administrations and then later as president, shared the REALTORS®' goal, telling them at a national housing conference he'd organized, "Our chief problem in finances relates to those

who have an earnest desire for a home, who have a job and therefore possess sound character credit, but whose initial resources run only 20 or 25 percent [of the cost of a home]."[3]

Relying heavily on policy recommendations drawn up by an NAR committee, Hoover started the ball rolling on a mortgage finance system by crafting and then pushing for passage of the Federal Home Loan Bank Act, which created the network of mortgage lenders and uniform lending standards that remain an underpinning of housing markets today. Throughout the Hoover administration and into the presidency of Franklin Roosevelt, other NAR recommendations were enshrined into law, most significantly the preference in federal lending programs—such as the Federal Housing Administration, created under Roosevelt in 1934—for the kind of planned, large-scale housing developments, subject to uniform quality

Two years before passage of the legislation that created Fannie Mae, NAR leaders lobbied for a national mortgage discount bank that would ensure a steady supply of mortgage funds for home buyers. Here, in January 1936, Wendell B. Barker, Herbert U. Nelson (executive vice president), Walter S. Schmidt, Edward A. MacDougall, and Walter W. Rose wait to testify before the Senate Finance Committee.

ORLANDO REGIONAL REALTOR® ASSOCIATION

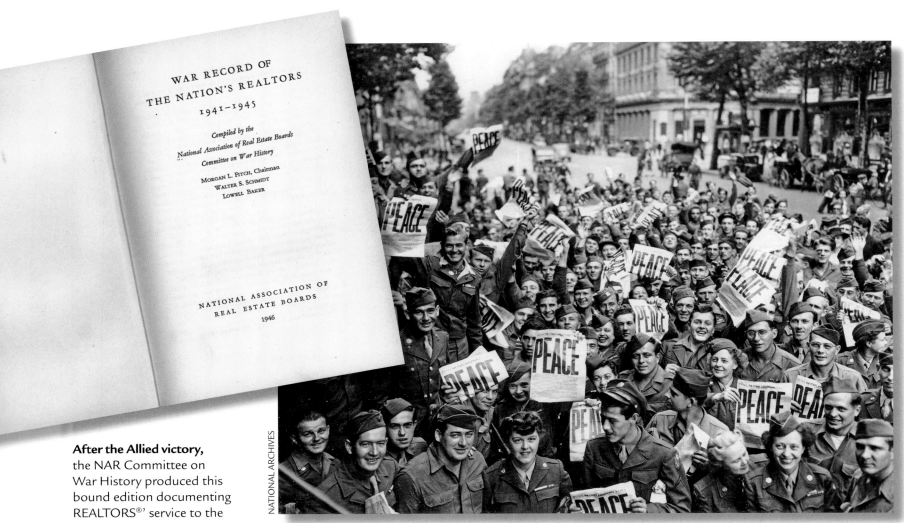

WAR RECORD OF
THE NATION'S REALTORS
1941–1945

Compiled by the
National Association of Real Estate Boards
Committee on War History

MORGAN L. FITCH, Chairman
WALTER S. SCHMIDT
LOWELL BAKER

NATIONAL ASSOCIATION OF
REAL ESTATE BOARDS
1946

After the Allied victory, the NAR Committee on War History produced this bound edition documenting REALTORS®' service to the nation during World War II.

standards, that came to dominate the American landscape beginning in the late 1930s.

Yet the modern-housing movement remained very much alive. The rapid migration of defense workers into urban areas during World War II created huge demand for affordable rental housing. To manage public-financed large-scale rental housing development, Congress in 1937 created the U.S. Housing Authority—the precursor to today's public housing operation in the U.S. Department of Housing and Urban Development. Backers of subsidized rental housing hoped the defense-housing effort would trigger a greater federal presence in

housing. But after the war, the government scaled back on the development programs and greatly expanded its REALTOR®-backed home loan efforts, adding mortgage insurance to the roster of services provided by the Veterans Administration (now the Department of Veterans Affairs) to accommodate millions of returning GIs.

Van Holt Garrett, 1945 NAR president, estimated the postwar demand for housing required building 1 million homes a year for the next 10 years. He and other NAR leaders warned that, without a freer hand, private enterprise couldn't meet the demand. Executive Vice President Herbert U. Nelson told the

Senate Housing Committee—headed by Senator Robert A. Taft of Ohio, son of former president William Howard Taft:

No category of small business is so oppressed, so restricted, so regulated and so hampered as is the real estate and building field. Courageous and drastic action by the federal government and by state and local government to remove obstacles is necessary. The mere fact that great need exists for all types of construction will not of itself produce real estate and building activity in any great volume. Before we can have any real action, private enterprise must be able to function freely and make a profit.[4]

Nelson outlined six suggestions, which included removing heavy tax burdens, eliminating rent controls that discouraged investment, getting rid of abusive building codes that also discouraged city planning and sound construction, and ending public housing, which hadn't accomplished its stated objectives.

Garrett said high taxes and rent controls "are nothing less than a high tariff policy on homes. We can have a million-houses-a-year program and cheaper houses if we do away with the artificial barriers," he said. He estimated that building costs could be cut by 20 percent—reducing the cost of a $6,000 home to $4,800 and saving the industry more than $1 billion in one year.[5] And removing the restraints offered another benefit—new jobs for thousands, including returning veterans.

TAKING ADVOCACY TO A NEW LEVEL

With its presence in Washington by this time well developed, although still without formal lobbying operations, NAR worked closely with

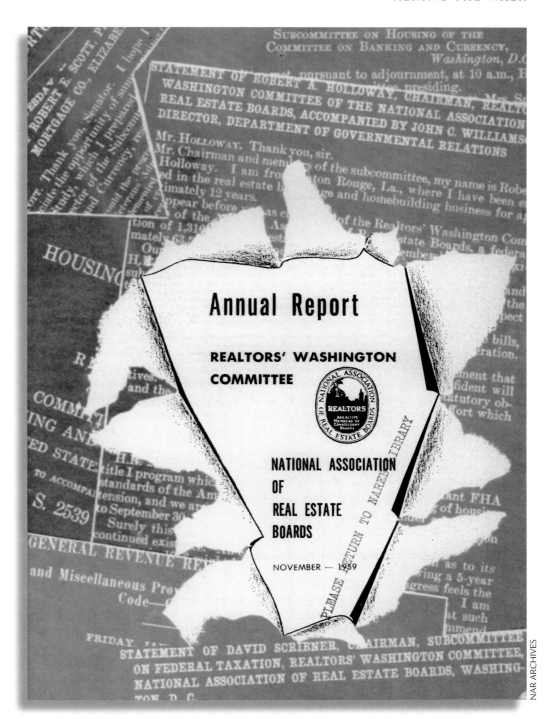

NAR ARCHIVES

The REALTORS®' WashingtonCommittee, established in 1942, was the first iteration of a permanent Washington, D.C., presence for NAR. Although their original purpose was to assist the U.S. government in the war effort, members of the committee also frequently met with federal officials on issues of concern to REALTORS®, including rent controls and gas rationing.

THE TRUTH

About the

Housing Shortage!

Listen Tonight

11:15 P. M.

Radio Station

WENR

HEAR

Herbert U. Nelson

Executive Vice-President

Natl. Assn. of

Real Estate Boards

The postwar period was a pivotal time for NAR, with Association leaders speaking out nationally and locally against the expansion of public housing. This Chicago newspaper advertisement urges readers to tune in to a radio address promoting the private sector's role in alleviating the nation's housing shortage.

At the NAHB convention in 1948, NAR Executive Vice President Herbert U. Nelson confers with REALTOR® and builder Joseph Merrion of Chicago, former president of the National Association of Home Builders. After World War II, REALTORS® and builders worked together to persuade government that private industry—not public housing—was key to solving postwar housing shortages.

The Contra Costa (California) Real Estate Board (today, the Contra Costa Association of REALTORS®) sponsored an open forum against socialized housing in 1950. The sound truck was used as a means of inviting area residents to attend the forum with members of the board of supervisors.

Congress and the expanding executive bureaucracy to enshrine the Association's preference for private-sector solutions into federal law.

Creation of the Farmers Home Administration, or FmHA (now Rural Housing Service), in the Housing Act of 1949 was one way. The act articulated the federal objective of a decent, safe, and sanitary home for every American household, and the new agency was seen as a way to expand FHA into rural areas for carrying out that objective. The Act also included funding for slum clearance, a priority for REALTORS®, who steadfastly maintained that redevelopment should be in the hands of the private sector, not the government.

In the meantime, the national debate over housing segregation and discrimination was heating up, fueled in part by riots coming out of those "slum" areas. The social chaos of the time led to passage of the landmark Federal Fair Housing Act in 1968, one week after the assassination of Martin Luther King Jr. Throughout the fair housing debate, REALTORS® made it clear they favored a law that would enshrine the principle of freedom of choice in housing for all people but without the federal government stepping in to integrate neighborhoods, which REALTORS® likened to "forced housing" laws that were then cropping up in states.

As passed, the 1968 act had what supporters and critics both acknowledged were weak enforcement provisions. The bill directed complainants—only after first trying to negotiate with the accused party an end to the discriminatory practice—to sue for injunction in federal court, a cumbersome process that was likely to dissuade many people from filing a claim. The only time the federal government could file a claim is when it suspected a pattern of discriminatory conduct by a party. That was considered a difficult standard to meet by legal experts.

In part as a result of the weak enforcement provisions, which caused complaints to drag on without resolution, REALTORS® in the years following the law found themselves painted in a bad light by fair housing advocates. It was another 20 years before REALTORS® could change the climate of opinion against them. NAR led an effort to create a clear enforcement path through passage of the 1988 Fair Housing Amendments Act. Jerry Giovaniello, who joined the Association staff in 1981 and has served as chief lobbyist since 2001, called it one of the most pivotal pieces of legislation for REALTORS® in the past 25 years. "We lobbied extremely hard on it and got the civil rights groups to realize we needed to work together as partners rather than as antagonists to get a satisfactory solution," Giovaniello said. (For more on NAR's role in fair housing, see Chapter 4.)

The groundwork for the 1988 victory had actually been laid shortly after passage of the 1968 Fair Housing Act, when NAR leaders saw the need to retool their approach to advocacy efforts. Among other things, the Association in 1969 launched its Real Estate Political Education Committee (later renamed the REALTORS® Political Action Committee) to collect donations from its members for the support of candidates who shared REALTORS®' free-market preferences.

PACs weren't new. They had been around since the early 1940s, but rules prohibiting the use of corporate money to cover operational costs severely limited the funds' usefulness. NAR felt this limitation as much as any other group, and it wasn't until two years after the creation of the Association's PAC—with the passage of the 1971 Federal Election Campaign Act—that PACs became cost-effective for groups like NAR. For the first time, groups could tap their own treasuries to operate a PAC and solicit voluntary contributions without

NAR leaders promoted the political action committee with buttons passed out at national meetings urging $99 donations from members.

> ## "NOT ONLY DID WE BECOME A NUMBER POWER, WE BECAME A MONEY POWER, AND OUR PRESENCE ON THE HILL WENT WAY UP."

having to set aside valuable donations to fund operations.

NAR was one of the first organizations to expand its PAC in the wake of the ruling—and it couldn't have done so at a more critical time. In a burst of activism, Congress in the late 1960s was significantly deepening federal involvement in housing, first by consolidating many of the government's major housing programs into a single, cabinet-level entity—the U.S. Department of Housing and Urban Development—and then by creating a number of development and rent subsidy programs, including the Section 235 home purchase and Section 236 rent subsidy programs.

Using its newly empowered PAC as a starting point, NAR leaders embarked on a series of reforms to its Washington operations, hiring the Association's first full-time lobbyist in 1973, opening membership to include sales associates rather than just brokers, and changing its name from the National Association of Real Estate Boards to the NATIONAL ASSOCIATION OF REALTORS®. The jump in membership that followed brought a greatly enlarged pool with which to drive the growth of RPAC.

"We became a powerhouse politically," said Harley Rouda Sr. of Columbus, Ohio, an NAR board member at the time and the Association's 1991 president. "Not only did we become a number power, we became a money power, and from that moment on our presence on the Hill went way up."

NAR's new lobbyist, Albert Abrahams, an old Washington hand who had honed his skills in the presidential politics of the early 1970s, ramped up the Association's operations over the next several years, adding additional lobbyists, hiring NAR's first policy analysts, and creating a staff of field representatives to mobilize members.

In one of the first fruits of that effort, Congress supported many NAR-backed initia-

tives to buttress housing during the midst of the high-inflationary 1970s by passing the Housing and Community Development Act of 1974. Among the initiatives in the law were higher loan limits and lower down-payment requirements for FHA and VA loans; eased rules on home loans for banks and thrifts; and higher Fannie Mae and Freddie Mac conforming loan limits. The legislation also created the landmark Community Development Block Grant program, which consolidated more than half a dozen categorical grants under a single umbrella and disbursed the funds annually to states and local governments on a formula-funded basis. Significantly, the bill also included an effort to move the federal government out of public housing—a long-sought goal of REALTORS®—by expanding tenant-based rental subsidies in private housing while curbing funding for public housing development.

The Association at the time also took up its first battle over the Real Estate Settlement Procedures Act, which started out as a modest reform effort in 1974 to boost competition in the title insurance business but then spiraled into a confusing and potentially industry-damaging regulatory regime. HUD further complicated matters by writing rules for the law that NAR and other groups complained were vastly too detailed, complex, and rigid. REALTORS® and members of other industry groups flooded House and Senate members with letters of concern, and Congress passed a quick-fix bill in 1975 that was much more palatable to REALTORS®. Among other things, the new bill removed provisions that implied that practices as integral to the industry as fee splitting among brokers could be called into question. Now in place for almost 30 years, RESPA continues to cause debate, most recently during the administration of George W. Bush. Bush's first HUD secretary, Mel Martinez, proposed sweeping changes to encourage one-stop shopping by consumers. NAR feared the proposal would give a competitive advantage to big lenders; it required bundled settlement-service packages to include a guaranteed interest rate, something only big lenders could control. In 2004 NAR and other concerned groups successfully tamped down that reform effort.

The distressed state of the nation's public housing projects convinced President Richard M. Nixon in 1973 to impose a moratorium on federally subsidized housing programs, a controversial move supported by REALTORS®. Nixon—pictured in inset with NAR President J. D. Sawyer of Middleton, Ohio—announced the moratorium at the Association's 1973 convention in Washington, D.C., less than a year before he resigned from office. Nixon's speech came in the midst of an energy embargo imposed by the Organization of Petroleum Exporting Countries in reaction to the Yom Kippur War in the Middle East. He talked about his administration's efforts to bring peace to the region and his goal of making the United States energy independent. He also told REALTORS®, "I believe in America, and I believe in America's real estate. That is why my money is in real estate." He was the first president since Dwight Eisenhower to address REALTORS®.

HEADLINES, NAR ARCHIVES

CORBIS/WALLY MCNAMEE

REALTORS® also welcomed Gerald R. Ford—then House Minority Leader from Michigan—to their 1973 convention. Ford was about to become vice president, following the resignation of Spiro Agnew. A year later, as president, Ford signed the Housing and Community Development Act, instituting Community Development Block Grants, now the longest-lasting example of federal revenue sharing. At the signing, he said, "In a very real sense, this bill will help to return power from the banks of the Potomac to people in their own communities."

A Year of Firsts

*"To everything there is a season, and
a time to every purpose under heaven."*

With those words from Ecclesiastes 3 as his clarion call,
J. D. Sawyer of Middletown, Ohio, traveled the country
in the year preceding his 1973 NAR presidency. His message: It's time to make the voices of REALTORS® heard in
Washington.

"From the very beginning of my career in real estate, I
knew the only way to make it was to have a voice that politicians would listen to," he told *Real Estate Today* magazine in
an interview conducted a decade after his presidency, "but no
one in Washington was listening to us."

By the time he took office, Sawyer had already scored a
political triple play—helping found the REALTORS® Political
Action Committee, quadrupling the Association's membership, and introducing a powerful, new brand, now widely
recognized as the trademarked "REALTOR® R."

The PAC's founders—13 REALTORS® from around the
country, including Ohioans Sawyer, Paul Everson of Euclid,
and Chet Sudbrack of Cincinnati—understood that fund-
raising was critical to promoting the agenda of REALTORS® in
Washington. Sawyer, a member of the Executive Committee
at the time, approached President Lyn Davis of Dallas at the
Association's 1968 convention in Washington, D.C., and
Davis threw his support behind the idea of a PAC. The group
drew up a plan based on the recently formed PAC of the
American Medical Association. "J.D. provided the leadership
and the strategy," Everson says. In 1969, the Ohio Association
of REALTORS® became the charter participant, signing an
agreement with NAR that covered the sharing of funds. (See
"Getting in the Game," page 96.)

BEHIND THE MEMBERSHIP SURGE

Even with the PAC in place, Sawyer knew that as a brokers-
only organization, the Association would never have the

J. D. Sawyer, 1917–2006

NAR ARCHIVES

REALTOR®

strong voice it needed to be heard on Capitol Hill. With
the blessing of 1972 NAR President Fred "Bud" Tucker of
Indianapolis, Sawyer began going state to state—on his own
dime—to educate his fellow brokers about the PAC and to
advocate for a change to the Association's constitution that
would enable salespeople to join.

Sawyer had to win over many, many skeptics, recalls
Everson, who acted as Sawyer's "first lieutenant" for many
years. Unlike a lot of Association presidents of his era,
Sawyer didn't come up through the ranks of the National
Institute of Real Estate Brokers (predecessor to today's
Council of Residential Brokerage Managers and Council
of Residential Specialists); he was an industrial specialist
who had served as president of the Society of Industrial
REALTORS® (today the Society of Industrial and Office
REALTORS®). Some of Sawyer's NIREB rivals feared that
opening the membership to salespeople would mean losing
control of the Association or creating havoc with member
record keeping.

Fortunately, Sawyer had his experience in Ohio to call on. As president of the Ohio Association of REALTORS® in 1967, Sawyer had made the same appeal to Ohio brokers. Two years later, with Everson serving as president, OAR became the first state association to welcome sales associates as members.

In time, Sawyer was able to not only bring the NIREB doubters around to his vision but also forge strong bonds with them, says his son John Sawyer, the third-generation president of Sawyer, REALTORS®, in Middletown, a city of about 50,000 located midway between Dayton and Cincinnati. The board of directors approved Sawyer's proposal in late 1972; in 1973, the National Association of Real Estate Boards became the NATIONAL ASSOCIATION OF REALTORS® with Sawyer as its president. The Association gained more than 400,000 new members. Symbolic of its newfound prominence, NAR welcomed both President Richard M. Nixon and Vice President-designate Gerald R. Ford to its 1973 annual convention in Washington, D.C.

With the name change under way, Sawyer charged Palmer Berge of Seattle, chair of the Public Relations Committee, with replacing the emblem that had been in place during the 67 years the Association was known as the National Association of Real Estate Boards. Berge's committee recommended the "REALTOR® R" logo, a design Sawyer embraced enthusiastically for its strength and simplicity.

Here again, Sawyer faced opposition—most notably, Everson remembers, from 1970 NAR President Rich Port of LaGrange, Illinois. Port, a former brigadier general with a legendary temper, insisted that the Association shouldn't abandon an identity that had been around almost since its founding. But Sawyer stood his ground and prevailed. To his great credit, Port came to the next board of directors meeting with a change of heart, saying the "REALTOR® R" was indeed a great brand for NAR, Everson says.

In his April 16, 1973, message in the weekly *REALTOR® Headlines,* Sawyer introduced the new logo, calling it "distinctive, memorable, and inimitable." The R, he said, symbolizes "not only REALTOR® and real estate but also readiness, responsibility, reliability, resourcefulness, right, and responsiveness."

PROPERTY RIGHTS: THE POWER OF OUR NATION

Sawyer had displayed all those characteristics in his rise to the presidency of NAR. He joined his father's real estate business during the Great Depression, obtaining a waiver in order to get a license at the age of 17. Middletown alone had more than 4,000 foreclosed properties, Sawyer recalled in the 1982 interview, and banks were anxious to get the properties back on the tax rolls. "They were even willing to put up a cash advance to help get the property in shape."

Following in the footsteps of his father and grandfather, Sawyer bought up property for investment. "In 1935, someone could buy a lot anywhere for $8 to $10," he recalled.

"Dad was a big believer in land," his son John said. "He was a salesman—he sold until 1955. But he also bought land and held it."

Real estate and politics were Sawyer's double passions. By 1949, he was a member of the REALTORS® Washington Committee, a group of influential members who carried out NAR's legislative agenda in the days before the Association had a professional lobbying staff. In the 1968 national election, Sawyer served as campaign manager for U.S. Senator William B. Saxbe of Ohio. Later, as attorney general in the Ford Administration, Saxbe appointed Sawyer associate U.S. attorney general, a position he held for one year following his NAR presidency.

It was Sawyer's belief in the sanctity of property rights that drove his political involvement. During his presidency, the Association vociferously opposed threats to property rights, including a proposal to reinstate federal rent controls and proposals to put federal control on land-use decisions.

Like William May Garland (page 84), J. D. Sawyer had the gift of vision—forecasting in 1982 that the Association would surpass 1 million members. It eventually did, in 2004.

Today, under the leadership of CEO Dale A. Stinton, the Association has begun to put more emphasis on its role as the voice for real estate consumers in America. It's a move Sawyer would have approved. In his annual report to members in 1973, Sawyer proudly called NAR "the world's largest business organization, speaking for 500,000 members and on behalf of . . . millions of property owners."

Getting in the Game

Before 1973, the NATIONAL ASSOCIATION OF REALTORS® was still a brokers-only group—and the roughly 87,000 members felt buffeted by a wave of federal activism in housing, not least of which—the 1968 Fair Housing Act—was drawing significant public criticism toward real estate practitioners.

To put it plainly, "we were getting legislated to death," said Chet Sudbrock, an Ohio REALTOR® who was part of the team that launched the REALTORS® Political Action Committee (RPAC) and one of its original trustees.

Labor unions had pioneered efforts to influence the political process. The first political action committee was started in the 1940s by the Congress of Industrial Organizations (later part of the AFL-CIO). By the 1960s, professional groups, including doctors and real estate practitioners, realized they needed to follow labor's lead.

From its start in 1969, the REALTORS®

Milestones in RPAC's 38-year history

1979

RPAC becomes the largest PAC in the United States, with more than $1 million in contributions to federal candidates in the 1977–1978 election cycle.

1980

The REALTORS® Independent Expenditure Program is launched as an extension of RPAC to offer significant electoral support to targeted candidates.

1982

With the signing of a cooperative agreement with Hawaii, all 50 states plus the District of Columbia have cooperative agreements with RPAC and have state PACs in operation.

1989

RPAC contributes $2.6 million to federal candidates in the 1987–1988 election cycle and begins its Opportunity Race Program, disbursing $40,000 on behalf of two candidates.

Political Action Committee has been a bipartisan organization dedicated to supporting both Democratic and Republican candidates who support REALTOR® positions.

The goal of RPAC, founded in 1969 as the Real Estate Political Education Committee (REPEC), was to support candidates who believed, as REALTORS® did, in free enterprise and the value of private property rights. The Ohio Association of REALTORS® was the first state to join REPEC and enter into a cooperative agreement outlining the raising of funds through voluntary contributions by members. All funds collected were split—as they are today—between national and state REALTOR® associations, enabling REALTORS® to support like-minded candidates at all levels of government.

In 1974—one year after sales associates were welcomed as Association members, quadrupling NAR's membership—the committee changed its name to RPAC and became an unincorporated nonprofit, bipartisan standing committee of NAR. Its first national goal was $10 per member.

Today, there are about 3,800 PACs in the United States, and RPAC consistently ranks number one in contributions to federal candidates.

1994–1998

Legislative Political Advocacy, a program funded with RPAC corporate dollars to educate the public and members of Congress about the importance of REALTOR® issues, contributes $1 million to NAR campaigns to save the mortgage interest deduction and lower capital gains taxes.

1995

With RPAC receipts falling, the committee kicks off its first national fund-raising plan. RPAC ups the split to state PACs to 70 percent (from 65 percent) and allows state associations to retain 100 percent of collected funds once they meet their national RPAC goal.

1999

RPAC once again establishes itself as the largest PAC contributor to candidates, meeting its "fair-share goal" of $10 per member for the first time in history.

2003

RPAC raises its fair-share goal to $15 per member and continues to meet its goal, raising over $4.4 million.

2004

All 50 states and four territories (Guam, Puerto Rico, the Virgin Islands, and the District of Columbia) meet their national RPAC goal, raising $5.4 million for federal elections. In that year more than 90 percent of REALTOR®-supported candidates win their races.

RPAC launched a "Golden R" program in 1986, requiring a $5,000 initial contribution. The Association's big donors in 1998 helped put the PAC back into the number one spot—and earned a place on the cover of *Today's REALTOR®* magazine. Those pictured include: *front row* (left to right), Terrence M. McDermott, NAR executive vice president; R. Layne Morrill, 1998 NAR president; and Gus Williams, 1998 National RPAC Trustees chairman; *middle row,* Larry Von Feldt, Martin Edwards Jr., Joe Hanauer, Alan Yassky, Randy McKinney, and Michael Schmelzer; *back row,* John Kretchmar, Jack White, Jim Imhoff, Richard Mendenhall, and David Hemenway.

REALTORS® attending a meeting in Washington, D.C., in 1981, met with President Ronald Reagan to express support for reductions in federal spending. Reagan, in turn, vowed to turn more attention to the needs of the housing industry. NAR President John R. Wood of Naples, Florida, to Reagan's right, called for federal tax relief to stimulate personal savings and investment. Less than a year later, with interest rates crippling housing, the Association launched "Paralysis in Government," or PING, a campaign to get Congress to limit government spending and reduce rates. Julio Laguarta of Houston, 1982 NAR president, called it "the largest grassroots campaign in the 74-year history of the National Association, and possibly the largest grassroots campaign ever for any trade association."

NAR ARCHIVES, COURTESY NANCY WILSON SMITH

INSIDE

surance coverage can avoid problems 2

r investment-property in 1990—page 8

South boost quarterly activity—page 11

NAL ASSOCIATION ALTORS®

Voice for Real Estate™

First-time affordability .... page 12

REALTOR NEWS®

All-Member Issue

Volume 10, Number 23   Week of November 20, 1989

PDATE

he typical 2,000 square-foot, three-ily home in a desirable neighbor-ket an average of 97 days before it er than last year's national aver-ter Homes and Gardens Real Es-

n the West sell fastest, averaging while homes in the Midwest sell es. In the Middle-Atlantic states, on the market, while homes stay age of 99 days in the Northwest st stay on the market an aver-in New England and the South longest shelf life, averaging 127 cording to Better Homes and

. Census Bureau is gearing up hecking its housing count fig-, towns and Indian tribal gov-s sent its block-by-block lists viewed by the local govern-s will be counted when the I.

expected to use property tax demolition permits, utility canvasses to compare their of the federal agency and bureau by Jan. 5. If local federal bureau staff will re-ct field checks to amend

o-tiered property tax ap-the supply of affordable

Bush unveils plan of HOPE

Housing program uses IRA downpayment idea

DALLAS—President Bush's new housing initiative, unveiled in a major policy speech at the 1989 NAR annual convention here Nov. 10, is a forward-looking first step toward alleviating the nation's housing affordability problems and underscores NAR's pro-active role as "The Voice for Real Estate," according to top officials of

More on Bush's speech, Dec. 4 issue

the NATIONAL ASSOCIATION OF REALTORS®.

Bush's announcement of the program—Homeownership and Opportunity for People Everywhere (HOPE)—was viewed by an estimated 6,000 REALTORS® and guests packed into two ballrooms at the Loews Anatole Hotel and received extensive national news coverage.

Association President Ira Gribin, who introduced Bush, said the president's speech made it clear that "housing affordability is a critical national issue, which is something NAR has been . . . for a long time.

1989 NAR President Ira Gribin presents President George Bush with a crystal eagle . . .

RANDY SANTOS

Thanks to the central role of home ownership in American culture and the bipartisan appeal of REALTORS®' issues in Washington, NAR meetings have been a popular place over the years for presidents and presidential hopefuls to seek out an audience. "There's no greater goal for America's families than to be able to live in their own homes," President William J. Clinton told REALTORS® at the Association's Midyear Legislative Meetings in Washington in 1993. "I'm proud to be with people who are on the front lines of America's real economy." Among the presidents and presidential hopefuls who've met with REALTORS® (counterclockwise, beginning from bottom left of previous page) are President George H.W. Bush, pictured in a *REALTOR® News* article with 1989 NAR president Ira Gribin; Newt Gingrich in 1991, when he was serving as minority whip of the U.S. House, talking with commercial practitioner Jim Righeimer of Huntington Beach, California; President Clinton making his 1993 address; Sen. Hillary Rodham Clinton of New York, talking with NAR Senior Vice President of Communications Frank Sibley and New York State Association of REALTORS® Executive Vice President Chuck Staro at the 2002 Midyear Meetings; and President George W. Bush (with back turned) as a candidate in 1999, greeting the late Tim Corliss, of Murphys, California, and Jorge Cantero of Miami, Florida, and again at NAR's 2005 Midyear Meetings.

ALL PHOTOS: RANDY SANTOS

RPAC HALL OF FAME

WITH DEEP APPRECIATION TO THESE MEMBERS FOR THEIR DEDICATION
AND CONTRIBUTIONS OF AT LEAST $25,000

NED WARD
NEW JERSEY

WILLIAM WATSON, JR.
FLORIDA

NESTOR WEIGAND
KANSAS

CATHY WHATLEY
FLORIDA

WALLACE WOODBURY
UTAH

❧ 2003 ❧

MARY FRANCES BURLESON
TEXAS

JACK WOODCOCK
NEVADA

❧ 2004 ❧

DAVID ALPHIN
ARKANSAS

GARY CLAYTON
ILLINOIS

TOM STACY
TEXAS

ALLEN TATE
NORTH CAROLINA

WAYNE WYVILL
MARYLAND

❧ 2005 ❧

CHERYL FERRIER
WASHINGTON

BOBBI GILLIS
TENNESSEE

JOHN HARR, JR.
UTAH

JIM JOHNSTON
IDAHO

PEGGY KAYSER
ILLINOIS

AUDREY LIVINGSTONE
NEW YORK

BENNY McMAHAN
TEXAS

GEORGE PEEK
NEVADA

GERALD PERLOW
ILLINOIS

AUBREY RICHARDSON
SOUTH CAROLINA

LAURA SHIFRIN
MASSACHUSETTS

WILLIAM SNYDER
KENTUCKY

BILL WATTS
ALABAMA

RANDY SANTOS

REALTORS® who serve as president of NAR maintain a visible presence in the nation's capital and lead by example when it comes to RPAC fundraising. Top, 2003 President Cathy Whatley attends an RPAC Hall of Fame reception. Right, 2004 President Walt McDonald testifies before a House committee about NAR's concerns over proposed reforms to the Real Estate Settlement Procedures Act.

PATRICIA FISHER, 2004

A POWER LIKE NO OTHER

Through the 1970s, REALTORS® continued to expand their Washington operations. Contributions to the PAC grew to about $1 million annually, and a corps of federal political coordinators was recruited, giving NAR a systematic grassroots mobilization tool. The FPCs—REALTORS® with ties to their area's federal lawmakers—serve as the first point of contact when NAR mobilizes its federal legislative and regulatory advocacy operations.

From the beginning the rules governing contributions to the PAC recognized the importance of the three-way agreement among REALTOR® organizations, with state associations and local boards each retaining 30 percent of the funds collected in their jurisdictions for contributions to state and local candidates, and the remaining 40 percent going to the national PAC. As the receipts grew, the formula was changed to a 35-35-30 split, giving state and local associations the bigger share of donations. Even with the new split, dollars flowed into NAR coffers; by the early 1980s, national receipts totaled $1.5 million and continued to grow.

Left, President Al Mansell presides over the board of directors meeting at one of the Association's annual legislative meetings in Washington. Below, 2006 President Thomas M. Stevens thanks state leaders for their support of RPAC.

RANDY SANTOS

Its PAC now firmly established, NAR began efforts to enhance the effectiveness of REALTORS®' advocacy efforts, not just nationally but at the state and local levels as well. A new Issues Mobilization Committee gave REALTORS® a platform for tackling public policy issues—like new state and local transfer taxes. Leveraging the Association's resources at the state and local levels helped NAR act more effectively nationally by enabling REALTORS® to tamp down issues that threatened to bubble up across states. In 1989, the NAR Board of Directors unanimously approved The Voice for Real Estate® as the Association's unifying theme.

By the 1990s, NAR had widened efforts to help states and localities with several programs for sharing resources. Through a popular land-use initiative, for example, NAR splits costs with state and local associations for legal analyses of land-use proposals. A shared government affairs director program enables smaller associations to tap professional lobbying assistance by pooling resources to hire a government affairs specialist.

RANDY SANTOS

ROBERT VISSER

At a 2006 U.S. House hearing, Pat V. Combs, then president-elect, responds to U.S. Justice Department charges of anticompetitiveness, saying the real estate business is more competitive than she's seen in her career.

Today, REALTORS® can respond instantaneously to Calls for Action through the NAR Action Center at REALTOR .org. One 2006 call, sent out in the weeks before an important Senate vote on NAR-supported small-business health insurance legislation, drew more than a quarter million letters, a response from almost 15 percent of the Association's membership, which at the time stood at just under 1.3 million.

NAR

On the national stage, NAR sought to help REALTORS® expand their support for federal candidates without running up against statutory limits on candidate contributions through what's known as "soft money" support. Under two programs—the independent expenditure initiative launched in the early 1980s and the opportunity race program launched in the late 1980s—NAR deploys corporate contributions to build candidate support in ways other than

donating money to their campaigns. Using independent expenditures, NAR speaks directly to consumers about its views through print and TV ads and other communications. Through opportunity races, NAR provides assistance to REALTORS® to solicit support from other REALTORS®, not the general public.

Meanwhile, contributions to RPAC continued to grow, exceeding $6 million by 2005, and its donations to federal candidates made it one of the top PACs in the country. In the late 1990s, *Fortune* magazine listed NAR among the top 25 most powerful lobbying groups in the country. By 2001, the magazine was calling NAR one of the 10 most powerful groups.

NAR demonstrated its strength in the 2004 national elections, when more than 90 percent of the candidates it supported won their races. Among them was Johnny Isakson. The three-term congressman—in the district once held by former House Speaker Newt Gingrich—became the first REALTOR® to be elected to the Senate. Isakson, whose father was one of the founders of the Georgia Association of REALTORS®, was one of the nation's largest brokers before selling his brokerage to NRT Inc. in 2002, and had been an NAR director. Having elected someone with this depth of involvement in the Association gave REALTORS® who'd supported his candidacy good reason to celebrate at Isakson's victory party.

The huge success of RPAC only partly explains NAR's growing grassroots power, though. Technology also plays a role. By the middle of this decade NAR had in place an electronic system that enabled it to generate a broad-based response from its members almost instantaneously. "For the first time, NAR could reach out directly to its members to enlist their help cost-effectively," said Giovaniello.

By 2006, the show of grassroots strength that NAR was demonstrating again and again was recognized across Capitol Hill. Representative Paul E. Kanjorski of Pennsylvania said, "No one can muster grassroots support like the REALTORS®."[6] Kanjorski is a cosponsor of the NAR-backed Community Choice in Real Estate Act, which would prohibit entry into real estate brokerage and property management by national banking conglomerates.

Still, one thing technology can never do is put REALTORS® face-to-face with members of Congress. That's accomplished each spring, when REALTORS® travel to Washington, D.C., for the Association's Midyear Legislative Meetings. Between meetings, NAR leaders and staff literally follow in the footsteps of those early NAR leaders who came to Washington to serve the nation during World War I.

"We approach issue advocacy the same way REALTORS® approach their business," said Giovaniello, "by wearing out a lot of shoe leather. In contrast to other groups, which might have business before one committee in Congress, we speak for all communities and property owners, so we have business with committee after committee."

NAR's new environmentally sustainable office building supports the Association's shoe-leather approach to advocacy: It's just a two-block walk to the Capitol. Not only does it raise the NAR profile in Washington but it demonstrates the commitment of REALTORS® to communities. It's built on a former brownfield site that sat vacant for years. Now it's a hub of economic activity, with a restaurant and coffeehouse, multiple tenants, and a rooftop deck that's become a favorite of lawmakers. "We hosted 150 to 200 events in just the first two years, including many by and for members of Congress," said Giovaniello. "They love the building, but more importantly, it completes the connection for them about what REALTORS® stand for. They know REALTORS® stand for communities and we see Congress as our partner in protecting them."

Georgia Senator Johnny Isakson at his victory party in 2004 and meeting with REALTORS® outside the Capitol building in 2005. If the successful campaign to preserve the mortgage interest deduction (the subject of a mid-1990s rally with Senator Don Nickles of Oklahoma) cemented REALTORS®' reputation on Capitol Hill, Isakson's victory marked another milestone for NAR. He was the first REALTOR® elected to the U.S. Senate.

Looming Large

In 2004 the NATIONAL ASSOCIATION OF REALTORS® opened the doors to one of the first environmentally green buildings in the nation's capital. The 12-story triangular building is sheathed in blue-green glass and topped with a tower that extends 40 feet above the District's height line.

Ten years earlier, in 1994, NAR had moved out of its building at 777 14th Street NW and rented space in the building of law firm Williams & Connolly. The W&C building, though centrally located Class A office space, was far from Capitol Hill and offered little visibility for REALTORS®.

All that changed in October 2002, when Association leaders broke ground on the new building, which stands just two blocks from the Capitol. NAR President Martin J. Edwards of Memphis said at the ceremony, "The location makes a statement about NAR's commitment to participate actively in federal policymaking."

The building's unique design, by Graham Gund Architects of Cambridge, Massachusetts, was the result of a competition that attracted some of the top architectural firms in the country. Submissions were judged by a seven-member panel that included George White, former Architect of the Capitol.

During construction, REALTORS® enthused about the building's aesthetic. "The architecture is dramatic and dynamic and stands out from everything around it," said Richard Rosenthal, a REALTOR® from Venice, California, in a May 2004 *REALTOR Magazine* article. "It's a new landmark."

Rosenthal chaired a subcommittee of the Association's Real Property Operations Committee that oversaw development of the building. He, along with RPOC Chair Dale Colby of Glendora, California, and Vice Chair Jim Helsel of Lemoyne, Pennsylvania, participated in judging the designs.

"A SLICE OF KEY LIME PIE"

After the building opened in October 2004, *Washington Post* columnist Jeffrey Birnbaum declared, "Depending on your perspective, the $46 million edifice looks like a gigantic slice of key lime pie or a blue-green battleship that has the Capitol dome in its wake. Either way, the REALTORS®' dazzling structure, just a few blocks from Congress, stands as a potent statement. It says: "We are a serious lobby, here to stay."

It wasn't just design and location that captured the fancy of the NAR Board of Directors. The total cost of the project was about $46 million, $15 million of which came from a fund established by the NAR when it sold the 14th Street building. The rest came from two low-interest bond issues that the Association qualified for because the surrounding neighborhood was designated an enterprise zone. The combined interest rate on the issues was 4.3 percent, about 2 percentage points less than a regular financing arrangement. NAR CEO and Executive Vice President Dale Stinton, who was chief financial officer at the time of the transaction, said NAR would save about $6 million in financing costs over the 20-year term.

The LEED-certified Washington, D.C., building at 500 New Jersey Avenue, N.W., is a short walk from the Capitol and provides a dramatic statement to federal lawmakers.

THE GREENING OF CAPITOL HILL

The design was driven in part by the Association's pursuit of green-building certification through the U.S. Green Building Council, a coalition of building industry leaders committed to using environmentally friendly materials and features.

"We decided that we needed to put our money where our mouth is," Helsel said during the building's construction. "This building demonstrates to Congress REALTORS®' commitment to environmental issues."

At the time, fewer than 200 buildings nationwide were certified. The building earned a Silver Leadership in Energy and Environmental Design (LEED) certification in May 2005, making it one of the first green-certified buildings in the District. Among the building's green features are a high-performance glass-curtain wall that reduces energy use by as much as 30 percent, efficient HVAC systems, the use of recycled building materials, a

NAR ARCHIVES, 1975

landscaping plan that includes native plant species, and an irrigation system that relies on recycled rainwater.

"NAR is the largest trade association in the world. Our goal is to promote real property ownership," Helsel said in the 2004. "What better way to do that than by owning a great building in Washington, D.C.?"

JULIE FOURNIER, 2004

HONORS FOR 500 NEW JERSEY AVENUE, N.W.

American Architecture Award, 2005 (Chicago Athenaeum Museum of Architecture & Design)

Best Architecture Award and Best Financing Award (*Washington Business Journal's* Best Real Estate Deals of 2003)

Bronze Award, 2005 (*Building Design & Construction* Magazine)

Digie Award, 2005 (Realcomm)

Energy Efficiency Award (The National Energy Resources Organization)

Honor Award, 2005 (Boston Society of Architects)

LEED Silver Certification (U.S. Green Building Council)

Peoples Choice Award, 2006 (AIA New England Design Awards)

Presidential Citation for Sustainable Design, 2006 (Washington, D.C., Chapter of the American Institute of Architects)

Sustainable Design Award—Design Excellence Citation, 2005 (Boston Society of Architects/New York City Chapter of the American Institute of Architects)

Vision Award, 2005 (The Committee of 100 of the Federal City)

Sweet Home Chicago. Although the new building has raised NAR's profile in Washington, D.C., the Association remains headquartered in Chicago in the 430 N. Michigan Avenue building it bought in 1974. The Chicago building, pictured at left in 1975, is famous for its appearance in the opening of the "Bob Newhart Show," a CBS comedy that aired from 1972 to 1978. The show was commemorated in 2004 by cable channel TV Land with a life-size bronze statue of Newhart's character—psychologist Robert Hartley—sitting next to a couch. The statue was unveiled in front of the Chicago building, with Newhart making a guest appearance. Later, the statue was moved to Chicago's Navy Pier.

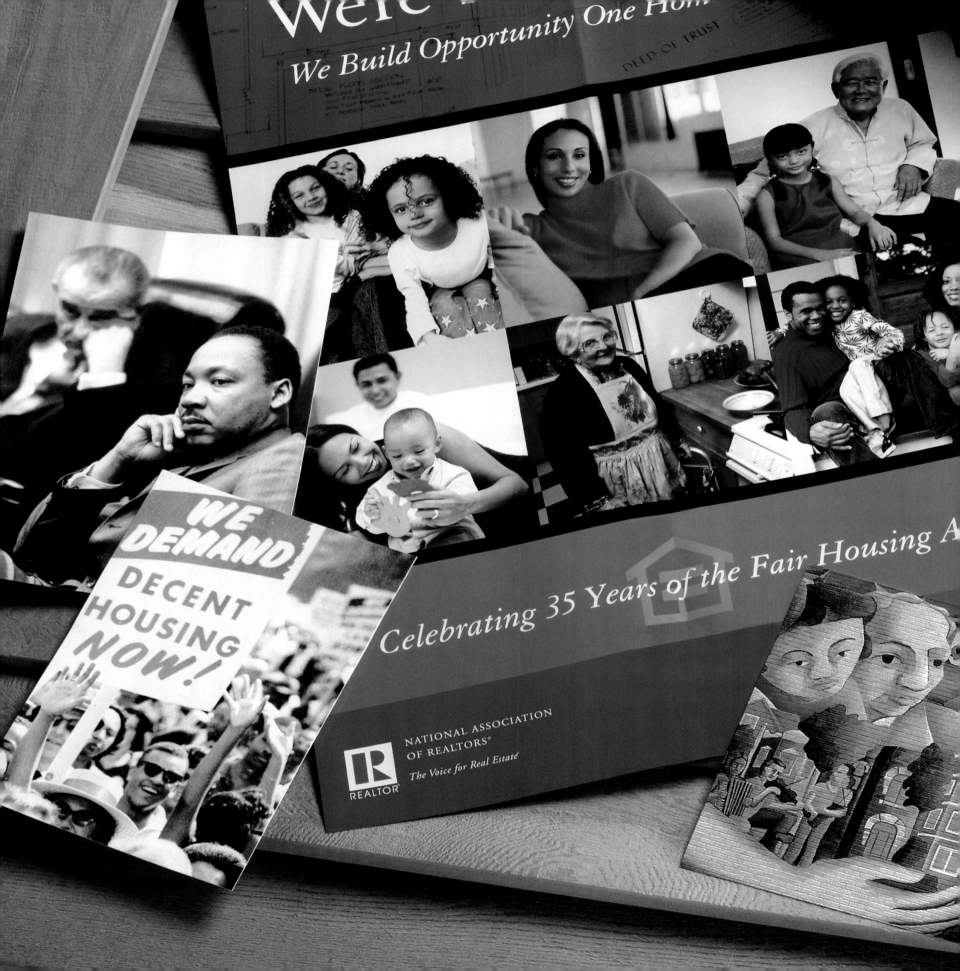

CHAPTER FOUR

Evolving Conscience

In his seminal novel *Native Son*, published in 1940, Richard Wright describes a Chicago where African Americans live in a Black Belt with poor housing conditions and inflated prices. Wright traces the anger of his protagonist, the murderous Bigger, directly to the real estate industry. "No white real estate man," Bigger thinks, "would rent a flat to a black man other than in the sections where it had been decided that black people might live."[1]

More than a decade before the NATIONAL ASSOCIATION OF REALTORS® was founded, the U.S. Supreme Court laid the groundwork for segregation, establishing the "separate but equal" doctrine in *Plessy v. Ferguson*. And for the first half of the twentieth century, the "separate" part was taken as a matter of course in real estate. Land developers routinely declared "No Negroes" in their marketing materials and imposed restrictive covenants to prevent owners from reselling to blacks and other minorities. Even after such covenants had been struck down in court, minorities faced discrimination in the purchase and financing of homes, and Association leaders trod awkwardly over how a fair housing law would impact owners' rights.

In the 39 years since passage of the Fair Housing Act, however, the Association has evolved into a leader in the promotion of equal housing opportunity—developing landmark education for its members, seeding programs for minority home buyers, seeking out a more diverse membership, and building bridges with minority real estate associations. NAR today celebrates the country's racial and ethnic diversity and strives to make the benefits of real property ownership available to all.

"WE HOLD THESE TRUTHS TO BE SELF-EVIDENT, THAT ALL MEN ARE CREATED EQUAL; THAT THEY ARE ENDOWED BY THEIR CREATOR WITH CERTAIN INALIENABLE RIGHTS; THAT AMONG THESE ARE LIFE, LIBERTY, AND THE PURSUIT OF HAPPINESS."

U.S. DECLARATION OF INDEPENDENCE

The National Association of Real Estate Exchanges, later to become the NATIONAL ASSOCIATION OF REALTORS®, was founded at the height of the Progressive reform era. It was a period when leaders in every sector of civic life converged on a family of ideals that today we recognize as characteristically American: efficiency, organizational planning based on the precise assessment of outcomes, and the prudent balance of tradition with innovation.[2]

From the point of view of the real estate business, however, the residential landscape of early-twentieth-century America resembled its past more than its future. With industrialization having just taken hold in the Northern states, even residents of large cities like New York and Chicago could mistake their neighborhoods for small towns. The average city dweller lived in a low-density neighborhood, walked most places, and didn't draw strict boundaries between areas of work and residence. The South, meanwhile, continued to rely on agriculture for its economic base.[3]

Perhaps surprisingly, residential segregation by race was the exception, not the rule, in both the North and the South. Before 1900, the Northern black population was too sparse and widely distributed to constitute a majority in any particular area. Most blacks lived in the South, where farmwork kept them in close daily contact with whites. In the North, racism usually took the form of employment discrimination, whereas Southern whites maintained their dominance through Jim Crow laws and social custom. In Southern cities, for example, blacks were often expected to travel along alleys and side roads, leaving main thoroughfares for whites.[4]

Apart from the fact that they favored liberal immigration policies, leaders of the newly minted profession of real estate brokerage had little to say about race, ethnicity, or religion. They were focused, instead, on reshaping the public perception of their business in the image of law and medicine. The Association's Code of Ethics, adopted in 1913, encompassed the fair business practices and standards of entry into the profession that would, they hoped, distinguish them from the unscrupulous land speculators of popular myth.[5]

But real estate professionals of the era were not immune to the racial and ethnic prejudices then common among Americans. The organization's first 30 years saw the largest and most abrupt demographic transformation within the United States ever: U.S. involvement in World War I set the North's industrial economy on the track of unprecedented expansion. Southern crop failures drove poor blacks north to fill the increasing demand for workers in the North's urban centers, where they faced hostility from Northern whites fearful of competition in the labor market. Racism among Northern whites

Real estate ads like this one (circa 1915) routinely prohibited purchase by blacks and foreigners.

became more aggressive—riots broke out in many cities—and gave rise to a new brand of economic and cultural separatism.[6]

The country's racial tension was reflected in a provision in NAR's Code of Ethics—Article 34, adopted in 1924—that prohibited its members from "introducing into a neighborhood . . . members of any race or nationality . . . whose presence will clearly be detrimental to property values in that neighborhood." This addition to NAR policy helped establish the notion that a neighborhood's dominant "race or nationality" should play a role, comparable to that of the social class or financial means of its residents, in determining its property values.[7]

The principle that the stability of a neighborhood's property values depended on its racial, ethnic, and religious homogeneity was first set down by Chicago appraiser Frederick M. Babcock in his 1924 book *The Appraisal of Real Estate*, endorsed by the National Association as part of its "Standard Course in Real Estate." According to Babcock, social order depended on the stability of land values; the role of the real estate practitioner, then, was to conduct business so as to maintain those values.[8] Historian Jeffrey Hornstein interprets Article 34 as, in part, a "reflection of the tendencies of its time." He writes,

The war exacerbated racism and nativism, and by the early 1920s there was overwhelming popular support for the restrictive Immigration Act of 1924. At the same time, the eugenics movement enjoyed renewed popularity, and its assumptions of racial hierarchy were shared even by ostensibly enlightened intellectuals like Richard T. Ely, a well-known economist of his day who served as an early consultant to the Association and edited the "Standard Course in Real Estate."[9]

Whatever Babcock's intentions, the justification of racial exclusion on economic grounds was to become a linchpin of federal housing policy. Babcock was appointed head of the underwriting division of the Federal Housing Administration (FHA), created by the National Housing Act of 1934. FHA insurance brought home ownership within the reach of an unprecedented number of Americans. Ironically, the agency's commitment to equitable housing opportunities went hand in hand with discrimination. Babcock also drafted the FHA's influential *Underwriting Manual,* which introduced into federal housing policy the principle that the stability of property values required social homogeneity.[10] "If a neighborhood is to retain stability," the *Manual* read, "it is necessary that properties shall continue to be occupied by the same social and racial classes."[11] From 1934 on, two FHA-recommended underwriting practices would mold the physical and social landscape of residential development: the insertion of "restrictive covenants" into deeds and "redlining."[12]

A typical restrictive covenant was a contract among property owners prohibiting sales to blacks or other minorities for a period of time, usually 20 years. This technique of discrimination was favored by the influential Chicago Real Estate Board, which in 1927 led a "special drive to ensure its adoption by all of the 'better' neighborhoods in the city."[13]

During the 1930s, civil rights lawyers began challenging restrictive covenants in court, with limited success. But in the 1940s, the upheaval of World War II and the military service of nearly a million black men and women led to rapid growth in the young civil rights movement. President Franklin Roosevelt banned discrimination in the war industries, the nonviolent Congress of Racial Equality was founded, and the National Association for the Advancement of Colored People (NAACP) launched a campaign against all types of legal discrimination,

NATIONAL ARCHIVES

The large-scale movement of Southern blacks to the North in search of jobs led to fear among white property owners and an increase in segregationist housing policies in the early 1900s.

In 1924 NAR added a measure to its Code of Ethics—amended in 1950 and later removed entirely—that essentially forbade REALTORS® from selling to blacks and other ethnic minorities in white neighborhoods. REALTORS®' key concern: maintaining property values. The provision also was said to protect neighborhoods from the unscrupulous practice of blockbusting, moving a black family into a neighborhood for the sole purpose of getting white residents to sell at deflated prices.

led by its chief counsel, Thurgood Marshall.[14] The campaign's first significant success came in 1948, when the U.S. Supreme Court, in *Shelley v. Kraemer* [334 U.S. 1 (1948)], prohibited state courts from enforcing restrictive covenants.[15] The decision stated: "Restrictive agreements of the sort involved in these cases have been used to exclude other than Negroes from the ownership or occupancy of real property. We are informed that such agreements have been directed against Indians, Jews, Chinese, Japanese, Mexicans, Hawaiians, Puerto Ricans, and Filipinos, among others." Later that year, *Hurd v. Hodge* applied the same ruling to federal courts. And in 1950, a campaign to integrate the New York public-private development called Stuyvesant Town led to the birth of the National Committee Against Discrimination in Housing.[16]

William North, NAR chief counsel and later executive vice president, noted in his 1986 book *Passwords and Prejudice*, however,

It was a full two years after the Shelley *and* Hurd *decisions that the FHA and VA [Department of Veterans Affairs] finally reversed their long-standing policy of insisting that restrictive covenants be enforced as a condition of insurability and instead prohibited insurance of mortgages of property encumbered by such covenants. But, even then, such a reversal of policy applied only to mortgage insurance on properties encumbered by restrictive covenants after February 15, 1950, but not before. The effect of government policy on minority access to FHA financing was such that, even as late as 1960, blacks had received barely 2 percent of the FHA mortgage insurance commitments made.[17]*

It took the same two years before NAR, in 1950, followed suit and amended Article 34. Renumbered as Article 33, it now said, "A REALTOR® should not be instrumental in introducing into a neighborhood a character of property or use which will clearly be detrimental to property values in that neighborhood."[18] Even with the specific reference to race deleted, many REALTORS® continued to understand Article 33 as having a racial intent. As historian William Brown wrote in a 1972 article on the role of the real estate industry in maintaining segregation,

Not until 1959 did a REALTOR® bring the issue to a head by going to court over a charge of unethical conduct concerning his introduction of a nonwhite buyer into a white neighborhood. When the court ruled in the REALTOR®'s favor, and against the local board, "it caused inquiry from some boards surprised to learn that REALTORS® no longer could be subjected to disciplinary action if they assisted minority families in finding homes in all-white neighborhoods."[19]

One black broker testified before the U.S. Commission on Civil Rights in 1964:

One and a half years ago we became members of the Oakland Real Estate Board.... I was amazed to discover that the OREB used "Caucasians Only" on their multiple listings.... I related to the OREB my concern about this situation.... The only response I had was a phone call from the executive secretary during which conversation he disagreed with my interpretation of the laws and furthermore informed me that it was incumbent on an office such as ours that is well known for its integrationist philosophy to check with brokers prior to showing a property in an area which might be all-white in character. He stated that it was our ethical duty to our fellow REALTORS® to inform them of the color of the buyer before showing a multiple listing.[20]

In order to serve blacks, an increasingly distinct segment of the real estate market, a group of black real estate practitioners in 1947 had founded the National Association of Real Estate Brokers Inc., a move recognized and supported by NAR leaders. As a separate organization, however, black real estate brokers lacked access to local real estate boards' multiple listing services. When they were able to join local boards, black brokers were shut out of policymaking committees and expected to follow NAR guidelines, which, as illustrated earlier, were widely understood to prohibit selling property in white neighborhoods to black buyers. Suburban real estate boards—kept all-white in part through the use of steeper fees than those of the cities

they surrounded—sometimes created private listing services for all-white neighborhoods. Black brokers were also excluded through hiring discrimination: White brokerages rarely employed black salespeople, making it more difficult for aspiring black real estate salespeople to accrue the field experience often required in applying for a real estate broker's license.[21]

The end of restrictive covenants did not mean the end of federal involvement in housing discrimination. The systematic denial of credit to residents and developers in racially and ethnically mixed neighborhoods, known as *redlining*, drove the continuing consolidation of blacks into isolated and impoverished neighborhoods throughout the 1940s, 1950s, and 1960s.

Redlining took its name from the credit-rating system instituted in 1933 by the Home Owner's Loan Corporation (HOLC), a New Deal program that provided low-interest loans to urban property owners who had lost their homes to foreclosure or were in danger of losing them. The HOLC's "Residential Security" maps gave neighborhoods one of four ratings. The lowest rating ("red") was invariably given to neighborhoods of mixed racial or ethnic composition. The direct impact of the HOLC's lending practices was limited, since the program affected relatively few areas. But the practice of redlining by lending institutions continued; the federal government included prohibitions to prevent redlining in the 1968 Fair Housing Act and the 1977 Community Reinvestment Act.

SLUMS, PUBLIC HOUSING, AND BLOCKBUSTING

Shut off from both publicly and privately insured financing, urban neighborhoods fell into disrepair while white central city residents fled

For years, developers advocated the use of restrictive covenants, private agreements to prevent minorities from buying into a neighborhood. This St. Louis property was the site of a landmark case, *Shelley v. Kraemer,* that marked the beginning of the end for such restrictions. The U.S. Supreme Court said in 1948 that the Fourteenth Amendment prevented state courts from enforcing restrictive covenants.

Index of Dissimilarity

Social scientists use a statistical calculation known as the *index of dissimilarity* to measure minority segregation.

A region's index of dissimilarity is equal to the percentage of a given minority's population that would have to move in order for that minority to become equally distributed across that region. For example, if a social scientist determines that the Hispanic population of a city has an index of dissimilarity of 25, it means that 25 percent of Hispanics would have to move from their current residences in order to achieve even distribution throughout the city. The minimum value is 0, indicating perfectly even minority distribution (i.e., no minority group member would have to move). The maximum value is 100, indicating total segregation.

Changes in the index over time show that the movement toward residential segregation by race began to accelerate at the turn of the twentieth century. Around 1860, the index of dissimilarity for free blacks in Chicago was 50,* meaning that 50 percent of Chicago's blacks would have had to move to achieve even distribution throughout the city. By 1910, Chicago's index of dissimilarity had risen to 66.8. Similar increases in segregation occurred over the same period in Cleveland (from 49 to 69), Milwaukee (59.6 to 66.7), and St. Louis (39.1 to 54.3). Segregation in southern cities increased more slowly during the same period, averaging an index of 29 in 1860 and rising to 38.3 in 1910.† But in the wake of the social and political upheaval spurred by American involvement in World War I, residential segregation was the rule everywhere by 1940, when northern cities averaged dissimilarity values of 89.2 and southern cities averaged 81.‡

As Alexander von Hoffman writes, the index of dissimilarity indicates a recent decline in segregation: "For the period between 1970 and 1990, the index of dissimilarity fell in 27 of the 30 metropolitan areas with the largest black populations. The average index dropped eight points to 67 for all the areas, by seven points in the north to 78, and nine points in the south to 66. In 12 areas—Atlanta, Baltimore, Washington, Norfolk–Virginia Beach, Tampa–St. Petersburg, Miami, Boston, Kansas City, Dallas, Houston, San Francisco, and Los Angeles—the index dropped by ten or more points."§

---

*Massey, Douglas S. and Denton, Nancy A. *American Apartheid: Segregation and the Making of the Underclass.* Cambridge and London: Harvard University Press, 1993, p. 21.

†*Ibid.*

‡*Ibid.*

§von Hoffman, Alexander. "Like Fleas on a Tiger? A Brief History of the Open Housing Movement." Joint Center for Housing Studies, Harvard University, 1998, p. 45.

to the burgeoning suburbs, taking with them their access to financing for home buying and commercial development. Meanwhile, black migration from the South to Chicago, Detroit, New York, Cleveland, Philadelphia, and other cities in the North and Midwest continued throughout the 1940s and 1950s, leading to the growth of disinvested slums as well as historically unprecedented levels of racial segregation.[22] Congress responded by mandating, in the Housing Act of 1949, the clearance of slums and subsequent construction of public housing.

NAR opposed the 1949 act because of its public housing provisions and successfully lobbied for maximum local control of public housing subsidies. Accustomed to the fact of residential segregation and eager to contain the slums, local governments usually chose to build public housing—characterized by high density and inexpensive construction—on cleared slum sites. The results were generically styled brick housing projects, monuments to this day of black residential segregation and its troubling persistence.[23]

Among a few real estate practitioners, racial turnover at the borders between predominantly white and predominantly black neighborhoods led to the practice of blockbusting. Introducing a black resident into a neighborhood (i.e., "busting" the block) led white home owners to sell their properties quickly at relatively low prices, freeing up property to meet black demand; the blockbusting agent would then resell the property at a higher price to black buyers. According to urban historian Alexander von Hoffman, however, the much-maligned figure of the blockbusting real estate practitioner concealed a complex social and economic reality. "Blockbusting . . . was a product, not a cause, of the . . . forces that induced the races to settle in different areas of the city," wrote von Hoffman. "Blockbusters carried out an economic function for which there was a demand—in this case, selling property to African Americans."[24]

In her 1969 study, *Racial Policies and Practices of Real Estate Brokers,* sociologist Rose Helper interviewed practitioners who sold and rented property to blacks in transitional neighborhoods during the 1950s. They reflected openly on their motives for engaging in the practice. "The Negro family I put in the house at X was the first in the block," explained one. "No, I wouldn't do it in Area C, but here, yes, because it is the inevitable trend." Another practitioner expressed a similar view: "When [blacks] were coming closer . . . the people who had the means to move, they moved. . . . [When the] Negroes were a mile or two miles away . . . then we were forced."[25]

Real estate salespeople possessed a familiar vocabulary of neighborhood turnover. Helper wrote that an approaching black population caused white neighborhood residents in a given area to feel "concerned," "jittery," "up in the air." Rumors of black influx scared off whites who would otherwise have bought homes there, halting property sales and sending brokers' business into the "doldrums," "twilight zone," "stagnation zone," or "stalemate period" when the first home was sold to blacks and the block was "broken."[26]

Helper, like von Hoffman, concluded that most individual real estate practitioners could do little to resist a process of racial turnover dictated by large social and market forces. In one Chicago suburb of 71,689 people, for example, 23,162 black residents arrived in lieu of 19,989 white residents who left in a span of just six years.[27] Local real estate boards, however, had substantial collective influence. "Interviews indicated that the board wields a particular kind of influence—one of professional and moral authority," Helper wrote. "The board reserves for itself the right to define the broker's role in the community."[28] Although discriminatory practice was no longer explicitly required by the Code of Ethics after the amendment of Article 34 in 1950, Helper argued, the Code continued to define real estate brokers' roles in the community: If their clientele favored racial, ethnic, or religious discrimination, brokers were tacitly expected to comply.[29]

MOVEMENT TOWARD INTEGRATION

The beginning of the end for discriminatory FHA housing practices came in 1954, when the U.S. Supreme Court ruled in *Brown v. Topeka Board of Education* that the Fourteenth Amendment's guarantee to all citizens of "equal protection of the laws" prohibited the Topeka (Kansas) Board of Education from segregating its public schools. In his Opinion of the Court, Chief Justice Earl Warren rejected the "separate but equal" doctrine set down in 1896 in *Plessy v. Ferguson,* writing that to separate black children "from others of similar age and qualifications solely because of their race generates a feeling of inferiority as to their status in the community that may affect their hearts and minds in a way unlikely ever to be undone." Consequently, "separate educational facilities are inherently unequal" [347 U.S. 483 (1954)]. The implications for FHA-sanctioned housing segregation and practices such as redlining were clear.

Both candidates for president in 1960 included open-housing planks in their platforms. In 1962, President John F. Kennedy signed Executive Order 11063. Echoing *Brown,* it declared, "Discriminatory policies and practices result in segregated patterns of housing and necessarily produce other forms of discrimination and segregation which deprive many Americans of equal opportunity in the exercise of their inalienable rights to life, liberty, and the pursuit of happiness." The order's practical effects were negligible, however—it covered only housing to be built in the future, leaving existing segrega-

Fair in Deed

While attending synagogue in the early 1960s, Maryland REALTOR® Malcolm Sherman heard his rabbi assert that if the Holocaust had taught any lesson, it was that one should never ignore injustice done to one's neighbor. The next day, he publicly announced his intention to buy, sell, and rent to anyone, regardless of race, creed, or color. "This was totally contrary to NAR policy at the time," Sherman later recalled. "When I consulted my attorney about the decision, he said, 'You'll commit business suicide.' " Sherman decided the risk was worth it.

Legendary Baltimore Orioles outfielder Frank Robinson was one of Sherman's clients. During the baseball season, Robinson lived in a mostly black Baltimore neighborhood near the Orioles' Memorial Stadium. But in 1966, after leading the Orioles to a World Series victory, Robinson informed his team that he wouldn't return next season if he had to continue living in a segregated neighborhood. When Sherman eventually found him an apartment in a predominantly white neighborhood, local brokers accused Sherman of blockbusting. His business suffered for the next several years.

Sherman encountered similar resistance from white homeowners while arranging the purchase of a home for NFL hall-of-famer John Mackey and his wife, Sylvia, in the Baltimore suburbs during the 1960s. Sherman said that when the Mackeys attended their first neighborhood association meeting, the neighbors asked the Mackeys why they felt they needed to buy a house in an all-white neighborhood. "Sylvia Mackey answered with a question of her own—'well, why did *you* buy a home here?' They recited the usual list of things that makes a neighborhood attractive," Sherman said, "safe streets, good schools, well-built homes. 'Right,' Sylvia explained, 'that's what we want, too.' " To Sherman, the story's lesson was clear: No matter a person's race, creed, or color, people want pretty much the same thing from their neighborhood.

Sherman's leadership in the fight for nondiscriminatory housing practices led President John F. Kennedy to

GREATER BALTIMORE BOARD OF REALTORS®

Malcolm Sherman

appoint him head of the National Committee for Equal Opportunity in Housing. Having served as president of the Maryland Association of REALTORS® (then the Maryland Real Estate Board) in 1962, Sherman wielded clout in the profession. "I was an oddball," he said. "I'd been president of a state association—I wasn't some protestor."

Sherman also recalled the "gentlemen's agreement" among brokers in one Baltimore neighborhood that prohibited sales and rentals to Jews in the 1950s. Surprised to discover that the neighborhood's development was strongly influenced by a prominent Jewish businessman, Sherman—accompanied by a rabbi—visited the businessman's office. "Will you work with us so that all people will live under the same law?" Sherman asked. The businessman declined, replying that the status quo had served his business well. Sherman said that reflecting on such moments brings to mind a favorite line of his from James Baldwin's *The Fire Next Time,* "Whoever debases others is debasing himself."

Life Achievement Award

PRESENTED TO

MALCOLM SHERMAN

MARYLAND REALTOR® SPOKE WITH

MAL SHERMAN,

1999 MARYLAND ASSOCIATION OF REALTORS®

LIFE ACHIEVEMENT AWARD WINNER, ABOUT HIS

FAIR HOUSING ACTIVITIES IN REAL ESTATE.

Malcolm Sherman began his career in real estate in 1949. Only brokers licensed for two years were allowed membership in the MLS, and a one-page contract of sale was standard.

Real estate has changed significantly in the 51 years since. And Mal Sherman, recipient of the 1999 Maryland Association of REALTORS® Life Achievement Award, has been both eyewitness and activist. He has been a leader in changing neighborhoods, changing viewpoints and changing lives.

"I had always been interested in houses and land," Mal says. "I thought I could help people make a decision. I wanted to help families find a better quality of life. It was a way for me to combine business and social work all in one." His firm, Mal Sherman REALTOR®, had 18 women and 18 men, at a time when there were very few women selling real estate.

Mal remembers clearly the anti-semitism in Baltimore in the early 1950s, as well as the segregated neighborhoods that were the norm and the law. "As a Jewish real estate broker, I was not allowed to show property east of Falls Road," Sherman says. "Jewish retailers were not allowed in Roland Park."

Nevertheless, real estate was a very good business for the young entrepreneur. As Jewish families moved further into the suburbs, Gentiles fled. "Speculators were blockbusting," Sherman says. He remembers the first time he tried to stabilize a neighborhood. It was 1953, and black families had starting buying in an area with very nice townhouses. As they moved in, white families started moving out. "I remember going to a meeting with white families, begging them to stay. But they moved out anyway." Sherman's business was affected; many did not want to do business with someone who was trying to end segregation.

In 1956, the Supreme Court handed down its landmark Brown vs. Board of Education decision, declaring unconstitutional the "separate but equal" policies that segregated public schools. Following the decision, deed restrictions were lifted.

Discrimination was still a way of life and as a result Jewish buyers were closed out of non-Jewish communities. Sherman sold property in Northwest Baltimore to Jewish families. "Of course, the Rabbi loved it because it created a community around the synagogue," Sherman explained, "just as Catholics lived around their churches. Prices rose because there was more demand than supply."

His business was doing well when Mal went to synagogue one evening and heard Rabbi Leiberman discuss human rights in the context of Nazi concentration camps in World War II. "We can't turn the other cheek. We've got to stand for everyone's liberty," the Rabbi said. Sherman remembers being so moved that afterwards he asked the Rabbi, "What can I do?"

For his leadership in fair housing, Mal Sherman received the Maryland Association of REALTORS®' Life Achievement Award.

By 1963, the federal government had already outlawed discrimination in housing owned by the federal government. In the face of calls for wider government intervention, REALTORS® published a controversial Property Owners' Bill of Rights, asserting that all Americans, regardless of race, color, or creed, be allowed to occupy and dispose of property without government interference.

PROPERTY OWNERS' BILL OF RIGHTS

In 1789, the people of America were fearful that government might restrict their freedom. The first Congress of the United States, in that year, proposed a Bill of Rights.

The Bill of Rights, essentially, tells the government what it cannot do. The statements comprise the first 10 amendments to the United States Constitution.

The Bill of Rights has had a profound impact upon the history of the world.

Forty million immigrants gave up much to come to this land, seeking something promised here — and only here. Many countries have abundant natural resources, vast vacant lands, and climate as good as America.

They came here for the promise of security — the promise of freedom — for the precious right to live as free men with equal opportunity for all.

In July of 1868, a new guarantee of freedom was ratified. Its purpose was to guard against human slavery. Its guarantees were for the equal protection of all.

This new guarantee of freedom is the 14th Amendment. It reads, in part, as follows:

"No state shall make or enforce any law which shall abridge the privileges or immunities of citizens of the United States; nor shall any state deprive any person of life, liberty, or property without due process of law, nor deny to any person within its jurisdiction the equal protection of the laws."

The vital importance of these federal laws was re-emphasized in a recent statement of the Chief Justice of the United States in which he urged the retention of "government of laws in preference to a government of men."

Today, the rights and freedoms of the individual American property owner are being eroded. This endangers the rights and freedom of all Americans. Therefore, a Bill of Rights to protect the American property owner is needed.

It is self-evident that the erosion of these freedoms will destroy the free enterprising, individual American.

It is our solemn belief that the individual American property owner, regardless of race, color, or creed, must be allowed, under law, to retain:

1. The right of privacy.

2. The right to choose his own friends.

3. The right to own and enjoy property according to his own dictates.

4. The right to occupy and dispose of property without governmental interference in accordance with the dictates of his conscience.

5. The right of all equally to enjoy property without interference by laws giving special privilege to any group or groups.

6. The right to maintain what, in his opinion, are congenial surroundings for tenants.

7. The right to contract with a real estate broker or other representative of his choice and to authorize him to act for him according to his instructions.

8. The right to determine the acceptability and desirability of any prospective buyer or tenant of his property.

9. The right of every American to choose who in his opinion are congenial tenants in any property he owns — to maintain the stability and security of his income.

10. The right to enjoy the freedom to accept, reject, negotiate, or not negotiate with others.

Loss of these rights diminishes personal freedom and creates a springboard for further erosion of liberty.

Published as a Public Service by
National Association of Real Estate Boards
36 So. Wabash Ave., Chicago, Illinois
Officially Approved June 4, 1963.

tion unaffected, and it applied only to housing owned by the federal government, which accounted for a tiny number of units.[30]

The practical effect of segregation was to deny blacks access to new housing, especially new homes built in the suburbs. Middle-class black families could move into city neighborhoods formerly occupied by whites, but they could not follow when whites fled to the suburbs. This artificial constraint on the market meant that blacks often ended up paying more for worse, sometimes dilapidated housing.[31] In

1961, the U.S. Commission on Civil Rights reported to the president and Congress,

Each year a constant stream of migrants flows from the countryside, increasing their size and their burdens. And as the poor, ill-educated, and unadapted migrants move into the central cities, there is an exodus of the wealthier, more stable, middle class into the expanding suburbs. The migrants, largely nonwhites, are fenced off into the older, deteriorating

On August 28, 1963, hundreds of thousands of civil rights activists attended the March on Washington where Martin Luther King Jr. made his famous "I have a dream" speech and Whitney Young, addressing future civil rights activists, said, "They must march from the rat infested, overcrowded ghettos to decent, wholesome, unrestricted residential areas dispersed throughout the cities."

neighborhoods and the tempo of decay increases. . . . The middle class, which in the past has provided stability, leadership, and a firm fiscal base for municipal taxes, is fleeing to the "white noose" of the suburbs, where its members are largely beyond the reach of municipal taxing power, although they work in the city and require many urban services which municipal government must help provide.[32]

And, apart from the measurable harms to its victims, housing discrimination was simply unjust:

[Denial of equal housing opportunity] involves more than poverty and slums, for it extends to the denial of a fundamental part of freedom: choice in an open, competitive market.[33]

By early 1965, there was a law on the books that outlawed discrimination in employment and public services, and civil rights advocates were well on their way to passage of the 1965 Voting Rights Act, designed to stop discrimination against blacks at the voting booth. So the National Committee Against Discrimination in Housing and the NAACP began a nationwide push for integration in housing. The theme was taken up by Martin Luther King Jr. the following year when he came to Chicago in the first explicitly northern campaign of the civil rights movement, the Chicago Freedom Movement. The proponents of that movement argued that the government of Chicago could end segregation by forcing real estate practitioners to change their ways.[34]

Although the marchers were pledged to nonviolence, the community was not. Each march saw an escalation of violence, until the chief of police asked city hall to seek an injunction because his resources were being stretched.

Eve Lee was one of the few REALTORS® who participated in that campaign. She later recalled,

A representative from the Leadership Council for Metropolitan Open Communities walked into my office and asked me to be a liaison between the NAR and the Leadership Council. As a student at Middlebury College in the early 1960s, I stepped down as president of my sorority because it refused to admit a black member. I felt that everybody else was just as good as I was. My parents taught me how to walk away from bigotry. In the summer of 1966, Mayor Daley called on the leaders of Chicago's top organizations to "do something" about the state of race relations in his city. The Leadership Council was formed under the leadership of Dr. Martin Luther King Jr. for the specific purpose of monitoring, controlling, and testing real-estate agents.

During the summer of 1966, the Chicago Freedom Movement staged a number of marches in white communities to protest housing discrimination.

BERNIE KLEINA, 1966

President Lyndon Baines Johnson met with civil rights leader Martin Luther King Jr. in March 1966, just two months after King kicked off the Chicago Freedom Movement, appealing to the city's real estate practitioners for open housing.

LBJ LIBRARY. PHOTO CREDIT: YOICHI R. OKAMOTO, WHITE HOUSE, 1966

Eve Lee of Chicago participated in support of open housing in the city during the 1960s. Later, in 1986, she became the first woman and the first REALTOR® to chair the Leadership Council for Metropolitan Open Communities, a Chicago fair housing organization founded in 1966. This 2003 REALTOR® Magazine article came after NAR President Cathy Whatley named Lee a "Hometown Hero" for her longtime efforts to end housing discrimination.

Other real estate practitioners resisted open-housing campaigns strenuously. After the California state legislature passed a fair housing law known as the Rumford Act in 1963, the California Real Estate Association (now the CALIFORNIA ASSOCIATION OF REALTORS®) led the effort to invalidate the law through Proposition 14, a voter initiative to amend the state constitution. The measure decreed, "[n]either the state nor any subdivision or agency thereof shall deny, limit or abridge, directly or indirectly, the right of any person who is willing or desires to sell,

lease or rent any part or all of his real property, to decline to sell, lease or rent such property to such person or persons as he, in his absolute discretion, chooses." The initiative won at the ballot box but was voided by the California Supreme Court, a decision reaffirmed on appeal in 1967 by the U.S. Supreme Court in *Reitman v. Mulkey* [387 U.S. 369 (1967)].

THE FAIR HOUSING ACT

In 1968 President Lyndon Johnson created the National Advisory Commission on Civil Disorders to investigate the causes of what had by then been four years of urban riots. The Kerner Report, named after the commission's chair, Governor Otto Kerner of Illinois, blamed the violence on racial ghettos and argued that the only way to stop it was to integrate poor African Americans into other neighborhoods. The commission recommended a national open-housing law. Such a bill had already been introduced and stalled, but the riots following the assassination of Dr. King lent the effort a new urgency. The legislation passed quickly, and Johnson signed Title VIII of the Civil Rights Act of 1968—the Fair Housing Act—just five days after King's death.[55]

The original Fair Housing Act banned housing discrimination and redlining on the basis of race, color, religion, or national origin. It also made it illegal to "deny any person access to or membership or participation in any multiple listing service, real estate brokers' organization or other service, organization, or facility relating to the business of selling or renting dwellings" on the basis of race, color, religion, or national origin.

According to William North, NAR's chief legal counsel in 1968, REALTORS® wielded little influence over federal housing policy in the period leading up to the Fair Housing Act. "We

REALTOR® MAGAZINE, MAY 2003

REALTOR® Hometown Hero | BY LESLIE CUMMINGS

The equalizer

Eve Lee, president of Eve B. Lee & Associates Inc. in Grayslake, Ill., remembers the first stand she took against racial injustice.

As a student at Middlebury College in Middlebury, Vt., in 1964, the popular Lee was president of her sorority. But when the sorority refused to admit black women, she stepped down. "My mother taught me everyone's equal," she says.

Lee became a real estate practitioner in 1965—and she's been taking stands for equal opportunity ever since. In 1986, she became the first woman and the first REALTOR® to chair the Leadership Council for Metropolitan Open Communities, a Chicago fair housing organization founded in 1966 as the result of a campaign for open housing led by Martin Luther King Jr. Lee's now a member of LCMOC's executive committee and counsels former residents of subsidized housing in Chicago on how to find affordable alternatives.

In 1978, she founded a not-for-profit corporation that provides housing for low- and moderate-income households. Her most recent project: turning an apartment building into a transitional home for women leaving jail with addictions.

For her lifetime involvement in affordable housing and equal opportunity issues, Lee's been named a REALTOR® Hometown Hero by NAR President Cathy Whatley. "I cried when I found out, because this road has been difficult at times," Lee says.

In 1985 for instance, LCMOC was filing lawsuits against real estate salespeople on behalf of people who said they'd been discriminated against. "It was controversial to have a real estate salesperson involved in a fair housing group at the time," she says. "Many people in the real estate industry wouldn't even talk to me."

Through it all, Lee's been a sales leader in her area, serving a wide range of income levels. "A coworker saw me work on transactions for a $300,000 home and a $30,000 home in the same day and said, 'You really do treat everyone equally.' That made me feel great about what I do." RM

To nominate someone for Hometown Hero, click **Current Links** at *REALTOR.org/realtormag*.

"Without affordable housing for people of all income levels there'd be no fair housing."

Dossier: Eve B. Lee, Eve B. Lee & Associates Inc., Grayslake, Ill. **E-mail:** EveBLee@aol.com **Claims to fame:** First woman and only REALTOR® to chair the Leadership Council for Metropolitan Open Communities. Served as president of the Lake County Association of REALTORS® and on NAR's Equal Opportunity Committee. **Also serves as:** Board member, Lake County Fair Housing Advisory Committee **Lately:** Holding forums in the Chicago suburbs to educate communities about affordable housing and marketing Prairie Crossing, a ... and economically diverse "conservation community" she ...

hired one legislative representative and had half of his time in Washington, D.C.," he recalled. "We operated more at the state level." Once fair housing legislation took hold, however, NAR became a vital stakeholder in the outcome of the national debate over how to implement and interpret the ideals underlying Title VIII. One provision of Title VIII, known as Mrs. Murphy's Exemption, exempted from fair housing compliance both single-family homes sold or rented by the owner and dwellings of four or fewer units where the owner resided in one of the units.

"This created real problems," he said, "because when a REALTOR® would go out and get a listing, the person would say, 'My neighbors . . . would be most offended if I sell to somebody other than one like us.' The real estate broker would say, 'Well, I'm bound by the Fair Housing Act.' Well, that's fine; it'll be a sale by owner—or a wink and a nod."

Two months after passage of the Fair Housing Act, the U.S. Supreme Court, in *Jones v. Alfred H. Mayer Co.*, drew on the Civil Rights Act of 1866 to rule that racial discrimination

On April 5, 1968, one day after the assassination of Martin Luther King Jr. in Memphis, President Lyndon Johnson met with civil rights leaders in the White House. Seated to his right was Supreme Court Justice Thurgood Marshall. To his left was civil rights leader Clarence Mitchell Jr. Four days after the meeting, Johnson signed the Fair Housing Act into law.

LBJ LIBRARY. YOICHI R. OKAMOTO, WHITE HOUSE, 1968

In his book *Passwords and Prejudice,* published in 1986, the Association's general counsel—and later executive vice president—William North captured the dilemma faced by real estate practitioners with regard to the sometimes opposing goals of fair housing—integration and freedom of choice.

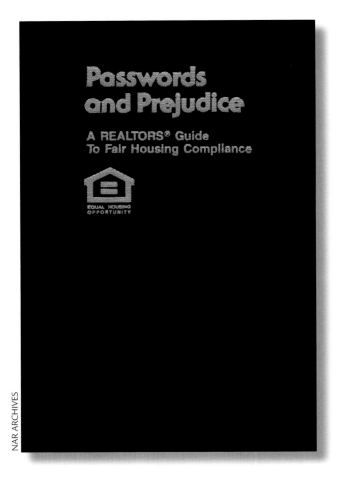

NAR ARCHIVES

Passwords and Prejudice

A REALTORS® Guide
To Fair Housing Compliance

EQUAL HOUSING
OPPORTUNITY

was illegal in any housing transaction, including those covered by Mrs. Murphy's Exemption.[36] But the Department of Justice and the recently created Department of Housing and Urban Development, the two governmental agencies most responsible for administering fair housing law, differed in their interpretations of the act's basic intent. "The Department of Justice took the position that fair housing meant equal opportunity in housing," says North. "The essence was that everyone had an equal opportunity to buy a house consistent with their means, no matter where it was or what the racial composition of the community was. HUD took the position that fair housing meant integrated housing and that it could authorize or require techniques of integration."

HUD's commitment to integration enforcement created significant legal confusion for Realtors®—notably in Oak Park, Illinois, a suburb of Chicago, which implemented an "integration maintenance" program in the 1970s. In the late 1960s, the adjoining neighborhood of Austin had undergone rapid transformation to become nearly all black and lower-income, and Oak Park residents were concerned that panic selling by whites could spread to their village. Oak Park adopted a series of measures designed to promote smoother integration, including the creation of the Oak Park Housing Center, which "induces house-hunting whites to settle in areas where there are blacks, and house-hunting blacks to settle evenly throughout the village." Of the program, Chester McGuire, assistant secretary of the U.S. Department of Housing and Urban Development, said, "There are some who still would say that there should not be any control or attempted management, that integration should just be a laissez-faire operation. But the market is currently stacked against that."[37]

But such activities, noted von Hoffman, "came uncomfortably close to the sort of discriminatory racial steering and quotas that had been used to keep blacks out."[38] In a strange paradox, the Fair Housing Act appeared to make racial steering illegal, yet the goal of integration seemed to require it. In 1986, NAR's North responded with a book on the subject, *Passwords and Prejudice.*

> *It is precisely because the Realtor® must obey the law that he must know what the law requires of him in terms of practice and procedure.... Realtors® cannot participate in integration maintenance activities if by doing so they become liable to damages and loss of license for conduct violative of the fair housing laws. This is why the National Association has actively pressed for both legislative and*

*judicial decisions regarding the legality
of integration maintenance programs
and practices and will continue to do so.*[39]

Throughout the 1970s, proponents of integration viewed NAR as hostile to their efforts. Bob Schwemm, a trial lawyer for the Leadership Council during the 1970s, recalls, "NAR was active in the courts. The Association drafted *amicus curiae* briefs [or 'friend of the court' statements] that would expound upon the implications of a decision the court was making—usually, these briefs would support the actions of the REALTOR® on trial." Eve Lee, the only member of the Leadership Council who was also a REALTOR®, has led efforts to facilitate understanding and collaboration between the two organizations since the early 1960s. Lee recalls the widespread perception that NAR viewed the Leadership Council "as an impediment to profitable business practice."

REALTORS® saw it differently. "What we were looking for," says North, "was a systematic procedure whereby we knew what the law required of us." Anxious to set a clear definition of fair housing compliance for its members, NAR negotiated with HUD to establish an affirmative marketing agreement. These negotiations initially stalled, according to North, because the terms HUD proposed—which included standardizing application forms for renters and buyers, prescribing the number of minority group members that real estate companies had to employ, and requiring companies to place weekly advertisements in minority media outlets—were too onerous to accept. In 1972, NAR unilaterally instituted its own Affirmative Marketing Agreement, which, says North, was "fair, honest, and consistent with the Fair Housing Act of 1968."

NAR finally achieved a breakthrough in its collaboration with HUD in November 1975 at its national convention in San Francisco. NAR President Arthur Leitch—who in 1963 led the California Real Estate Association's drive to pass Proposition 14—startled his colleagues with a sharp reversal. He campaigned for ratification of an agreement between NAR, HUD, and the Department of Justice to actively facilitate fair housing compliance among REALTORS®. "There was tremendous division about it among our leadership," former NAR Senior Vice President Nancy Wilson Smith told an interviewer in 2001. "[Leitch] was a quiet, gentle person, but he took the tiger by the tail on this issue."[40] At the 1975 convention, North remembers, "there was a very strong feeling that NAR should not, in essence, get involved in substituting their judgment for [that of] potential buyers and . . . sellers as to whom they want to sell to and buy from." Yet despite these potent reservations, North adds, NAR pioneered antidiscrimination measures: "It wasn't until eight or nine years later that the mortgage bankers . . . undertook anything comparable."

STEPS FORWARD, STEPS BACK

Leitch's success at the 1975 convention led to the agreement between NAR, HUD, and the Justice Department known as the Voluntary Affirmative Marketing Agreement, a set of guidelines that clarified for REALTORS® the rights and responsibilities given them by the Fair Housing Act. The VAMA was intended to strengthen the federal Fair Housing Act by ensuring that NAR take active measures to promote compliance within its ranks. The agreement called for HUD and NAR to "work out programs of voluntary compliance and of enforcement."[41]

The VAMA emphasized the importance of educating REALTORS® in fair housing compliance. Signatories committed to nondiscriminatory real estate practices, which would ensure that people of similar financial means had access to

Change of Heart

If one person can represent the transformation of an entire organization, when it comes to fair housing and the NATIONAL ASSOCIATION OF REALTORS®, that person is Arthur S. Leitch, the Association's 1975 president. His courageous leadership helped NAR move toward embracing and eventually leading the drive for fair housing.

Leitch became NAR president seven years after passage of the 1968 Fair Housing Act. In those years, however, many NAR leaders remained at odds with the U.S. Department of Housing and Urban Development. They didn't dispute the aim of the law—equal opportunity in housing. But they strongly disagreed with HUD's proposed rules for implementing fair housing. And many practitioners were still adamant that owners should be able to decide to whom they would rent or sell their property.

That was a position Leitch, a San Diego practitioner, had advocated in 1964 when he was president of the California Association of REALTORS®. In that year California REALTORS® sponsored a state ballot measure, Proposition 14, that guaranteed property owners the right to sell or rent to the person of their choice. The measure—prompted by the passage of a state fair housing law in 1963—was approved by the state's voters but later declared unconstitutional by the U.S. Supreme Court.

With the passage of the federal law four years later, however, Leitch had a change of heart. He was determined to bring NAR into compliance with national policy. The *Los Angeles Times,* reporting on his death in 2001, credited Leitch with "spearhead[ing] the campaign to support equal housing opportunities."

Indeed, at NAR's 1975 convention in San Francisco, Leitch asked his fellow NAR directors to approve a Voluntary Affirmative Marketing Agreement (VAMA) with HUD, which required every board of REALTORS® to support equal housing opportunity. His predecessors, 1973 president J. D. Sawyer and 1974 president Joe Doherty, had started the effort to work out an agreement

NAR ARCHIVES

Arthur S. Leitch, 1911–2001

with HUD, but negotiations had broken down. Leitch renewed the effort and, working with HUD undersecretary Jim Blair, came to terms with the department. The agreement eliminated provisions in a HUD proposal that NAR felt were onerous and possibly counter to antitrust law.

Although Leitch wasn't alone in his conviction, not everyone shared his priority. Despite the modifications that Leitch had negotiated, the Board of Directors debated the proposal for three hours. Leitch faced "widespread and ferocious opposition," Bill North told *The San Diego Union-Tribune* in 2001. In the end, however, he won the support he needed. North, who was the organization's general counsel at the time, recalled in the *Union-Tribune* article, "Not only did Art achieve a winning vote, but he was able to keep the organization together, minus any splinter groups that could have caused damage."

In an unpublished interview with *Real Estate Today* magazine in 1982, Leitch, in his characteristically humble manner, credited another HUD undersecretary, Robert Crawford, with the idea for the affirmative marketing program. "It was Crawford," he said, "who suggested that the industry try to police the problem, getting our own people to sign up and agree to practice under the Fair Housing Act."

THE AGE OF THE CONSUMER

Fair housing wasn't the only issue on which Leitch's leadership skills came to bear. In the mid-1970s, "consumer protection was a very heavy concern," Leitch told *Real Estate Today*. "It still is and should be. REALTORS®—if only people would study their history—have been on the side of consumer safeguards for years."

Leitch waged a successful battle over the proposed implementation of the Real Estate Settlement Procedures Act, a law that had been passed in 1974 to prevent kickback payments in the delivery of real estate settlement services. To protest all the dos and don'ts in the regulations—which he said "would tie the industry in knots"—Leitch set up a flying panel to travel the country to argue that the rules would cost consumers more, not less. Eventually he succeeded in getting major modifications to the law.

During his presidency, Leitch also encouraged the use of home inspections and home warranties, both new concepts to many consumers. And along with his successor, Phil Smaby of Minnesota, Leitch fought successfully to retain independent contractor status for real estate salespeople.

With interest rates and inflation on the rise in 1975, Leitch foresaw the affordability problems that would grip buyers in the United States, particularly his home state of California, in the coming decade. "The word you'll hear more and more in the future is affordability," he said.

LIFETIME OF ACTION

Leitch began his real estate career after working nearly two decades in the dental field. Three years before he changed careers, he had served as president of the Southern California Dental Laboratory Association. It wasn't long before he was making his mark in his new profession. Along with several colleagues from California—including Art Godi and Ira Gribin, who would also become NAR presidents—he developed a management training program and later a sales training program that would become the underpinning for today's Certified Residential Broker and Certified Residential Specialist training.

Before becoming president of the California Association, Leitch served as chairman of the California Real Estate Association Insurance Committee, developing the first errors and omissions insurance program available in the real estate industry.

During the 1970s Leitch owned 17 offices in San Diego County, developed property, and taught real estate and development courses at the University of California at San Diego.

Having spent more than a half century in the real estate business, Leitch left a legacy of progress, but most enduring in the minds of many NAR leaders was his championing of the VAMA. It was the prototype for programs later adopted by the National Association of Home Builders and the Mortgage Bankers Association, and as North told the *Union-Tribune*, "It also had the effect of creating new opportunities for minorities to become REALTORS® and make a living in the real estate business."

Gribin, who as 1989 NAR president lobbied strongly for increasing the diversity within the Association, remembered his friend in a 2002 interview with *REALTOR® Magazine* as not only a great leader but "an incredibly good human being."

the same housing choices in their area.[42] Local boards of REALTORS® pledged to develop educational materials and training courses on fair housing for their members, to place affirmative marketing advertisements in local newspapers, to encourage minorities to join the real estate industry and provide these newly recruited real estate professionals with training seminars, to establish equal opportunity committees, and to work with their communities to achieve and promote fair housing.[43]

In addition, each NAR state association was charged with establishing an equal opportunity committee to explain and promote the VAMA to its member boards, to conduct seminars on the VAMA and fair housing, and to monitor the implementation of the VAMA across the state and report on its findings annually to NAR.[44]

REALTOR® Hazel Lewis said the VAMA was a turning point in the relationship between NAR and the federal government. "When we started really working with HUD as a team," she recalled, "it opened the window for clearer communication between the federal government and NAR. There was no longer a 'fox in the henhouse' adversarial relationship. It was a team working together for the same end, and that was fair housing for all."

Controversy persisted, however, over the practice known as testing. Fair housing organizations would send applicants of different racial or ethnic backgrounds, but who claimed similar economic means, to the same real estate company and then compare their experiences to determine whether the minority tester suffered discrimination.

For several reasons, NAR viewed testing as unfair. "Number one," said North, "HUD didn't do the testing itself; it farmed it out to organizations that had a vested interest in the outcome." The premise that testing could be an accurate gauge of discrimination was flawed, too, according to North. "If you take any two buy-

ers, they aren't exactly the same," North said. "Personalities are different; their explanation of their desires and wants, their interests, are not the same. And then, often, one of the things that we really had problems with was that the testers didn't test the same salesperson, and every salesperson was different." If testing had to be done, North argued to HUD, testers should at least check the same salesperson rather than merely sending testers to the same company. HUD and civil rights organizations objected on the grounds that the same salesperson might not be available for both buyers, North says, or because that salesperson "would perceive that [testers were] engaged in testing and modify their conduct accordingly." To North, such arguments failed to address the inherent unreliability of testing different salespeople.

In 1985 a bill was proposed in Congress to provide $4 million to private organizations to conduct testing of real estate firms. The bill was defeated in Congress, and NAR's opposition to the measure provoked negative attention in the media. Headlines from *The Washington Post* included, "HUD, REALTORS® Group Do Battle" and "REALTORS® Oppose HUD Proposal for Enforcing Fair Housing Laws."[45] Yet NAR's primary objection to testing by private organizations was unrelated to fair housing as such, but about basic due process, says Fred Underwood, manager of NAR's diversity programs. The HUD administrative process for enforcement of offenses based on testing didn't require fair housing organizations to disclose their methods or results to real estate companies until after the complaint was settled.

In the early 1980s, the local real estate board of Grand Rapids, Michigan, initiated a program in which real estate companies conducted tests of their own salespeople. Led in part by Pat Vredevoogd Combs, who in 2007 became president of NAR, the Grand Rapids program demonstrated that self-testing could

Gordon H. Mansfield Jack Kemp Dorcas Helfant Jean M. Yassky

COURTESY FRED UNDERWOOD

yield benefits for real estate professionals. "I think the value comes in seeing what I might be doing inadvertently, or what somebody at my company is doing, that I should be aware of," Underwood said. "It's a risk management tool for brokers." The Grand Rapids program inspired a similar one on the south side of Chicago in the mid-1980s, this time in collaboration with the Leadership Council. The tests were used for education, not enforcement, says Underwood, and they provided a lot of the material that was later used to help develop fair housing training for REALTORS®.

NEW ACT FOR NAR

The period of negotiation between NAR and HUD to ensure that the fair housing law was also fair to REALTORS® culminated in 1988 with the passage of amendments to the law. The amendments were the product of a compromise between civil rights groups, which wanted the original fair housing act to cover families and the disabled, and NAR, which decided that its core requirement for any fair housing legislation was that it would protect the right of real estate professionals to due process.[46] Congress passed

HUD secretary Jack Kemp and NAR President Dorcas Helfant, center seated, signed NAR's last voluntary affirmative marketing agreement in 1992.

Opening the Lines of Communication

Hazel Lewis-Wiltz

Hazel W. Lewis-Wiltz owes her interest in real estate to her uncle, Sampson B. Odell. She remembers looking forward to her uncle's visits to her home state of Texas, where the National Association of Real Estate Brokers (NAREB) sometimes held its annual convention.

NAREB's members, referred to as Realtists, include real estate brokers, sales associates, developers, appraisers, mortgage brokers, lenders, and educators. Though they are typically minorities and mostly African American, NAREB is open to all qualified practitioners committed to achieving the Realtist mission: ensuring that all citizens have the right to equal housing opportunity, regardless of race, creed, or color; serving the underserved; and seeking the economic improvement of NAREB's membership and the minority communities it represents.

Lewis-Wiltz's uncle, the founder of the California Realtist organization, taught her to value flexibility and encouraged her to pursue education and employment in a variety of communities. "You don't want to get type-cast," she said in a 2006 interview, "because then you lose opportunity."

With her uncle's encouragement, Lewis-Wiltz attended the University of Texas at Arlington. Learning in Dallas and Fort Worth taught her how to succeed as a minority student in a predominantly white environment. After graduating, she went to work at a minority real estate firm in 1976, again with her uncle's encouragement. "You have to stand up for who you are," she explained, "but not get hung up on who you are."

Despite the National Association's history of low minority representation, Lewis-Wiltz became a REALTOR® in 1979 because, she says, NAR represented professionalism. It held its members to high standards and provided them with the best services available: multiple listing services, professional education, and networking opportunities.

In 1987, Lewis-Wiltz became a member of NAR's Equal Opportunity Committee, which suffered from what she called a "back-of-the-room position." Lewis-Wiltz played an integral role in getting the committee the attention it deserved, in part by reformulating its message.

Her first task, she thought, was to convince members that discrimination was not something shameful, but an organizational problem like any other—something that could be talked about and dealt with. "Few people believed that they discriminated," she said, "and the rest believed that if they didn't discriminate, they'd have a serious problem. One of the things that helped me help the Association was not pointing fingers at our membership. People get tired of hearing that and turn a deaf ear. When presenting and talking to our committee, or for our committee, I would always turn the tables and show the ways in which I had discriminated, or ways in which I could have discriminated."

After establishing an atmosphere of more open discussion about diversity and discrimination issues, the committee needed to "get equal opportunity on the map." This meant, Lewis-Wiltz explained, "that when we went to our National Association convention, Equal Opportunity would have to draw a packed house—the room would have to be as full as it was for the policy committees or the political fund."

Lewis-Wiltz, who was chairing the National Fair Housing Month Committee, had a plan: She booked HUD secretary Jack Kemp to speak at the convention. Before Kemp's 1991 speech, only 50 to 100 people regularly attended the Equal Opportunity Committee's luncheon meetings. Afterward, the meetings consistently accommodated more than 400. "Everyone was looking forward to coming to our luncheons," Lewis-Wiltz remembered, "because they weren't about federal affairs or policy; they were about fair housing. From that point on, we had the respect of the organization."

A BREAKTHROUGH WITH HUD

In addition to raising the profile of the Equal Opportunity Committee, Lewis-Wiltz initiated a partnership with HUD that represented a shift in the way NAR began to think of its role in fair housing: from simple cooperation toward participation and support. She worked with HUD to devise a motto that would testify to the partnership between HUD and NAR: "Fair Housing Opens Doors and REALTORS® are the key."

From this initial breakthrough at the national convention, more open communication flowed between HUD and NAR. By opening itself to scrutiny and to HUD's involvement, NAR found that it actually received less criticism, not more.

In 1993 Lewis-Wiltz became the chair of NAR's Equal Opportunity Committee and has gone on to serve in other leadership positions, including on NAR's board of directors.

Lewis praised her colleagues for making her work possible—NAR presidents Bill Chee and Ira Gribin are first on her list. "They were sensitive to our agenda. And it's quite a credit to our organization that they came to leadership positions."

Lewis-Wiltz no longer serves on the Equal Opportunity Committee, but she continues to be active both as REALTOR® and Realtist. Most members of NAREB, she said, are also members of NAR. Lewis-Wiltz believes that the partnership between these organizations benefits them both. "For example," said Lewis-Wiltz, "both organizations represent private property rights. If NAREB is working on a case in which a black community's property rights are being in-

Lewis-Wiltz, left, welcomed Jack Kemp to the Equal Opportunity Committee luncheon in 1991. Kemp, secretary of the U.S. Department of Housing and Urban Development under President George H. W. Bush, advocated for the creation of Enterprise Zones to encourage entrepreneurship in impoverished neighborhoods and for the expansion of home ownership among the poor as a means of wealth creation.

RANDY SANTOS

fringed upon, it is also in the best interest of NAR to contribute and support NAREB's reclamation of those property rights . . . because when property rights are weakened in one area, regardless of the demographic, they are weakened across the board." In addition, said Lewis-Wiltz, joint members of NAR and NAREB have access to a wider variety of real estate markets and communities.

"I have been so proud to be a REALTOR® member because I am keenly aware . . . of discrimination in this nation," said Lewis-Wiltz. "So it is . . . valuable to me when I say that our organization has worked hard to include, and promote, and make the opportunity for African Americans and African-American neighborhoods."

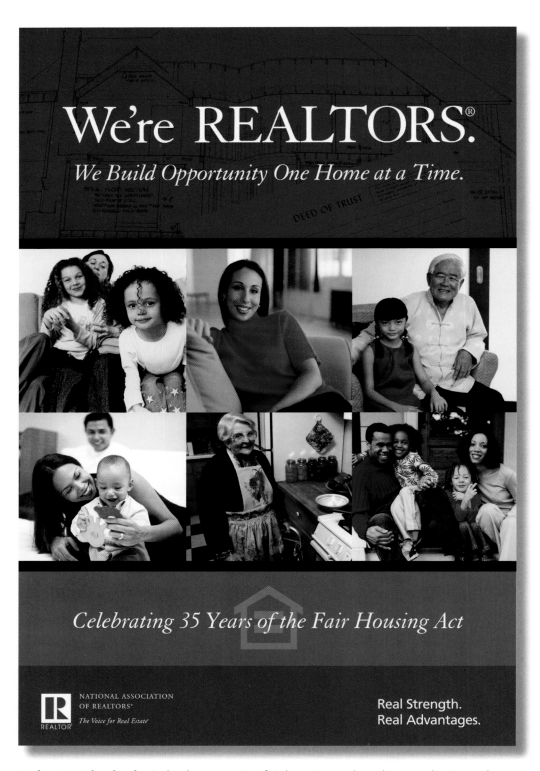

We're REALTORS.®

We Build Opportunity One Home at a Time.

Celebrating 35 Years of the Fair Housing Act

NATIONAL ASSOCIATION
OF REALTORS®
The Voice for Real Estate
REALTOR

Real Strength.
Real Advantages.

Today, NAR is a leader in both promoting fair housing and working to eliminate the barriers to minority home ownership.

the bill overwhelmingly and—three months after the historic agreement between NAR leaders and Ralph Neas, then executive director of the Leadership Conference on Civil Rights—President Ronald Reagan signed the Fair Housing Amendments Act of 1988. In addition to streamlining and strengthening the administrative and judicial enforcement process for HUD complaints, the 1988 act added two protected classes—familial status and mental or physical handicap—and provided for monetary penalties when housing discrimination was found.[47]

Meanwhile, NAR continued its joint education efforts with HUD, renegotiating the 1975 VAMA several times. In 1996, the VAMA was replaced with a new HUD/NAR Fair Housing Partnership agreement and a new focus on identifying and eradicating the causes of housing discrimination. It was signed by NAR President Russ Booth; HUD Secretary Henry Cisneros; Michele Smith of St. Louis, chair of NAR's Equal Opportunity Committee; and Elizabeth Julian, HUD assistant secretary for fair housing and equal opportunity. The Fair Housing Partnership, says Underwood, was "part of a shift . . . in the culture and viewpoint of the leadership of the Association and the members, where members were saying, 'Look, I *believe* in fair housing, I *want* to accomplish this.' " Working to eliminate discrimination wasn't just right, NAR leaders reasoned, it also made good business sense. With the country's minority population growing rapidly, the more adept REALTORS® became at nondiscriminatory practices, the more they'd succeed in this vital market.

The partnership gave local real estate associations more flexibility to respond to the specific housing discrimination issues within their community. At the national level, HUD and NAR continued to meet regularly to identify national issues and concerns, develop joint strategies and actions to address housing discrimination, and review successes.

With the new emphasis on eliminating barriers, NAR began extending its advocacy beyond its traditional areas of concern, lobbying for consumer-friendly practices in the credit industry. In the early 1990s when credit rating agencies began producing credit scores, home buyers without top-quality credit were often left little choice but to seek subprime loans. Prospective buyers had a difficult time learning the reason for their credit scores and how to improve them, and the subprime market tended to exploit borrowers already in compromised financial positions. Both of these problems took a disproportionate toll on urban, often predominantly minority, communities. The California Association of Realtors® joined with the California Realtist organization, successfully lobbying the state legislature to pass a bill that required credit reporting agencies to disclose to consumers the reasons for their credit scores. And NAR began a campaign to warn consumers about the practice of predatory lending.

REACHING OUT
TO A BROADER MARKET

While fair housing legislation has doubtless resulted in fairer treatment for minorities in the market for property, it has not resulted in the widespread integration that open housing activists hoped for in the 1960s. The open housing movement favored active measures to promote racial integration in housing, but as Alexander von Hoffman has written,

> *For all their assertiveness, the open housing leaders failed to recognize that many African Americans were unenthusiastic about living in integrated neighborhoods. A 1964 study of a Boston urban renewal district found that only four percent of the 250 middle-class families in the sam-*

In recent years, NAR has increased its outreach to minority communities, working with partners such as the U.S. Department of Housing and Urban Development and the Center for Responsible Lending to produce a series of educational brochures on mortgage financing.

Diversity Champion

The career of REALTOR® Allen Okamoto exemplifies the change that NAR has undergone since passage of the Fair Housing Act of 1968. Okamoto's father, Takeo, who became a real estate licensee in the mid-1950s, was initially denied membership in the San Francisco Association of REALTORS® because he was of Japanese descent. Thirty-five years later, in 1990, his son Allen was elected president of that organization.

Okamoto is broker-owner of T. Okamoto & Co., a San Francisco real estate and insurance brokerage, specializing in single family homes, condos, and small commercial properties. He followed his father into real estate in 1965, soon after his graduation from San Francisco State University.

Although he didn't recognize it at the time, Okamoto experienced discrimination early in his career. "I would call other real estate associates to ask for cooperation in the sale of their listings, and they would flatly deny me access. I didn't realize until later that it was due to my name and face," he said. He managed to build a successful business working with Japanese Americans, African Americans, and Chinese Americans.

Okamoto became involved in diversity issues in the mid-1980s when Fred Underwood, the staff liaison to the NAR Fair Housing Committee, visited California to promote an NAR diversity initiative. In the 1990s, Okamoto served on the working group that developed the Association's "At Home with Diversity" course. He later chaired the Equal Opportunity–Cultural Diversity Committee.

Despite the progress within NAR, Okamoto joined with some colleagues in 2003 to found the Asian Real Estate Association of America (AREAA), the first national organization for Asian real estate practitioners. AREAA has almost 10,000 members in 23 states. Okamoto is a founding director of AREAA and serves as chairman of the board.

AREAA is "primarily interested in closing the housing gap," Okamoto said, citing census figures that demonstrate that Asian Americans lag behind the general American population in home ownership. "Many Asian Americans entered the hous-

Allen Okamoto

ing market after their native contemporaries. Cambodian and Vietnamese people who came to California in the 1970s as a result of the Vietnam War suffered from discrimination," he said. In addition, "Asian Americans suffer from the 'model minority' myth. Many believe that Asian Americans are rich and don't need assistance, but many do."

Like the National Association of Hispanic Real Estate Professionals, founded in 1999 by Ernest Reyes and Gary Acosta, AREAA is an organization that targets a diverse minority group. Such groups, Okamoto said, can help remove or lower the linguistic and cultural barriers minorities face. "One way in which we can do this is by partnering with NAR."

"The president of the CALIFORNIA ASSOCIATION OF REALTORS® came to speak at an AREAA event," he recalled. "The first question he asked the people attending was, 'What is the CALIFORNIA ASSOCIATION OF REALTORS®?' Many of them had no idea. They thought it was an organization that published a magazine. The point is, many Asian licensees are extremely alienated from the larger real estate community, and both organizations will benefit from cross-pollination."

RANDY SANTOS

The HOPE Awards—launched in 2001—recognize individuals and organizations that are helping make home ownership possible for more minorities. At the HOPE Awards Gala in 2005, PBS *NewsHour* senior correspondent Ray Suarez was the master of ceremonies. NAR today operates the awards program in partnership with the Asian Real Estate Association of America, the Chinese Real Estate Association of America, the Chinese American Real Estate Professionals Association, the National Association of Real Estate Brokers, and the National Association of Hispanic Real Estate Professionals.

ple moved outside the African-American area. A large majority never even looked at the lists of affordable housing in white neighborhoods which the renewal agency had provided them.[48]

Today, more than 40 years later, a gap persists between the beliefs most Americans profess to hold about the desirability of racial integration in their neighborhoods and their willingness to make the personal and political choices that would bring about such a result. Policy analyst Sheryll Cashin writes, "although in opinion polls the majority of all races say they would prefer an integrated neighborhood, similar majorities also state a preference for living in a neighborhood in which their own race is a majority or a plurality."[49]

Though the landscape is still segregated de facto in many places, minorities are finding increased opportunities to participate in the housing market. Government and industry

RANDY SANTOS

Today, NAR is helping its members recruit a more diverse sales force and better serve an ethnically diverse base of customers.

data indicate that two out of every three new households are being formed by foreign-born or minority persons, and by 2010 minorities are projected to account for more than 50 percent of first-time home buyers.[50] Yet even with increased opportunity, minority homeownership rates continue to lag behind those of whites. In 2005, more than 75 percent of non-Hispanic whites owned their own homes, compared with 48 percent of blacks and 49.5 percent of Hispanics.[51]

NAR has responded to this situation by taking steps to recognize REALTORS® and other real estate professionals for their efforts to ensure equal opportunity in the buying and selling of property. In 2001 NAR joined with several other real estate organizations to create the HOPE (Home Ownership Participation for Everyone) Awards, the first of their kind. Every two years, the HOPE Awards—offered in partnership with the California Association of Real Estate Brokers, the Chinese Real Estate Association of America, the Chinese American Real Estate Professionals Association, the National Association of Real Estate Brokers, and the National Association of Hispanic Real Estate Professionals—give $10,000 apiece to individuals or organizations whose programs have demonstrated a benefit to minority home ownership. Honorees present their programs at a symposium in Washington, D.C., and receive their award at a well-attended gala.

To reach these expanding markets, REALTORS® have also sought to diversify their own ranks. Diversity is now a strategic goal for NAR, which aims to prepare its members to thrive in a diverse market, to increase diversity in the real estate workplace as a whole, and to increase diversity among NAR's membership and leadership. Today, about 88 percent of NAR's membership is white[52], and though this figure shows an improvement in the organization's diversity since 1999—when a mere 5 percent of members identified themselves as minorities—NAR wants its roster of professionals to reflect more accurately the evolving racial and ethnic diversity of contemporary America and its housing market. The "At Home with Diversity®" course, the Diversity Toolkit (a collaboration between NAR and the California Association of REALTORS®), and the efforts of the Equal Opportunity–Cultural Diversity Committee have all been part of the mission to make REALTORS® leaders in a real estate environment that is rich with cultural variety.

Today, NAR's role in fair housing includes not only educating members and consumers but also promoting land-use decisions that provide greater housing choice for all people and encourage integration. The Association's Housing Opportunity and Smart Growth programs have been a means to that end. (The Housing Opportunity and Smart Growth programs are discussed in Chapter 2 and Chapter 5, respectively.)

Hazel Lewis, a past chair of NAR's Equal Opportunity Committee, sees the diversity agenda as another key to the Association's future success. "We're global now," she says. "As we expand our awareness of cultural diversity, REALTORS® must learn how different cultures prefer to be served—*need* to be served. Our job," she says, "is service."

In May 2007, Charles McMillan of Texas became NAR's first African American president-elect. He will serve as president in 2009.

Women Find a Home in Real Estate

The WOMAN REALTOR

REALTORS

APRIL 1955

REFER TO ARTICLE —
"OUR FLYING REALTOR"
SEE PAGE 11

In the twentieth century, real estate provided unparalleled opportunities for women. When this issue of *The Woman Realtor* was published, however, a few local associations were still grappling with whether to admit women members.

From before the founding of NAR, women were involved in the real estate business. As early as 1892, Cora Bacon Foster headed her own Texas real estate and builder's office and founded the first Houston real estate board. She also helped found the first national organization in real estate, the short-lived National Real Estate Association.

Yet there are no records of women being among NAR's founding members. The first recorded application for membership in NAR by a woman dates from either 1911 or 1912, depending on which source is considered more accurate. One account says an Omaha, Nebraska, woman applied in 1911. Another says 1912 applicants Corinne Simpson of Seattle and Frances Wines of St. Louis were the first.[53]

The U.S. Census counted 3,000 women brokers in 1910, approximately 2 percent of the total, but few belonged to local boards. Women who worked in the profession generally were active in small exchanges and in their own companies; often they were widows, wives, or daughters who had been pressed into emergency service, according to the late NAR historian Pearl Janet Davies. The braver women, however, were "fearlessly invading the cities," according to an early article about real estate as a profession for women. Among the pioneers was Lucile N. Chapman, who entered the profession after buying a small tract in a Chicago suburb, laying it out, and selling it for a healthy profit. She continued to buy and sell Chicago suburban realty, where she was known as one of the city's best-known developers. She later headed east to Long Island, New York.

Why were women attracted to real estate as a profession? Gary Krysler, executive vice president of the Women's Council of REALTORS® said the standard case made during the 1920s

Minutes of the first Women's Council meeting demonstrate that in 1938 women were already actively engaged in all aspects of real estate.

Minutes of the Organization Meeting
of the Women's Council
Hotel Schroeder, Milwaukee, Wis.
November 11, 1938

Attendance

The first meeting in connection with an annual convention of the National Association arranged especially for women in the real estate business was held at a luncheon on Friday, November 11, in Milwaukee, Wis., at the Schroeder Hotel. Thirty-eight women in all phases of the real estate business -- renting, buying, selling, and managing residential, farm, and income properties, and even building homes -- were present to discuss the unusual experiences and problems which they encountered as a result of their entering the real estate business. Nine states -- California, Georgia, Illinois, New York, Ohio, Oklahoma, Oregon, Pennsylvania, and Wisconsin were represented. Following is a list of those present:

Mrs. W. H. Wright, 5613 W. Lake St., Chicago, Ill., Chairman
Miss Bernice Elliott, Assistant Secretary, Los Angeles Realty Board, Calif.
Mrs. Grace D. Fletcher, 7650 Long Beach Blvd., Huntington Park, Calif. - residential sales and management.
Mrs. Niomi E. McCann, 5336 Lankershim Blvd., N. Hollywood, Calif. - general brokerage-own office.
Mrs. Henrietta T. White, 2932 S. Vermont, Los Angeles Calif. - general brokerage.
Mrs. Louise Peacook, Executive Secretary, Atlanta Real Estate Board, Ga.
Mrs. M. M. Crenshaw, Baird & Warner, Chicago, Ill. - Specializes in sales of income property.
Mrs. R. G. Knight, 4167 Irving Park Blvd., Chicago, Ill. - general real estate business.
Mrs. Mabel Moore, 5613 W. Lake St., Chicago, Ill. - saleswoman.
Peg Russell, Parker-Holsman, 1501 E. 57th St., Chicago, Ill. - renting.
Mrs. Jane A. Shreeve, 203 Morris Bldg., Joliet, Ill. - insurance, real estate and loans.
Mrs. Jean C. Miles, 8 N. LaGrange Rd., LaGrange, Ill. - Partner, F. D. Cossit & Co.
Mrs. Henry A. Miller, 23 N. Longcommon Rd., Riverside, Ill. - general brokerage.
Miss Marie Ratledge, 23 N. Fifth Ave., Maywood, Ill. - real estate, insurance and servicing of mortgages.
Miss Christine Baumann, 553 Lincoln Ave., Winnetka, Ill. - Brokerage and Management office.
Mrs. L. A. Laramee, 519 Marquette, Minneapolis, Minn. - Husband has general real estate business.
Miss Ysobel A. Muceeke, National Real Estate Clearing House, New York City
Miss Hazel M. Long, 2126 Lee Road, Cleveland, Ohio - specializes in rentals and sales.
Mrs. Blanche L. Shaffer, 120 E. Market, Warren, Ohio - general brokerage, farms, city property, and lots.
Mrs. R. B. Butler, 1347 S. Gary Place, Tulsa, Okla. - residential building and sales.
Mrs. Marion E. Hall, 1708 S. Gary Place, Tulsa, Okla. - general brokerage.
Mrs. Elva D. Cofer, 1535 S. W. Sixth Ave., Portland, Ore. - income properties and trades.
Mrs. Harry Hagmann, 2714 Liberty, Erie, Pa. - in charge of management department in husband's business.
Mrs. Mabel Hartwell, Lake Geneva, Wis. - brokerage.
Stephanie Bird, 229 E. Wisconsin Ave., Milwaukee, Wis. - broker and property manager.
Mrs. Joe Courteen, 110 E. Wisconsin Ave., Milwaukee, Wis. - residential renting.

WOMEN'S COUNCIL OF REALTORS®

Cora Ella Wright of Oak Park, Illinois, was a prominent Association member when she was tapped by 1938 NAR President Joseph Catherine to lead the first meeting of the Women's Council.

NATIONAL ASSOCIATION OF REAL ESTATE BOARDS

HERBERT U. NELSON
EXECUTIVE VICE PRESIDENT
22 WEST MONROE ST.
CHICAGO

October 4, 1939

Just three weeks from today real estate women from all over the country will be assembled at the Biltmore Hotel in Los Angeles for the second annual meeting of the Women's Council at the Annual Convention of the National Association of Real Estate Boards.

Here are a few of the items that have been planned for us on the Convention program: "Real Estate in War Time," "What Can We Do to Save Our Business Districts?," "An Appraisal of Our Times." . . . . Bread and butter discussions on "Visual Aids in Selling," "Rehabilitation of Old Houses," "Reviving Profits from Older Buildings," "How to Study and Interpret Rental Markets," "How to Obtain and Retain Management Business," and "It's Your Attitude" have been selected to give each of us some new slant or idea on how to improve and increase our business.

The Women's Council, whose initial meeting was held last year in Milwaukee, will meet again this year at luncheon on Wednesday noon, October 25. Women Realtors and saleswomen are invited to attend this meeting. This is the one national medium we have through which all of us engaged in this grand calling can get acquainted with one another, can "trade" and exchange our special ideas, and appraise and cash in on the woman's angle in selling, managing, financing, and building homes, apartments, offices, etc.

This year we are looking forward with especially keen interest to our get-together, because the women in the real estate business in the host state, California, have long had their own Women's Division (since 1924) and have been holding their own women's meetings in almost all of the Boards of that State. Doubtlessly they will have many helpful suggestions to impart to us.

May I count on seeing you in Los Angeles the week of October 23?

Sincerely,

Mrs. W. H. Wright, Chairman
Women's Council, N.A.R.E.B.

NAR ARCHIVES

through 1940s was that women were "somehow suited by their natures to sell homes—their appreciation of esthetics, their inclination to homemaking, their innate ability to empathize."

Krysler said the truth is probably closer to what Jeffrey Hornstein hypothesized in his 2005 book, *A Nation of REALTORS®* (Duke University Press). "Women—like men—were attracted because real estate was a paradigmatically middle-class profession at a time when the American middle class was in the process of formation," he said.

Some women entered the business through a back door, Krysler said, "for example, the broker's secretary who got her license in order to become more knowledgeable, then outsold some of the broker's male associates, or the widow or daughter who inherited a large brokerage and grew the company, making her impossible for the local board to ignore. But there were also ambitious young women like Ebby [Halliday] who saw opportunity and seized it. Then, of course, Rosie the Riveter came along, accelerating the entry of women into the larger American workforce."

From an early date, NAR published articles about successful women in its *Journal.* At the first convention of NAR's new specialty divisions in 1923, John G. Morgan, a REALTOR® from Boston, pointed out that women had shown their competence in the profession. "Already there are several buildings in the United States that are managed by women," he said, "and in justice to them I will say they are proving very successful in this field of work."

Groups of like-minded women began organizing. The Fort Wayne REALTORS®' Girls Club, formed in 1923, consisted of young female employees in the offices of Fort Wayne–area REALTORS®. These women received the endorsement of NAR board members. One of their duties was to see that REALTORS® in Fort Wayne

"were prompt and constant in their attendance at regular board meetings." The "girls" performed admirably.

Grace Perego worked as a builder of apartment houses as well as a general broker in San Francisco. At NAR's Seattle conference in 1927, Perego made a speech titled, "In What Type of Real Estate Activity Are Women Succeeding Best?" She refused to pigeonhole women into traditional real estate positions. "It would be as difficult to say in which particular line success would be assured to women as it would be to say in which particular line men would best succeed," she told the audience.

Still, women typically started their careers by selling homes. Some brokers felt homeowners preferred to deal with a woman. Women possessed an innate talent at home sales, said a 1941 article in *The National Real Estate Journal:* "A man sells largely by the process of elimina-

WOMEN'S COUNCIL
BULLETIN
OF THE
National Association
of
Real Estate Boards
▼

JUNE
1945

WOMEN'S COUNCIL OF REALTORS®

In 1945 the Women's Council began to charge dues and publish its *Bulletin,* a forerunner to today's *Connections* magazine.

Through its monthly news-letter, the Women's Council not only provided a voice for women but also strengthened the voice of the Association.

WOMEN'S COUNCIL OF REALTORS®

PHOENIX ASSOCIATION OF REALTORS®.
JOEY STARR

Despite having earned respect as real estate professionals, women for many years retained a uniquely female presence at NAR meetings. Marilyn Sharkey of Phoenix—boarding the Golden State Limited train—represented the Phoenix Real Estate Board (today the Phoenix Association of REALTORS®) as "Miss Phoenix REALTOR®" during the Association's forty-ninth annual convention in St. Louis. The year was 1956.

tion. A woman sells largely by the process of selection."

As women gained experience, they could enter "any branch they choose," Perego said in her 1927 speech. She'd started out as a builder of flats and moved on to apartments and commercial buildings.

California led the way in creating an organization to represent the interests of women members. The California Real Estate Association (now the California Association of REALTORS®) formed a Women's Division in 1924. Davies, who was director of NAR's pressroom at the time, credited CREA Executive Secretary Glenn Willaman with initiating the effort.[54]

On the train trip home from the Washington, D.C., convention in 1924, members of the California delegation discussed the

idea of creating a national women's organization. The discussion took place between CREA President Henry Barbour and Hazel Grant King of Pasadena, head of the CREA Women's Division. But 14 years would pass before the idea would become a reality. With the encouragement of the Association's 1938 president, Joseph Catherine, the women held their first national meeting at the 1938 convention in Milwaukee.

At that meeting, 38 women representing nine states shared their experiences. Cora Ella Wright, known to real estate boards all over the country as an authority on real estate advertising, led the meeting. She was associated with her husband, W. H. Wright, in a general real estate business in Oak Park, Illinois, and was business manager of the Illinois Association of Real Estate Boards.

Wright orchestrated state surveys on the status of women in real estate. Along with several female colleagues, she also pressed to keep the organization integrated with NAR rather than operated as a separate organization. Convention participants agreed: The Women's Council would meet annually at the NAR convention.

In 1942 the Women's Council took its first steps to formulate bylaws and adopt a formal statement of objectives. Its early goals were to offer educational advantages and training to women who entered the field and to implement NAR policies, aims, and objectives. The group sent its members a monthly publication titled, *What Women REALTORS® Are Doing.*

A St. Louis chapter became the first local Women's Council organized under national council guidelines. Within a year, there were 32 local chapters, and the council adopted a statement of long-term objectives, which included leadership, professionalism, education, and active involvement in NAR and its boards.[55]

Many boards, however, still didn't welcome women members. In 1948, the Pittsburgh board admitted women, followed by the Chicago board in 1950. Although 46 Chicago leaders voted yes to women, an overwhelming majority, eight men still voted no.[56] The St. Louis board admitted women in 1956. One of the last was the Columbus, Ohio, board, which finally admitted women members in 1961.[57]

In 1972, in conjunction with the impending National Association name change, the Women's Council changed its name from Women's Council of the National Association of Real Estate Boards to Women's Council of REALTORS®.[58]

At that time, the women's liberation movement was in full swing—*Ms.* magazine published its first issue in January 1972—and women around the country were seeking passage of the Equal Rights Amendment. However, women in real estate weren't likely to be among the country's bra burners. Texas REALTOR® Ebby Halliday spoke for many women real estate practitioners of the day when she presented "Women's Liberation Movement Never Needed in Real Estate Field" at the NAR convention in Chicago in 1970.

In honor of its fiftieth anniversary in 1988, the Women's Council published a hardcover book that chronicled the role of women in NAR. The book, by Sally Ross Chapralis, was titled *Progress of Women in Real Estate: 50th Anniversary, Women's Council of REALTORS®*.

By 1990, female members played a leading role in the industry, if not in Association leadership. An NAR study that year found that the typical member was a female who was involved in residential real estate sales, about 47 years old, with ten years in the business. "It has taken us women a long time to become the 'average' NAR member," commented Deborah Ahrens, president of the Missouri Women's Council, in a 1992 article.[59]

That year, 1992, was also the year a woman broke the glass ceiling at NAR. Dorcas T.

Helfant from Virginia Beach, Virginia, became the first female president in 1992. She was also the first woman to serve as president of her state association and only the second woman to serve as president of her local board.

At the time, Helfant said it was just a matter of time before other women began work-

During the 1970s, while the nation debated passage of an Equal Rights Amendment, women continued to make strides in real estate. At their 1974 Women of Achievement Luncheon, Seattle city leaders honored women in real estate.

Wednesday, February 20, 1974   The Seattle Times D 1

Real-estate women honored

The Past Presidents' Assembly honored five women for their work in the field of real estate at its annual Women of Achievement Luncheon yesterday at the Washington Athletic Club. The honorees are from left, seated, Mae Wunder Kemp, Betty Hall, Jean D. Veldwyk, and, standing, Evangeline Anderson, and Margie Scott. Each year the assembly honors women of achievement in a different field.—Staff photo by Jerry Gay.

By the start of the twenty-first century, women in all walks of life were examining how to have more balance in their lives. Many credited real estate with giving them substantial income opportunities and the flexibility to spend time with their families.

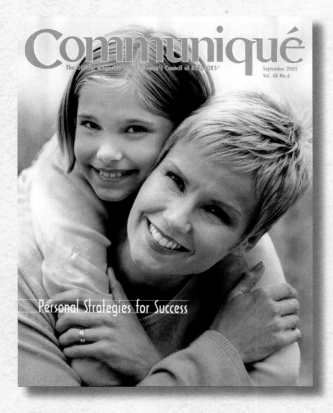

Mo Anderson was one of the first women to enter the executive ranks of real estate franchise organizations, serving as president and CEO of Keller Williams Realty for about a decade before being named vice chair in 2005.

ing their way into the leadership ranks of the profession, but progress at the national level has been slow. In the 15 years since Helfant's presidency, only three other women have risen to the top—Sharon A. Millett of Auburn, Maine (1999); Catherine Whatley of Jacksonville, Florida (2003); and Pat Vredevoogd Combs of Grand Rapids, Michigan (2007). The first and only female treasurer of NAR was Pat G. Kaplan of Portland, Oregon. Kaplan served from 2001 to 2003. She was president of the Oregon Association of REALTORS® in 1996 and the Washington County Association of REALTORS® in 1991.

Over roughly that same time frame, the growing influence of women in the home buying market was becoming more clear, with newspapers and television and radio commentators doing stories on the proliferation of single-women buyers.[60]

It was a trend that didn't surprise NAR members. "Women always had a strong influence on home purchases," commented Vredevoogd Combs in a 2007 interview. In fact, NAR had identified the trend three decades earlier. The September 16, 1974, edition of *REALTOR® Headlines* trumpeted, "Changing attitudes toward women in the work force apparently have contributed to an increasing percentage of real estate sales to single women, according to a report of the National Association. A random survey of REALTOR® boards has revealed that single women in many parts of the nation are purchasing homes, condominiums and investment property in increasing numbers." The article cited statistics from the U.S. Department of Housing and Urban Development showing that single women in the previous year purchased more FHA-insured existing homes than did single men. "HUD reported that in 1970, 5.5 percent of existing home mortgages insured by FHA went to single males, and 4.5 percent went to single females. Last year, single males had 7.3 percent of the market and single women, 7.7 percent."

By 1995, the percentage of total home buyers who were single women stood at 14 percent—and that number jumped to 22 percent by 2006, giving single women the second largest share of adult households that purchased homes.[61]

Meanwhile, with a few exceptions, such as Ebby Halliday, REALTORS®, in Dallas (see "From Hats to Houses," p. 218)—the largest real estate companies in the country continued to be run by men. Women made inroads in the franchise arena, however. Mo Anderson, served as president and CEO before becoming vice chair of Keller Williams Realty in Austin, Texas. At RE/MAX International in Denver, cofounder Gail Liniger also served as vice chair, and Margaret M. Kelly became RE/MAX's CEO in 2005 after sharing the role for a year with retiring CEO Daryl Jesperson. In 2006, Sherry Chris became chief operating officer of Coldwell Banker Corporation, part of the Parsippany, N.J.–based Realogy. And in 2007, Laurie Keenan was named president of Prudential Real Estate Affiliates Inc, a division of the Newark, New Jersey–based financial services giant. Keenan was chief operating officer for nine years before being named president.

Despite these gains, a significant income gap exists between men and women in the industry—even more so than in the general population. The Department of Labor reported in 2006 that women were earning 81 percent what their male counterparts earned.[62] Meanwhile, 2006 statistics from NAR showed that the female REALTORS® earned just 79 percent of what their male counterparts earned. The median income for a full-time female REALTOR® was $62,400, compared with $78,700 for a full-time male REALTOR®.

Today, about 55 percent of full-time REALTORS® are female—and women have come a long way from the days when Association members were called the nation's "real estate men." But as in so many arenas, true equality—at least as measured by income—remains elusive.

At a reception in 1999, NAR President Sharon Millett, center, and her husband Jerry greeted Dorcas Helfant. Helfant and Millett were the National Association's first women presidents, Helfant in 1992 and Millett in 1999.

Pat G. Kaplan served as NAR's first female treasurer from 2001 to 2003.

CHAPTER FIVE

City Sculptors

From the start, NATIONAL ASSOCIATION OF REALTORS® members have played a role in their communities that has extended well beyond facilitating real estate transactions. W. W. Hannan, 1909 president of the Association, likened the real estate man seeing "a vision of a city ten, twenty years hence" to a "sculptor [who] sees the imprisoned Venus in a block of marble, an artist [who sees] a Madonna looking out from the bare canvas."[1] REALTORS® were among the earliest community planners and continue to play an integral role in shaping their communities, whether serving on housing commissions or in other civic functions or volunteering their time for the community good.

The National Association has both facilitated and recognized REALTORS®' involvement in communities. The Association's early leaders helped lay the foundation for community planning. Much later, beginning in the late 1990s, NAR helped shape the burgeoning smart-growth movement in a way that recognized the rights of owners and the needs of future buyers.

To encourage and showcase community involvement by its members, NAR has instituted a range of programs, from the long-running annual REALTOR® Week campaign initiated in 1956 to today's Habitat for Humanity and REALTOR® Magazine Good Neighbor Awards programs.

"When you look at a city, it's like reading the hopes, aspirations, and pride of everyone who built it."

HUGH NEWELL JACOBSEN, architect

Henry Morrison Flagler, co-founder of the Standard Oil Company, has been called the man who built Florida. One thing is certain: The hotels and rail lines the tycoon built near the turn of the twentieth century put the out-of-the-way state on the map. By 1912, his Florida East Coast Railway ran the length of the state's Atlantic seaboard all the way to Key West. Drawn by the sunshine, palm trees, and beaches, tourists began flocking to south Florida. In the decades that followed, retirees joined the parade. So did waves of immigrants from the Caribbean and Latin America.

Flagler opened the door to paradise, and people have been pouring through ever since. Every day, south Florida welcomes another 160 residents. By 2020, the combined population of Broward, Miami-Dade, and Monroe counties is projected to reach 5.2 million, an increase of more than 3 million from 1970.[2]

It's easy to guess the upshot of such continuous growth. Sprawl. Congestion. Public services stretched to the brink. In 1985—about 100 years after Flagler built his first hotel in the Sunshine State—Florida passed one of the country's strongest statewide growth management laws, but issues such as

gridlock, loss of open space, and affordability remained.

And Floridians weren't alone in feeling overcrowded and overcharged. The same growth challenges facing Florida residents were playing out at various levels in metropolitan areas around the country. According to a 2001 report issued by the Reason Public Policy Institute, a Los Angeles think tank, state legislatures responded with a variety of statewide planning reforms.

From the perspective of the real estate industry, however, the reforms sometimes created more problems than they solved. In fact, the potential side effects—usurped property rights, diminished housing supplies, and inflated housing costs—were downright alarming.

NAR members were experiencing first-hand the onslaught of troubling growth management laws that were being adopted by cities, counties, and states nationwide. In Ventura County, California, for example, eight of ten cities approved laws that forbade extending city services outside City Urban Restriction Boundaries and required a public vote for development of any farmland or open space outside the line.[3]

The Reason report characterized many of the reform efforts as "driven by theoreti-

Palm Beach, Florida, circa 1915, was a golfer's paradise. Today, right, it's dense with development. The passage of slow-growth measures in Florida and other fast-growing states beginning in the mid-1980s led REALTORS® to take a lead in promoting smart growth.

JOSEPH MELANSON, SKYPIC.COM

COURTESY CATHY WHATLEY

FLORAL PARK
PALM BEACH FLORIDA
OWNED BY
J.R. & E.R. BRADLEY

LAKE WORTH

BEACH

cal concepts of urban planning and practice" and lacking a sound assessment of their consequences. "Nevertheless," the report continued, "the impacts on the quality of life for households and families can be significant. . . . This is probably most evident in the case of housing availability and affordability."[4]

When undoing the laws proved unattainable, NAR began encouraging local associations to push the concept of smart growth, a thoughtful philosophy of development emphasizing density, mixed use, and walkability. In south Florida, a REALTOR® named Sandra Goldstein made smart growth the cornerstone of her agenda when she assumed leadership of the REALTORS® Association of Greater Miami and the Beaches in 2000.[5]

Eager to jump-start better planning and development through smart growth, Goldstein began meeting with elected officials, planners, environmentalists, and anybody else with a voice in the region's future. The Greater Miami association then organized a conference to educate REALTORS® and others about smart growth and show community leaders that REALTORS® want to participate in community issues.[6]

In 2003, Goldstein became chair of the Florida Association of REALTORS'® new Smart Growth Council, which helped develop a smart-growth continuing education curriculum. "We tried to show that there's no prototype that will fit every community or every village in Florida," said Goldstein, president of a commercial brokerage and building management firm in Key Biscayne. "But what we can do is educate people and alert them to what the possibilities are and what success stories exist—and that can light a fire under them."[7]

FLORIDA ASSOCIATION OF REALTORS®

CREATING THE LANGUAGE AND METHODS OF PLANNING

For REALTORS® with long memories, Goldstein's leadership on smart growth reprises a historic role of the National Association: that of community builder. It's a role with 100-year-old roots and a proud legacy as midwife of the modern residential subdivision. The rise of local real estate associations and the formation of NAR were inspired by, among other issues, the need to "[improve] the pattern of urban land-use and quality of development to increase the attractiveness, security, and growth potential of real estate investment," according to Marc A. Weiss, author of *The Rise of the Community Builders.*[8]

At a smart-growth conference in 2003, Florida Association of REALTORS® Smart Growth Council Chair Sandra Goldstein, second from right, leads a tour of Abacoa, a Jupiter, Florida, community where developers combined compact design with open space restoration.

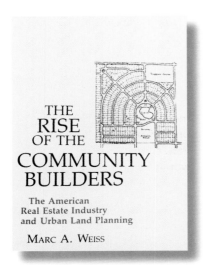

Marc Weiss's 1987 book, *The Rise of the Community Builders,* documents how land developers and subdividers at the start of the twentieth century—many of whom were REALTORS®—originated the science of community planning.

At the turn of the twentieth century, there was virtually no such thing as planning for growth—smart or otherwise. As cities grew outward, entrepreneurs bought large tracts of land on the fringe and subdivided the land into individual building lots as they saw fit, with little or no regulation and without much regard for a lot's ultimate use. The quality of those early subdivisions was all over the map. "Many consisted of no more than a few stakes in the ground, an ungraded road, an unrecorded plat, and a defective title. Others were elaborately landscaped, with full streets and utilities already installed."[9]

Seeking better control, coordination, and consistency in the development process, a band of REALTORS® involved in subdividing pioneered the basic tools of planning—zoning laws, street plans, building codes—elevating their status from mere subdividers to community builders and fundamentally changing the way that land is developed in the United States. "On the vital public issues of land planning and regulation for development of the urban periphery," Weiss writes, "the leading residential subdividers inside [NAR] were more active and influential lobbyists than any other organized group from the entire real estate industry."[10]

Although sometimes at odds with rival subdividers and rank-and-file NAR members, progressive subdividers such as J. C. Nichols believed that their approach—creating communities rather than just carving vacant land into lots—represented a win-win for themselves and the public. Nichols ushered in the new era with a landmark speech at the 1912 NAR convention. "The best manner of subdividing land should not necessarily mean the quickest sale. The destiny and growth of your town is largely affected by the foresight of the man who subdivides

the land upon which you live. The most efficient manner of platting land should be the plan which gives the greatest value and security to every purchaser, adds the greatest amount of value and beauty to the city as a whole, yet produces a big profit to the man who plats the land."[11]

Nichols, developer of the groundbreaking Country Club District in Kansas City, Missouri, called the subdividing work of early community builders "the foster mother" of urban planning—and he wasn't just bragging.[12] George Ford, president of the National Conference on City Planning, backed up the claim during a 1925 speech to NAR's Homebuilders and Subdividers Division. "It is the REALTOR® subdivider who is really planning our cities today, who is the actual city planner in practice."[13]

In fact, the leading subdividers were collaborating on site with professional engineers, landscape architects, building architects, and other urban designers to work out the nuts and bolts of good planning and establish the model for eventual public control of the process. In *The Rise of the Community Builders,* Weiss writes:

> *The classification and design of major and minor streets, the superblock and cul-de-sac, planting strips and rolling topography, arrangement of the house on the lot, lot size and shape, setback lines and lot coverage restrictions, planned separation and relation of multiple uses, design and placement of parks and recreational amenities, ornamentation, easements, underground utilities, and numerous other physical features were first introduced by private developers and later adopted as rules and principles by public planning agencies.[14]*

Presenting a Fully-Improved Subdivision--

PRINCESS PARK

Showing by Photographs the Different Stages of Development. Photographs Don't Lie---So This Information Is Convincing
Proof of the Claim That Princess Park Will Be One of the Very Finest Developments in Miami.

SEE HOW WE ARE EXPENDING $125,000 FOR IMPROVEMENTS

Step by Step this Forty Acre Tract is being transformed from a pine forest to an ideal residence section. On October 1st, 1920, the work of clearing was commenced. The pine trees were all cut down and removed from the property and the palmettos were all grubbed out and removed, at a cost of $6,000.

The next step was the surveying of the property by one

Clark & Sons about the middle of December, and work was begun on the grading the middle of January. There are 3,410 cubic yards of excavation in the grading of nearly two miles of streets and 26,950 square yards of rock base and asphalt surface for the paving, which is 30 feet wide on all streets. All of this grading and paving is done according to City Engineer's specifications and is costing fully $38,000.

This is the character of asphalt pavement that is being laid in Princess Park— 26,950 square yards of it.

Parkway in Miramar, the subdivision that has made more money for investors than anything in Miami. The Parkway in Princess Park will be a duplicate of this beautiful improvement.

Study well the character of homes that follow such improvements—asphalt paved streets, cement walks, cement curbs, grassed parking with ornamental trees and shrubbery, good water, electric lights and telephones. Princess Park will have all these this year.

NOW STUDY THE PICTURES SHOWING THE DEVELOPMENT IN SO-CALLED IMPROVED SUBDIVISIONS

MANY SUBDIVISIONS HAVE BEEN PUT ON THE MARKET IN A ROUGH CONDITION AND SOLD OUT AT CHEAP PRICES

DON'T CONFUSE PRINCESS PARK WITH THIS CLASS

Photographs are actual demonstrations. They tell the truth and cannot misrepresent. The photographs on the right show how cheap sub-divisions are "improved." The first shows a street grubbed out at a nominal cost. The second shows the rough rock dumped in the middle of the street. This rock is crushed and rolled down and advertised as paved streets. The total cost of such an improvement is from $1.00 to $1.50 a running foot as compared with a cost of about $14.00 a running foot in Princess Park.

The third picture shows a street close to some of the best development in Miami, where hundreds of thousands of dollars have been expended in fine homes. This street was cheaply rocked and sidewalks laid four years ago, but no houses have been built on it. Why?

The fourth picture shows the class of homes that follow these cheap "improvements." Such property is slow to increase in value, because the cheap aspect presented is repugnant to investors. No person wants to buy and build a good home when it will be forever surrounded by such cheap houses.

On the other hand, a finely developed subdivision attracts a good class of investors who build fine homes, and it is in this manner that values are made to increase rapidly.

Summary of Expenditures on Improvements in Cheap Subdivisions of Forty Acres	
Clearing two miles of streets	$ 500
Engineer's survey and staking lots	480
Rocking the streets 16 feet wide	7,920
Total	$8,900

Where sidewalks are laid, in entire subdivisions, add about $20,000.

PRINCESS PARK

"The Heart of Miami's Best Values" is being bought by substantial business men and women. Many of them will build and all of them will make money on their investments.

This is a street in a so-called improved subdivision, grubbed and ready to dump the rough rock on top of the ground without grading—photographed January 18.

This shows the rough rock dumped on the rough ground, nine feet wide, without any grading whatever—photographed January 18. This rock is simply crushed and rolled and called a paved street in many subdivisions.

Here is a street leading off Biscayne Drive that was partially improved four years ago. No houses have been built on this rough street although there are many fine homes around it.

This shows the character of houses that follow makeshift improvements. This street is only 14 blocks of centre of city. It takes years for values to increase in such surroundings.

REALTY MEN GIVE SUBSTANTIAL HELP IN CITY PROGRESS

Members of Seattle Association Play Big Part in Development of Present Metropolis of Northwest by Systematic and United Endeavor.

By B. L. LAMBUTH,
President Seattle Real Estate Association.

A BRILLIANT chapter in the history of Seattle has been written by her real estate men. They were a potent force in conquering the natural obstacles which confronted the small town in the course of its development into a great city. The fact that in this unequal contest they prepared themselves, professionally, to handle the complex real estate problems of a great city is perhaps their just and logical reward.

It has come to be conceded that the training of the competent real estate man who does a general brokerage business must be as elaborate and expensive as that of the lawyer or doctor. In addition, he must be trustworthy, as he is a fiscal agent in almost every transaction. And finally, he must be a sound business man in all that the term implies. Thoughtless criticism of the real estate broker is giving place to sincere commendation. Every day there are more people who appreciate the nature of the service which he has prepared himself to render.

Promote Development.

By far the largest part of the building development of the city, both commercial and industrial, has been promoted by the real estate men. Any successful office doing a leasehold and building business can account for hundreds of buildings which it has promoted during the last few years. One firm will specialize in apartments, another in industrials, another in warehouse and loft space. The promotion of each class of construction is a highly specialized business in itself. Private capital must be stimulated to make these improvements; the rates of rental return must be stabilized

What Seattle Has to Date in Improvements

Miles.		Cost
1,111.26 concrete walks;		
752.54 graded streets		$18,800,181
556.39 water mains		6,256,706
494.36 sewers		10,294,995
282.68 paved streets		13,072,512
153.06 planked streets		3,032,814
25.56 cluster lights		497,259
Steel and concrete bridges		840,050

Completed This Year.

30.35 miles of concrete walks.
21.70 miles of streets graded.
10.82 miles of water mains.
5.54 miles of sewers.
19.73 miles of streets paved.
3.89 miles of streets planked.
One-fifth of a mile of cluster lights.
Total expenditures for these improvements from January 1 to December 1, $2,151,308.

Contracts Under Way.

Steel and concrete bridge at 15th Ave. N. W.	$242,700
Steel and concrete bridge at Eastlake Ave.	$226,643
Wood bridge at West Spokane St.	61,606
Greenwood Avenue, concrete walks	23,000
47th Ave. S. W., sewers	43,000
E. 54th St., sewers	18,200
Latona Avenue, paving	28,000
Court Street, grading	13,600

SEATTLE-KING COUNTY ASSOCIATION OF REALTORS®

Real estate practitioners were hailed in this 1917 *Seattle Times* article for their contributions to the city's growth. The author, president of the local association, called his colleagues "a potent force in conquering the natural obstacles which confronted the small town in the course of its development into a great city."

NAR formed a City Planning Committee in 1914. Although most large subdividers did not buy in until the 1920s, the community builders on the committee quickly allied with other planning advocates through the NCCP. Together they began promoting the "science" of planning, or, as some called it, "realology." A 1914 article in the official magazine of the California Real Estate Association (today the CALIFORNIA ASSOCIATION OF REALTORS®) extolled the virtues of the science of planning. "The merits of a scientific town stand out. . . . It is so apparently superior to the old-fashioned community laid out more or less at random and left to itself to grow, that even the man of the least practical ideas can see for himself the great advantages of living and owning property in the scientifically planned community."[15]

The community builders were the rock stars of early-twentieth-century real estate. "The most lauded brokers in the national trade press were those who advocated planning and zoning and designed subdivisions with an eye toward permanency rather than quick profit," writes Jeffrey M. Hornstein in his book *A Nation of Realtors*®. "Most leaders of the National Association, at least in the first two decades, were firm believers in some form of controlled development."[16]

Nichols frequently took center stage. As developer of the Country Club District, a then 1,000-acre planned residential community that included a shopping center, Nichols walked the walk. And whenever he got the chance, he talked the talk, including a watershed 1916 speech to the NCCP.

Subdividing land solely for residential purposes was not the norm when Nichols and other early community builders began their careers. Most land was carved into building lots and sold for whatever use the new owner desired. The regulatory vacuum

"NOW, HOW IN THE WORLD CAN THE PRIVATE DEVELOPER, WITHOUT MUNICIPAL ASSISTANCE, EXPECT HIS PROPERTY TO SUCCEED IF HE IS TO WORK WITH UNREGULATED DEVELOPMENT ALL AROUND HIM?"

left the door open to numerous negative outcomes. One scam involved a sort of blackmail. First, speculators would buy land in a well-to-do neighborhood. Then they would announce plans to build a livery stable or some other nuisance. Residents would have to buy them out to stop construction.[17]

The main tool used by community builders to thwart such problems was private deed restrictions. Deed restrictions worked—but only within the confines of a given subdivider's tract. During his 1916 speech to the NCCP, Nichols made a case for taking the next step, increased public regulation, with this rhetorical question: "Now, how in the world can the private developer, without municipal assistance, expect his property to succeed if he is to work with unregulated development all around him?"[18]

Zoning was a novel concept when Nichols made his speech, but it was not unheard of—especially in the trendsetting state of California. With strong support from the local real estate board, Los Angeles had passed the nation's first major land-use zoning ordinance in 1908, which barred businesses from operating in residential districts. After Los Angeles had defeated several legal challenges in court, other California cities, such as Oakland, Pasadena, and Sacramento, adopted zoning laws patterned after the Los Angeles model.[19]

In their zeal to popularize zoning and other public planning tools, Nichols and

his cohorts discovered a sympathetic ear in Washington, D.C.—that of Herbert Hoover. As secretary of commerce, he established the Division of Building and Housing, which produced a plan of action for local civic groups to use in mobilizing forces to pass zoning laws. "Zoning spread rapidly in the 1920s, and many municipalities cribbed their ordinances directly from the primer," according to Hornstein. "Hoover attributed the success of the zoning initiative largely to the widespread exposure it received from organizations that distributed the primer, including . . . the National Association of Real Estate Boards [NAR]."[20]

The snowball was rolling, but it needed another push. Intended to protect neighborhoods, zoning laws were instead frequently being used promotionally for speculative purposes. In addition, subdivisions remained poorly regulated in most urbanizing areas, and most municipalities lacked long-range plans for roads, parks, and other major public improvements. The community builders in NAR recognized the problem but were wary of any solution that resulted in too much government control. Seeking to strike a "proper balance" between "private enterprise" and "the general good," they found the perfect vehicle in the Federal Housing Administration.[21]

Besides lighting a fire under a market frozen by the Great Depression, the FHA offered a way to shape development with

NAR ARCHIVES

J. C. Nichols in 1918.

a carrot, not a stick. On the basis of its *Underwriting Manual,* the FHA could deem properties in poorly designed or unprotected neighborhoods bad risks and deny loans on those properties. Since land-use restrictions, transportation, and public services were all important criteria for risk taking in the manual, their acceptance grew. The key was that compliance was voluntary. "The extensive requirements in the *Underwriting Manual,* including the property standards and neighborhood standards, were considered by the general public to be wise businesslike protections, rather than coercive intrusions."[22] Some of those same underwriting principles would prove controversial, however, as the civil rights movement gained steam. (See Chapter 4, "Evolving Conscience," page 106.)

By the 1940s, most of the goals for public and private land use that Nichols described in 1916 had been achieved. In terms of the heavy lifting needed to create modern development tools, the pioneering community builders of NAR—men such as Nichols; Edward Bouton, developer of Forest Hills Garden, New York; and Harry Culver, developer of Culver City, California, and 1929 Association president—could look back on a mission accomplished. Starting in the mid-1940s, the Urban Land Institute and the National Association of Home Builders—both NAR spin-offs—supplanted the Association's practical role in community building.

Far from abandoning the mission of vibrant communities, however, NAR leaders in the 1950s turned their attention to how to restore run-down urban areas. In fact, even before 1950, NAR had been keenly concerned about urban blight. "For years, the Association has advocated urban redevelopment and has been responsible for initiating 18 state laws on redevelopment," read a 1949 memo sent to the NAR Board of Directors by Executive Vice President Herbert U. Nelson. REALTORS®' ongoing concerns that the federal government would impose solutions on cities led Association leaders to launch the "Build America Better" program in 1952. The program focused on reenergizing run-down neighborhoods, with the goal of rehabilitating 10 million buildings. NAR sent experts to visit various cities, study city ordinances, schedule public meetings, and compile a comprehensive report with specific suggestions. By 1954, the program had gained wide recognition and was cited in the *Municipal Yearbook of International City Managers* as a major development in housing conservation. In some ways, the Build America Better campaign was working against a tidal wave of change. The growth

Herbert Hoover visits flood victims after the Great Mississippi Flood of 1927. Hoover, who was serving as secretary of commerce under President Calvin Coolidge, shared NAR's enthusiasm for community planning and zoning.

Harry Culver, pointing, announced in 1913 his plans to build a new community midway between Los Angeles and Venice, California. He promised "63 solid miles of new residences in 12 months," and proposed to wage "a selling campaign second to none in California for rapidity of sales." Culver City was incorporated in 1917, and Culver went on to serve as NAR president in 1929.

Visionary of the Midwest

Not many people know that an early NAR leader put the idea of community development on the map—and served as an inspiration to today's new urbanist developers. Jesse Clyde "J.C." Nichols of Kansas City, Missouri, was never an Association president, but he served on the NAR Board of Directors and was one of the Association's most influential leaders.

Nichols's name is synonymous with the Country Club District and Country Club Plaza mixed-use center in Kansas City. With those groundbreaking projects, he was the first to combine several real estate concepts within one site: a planned residential development with home association agreements; special events, such as an annual public Christmas lighting, to foster community spirit; percentage leases that provided the developer with a percentage of store receipts; and landscaping and

artwork. Nichols was considered a master salesman who espoused enthusiasm, truthfulness, and a belief in the properties he sold.[*]

Nichols, a native of Olathe, Kansas, received degrees from the University of Kansas and Harvard University. In 1905 he joined with fraternity brothers W. T. Reed and Frank Reed to sell land and build speculative houses. A few years later the three partners completed their first subdivision, Rockhill Park. They hired architects rather than builders to design the houses, a trend that architect Frank Lloyd Wright had helped initiate.[†]

In 1908, Nichols founded his eponymous company, the J.C. Nichols Company. With help from financial backers, he purchased a 1,000-acre site adjacent to the exclusive Kansas City Country Club and developed the Country Club District as a place where affluent buyers could escape the declining downtown.[‡] Nichols even developed a club—the Mission Hills Country Club—that was less restrictive than the old-line Kansas City Country Club.[§] Others without his vision may have passed up the site. As NAR's *National Real Estate Journal* described it, "It was beyond the

J.C. Nichols, here in a 1936 portrait, advocated "planning for permanence." His Country Club District in Kansas City was one of the earliest examples of a planned community, and his work was emulated by land developers in other cities.

---

[*] "Nichols' Notes on Selling," *National Real Estate Journal*, February 1939, p. 56.

[†] William S. Worley, *J.C. Nichols and the Shaping of Kansas City: Innovation in Planned Residential Communities* (University of Missouri Press, 1990), pp. xiv, 6, 65, 185.

[‡] Worley, p. 39.

[§] Robert Pearson and Brad Pearson, *The J. C. Nichols Chronicle: The Authorized Story of the Man, His Company, and His Legacy, 1880–1994* (The Country Club Plaza Press, 1994), p. 51.

"THERE IS NO SURER WAY OF DEPRESSING YOUR PRICES THAN TO FORCE MORE PROPERTY ON THE MARKET THAN CAN BE HEALTHILY ABSORBED."

transportation lines, without streets or utilities. Its neighbors were miserable shanties . . . stone quarries, trash dumps, and truck gardens."*

Mission Hills subdivision became the first automobile-oriented suburb in the area.† It was also among the first planned communities to replace a standard street plan with curving streets that better matched the topography. Nichols accented them with parks, sculpture, and water features.‡ And he insisted on a variety of housing styles by refusing to sell two adjoining lots unless his company received an agreement that the houses built would not be duplicates. His company awarded prizes for the most beautiful lawns, flower boxes, and parking spaces. Nichols insisted on not oversaturating a market. "There is no surer way of depressing your prices than to force more property on the market than can be healthily absorbed," Nichols explained at the NAREB convention in Louisville, Kentucky, in 1912.§

PLANNING FOR PERMANENCE

Nichols's aim was to foster good feelings among home owners about where they lived. He termed it "planning for permanence,"* and at the 1912 NAR convention, he was pleased to tell his fellow real es-

Among Nichols's tactics for building a strong community was an annual public Christmas lighting. It's a tradition that continues in communities throughout the country today.

---

* "Portrait of a Salesman: Jesse Clyde Nichols," *The National Real Estate Journal,* February 1939, p. 19.

† Pearson, p. 56; "Subdivisions and the Best Manner of Handling Them," *The National Real Estate Journal,* August 15, 1912, p. 460.

‡ "The Lessons of a Lifetime of Developing," *The National Real Estate Journal,* February 1939, p. 30.

§ "Subdivisions . . . ," pp. 461–462.

Nichols insisted on design conformity for his Country Club Plaza, a retail and apartment complex developed in the 1920s. Pictured here, in 1924, are the completed Tower and Wolferman buildings.

tate men that he was achieving his goal: "I believe that we have entirely changed the feeling that people have in Kansas City as to the possibility of building a home and retaining it in their family if they desire for a period of 50 years or 100 years or more."[†]

At the 1920 NAR convention in Kansas City, Association Secretary Tom Ingersoll declared, "The Country Club District . . . is the national model of high-class [residential] development. . . . It has elevated the entire real estate profession and is vitally affecting many of our larger cities."[‡]

In 1922, Nichols announced plans for Country Club Plaza, a Mediterranean-style development that combined apartments with retail. The first retail building opened a year later. Nichols insisted on design conformity through similar building heights, cornice lines, sign design, and placement. The purpose was to achieve an "orderly effect so generally praised in Paris and certain other European cities."[§] Nichols also wanted mostly one-story shops, rear unloading docks, and courts for stores to create a good traffic flow. The one-story heights eliminated steps for shoppers, though a few two-story buildings served as architectural punctuation marks.[¥] Once the plaza opened, Nichols began his tradition of having merchants put up Christmas trees and hang lights.

---

* *Community Builder: The Life & Legacy of J. C. Nichols,* Anderson Productions Ltd., Steven C. F. Anderson, Executive Producer, 2006, KCPT TV.

[†] "Subdivisions . . . ," p. 459.

[‡] Pearson, p. xv.

[§] Worley, pp. 247–249.

[¥] *Ibid.,* p. 247.

Nichols believed that parked autos would detract from the appearance of Country Club Plaza. He placed garages and parking stations apart from stores and camouflaged them with landscaping and decorations.* The growing popularity of autos influenced his thoughts on home design, too. Nichols decided the front porch was becoming obsolete because cars traveled too quickly for passersby to chat with sitters. He urged builders to put porches at the rear of homes.†

The pent-up demand for affordable housing before and after World War II pushed Nichols to develop land

---

* Worley, p. 258.

† Pearson, p. 52.

William S. Worley's 1990 book, *J.C. Nichols and the Shaping of Kansas City,* shows visitors lined up to see J. C. Nichols's "Mr. Blandings" model, inspired by the comic novel *Mr. Blandings Builds His Dream House* and the movie starring Cary Grant and Myrna Loy.

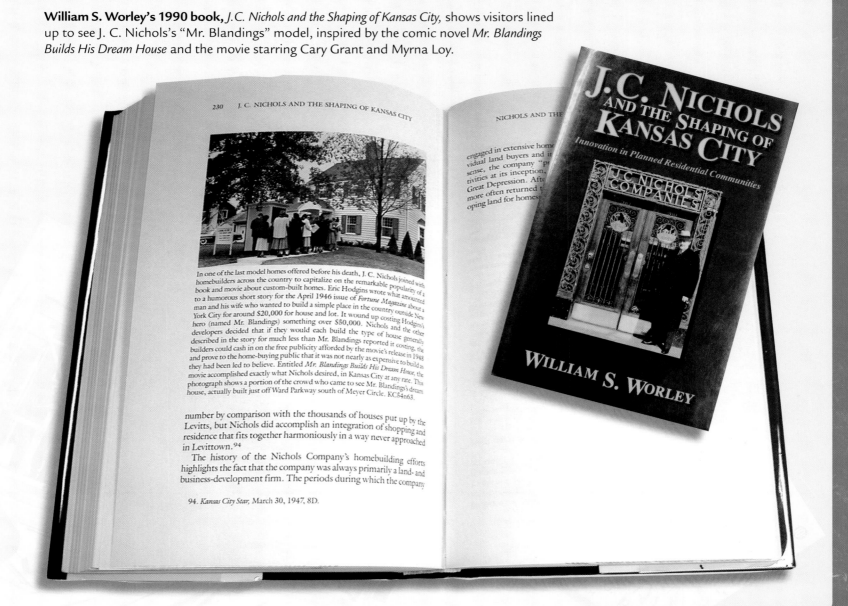

230   J. C. NICHOLS AND THE SHAPING OF KANSAS CITY

In one of the last model homes offered before his death, J. C. Nichols joined with homebuilders across the country to capitalize on the remarkable popularity of a book and movie about custom-built homes. Eric Hodgins wrote what amounted to a humorous short story for the April 1946 issue of *Fortune Magazine* about a man and his wife who wanted to build a simple place in the country outside New York City for around $20,000 for house and lot. It wound up costing Hodgins's hero (named Mr. Blandings) something over $50,000. Nichols and the other developers decided that if they would each build the type of house generally described in the story for much less than Mr. Blandings reported it costing, the builders could cash in on the free publicity afforded by the movie's release in 1948 and prove to the home-buying public that it was not nearly as expensive to build as they had been led to believe. Entitled *Mr. Blandings Builds His Dream House,* the movie accomplished exactly what Nichols desired, in Kansas City at any rate. This photograph shows a portion of the crowd who came to see Mr. Blandings's dream house, actually built just off Ward Parkway south of Meyer Circle. KC54n63.

engaged in extensive home... vidual land buyers and in... sense, the company "pr... tivities at its inception,... Great Depression. Afte... more often returned t... oping land for homes...

number by comparison with the thousands of houses put up by the Levitts, but Nichols did accomplish an integration of shopping and residence that fits together harmoniously in a way never approached in Levittown.[94]

The history of the Nichols Company's homebuilding efforts highlights the fact that the company was always primarily a land- and business-development firm. The periods during which the company

94. *Kansas City Star,* March 30, 1947, 8D.

J.C. NICHOLS AND THE SHAPING OF KANSAS CITY
Innovation in Planned Residential Communities

J.C. NICHOLS COMPANIES

WILLIAM S. WORLEY

Nichols—addressing his sales force in 1939 and in an interview with Kansas City's WHB radio in 1948—was beloved in the industry for his tireless efforts to spread the gospel of urban planning. Two months before his death in 1950, the *Kansas City Star* reported, "Nichols gives the impression of a man who would like to relax and sit around being a good fellow—just as soon as he gets some fifteen projects off his mind."

for middle-income home buyers. He and other developers of the time were inspired by the 1946 Eric Hodgins novel *Mr. Blandings Builds His Dream House* and the subsequent movie starring Cary Grant and Myrna Loy. Nichols built a model of Blandings's house off Kansas City's Ward Parkway, and crowds of sightseers queued up.*

One area in which Nichols wasn't ahead of his time was equal opportunity housing. His communities were governed by restrictive covenants that ensured that blacks and Jews wouldn't be able to buy homes there. The fear was that other residents would move out and values would plummet. At a conference, Nichols raised the question of selling to Jewish people. A Dallas developer said that he had sold to a few Jews but had "absolutely picked them." Under pressure from Jewish leaders, Nichols eventually sold to Jews.†

Nichols's actions should be considered within the context of his time. He was not alone or the first to institute such restrictions. In researching subdivisions in Baltimore, Boston, Philadelphia, and San Francisco, Nichols and colleague John Taylor came to believe that restrictive covenants and responsible home owner associations were among the best ways to maintain

---

* Worley, p. 230.

† *Ibid.*, pp. 147, 149, 152.

community values.* His beliefs were fortified by anticommunist feelings, which had a powerful hold on many Americans in his day. As Nichols told *Time* magazine in an article dated November 1, 1947, "When you rear children in a good neighborhood, they will go out and fight communism."†

"NEW URBANIST" PIONEER

After Nichols died in 1950, his oldest son, Miller, ran the company. In 1990, Jack Frost, Larry Wallace, and David Cooper acquired the majority interest in the residential brokerage arm of the J.C. Nichols Company and renamed it J.C. Nichols Residential Real Estate. Highwoods Properties Inc., a North Carolina real estate investment trust, acquired J.C. Nichols Company in 1998; the acquisition included Country Club Plaza. In 2002, the residential brokerage—by then a part of HomeServices of America—merged with J.D. Reece Company. The company today operates under the HomeServices umbrella as Reece & Nichols, with J.D. Reece founder Jerry Reece as CEO.

Of Nichols, Reece says, "He brought an artistic flair to development and design. If you look at what he touched and at all the innovations he brought to the world of residential and commercial development— hardscapes, statuary, fountains, pocket parks, architectural control—you know that he put Kansas City on the map."

Nichols generously shared his vision. Within NAR, he was active on the City Planning Committee. He was also founding president of the Association's Home Builders and Subdividers Division, which eventually would become the National Association of Home Builders. Along with other NAR leaders, Nichols helped found the Urban Land Institute. Today, ULI

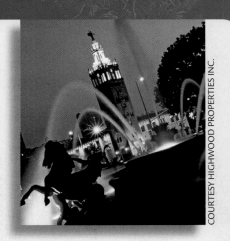

Taking a cue from the plazas of Europe, Nichols adorned Country Club Plaza with fountains and statuary, an idea widely adopted by shopping center developers. Today, Nichols's development remains a premier shopping and entertainment center for Kansas City residents.

COURTESY HIGHWOOD PROPERTIES INC.

gives a J.C. Nichols Prize for Visionaries in Urban Development.

"He was the one who crafted the concept of exchanging ideas and thinking about best practices in urbanism," said Richard M. Rosen, president of the Urban Land Institute, in a 2006 documentary about Nichols's life. Nichols directly influenced the development of other planned communities, including Beverly Hills in California and Cleveland's Shaker Heights, and he even wrote ULI's first book, *Community Builders Handbook.*

For 22 years, Nichols served on the National Capital Park and Planning Commission, working on the planning of metropolitan Washington, D.C. When failing health forced Nichols to resign in 1948, President Harry Truman held the resignation in abeyance for several weeks, hoping Nichols would change his mind.‡ On February 16, 1950, six months shy of his seventieth birthday, Nichols died of cancer.§

Today, his philosophies live on in the work of new urbanists—developers and planners who seek to make communities more attractive, livable, and spirited places to live and work. In the documentary *Community Builder: The Life and Legacy of J.C. Nichols,* Paul Goldberger, Pulitzer Prize–winning architecture critic and writer, called Nichols "the spiritual father of new urbanism."

---

* Pearson, p. 57.

† Worley, p. 154.

‡ Garnett Laidlaw Eskew, assisted by John R. MacDonald, *Of Land and Men,* Urban Land Institute, 1959, p. 156.

§ Pearson, p. 188.

MCCREA PHOTOGRAPHY

CHARLES F. TEED

NATIONAL ARCHIVES/LEIGH WYCKOFF CO.

NAR expressed bitter opposition to the public housing developments made possible by the Housing Act of 1949. Photographs taken between 1952 and 1955 show new public housing in St. Louis; Binghamton, New York; and Detroit.

of suburbs was changing the racial and economic composition of cities—and the creation of interstate highways was speeding up the process. Mayors pushed for assistance to save their central cities, and the federal government responded with the Housing Act of 1961, which authorized funds for expansion of conventional mortgage subsidy programs and grants for slum clearance.

By 1970, however, more homeowners lived in the suburbs than in cities or rural areas, and the percentage of city residents who were nonwhite had jumped to 56 percent, from 43 percent in 1950. Build America Better was sunset in 1974. Still, REALTORS® generally prevailed in convincing government to favor local solutions over federal solutions to urban decay. It was also 1974 when U.S. President Gerald Ford signed legislation authorizing the Community Development Block Grant program. Ford's predecessor, Richard Nixon, citing corruption and inefficiency, had put a freeze on federally subsidized housing programs. The grant program, Ford said at the signing, "will help to return power from the banks of the Potomac to people in their own communities."

SETTING GROWTH ON THE RIGHT PATH

After 1974, REALTORS® continued to promote solutions to urban decay through a separate program called Make America Better.

Unlike Build America Better—which had involved sending advisory teams to study urban areas—Make America Better encouraged boards and individual members to sponsor and participate in civic activities. The focus was not just on rehabilitating real estate and infrastructure but also on solving societal ills, such as lack of educational opportunity, vandalism, delinquency, and disrespect for law enforcement. Make America Better received plaudits from the Nixon Administration for its positive approach, and NAR continued the program until 1986, when it became the REALTORS® Community Service Committee. That, in turn, was absorbed into the Public Relations Committee in 1994. Efforts to promote REALTORS® community service would pick up steam again in 2000 when the Association embarked on a new wave of community service programs (see page 182).

In the meantime, NAR was beginning to reemerge as a leader in community planning. Even with the stagflation and steadily rising interest rates, the suburbs were continuing their seemingly boundless growth. It was becoming evident that the tools created by the community builders, which laid the foundation for postwar suburbanization, had in some ways worked too well. When combined with construction of new highways and the expansion of automobile use, the tools were an agent of sprawl.

The extreme growth-management measures that were being adopted around the country—including development moratoriums, urban growth boundaries, and sweeping downzones—were having a direct impact on real estate practitioners' businesses. In 1985, Boulder County, Colorado, downzoned 25,000 acres, "and 56 of those acres were mine," said Ron Myles, a two-time vice president of NAR and president of Myles

KENT STATE UNIVERSITY
KENT, OHIO 44240   TELEPHONE 216-672-2982

OFFICE OF THE VICE PRESIDENT
UNIVERSITY RELATIONS AND DEVELOPMENT
ADMINISTRATION BUILDING

July 29, 1966

Mr. J. William Venable
Staff Director
National Association of
  Real Estate Boards
1300 Connecticut Avenue, NW
Washington, D.C. 20036

Dear Bill:

As I reflect upon the "fallout" following the departure of the BAB team members, and as I listen to others who were touched by their penetrating inquiry, I find virtual unanimous agreement that the entire effort was of immense benefit to all of us. In the personal sense, it was a most enriching experience for me. I shall remain forever grateful to all of you for permitting me to share in your wisdom.

If the occasion should ever arise at which I might be able to convey personal testimony regarding the effectiveness of this approach, I hope that you will permit me the opportunity to do so. Until I see you in Washington or in these environs, I extend again warmest regards and best wishes.

Sincerely,

Ronald W. Roskens/ms

Ronald W. Roskens
Vice President,
University Relations and
Development

NAR ARCHIVES

Enterprises Inc. in Littleton, Colorado. Although the measures may have worked to curb rampant growth, said Myles, "they were affecting the affordability of home ownership, and they weren't really accomplishing the goal of building better communities. They were just an 'anti-' approach to solving growth issues."

NAR called for new affordability measures, such as mortgage revenue bonds to finance below-market-rate mortgages. On behalf of property owners, the Association

For 22 years beginning in 1952, through NAR's Build America Better program, REALTORS® provided cities with guidance on rehabilitating run-down areas. After meeting with a BAB advisory team, an official of Kent State University in Kent, Ohio, called the experience "enriching" and "of immense benefit."

Smart Growth Defined

The smart growth movement reflects a convergence of numerous interests with overlapping agendas. The Smart Growth Network, a coalition organized in 1996, includes members ranging from the Environmental Protection Agency to the Institute of Transportation Engineers to the American Planning Association. NAR joined the coalition in 1999. Since then, REALTORS® have made a big impact "in helping to frame the debate, in finding common ground, in being a good representative for the housing industry," Geoff Anderson, manager of the EPA's Smart Growth Program, said in 2006.

Perhaps NAR's biggest contribution has been to help define smart growth. In the beginning, said NAR's Joe Molinaro, smart growth was all about stopping sprawl—period. Through their involvement, REALTORS® helped add housing to the agenda. The Smart Growth Network, for example, lists creating "a range of housing opportunities and choices" as one of its ten principles of smart growth, stating: "Providing quality housing for people of all income levels is an integral component in any smart growth strategy."

10 Principles of Smart Growth

1. A range of housing opportunities and choices
2. Walkable neighborhoods
3. Community and stakeholder collaboration
4. Distinctive, attractive communities with a strong sense of place
5. Predictable, fair, and cost-effective development decisions
6. Mixed land uses
7. Preservation of open space, farmland, natural beauty, and critical environmental areas
8. Varied transportation choices
9. Emphasis on development in existing communities
10. Compact building design

SOURCE: SMART GROWTH NETWORK

waged a campaign against excessive transfer taxes and impact fees, said Myles. However, by the mid-1990s, REALTOR® associations around the country were clamoring for more assistance on how to influence local land-use decisions. NAR launched a Land Use Initiative in 1998, retaining the law firm of Robinson & Cole to help local associations battle growth-management legislation they opposed. Soon, however, NAR leaders concluded that taking potshots at objectionable legislation was not enough. The feeling was, "We can't just be on the opposing side," said Myles. "We've got to get engaged."

In 1999, NAR President Sharon Millett of Auburn, Maine, formed a Smart Growth Presidential Advisory Group to explore how the emerging concept of smart growth might offer local associations a way to make growth management work positively for everybody. Myles, a commercial practitioner and Certified Commercial Investment Member (CCIM) with extensive development experience, chaired the group. He found that the term *smart growth*, a fluid buzzword that was still jelling, meant different things to different people. "We decided we would help define it ourselves," he recalled.

The Presidential Advisory Group developed five "Guiding Principles for REALTORS® and Smart Growth," which were adopted by NAR:

1. Provide housing opportunity and choice.
2. Build better communities.
3. Protect the environment.
4. Protect private property rights.
5. Implement fair and reasonable public sector fiscal measures.

After adopting the principles, NAR launched a formal Smart Growth Program in 2000. It is overseen by a 14-member advisory group and provides training, polling, networking, legislative, and research services to local associations. Through the program, the Association also publishes *On Common Ground,* a twice-yearly magazine devoted to smart growth.

In 2003, Myles again took a leadership role, this time in a work group that reviewed the progress of NAR's smart-growth efforts. "We were quite pleased with the progress we had made," he said. "What we're seeing happening is that some areas have caught fire because there were strong leaders who got engaged."

Success stories include that of the Realtors® Association of New Mexico, which used the program's customized legislation service to pass two amendments to the state's planning and zoning laws.[23] More common examples involve Realtors® in educational roles. In Ventura County, California, where development outside most cities is severely restricted, the Ventura County Coastal Association of Realtors® helped found Housing Opportunities Made Easier (HOME). The nonprofit group, led for three years by commercial practitioner Fred Ferro, promotes smart-growth practices such as urban infill and increased density as a way to ensure that the cities of Ventura County can provide a mix of housing options.

In 2002, NAR launched another program aimed at expanding housing choice—the Housing Opportunity Program (see Chapter 2, "Home Ownership in America"). Both programs, said Joe Molinaro, manager of NAR's Smart Growth Program, reflect "our long-term desire to see high rates of home ownership and better housing for everyone."

Since embracing smart growth, NAR has expanded its public policy agenda beyond housing to include related community is-

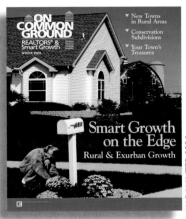

sues, most notably transportation. In 2002, the Association developed policies directed at the federal government's six-year funding package for highways and transit, said Molinaro. A working group is now studying the issue of education.

For Realtors® involved in these efforts—whether through NAR, their state or local association, or on their own—it's a terrific way to reach their ultimate goal: strong communities.

NAR joined the Smart Growth Network in 1999 and helped define the coalition's smart-growth principles, which emphasize factors such as walkability, a range of housing choices, varied transportation options, and a strong sense of place.

Cities Rising Tall

It's telling that delegates to the first meeting of the National Association in 1908—which included representatives from such major business centers as Chicago, Boston, Philadelphia, Cincinnati, and St. Louis—made no distinction between commercial and residential real estate in the organization's founding documents.

In the years leading up to NAR's founding, in all but a handful of large cities, there was no commercial real estate specialty. The central business district of a typical small- to medium-sized town consisted of a street of storefronts, a hotel, a train station, and a block of three- or four-story office buildings for professionals. Very little of that property changed hands in the course of a year, nor did it require extraordinary efforts to lease or manage. Even in large cities, residential and commercial real estate tended to be intermingled. Shopkeepers often lived over their stores, and it was not unusual for houses and commercial buildings to alternate on the same block.

That all began to change as the United States started its transformation from a pre-

The sidewalks of New York in 1906: Commercial real estate had emerged as a specialty in only a handful of cities.

ANDY KINGSBURY/CORBIS

dominantly rural society to the urban and suburban world we know today. Technology played a key role in the transformation. Two inventions—the skyscraper and the automobile—were especially important from a commercial real estate perspective. The skyscraper had its greatest impact in the late 1800s and early 1900s and the automobile was a significant factor after 1910.

By the late 1800s, companies of all kinds were getting larger, creating a rising need for office space. Central business districts were growing ever more expensive. The answer, ultimately, was taller buildings. The world's first steel-frame skyscraper—the nine-story Home Insurance Building in Chicago—was erected in 1884 and was immediately followed by numerous others.

"At a time when neither London, the world's largest city, [nor] Berlin or Paris boasted a single high-rise, steel-framed towers were rising in . . . places [such] as Bangor, Maine; Tulsa, Oklahoma; and Galveston, Texas," said urbanologist Joel Kotkin, author of *The City: A Global History*.

In *Downtown: Its Rise and Fall 1880–1950,* author Robert M. Fogelson describes the ambivalence many in the real estate industry felt at the dawn of the skyscraper age: "For property owners, skyscrapers offered a splendid opportunity to increase rental income and raise real estate values. But [skyscrapers] also posed serious problems. Given their capacity to house thousands of tenants, they centralized office work, thereby reducing property values on the fringe of the business district. They also displaced tenants from older and less up-to-date buildings, thereby reducing rental income of the structures, but not necessarily the assessed value of the land. And they lowered the value of adjacent buildings by depriving them of light and air."[24]

To sort out the consequences, property owners needed in-depth knowledge of property values and performance ratios. It's no coincidence that during this period, real estate brokers suddenly became far more important in the business world.

"The real estate broker everywhere is the pioneer in the development of great enterprises," said Benjamin M. Weil, one of Milwaukee's leading real estate professionals at the turn of the century. "He points out the opportunity and organizes the forces whereby latent energies of nature are transferred into tangible forms of wealth."[25]

The men who gathered in Chicago in May 1908 certainly saw the radical changes that were taking place in their cities and how their organization might influence the cities' commercial development for the better through urban planning.

Although the National Association formally embraced planning for residential subdivisions, it was more divided when it came to the zoning of commercial districts. In New York, a city with fully half of the nation's tall buildings in the early part of the twentieth century (tall being defined as 20 or more stories), the local real estate board actively campaigned for height restrictions. Other boards, however, felt differently. "What right," asked Horace Groskin, director of the Philadelphia Real Estate Board during that time, "has a zoning commission to set itself up as the judge and distributor of property values? To take the value away from one property owner and give it to another, or not to give it to anyone but to destroy it entirely for the imaginary benefit of the community, strikes me as coming mighty close to socialism."[26]

Ultimately, however, the Association embraced the practice as a way to stabilize property values at a time when older neigh-

"SPACE AND LIGHT AND ORDER. THOSE ARE THE THINGS THAT MEN NEED JUST AS MUCH AS THEY NEED BREAD OR A PLACE TO SLEEP."

Le Corbusier

New York's Equitable Building, a 40-story high-rise built in 1915, was widely reviled and prompted passage of the country's first citywide zoning ordinance.

EMPORIS

borhoods were being drastically affected by indiscriminate development.

The tipping point in the national debate over zoning was the Equitable Building in New York, a 40-story high-rise erected in 1915 at the corner of Broadway and Cedar streets. "It was said that the Equitable blocked ventilation, dumped 13,000 users onto nearby sidewalks, choked the local transit facilities, and created potential problems for firemen," said architectural historian Sally A. Kitt Chappell.

The 1.2-million-square-foot behemoth also cast its shadow on buildings four blocks away and caused real estate values in the surrounding neighborhood to decline by about 30 percent.

That did it. The next year, New York enacted the country's first citywide zoning ordinance, which included extensive restrictions on building height and usage. Over the next decade, two-thirds of the country's largest cities followed suit, with most of the new ordinances being modeled on New York's example.

The 1920s were the economic heyday of downtown business districts. "Fueled by almost a decade of tremendous, if uneven, economic growth, downtown business interests built more and bigger skyscrapers, hotels, and department stores in these years than at any other time in American history," said Fogelson.[27]

During that period, the U.S. Treasury Department asked REALTORS® to make a study of depreciation and obsolescence of commercial real estate. The results, published in 1927, were used to establish tables for computing depreciation.

But even as downtowns approached their commercial zenith, a countertrend was under way. As land values escalated in central business districts, industrial companies began relocating, first to the outskirts of cities and then to the suburbs and beyond.

Ford Motor Company's River Rouge plant, for instance, which was completed in the late 1920s, was the world's largest manufacturing complex. It occupied 1,100 acres in Dearborn, a then-distant suburb of Detroit, and employed more than 75,000 workers. The way people lived and worked was changing, and the automobile played a disproportionate role in the transformation. In the past, commercial and residential development in most cities tended to be concentrated around train stations, streetcar lines, and other forms of public transportation. With the rise of the automobile, however, roads—both inside and outside

Streetcars and automobiles enabled companies to locate facilities outside central business districts. This Ford Motor Company plant (top) was built in Dearborn, Michigan, in the 1920s. The boom in automobile use led NAR to call for improvements to the public highways.

BETTMAN/CORBIS

BETTMAN/CORBIS

the city—became far more important. The members of NAR were among the first to recognize the importance of that shift.

Not long after the Association's founding, NAR leaders issued a declaration calling for "the immediate and permanent improvement of the main public highways to the standard required for twentieth-century conditions" to be paid for by "federal and state governments cooperating with the respective counties."[28]

The suburbs were the new frontier. A telling statistic from Chicago: Between 1910 and 1928, commercial property values outside the Loop went up eight times faster than those within the district.

That decentralization impulse, however, was basically put on hold as the country plunged into two world wars and the economic upheaval of the Great Depression. Among the many causes that economists have identified for the downturn were overexpansion, rampant speculation on Wall Street, and a precipitous drop in agricultural prices.

By the early 1930s, commercial rents in many U.S. cities were off 30 percent from their 1920s peaks; overall property values had declined by 50 percent or more. Department stores sales, the linchpin of most downtown retail districts, fell by 40 percent, and 80 percent of downtown hotels ultimately wound up in bankruptcy. "By almost any standard," says historian Robert S. McElvaine, "the United States was in its worst crisis since the Civil War."[29]

NAR's response to the economic crisis included a largely successful campaign to limit property taxes and to shift responsibility for schools and roads to the state level. Late in the decade, it also created one of the first urban think tanks, the Urban Land Institute, to study the twin problems of blight and decentralization. The Washington, D.C.–based research group was spun off in 1940 and continues to be a major player in the field of urban studies.

Recovery from the Depression was slow and at first was limited almost exclusively to an extensive public works program instituted by the federal government. The program, the Public Works Administration, was responsible for the numerous classically inspired libraries, post offices, city halls, courthouses, and other public buildings that even now are a distinctive feature of many U.S. cities.

POSTWAR CITIES

With the advent of World War II, "the country needed to utilize its full potential," said Pearl Janet Davies, the late NAR historian in *Real Estate in American History*, her book commemorating NAR's 50-year anniversary. "A vast amount of communica-

Of Land and Man tells the story of the REALTORS® who founded the Urban Land Institute. Their mission: to study urban land use and provide solutions to urban decay.

tion was needed between the loosely knit real estate-construction-financing-materials industry and the federal government."

According to Davies, NAR played a leading role in coordinating that communication. Shortly after the Japanese attack on Pearl Harbor on December 7, 1941, the recently formed Society of Industrial REALTORS® was asked by the federal government's War Production Board to compile a comprehensive list of vacant commercial and industrial properties around the country. SIR also developed a standard formula the government could use for measuring factory and warehouse properties.[30]

"REALTORS® aided extensively in the difficult problems of land assembly for cantonments, airfields, docks, yards . . . as well as in the leasing of properties already built and in appraisal problems," said Davies.[31]

Early in the war, the Association was also instrumental in killing a federal bill that would have established rent controls for commercial and industrial properties. In a move that acknowledged the realities of modern warfare, the Association's Institute of Real Estate Management published guidelines for blacking out hotels, office buildings, hospitals, and other buildings.

The United States emerged from the war in much stronger economic shape than it had been in when it entered it. During the five-year period between 1940 and 1945, the country's gross national product more than doubled, to $213.6 billion. By 1955, the total was $360 billion. The next 20 years would prove to be a real estate golden age as cities embarked on extensive urban renewal efforts, and suburbs took off first as bedroom communities and ultimately as thriving business centers in their own right.

It was also an era when, because of the increasing size and complexity of the

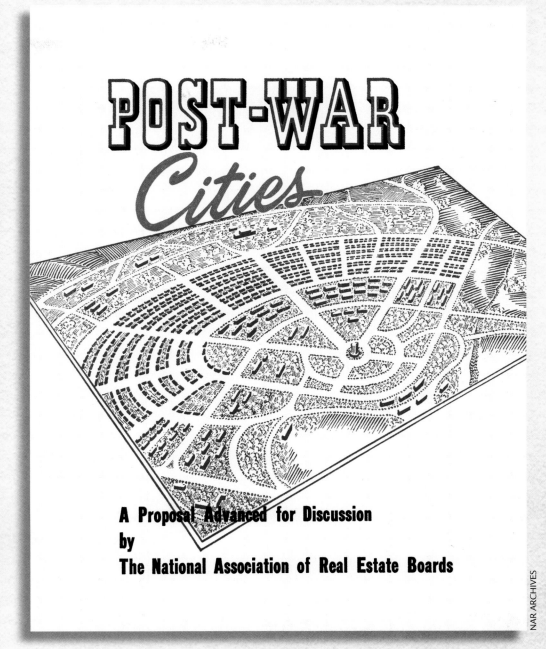

POST-WAR Cities

A Proposal Advanced for Discussion by The National Association of Real Estate Boards

NAR ARCHIVES

market, commercial real estate definitively branched off from residential and became its own business. All five of NAR's current commercial affiliates—the CCIM Institute, the Counselors of Real Estate, the Institute of Real Estate Management, the REALTORS® Land Institute, and the Society of Industrial

Even before the end of World War II, NAR members were discussing and writing about how to ensure that post-war construction would fall into the hands of private developers, not the federal government.

and Office REALTORS®—either began or experienced significant growth in the postwar years. It would be another three decades, however, before the Association effectively reorganized itself to acknowledge the divide. During the 1930s and 1940s, various commercial committees were formed and dissolved. Judging from the existing records, commercial matters tended to be regarded as an adjunct to the Association's far more numerous residential activities.

That hardly seemed to matter in the years following the war, however, because commercial real estate was doing very nicely on its own. Between 1945 and 1950, about 30 million square feet of new office space was constructed in the United States, an increase of 14 percent. Most of the building occurred in traditional downtown central business districts, with Chicago, New York, and San Francisco leading the way.

Still, the postwar years were a time when talk of the need for urban renewal programs became far more urgent in the real estate industry. This urgency was fueled by a number of troubling statistics from around the country. In Chicago, for instance, the number of people going downtown on an average day to work or shop fell by 20 percent between 1948 and 1952. In Baltimore, downtown retail sales fell 2 percent between 1948 and 1954 at a time when total retail sales for the metropolitan area as a whole were up 25 percent. During the same period in San Francisco, downtown property values still lagged behind their 1920s peaks at a time when suburban business districts were rapidly appreciating. Those and similar statistics from other cities seemed to indicate that traditional downtowns were losing their luster as commercial centers and that action was needed if they were to compete with their suburban competitors.

What finally emerged was a two-pronged initiative that involved numerous freeway construction projects to relieve downtown congestion, along with extensive slum clearance programs to reverse urban blight. Needless to say, both initiatives required major government input and funding. Of the two, slum clearance—which involved bulldozing blocks of blighted homes and businesses and replacing them with modern high-rises in landscaped settings—proved to be the most controversial.

"There is nothing economically or socially inevitable about either the decay of old cities or the fresh-minted decadence of the new un-urban urbanization," wrote urbanologist Jane Jacobs in the 1960s. "Extraordinary governmental financial incentives have been required to achieve this degree of monotony, sterility, and vulgarity."[32]

NAR's involvement in those efforts was mixed. On the one hand, the Association was a longtime advocate of more and better roads. But the wholesale destruction of inner-city neighborhoods was something Association leaders had a hard time embracing.

NAR's "Build America Better" program, launched in 1952, stressed renovation and enforcement of existing building codes. Build America Better Advisory Teams sought holistic solutions that would reverse the decline of the nation's urban centers. In addition to promoting rehabilitation of existing housing stock, they looked at transportation, distribution of tax revenues, and planning and zoning laws. In a speech explaining the program, 1952 NAR President Joseph W. Lund made it clear that the focus must be on commercial as well as residential interests.

Lund was particularly passionate about solutions that preserved mass transit options. Although earlier Association leaders

World War II's end coincided with skyrocketing suburban home development, but central cities continued to be centers of business and retail.

RETROFILE/GETTY IMAGES

ARCHIVES HOLDING INC./THE IMAGE BANK/GETTY IMAGES

Brockton *Daily Evening* Enterprise

AND BROCKTON TIMES

REG. U. S. PAT. OFF.

BROCKTON, MASS., TUESDAY, SEPTEMBER 10, 1963—

REALTY EXPERTS TOUR BROCKTON Arnold B. Tofias of Brockton, chairman of the Build America Better Committee, locally, at left, and General Chairman F. Lawrence Dow of Hartford discuss Brockton trip of real estate experts held Monday.

'BULLDOZER ISN'T ENTIRE ANSWER'

Team Maps Way to Stop Blight in City Areas

By BRUCE P. SMITH
Staff Reporter

A five-member team of real estate experts is making a comprehensive study of Brockton to pinpoint danger spots of deterioration that threaten to spread and develop into blighted areas.

The study team, sponsored by the Build America Better Committee of the National Association of Real Estate Boards, will make preliminary recommendations for the city's development to a luncheon of civic leaders Thursday and present a complete written recommendation in about eight weeks.

"The bulldozer isn't the entire answer to urban renewal," said F. Lawrence Dow, a Hartford, Conn., industrial and commercial realtor, chairman of the study team.

Dow, speaking today at the team's headquarters at the Hotel Bryant, emphasized that there is a great field for neighborhood re-

habilitation and conservation programs, rather than complete clearance projects.

"Rehabilitation of individual property can save entire neighborhoods from blight," Dow pointed out.

Another study team member, Laurel G. Blair, a Toledo, Ohio realtor, commented that the rehabilitation of blighted property is like a stone thrown into clear water. "It ripples out and more and more people in the neighborhood start fixing up their property, Blair specializes in the commercial and housing subdivision field of real estate.

The study team, armed with preliminary findings gathered by the team's professional member, Mechlin D. Moore of Washington, arrived in Brockton Sunday and made a bus tour of the city Monday along with a group of local realtors, bankers, manufacturers, merchants and civic leaders.

Non-paid, the team members are part of a pool of members of the National Association of Real Estate Boards who have conducted similar studies in 24 other cities. They came to Brockton at the invitation of the local Real Estate Board and Mayor F. Milton McGrath.

The only woman member of the study team, Miss Agnes Coleman of Newark, N.J., was impressed in yesterday's tour of the city that she didn't see any slum housing areas. She added, however, that she hadn't yet visited the Crescent-Court Urban Renewal project area.

Rental Housing

Miss Coleman, long-time chairman of the Newark Commission for Neighborhood Conservation and Rehabilitation, stressed that she was interested in inspecting the quality of rental housing available in the city and determining what can be done to rehabilitate it if necessary.

Dow, the team chairman commented on the spirit of cooperation and friendliness evident Monday afternoon when the team met with city department heads. The department heads outlined some problems as they saw them, and what their respective agencies and departments were doing about them.

Downtown Emphasis

"I'm especially interested in the downtown area," commented Earl C. Kester of Pottstown, Pa., former chairman of that city's Planning Commission and Redevelopment Authority.

"When valuation is lost in downtown areas due to deterioration, the loss is passed on to homeowners in the form of increased real estate taxes," he said.

For that reason, the team will take a particularly long look at the downtown area and offer concrete proposals to rectify adverse conditions.

"Downtown is the very heart of the city and must be preserved," Chairman Dow added.

The team was due for an extensive tour of the city's planned urban renewal area today, accompanied by Brockton Redevelopment Authority officials.

Moore, the team's professional, emphasized that the study group wouldn't recommend any broad changes in the UR plan, but might offer some suggestions for future use of the property.

"We study urban renewal and consider its overall effect on the city," Moore said. "We will take a special look at other older neighborhoods

REALTORS WHO SERVE ON BUILD AMERICA BETTER ADVISORY TEAMS

John F. Havens, Columbus, Ohio, Chairman of the Build America Better Committee, whose work in relocating displaced families through ownership of rehabilitated homes focused nationwide attention upon the importance of FHA Section 221, which provides insurance of mortgage loans for no-down payment home ownership for relocating families.

Paul B. Guthery, Charlotte, N. C., civic leader who took a major part in building support for enforcement of modern housing standards which has affected approximately one-third of all the dwellings in Charlotte; Past President North Carolina Association of Real Estate Boards; Former Chairman of Realtors' Washington Committee; Former NAREB Director; served on Charlotte Zoning Commission and Planning Board.

Guy T. O. Hollyday, Baltimore, Md., leader in establishing his city's housing rehabilitation program and Fight Blight Fund, nationally known mortgage banker; former Commissioner of the Federal Housing Administration; Vice-Chairman of the Board, Title Guarantee Co., Baltimore; Past President, Mortgage Bankers Association of America.

R. Gordon Tarr, Cincinnati, Certified Property Manager and a founder of what is now the Build America Better Committee, is chairman of the Cincinnati Rehabilitation Committee, former Vice-President of the Cincinnati Real Estate Board, and member of Board of Governors of the Institute of Real Estate Management.

Walter S. Dayton, Bayside, New York, former Chairman of the Build America Better Committee; appraiser and broker; former President of National Institute of Real Estate Brokers; former Chairman of Realtors' Washington Committee, and a past President of the New York State Association of Real Estate Boards.

Miss Agnes Coleman, Newark, N.J., is a Past President of the Real Estate Board of Newark, and is the only woman to have served in that capacity. She also is the only woman member of the Housing and Home Finance Agency's National Advisory Committee on Housing Studies, and is a charter member and Chairman of the Newark Commission for Neighborhood Conservation and Rehabilitation.

Harold S. Goodrich, Springfield, Ohio, appraiser, whose work in cooperation with real estate boards in 1952 as Chairman of the NAREB committee on Rehabilitation was a major factor in the postwar movement of cities into more aggressive enforcement of health, safety, and sanitary standards for housing.

John A. Dodds, Detroit, Mich., Past-President of the Detroit City Plan Commission, is one of the most active leaders in his city's well-advanced urban renewal program. He is a real estate lecturer at the University of Michigan and a Director of the Trustee Citizens Redevelopment Commission.

Through the Build America Better Committee, advisory teams traveled to cities in order to make customized recommendations (at right). The underlying agenda didn't vary: They promoted the use of the hammer over the bulldozer, urging investors to champion alternatives to public housing and mortgage bankers to fund rehabilitation projects.

had favored improved roads as a means of expanding residential development outward, Lund said the nation's central business districts were now caught in the "ever tightening spring of useless auto traffic. When we have to tear down one-third to one half of our central areas to provide highways and parking, we have gone a long way toward making our cities unattractive places for working and unprofitable sites for carrying on business. . . . In our worship of the auto," he continued, "we have forgotten the very simple fact that exchange of goods and ideas by people has built our standard of living."[33]

Lund's exhortations did little to turn the tide on automobile use or highway development. The federal Highway Act of 1956—which created the Interstate Highway System—resulted in wide swaths being cut through many established urban neighborhoods, affecting residents and commercial businesses alike.

The highway expansion enabled businesses, including real estate practitioners, to follow residents to the burgeoning suburbs. But there was one area in which the Association turned out to be prescient: that is, in its policy of favoring rehabilitation—which Lund called slum "curance"—over slum clearance. The policy was derided as overly conservative at the time. Beginning in the early 1960s, however, there was a backlash against large-scale urban renewal projects that continues to this day.

GUIDING CHANGE IN BERWYN-CICERO

AN ADVISORY TEAM REPORT ON BERWYN AND CICERO, ILLINOIS
Build America Better Committee
National Association of Real Estate Boards

Brockton on the Move

AN ADVISORY TEAM REPORT TO THE CITY OF BROCKTON, MASSACHUSETTS
Build America Better Committee
National Association of Real Estate Boards

CAMPBELL COUNTY'S COMING ADVANCE

AN ADVISORY TEAM REPORT ON CAMPBELL COUNTY, KENTUCKY
Build America Better Committee / National Association of Real Estate Boards

A HOUSING PROGRAM FOR DEKALB COUNTY

AN ADVISORY TEAM REPORT TO DEKALB COUNTY, GEORGIA
Build America Better Committee / National Association of Real Estate Boards

POCATELLO, IDAHO SEEKS A MISSION FOR PROGRESS

AN ADVISORY TEAM REPORT TO POCATELLO, IDAHO
Build America Better Committee   National Association of Real Estate Boards

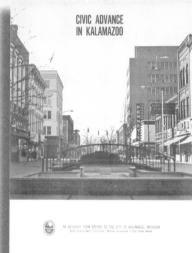

CIVIC ADVANCE IN KALAMAZOO

AN ADVISORY TEAM REPORT TO THE CITY OF KALAMAZOO, MICHIGAN
Build America Better Committee / National Association of Real Estate Boards

A MANDATE FOR PROGRESS IN MODESTO

AN ADVISORY TEAM REPORT TO THE CITY OF MODESTO, CALIFORNIA
Build America Better Committee / National Association of Real Estate Boards

CONSERVING THE CITY BEAUTIFUL

AN ADVISORY TEAM REPORT TO THE CITY OF ORLANDO, FLORIDA
Build America Better Committee / National Association of Real Estate Boards

SAN JOSE CITY HALL

SANTA CLARA CITY HALL

NEW GOALS FOR RENEWAL IN SAN JOSE AND SANTA CLARA

AN ADVISORY TEAM REPORT TO THE CITIES OF SAN JOSE AND SANTA CLARA
BUILD AMERICA BETTER COMMITTEE / NATIONAL ASSOCIATION OF REAL ESTATE BOARDS

SEATTLE IN TRANSITION

AN ADVISORY TEAM REPORT TO THE CITY OF SEATTLE, WASHINGTON
BUILD AMERICA BETTER COMMITTEE / NATIONAL ASSOCIATION OF REAL ESTATE BOARDS

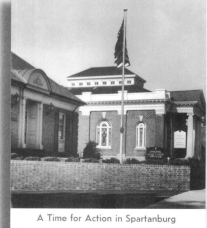

A Time for Action in Spartanburg

AN ADVISORY TEAM REPORT TO SPARTANBURG, SOUTH CAROLINA
Build America Better Committee / National Association of Real Estate Boards

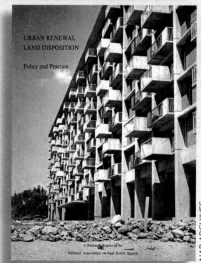

URBAN RENEWAL LAND DISPOSITION

Policy and Practice

A Research Report of the
National Association of Real Estate Boards

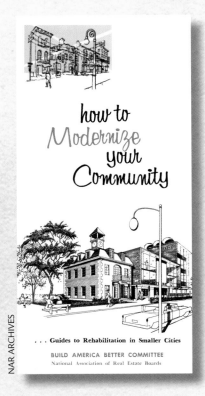

NAR's Build America Better Committee offered guidance for restoring downtown as the commercial, cultural, and professional center of the city. Cities should take a cue from the suburban shopping center—"one of the most successful creative achievements in real estate during the twentieth century," the booklet said—employing harmony of design, allowing for adequate off-street parking, and creating a degree of separation between pedestrians and drivers.

how to
Modernize
your
Community

. . . Guides to Rehabilitation in Smaller Cities

BUILD AMERICA BETTER COMMITTEE
National Association of Real Estate Boards

A NEW SERVICE IN

NEIGHBORHOOD CONSERVATION

Through Advisory Visiting Teams

Organized by the

BUILD AMERICA BETTER COMMITTEE

NATIONAL ASSOCIATION OF REAL ESTATE BOARDS

The other major trend in postwar commercial real estate, suburban development, evoked far less controversy. For most of the 1950s and 1960s, the suburbs—in commercial terms—meant one thing: shopping centers.

"The huge shopping center, surrounded by wide parking lots, has done much to build the new markets," said *Time* magazine in a 1954 article on the growth of the suburbs. "There are already 93 such centers around the 20 largest U.S. cities, and at least 25 more on the drawing boards. The investments run high—$20 million at Chicago's Park Forest suburban development, $30 million at San Francisco's Stonestown, $100 million at Los Angeles' Lakewood. And an increasing number of big city department and specialty stores, sensing the trend, are building their own suburban branches."[34]

In 1954, all the centers were open-air. Two years later, however, came Southdale in suburban Minneapolis, the world's first enclosed mall. It's safe to say the world has never been the same.

"They float on the landscape like pyramids to the boom years, all those Plazas and Malls and Esplanades," wrote author Joan Didion in the late 1970s when mall development was experiencing what proved to be a temporary lull. "All those Squares and Fairs. All those Towns and Dales, all those Villages, all those Forests and Parks and Lands. . . . They are toy garden cities in which no one lives but everyone consumes. . . ."[35]

So they were. So they are.

The 1970s and 1980s saw increasing numbers of people fleeing the turmoil and decline that plagued cities in search of fresh starts in newly built subdivisions. Some central cities—particularly those in the East and the Midwest—saw their populations drop by half or more.

There was also a national demographic shift, with cities in the South and West—such as Atlanta, Houston, Las Vegas, Los Angeles, and Phoenix—growing at much faster rates than those in the Midwest and Northeast.

It was also a period marked by more than the usual number of economic ups and downs. For the commercial real estate industry, the late 1970s and early 1980s were among the worst periods since the Depression. A stubborn recession took hold, and interest rates soared. Construction of all kinds—commercial as well as residential—slowed to a crawl.

However, the 1980s brought an unprecedented amount of foreign, especially Japanese, investment, creating a far more favorable environment. Indeed, the downtowns of many U.S. cities received their biggest makeovers since the 1920s. Atlanta, Chicago, Houston, Los Angeles, and New York all saw the construction of dozens of new office towers and other improvements.

Many of the buildings were designed in the new postmodern style, a deliberate attempt to revive the lively architectural eclecticism of the 1920s. After three decades of often-nondescript glass boxes, U.S. cities were once again awash in pillars, pediments, turrets, and cupolas. It remains to be seen whether those structures will achieve the enduring popularity of their 1920s counterparts.

Meanwhile, the suburbs created the concept of *edge cities,* basically minidowntowns crammed with new high-rises and located at the urban periphery or in neighboring suburbs. In some instances, edge cities replaced downtowns as commercial centers. In Detroit, for example, central business districts in suburban Troy and Southfield took over from downtown as the twin business hubs for the region.

The end of the 1980s boom came with a change to the federal tax code known as the Tax Reform Act of 1986. The new law—which did away with tax benefits for passive real estate investors—was particularly onerous for the syndication business. The Association's new executive vice president at the time, William D. North, told a Chicago newspaper, "If this law passes, who is going to invest in real estate again?"[36]

Clark Wallace of Moraga, California, 1986 NAR president, recalled the efforts made by NAR leaders to turn the tide on tax reform. "I was in the neck of it," Wallace

By the 1980s, "urban renewal" was passé, but foreign investors were pouring money into U.S. cities. The 1980s also marked a break from boxy modern architecture. Among the postmodern additions to the skyline of Chicago—NAR's headquarters city—were the Diamond Building at 150 N. Michigan Avenue, 900 N. Michigan Avenue (not pictured), the AT&T Corporate Center at 227 W. Monroe Street, 311 S. Wacker Drive, and 77 W. Wacker Drive.

311 S. Wacker 1990

227 W. Monroe 1989

77 W. Wacker 1992

150 N. Michigan 1983

DIGITAL STOCK

said in 2006. "I flew into Washington, D.C., maybe 20 times. I probably met with 150 senators; the secretary of the treasury, Jim Baker; Dick Cheney."

But Bob Packwood of Oregon, Republican chairman of the Senate Finance Committee, "locked up the 20 members of the committee late in the legislative year, and they came out with a pact . . . and none of us could get to him," Wallace said. Wallace did meet with Packwood's chief of staff, telling him, "This is going to kill us." His answer, Wallace recalls, was, " 'Well, my boss is going to stick to his guns. He got this passed out to the Senate Finance Committee, so go ahead and defend yourselves.' And that's how it ended."

There was little NAR could do. "We brought it on ourselves—not the REALTORS® per se but the developers, with wild excesses

> "[DEVELOPERS] CREATED AN ATMOSPHERE FOR EXCESS AND THEN ENJOYED THE RIDE—AND '86 WAS THE PAYBACK."
>
> –Clark Wallace

of building—all over Texas, the West, the South, Atlanta," said Wallace. The rampant overbuilding led to statements in Congress about "see-through buildings" built purely as tax shelters.

"[Developers] were getting tax benefits really going back to 1981. We created an atmosphere for excess and then enjoyed the ride—and '86 was the payback."[37]

When NAR failed to stop the passage of "TRA '86," leaders of NAR's commercial affiliates felt betrayed. Within four years, one affiliate, the Real Estate Securities and Syndication Institute, disaffiliated with NAR.

Perhaps it's no coincidence, then, that in the late 1980s, NAR took steps to organize a commercial division and provide distinct services to commercial practitioners. Unfavorable tax reform was hardly the only reason. Most important was the recognition that the local associations that formed the heart of NAR weren't equipped to provide the kind of specialized education and services required by the commercial sector.

"Except in the area of government affairs, the commercial firms were not perceiving any value to being involved with NAR," said Ron Myles, a broker from Denver. In the late 1980s, Myles was part of a task force that produced a report calling for the Association to take a new approach to commercial activities.

The new approach ultimately included the creation of commercial overlay boards, which coexist and share in a geographic jurisdiction with one or more REALTOR® associations to better serve members in a commercial market area.

At the same time, NAR played an important role in sorting out the savings and loan crisis that had resulted from the overbuilding of the previous decade. Deregulation of savings and loan institu-

tions in the early 1980s had enabled them to make far larger and more risky investments, many in real estate. Ultimately, more than 1,000 institutions collapsed, and $150 billion in equity vanished. The government bailout that followed left a $100-billion-plus hole in the federal budget that was not filled until the late 1990s. Part of the bailout effort involved disposing of thousands of failed real estate parcels and projects. After considerable lobbying from NAR, the government agreed to employ private commercial brokers for that purpose, which not only speeded up the process but also provided a livelihood for salespeople struggling to adjust to the recession that gripped the country in the early 1990s.

In fact, when the market began to recover, the driver was residential. One of the more unusual developments at the time, which extends to the present day, was the redevelopment of many downtown commercial districts as mixed-use neighborhoods, with significant amounts of residential space. After 75 years of decentralization, downtown living was back in style again in many cities.

Meanwhile, the suburbs, following the dictates of New Urbanism, were being recast as modern versions of early-twentieth-century small towns, with commercial and residential space closely intermingled.

It was during the 1990s that real estate investment trusts became far more ubiquitous and influential in the real estate world. REITs had been a factor in the market since 1960, when President Dwight Eisenhower, after lobbying from NAR, signed a bill that eliminated double taxation of real estate trusts. REITs remained minor players, however, until two pieces of legislation were passed. The 1986 Tax Reform Act allowed REITs to manage as well as own their properties. In 1993, the government eliminated laws that had discouraged pension funds—a major source of development money—from investing in REITs. Together, those two pieces of legislation opened the floodgates.

In the past, the great commercial real estate empires tended to be family owned or controlled and concentrated in particular cities or regions. With the growth of publicly traded REITs, however, real estate came to be regarded as an investment not that different from the stock market. Large REITs like Equity Office Properties and Vornado Realty Trust bought and sold hundreds of properties in cities across the country. REITs were an $8.7 billion business in the early 1990s. Today, that figure is $475 billion.

In 2000, NAR renamed its commercial division the REALTORS® Commercial Alliance. The RCA represents the collective commercial real estate constituencies of NAR, including the affiliated commercial organizations—the CCIM Institute, the Counselors of Real Estate (CRE), the Institute of Real Estate Management (IREM), the REALTORS® Land Institute (RLI), and the Society of Industrial and Office REALTORS® (SIOR). The RCA works to serve the needs of commercial practitioner members through development of business-focused materials, including a quarterly newsletter, *RCA Report,* in-depth reports on current business issues, and audio interviews with industry leaders. In 2006, the RCA held the first online convention for commercial real estate; CommercialSource (*www.commercialsource.com*) became a destination site for real estate professionals from novice to experienced. Today, RCA is working to facilitate and deliver a national commercial information exchange to provide market-relevant access to commercial real property information.

In embarking on its distinct mission, the RCA is helping REALTORS® carry on the work described 50 years earlier by Pearl Janet Davies in *Real Estate in American History.* "Whatever may be ahead in world affairs, in scientific advance, in economic change," Davies said, "the real estate problem of that future is likely to be essentially the same as the problem of today: to provide the home, the workshop, the mart of trade, the places for community life; and to make their ownership sound and safe; to relate each to each with efficiency, and in a setting that gives satisfaction to the individual human spirit. Beyond, on a new frontier, to link more efficiently the central city and its far-scattering satellite communities. That is real estate achievement."[38]

Today, the REALTORS® Commercial Alliance serves more than 60,000 commercial specialists with the quarterly RCA Report; a virtual conference; in-depth Hot Topics reports; and technology briefings delivered via CD.

The September 11, 2001, terrorist attacks on the World Trade Center towers and Pentagon prompted NAR leaders to launch the REALTORS® Housing Relief Fund to provide temporary mortgage and rental payment relief for those who lost a breadwinner in the attacks.

NEW YORK STATE ASSOCIATION OF REALTORS®

A MISSION TO SERVE

Throughout NAR's history, REALTORS® have mobilized to help others in need—both individuals within their own towns and those struck by calamity in other areas. For REALTORS®, community building and community service go hand-in-hand.

One of the most poignant examples came in the months after the September 11, 2001, terrorist strikes.

"At first I was stunned, like the rest of America," 2001 NAR President Richard A. Mendenhall of Columbia, Missouri, said in an interview a year after the attacks. "Then I realized that as REALTORS® we must respond immediately by saying, 'No victim's family will lose their home as a result of the tragedy.'"

One day after terrorists hijacked and crashed four jetliners, killing thousands of people, NAR leaders established the REALTORS® Housing Relief Fund—seeding it with $1 million from Association reserves—to help surviving family members make their mortgage and rent payments in the wake of the attacks.

REALTORS® began delivering checks within just a few days. "I delivered checks to the wives of five victims," George A. Naylor Jr., a REALTOR® from Southampton, Pennsylvania, said in 2002. "It was the first assistance they received, and it meant a lot. One was already behind in her mortgage payments. I don't know if we [the real estate industry] got much notice for what we did; and I don't know that we should. In our hearts we know we did the right thing."

Ultimately, the REALTORS® Housing Relief Fund collected and distributed more than $8 million to surviving fam-

182 THE NATIONAL ASSOCIATION OF REALTORS®

ily members. "It's made a major difference in my life," widow Debra Roberts told *REALTOR® Magazine* in December 2001.

In that same year, another major philanthropic project was already under way—a national partnership with Habitat for Humanity International.

The partnership was officially launched at the REALTORS® Conference & Expo in Chicago held in November 2001. Through the partnership, REALTORS® fund and help build a home each year in the conference city—as well as in select cities around the world.

In a major international joint effort, NAR teamed up with Habitat to help restore housing destroyed by the December 26, 2004, South Asian tsunami. REALTORS® and

friends donated more than $1.5 million to help Habitat build homes for displaced residents, and 2005 NAR President Al Mansell of Midvale, Utah, who toured some of the sites where construction was under way, later thanked members for their generosity. "As I watched the slow rebuilding taking place," he said in the October 2005 issue of *REALTOR® Magazine*, "I saw how your generosity was helping give the survivors the will they needed to go on with their lives."

Mansell's column, while thanking REALTORS® for their contributions after the tsunami, was actually a plea for REALTOR® assistance after another natural disaster: the devastation of the Gulf Coast caused by Hurricane Katrina in August 2005. Since

Since 2001, NAR has worked with Habitat for Humanity International to fund and build a home each year in the city that hosts the REALTORS® Conference & Exposition. Bottom, a wall-raising in San Francisco in 2005; inset, Martin J. Edwards Jr. turns over the keys to a New Orleans resident in 2002.

NAR

NAR/CONVENTION

Al Mansell's year as NAR president was punctuated by several natural disasters—the South Asian tsunami in December 2004 and Hurricanes Katrina, Rita, and Wilma in 2005. Mansell visited storm-damaged areas in Thailand and the U.S. Gulf Coast and called on REALTORS® to provide aid to victims. As they had after 9/11, REALTORS® and friends contributed millions of dollars. In Kao Lak, Thailand, in 2005, from left, are Marguerite Mansell; 2007 NAR President Pat V. Combs; videographer John Ringstad; Mansell; translator Phanmanee Suphoti; and survivor Supachai Srisawat. The group is standing in the spot where Srisawat's small restaurant was located. The tsunami killed his wife and daughter and washed away his restaurant. With money from NAR, Habitat for Humanity International built Srisawat a new home, where he lives with his young son. One month after his trip to Thailand, Mansell, left, got a firsthand look at Hurricane Katrina's devastating effects. His tour guide was John Phillips of Prudential Gardner, REALTORS®, in Biloxi, Mississippi.

COURTESY JOHN RINGSTADT

then, the Association's Gulf Coast recovery efforts—most in conjunction with Habitat for Humanity International—have been its most ambitious philanthropic project to date.

With the REALTORS® Conference planned for New Orleans in November 2006, Association leaders asked REALTORS® to use some of their down time to help residents of the city. While at the conference, more than 2,000 attendees put in 8,364 hours of volunteer work. Volunteers framed new homes and did reconstruction work. Others engaged in such rehab projects as cleaning up a New Orleans public library and painting a local school.

But those volunteer efforts tell just part of the story. All told, by early 2007, REALTORS® and REALTOR® organizations across the country had contributed supplies, volunteer labor, and more than $4.6 million to directly help victims of the hurricanes. Early in his term, 2006 NAR President Thomas M. Stevens of Vienna, Virginia, challenged REALTOR® associations in the 50 states and four territories to raise $75,000 each to sponsor a Habitat for Humanity house in the Gulf Region. In a program dubbed "Operation Home Delivery," REALTORS® in each of NAR's 13 regions built two "homes in a box" to be shipped to affected areas. And the work continued in 2007, with REALTOR® volunteers traveling to the Gulf Region to work with Habitat on the construction of more homes.

"REALTORS® build communities, helping families find their dream homes every day," said 2007 NAR President Pat V. Combs of Grand Rapids, Michigan, in an NAR statement released in March 2007. "More than 18 months after the storms hit, thousands of homes in the affected areas remain untouched because many of their owners cannot afford to rebuild them. We are committed to helping those families find a new place to call home."

NAR/CONVENTION

During the REALTORS® Conference & Expo in November 2006, REALTOR® volunteers participated in the building of Musicians Village, a community created by musicians Harry Connick Jr. and Branford Marsalis in partnership with the New Orleans Area Habitat for Humanity.

REALTORS® around the country lent a hand in Gulf Coast relief. Through a program called Operation Home Delivery, NAR members framed homes and shipped them to the Gulf Coast in trucks.

REALTORS® are community boosters, working through more than 1,200 local, state, and territorial associations to improve housing conditions and the lives of others where they work and live. In this 1987 photo, members of the Greater Baltimore Board of REALTORS® present a check to benefit the homeless. Pictured, left to right, are Sid King of WBAL Radio and Donna Lee Frisch, cochairs of Project Shelter with REALTORS® Jan Hayden and Ann Neumann, chair and vice chair, respectively, of GBBR's Public Relations Committee.

RECOGNIZING REALTORS® AS GOOD NEIGHBORS

NAR's good works—beginning with the creation of the REALTORS® Housing Relief Fund and continuing through its ongoing partnership with Habitat for Humanity—represent just a sliver of the community service work of REALTORS® around the country. That's why, since 2000, *REALTOR® Magazine,* the monthly magazine of NAR, has recognized exemplary service to the community with its Good Neighbor Awards program. Winners are chosen for the breadth and impact of their volunteerism, as well as the leadership and determination needed to change the quality of life for others in a meaningful way. Their volunteer work may be related to housing or real estate, or it may serve

another community need, such as caring for the elderly or guiding troubled teens. First-year winner Jill Rich of Tucson, Arizona, summed up the feelings of many Good Neighbor Award winners: "Volunteering keeps me centered and gives me a more realistic view of the world," she told *REALTOR® Magazine* in 2000. "I couldn't imagine a life without it."

The program was the brainchild of NAR Senior Vice President Frank J. Sibley and Vice President (then editor) Pamela Geurds Kabati. It started as a vehicle for the magazine to cover, once a year, the good works of REALTORS® in their communities. Nurtured in its first year by the support of Martin J. Edwards, who would become NAR president in 2002, the program grew. Today, it draws more than 300 nominees per year. By 2006,

REALTOR® Magazine's Good Neighbor Award Winners

2000
Linda Booker, Arizona
Oral Lee Brown, California
Gil Gillenwater, Arizona
Joseph Pitts, Florida*
Jill Rich, Arizona

2001
Doris J. Attebury, Texas
Jean Clary, Virginia
Craig C. Conant, Missouri
Debra Parmenter, Colorado
Matthew J. Schrum, Pennsylvania

*Deceased.

For the current list of *REALTOR® Magazine*'s
Good Neighbor Award Winners and Honorable
Mentions, see REALTOR.org/realtormag.

2002
Hal Ehretsman, Ohio
John M. Green, Tennessee
Linda W. Norton, Colorado
Cynthia J. Shafer, Florida
Annemarie Torcivia, Massachusetts

2003
James N. Austin Jr., Texas
James H. Bess Sr., California
Claudia Deprez, Florida
James Pacheco, California
Bobbie Tugwell, Louisiana

During the REALTORS® Conference & Expo, 2003 Good Neighbor Award winner Jim Bess, right, accepts his award from the corporate sponsors.

2004
Thomas Bush, North Carolina
Robin Croft, Rhode Island
Ned C. Li, Maryland
Thomas Maloney, Massachusetts
Diane Mintz, California

2005
David Forward, New Jersey
Howard Freeman, Florida
Greg Garrett, Virginia
Carole Sharp, Illinois
Ouida Spencer, Georgia

2006
Ernest "Chuck" Ayala, California
Rob Cronin, Idaho
Sharon Friend, Nevada
Lolita Junk, Illinois
David Sonenberg, Georgia

70 REALTORS® had been recognized with either the Good Neighbor Award or a Good Neighbor honorable mention. Each year, five award winners receive $10,000 grants, and five honorable mentions receive $2,500 grants for their cause. The grants are supported by contributions from sponsors. "I get energized by what REALTORS® are accomplishing at the grassroots level to help their communities," said founding sponsor Stuart Siegel, CEO of e-Neighborhoods in Boca Raton, Florida, in 2006. "What I find most incredible about Good Neighbor recipients is the amount of personal time they devote to their projects [a combined total of 7,000 hours in 2006], and how they unanimously feel they would be less successful without integrating community service into their day-to-day businesses."

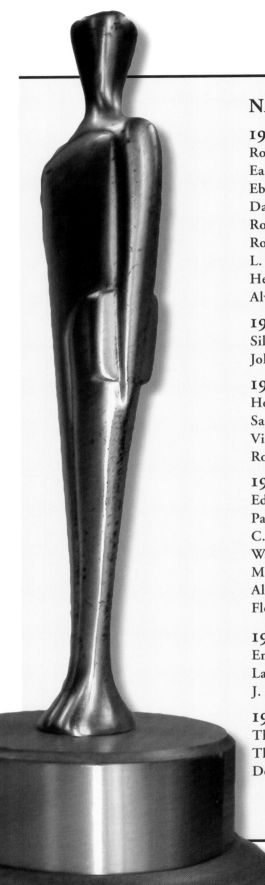

NAR Distinguished Service Award Winners

1979
Robert S. Curtis,* New York
Earl A. Espeseth, Wisconsin
Ebby Halliday, Texas
Daniel C. Hanrahan,* New Jersey
Robert A. Holloway,* Louisiana
Robert N. McGuire,* Illinois
L. Allen Morris,* Florida
Henry E. "Bud" Pogue IV, Kentucky
Alvin J. Wolff, Washington

1980
Silas Albert,* Michigan
John Carpenter,* Kentucky

1981
Howard C. Babcock Jr.,* Florida
Sam E. Brown,* New Mexico
Victor L. Lyon,* Washington
Roland Randall,* Pennsylvania

1982
Edward E. Branter Jr.,* Indiana
Paul Everson, Ohio
C. Larry Hoag,* California
Walter Scott,* Georgia
M. Edward Smith,* Illinois
Albert V. Vincent,* Hawaii
Florence Willess,* Texas

1983
Emmette T. Gatewood Jr., California
Lawrence E. Mabry,* Washington
J. Alton Stanford,* North Carolina

1984
Thaddeus S. Cwik, New Jersey
Thomas C. Laswell Jr.,* Kentucky
Don H. Mason, Texas

1985
Frederick R. Hunter,* Indiana
Wallace R. Woodbury, Utah

1986
Joseph B. Carnahan, California
Budd Krones,* Arizona

1987
Jamie O'Neill,* Oklahoma
Chester C. Sudbrack Jr., Ohio

1988
Roland J. Ledebuhr, Michigan
Phillip C. Stark, Wisconsin

1989
Vincent T. Aveni, Ohio
Max L. Hill Jr., South Carolina

1990
B. E. Grantham Jr.,* Mississippi
Jack I. Korenblit,* Florida

1991
Stuart A. Davis,* Missouri
Angeline A. Kopka, New Hampshire

1992
Al H. Jennings Jr., Georgia

1993
C. Dan Joyner, South Carolina

1994
Jerome Blank,* California
Owen V. Hall, Ohio
John W. Steffey Sr., Maryland

1995
Betty Kissock, Montana
David Schoepf, Kentucky

1996
David W. Bradley, Massachusetts

1997
Benjamin Blair, Kansas
Janet Scavo, Colorado

1998
Montie Box, Oklahoma
Robert Wertheimer,* Texas

1999
Leo Saunders, California
Michael Schmelzer, New York

2000
Joan Ballantyne, Iowa
William F. Overacre, Virginia

2001
Theodore A. Bryant, Colorado
Dale Colby, California

2002
Thomas Jefferson III, Virginia
Paul Scott, Michigan

2003
Virginia Cook, Texas
Alan Yassky, New York

2004
Stephen Hoover, Virginia
Ron Myles, Colorado

2005
Stephen R. Casper, Ohio
Richard J. Rosenthal, California

2006
Robert Arkley, Vermont
Joseph K. Funkhouser II, Virginia

2007
Henry Ray, Alabama
George Peek, Nevada

*Deceased.

View a current list of DSA winners at
REALTOR.org.

The Good Neighbor Award has been adopted by many state and local associations as a way to identify local heroes for nomination to the national award. And it's just one of the ways the REALTOR® organization honors REALTORS® who give back. Each REALTOR® association in the 50 states and four territories and many local associations also honor a REALTOR® of the Year for distinguished service to the organization.

DISTINGUISHED IN SERVICE

In 1979, NAR established the Distinguished Service Award to honor REALTORS® who have provided outstanding contributions and service to the real estate industry.

Rich Port of LaGrange, Illinois, 1970 NAR president, established the award. His goal was to honor the many members who served with distinction at the local, state, and national levels in organized real estate and who had the qualifications for the NAR presidency but never sought the position.

REALTORS® who receive the award have shown meritorious service for at least 25 years. They have also been recognized as local leaders whose performance and involvement in political and community activities have been extraordinary. Many have held leadership positions in the National Association and its institutes, societies, and councils, as well as in their state and local association. The Distinguished Service Award was first presented in 1979 to nine recipients. To date, 72 individuals have received the award.

CHAPTER SIX
The March of Progress

From hopeful but modest beginnings, the NATIONAL ASSOCIATION OF REALTORS® today is recognized as a world leader in the promotion of private property ownership and a champion of innovation. Today, the real estate business is a huge factor in the national economy—together, residential and commercial real estate represent more than 19 percent of the nation's gross domestic product—and NAR is the largest association representing the business. The membership is a complex stew of large companies, small businesses, and independent contractors working in a variety of specialties and an array of business models, but all attracted to the promise of succeeding in a profession that offers unlimited earning potential. NAR's ability to keep all those elements working toward common goals says a lot about the wisdom of the Association's structure—with local and state associations working together with the National Association to serve members and consumers. But the Association's strength also comes from its ability to embrace and lead through change. Starting with the push for licensing and professional standards and continuing through the sweeping technological advancements of the past 15 years, the Association has been at the forefront of many of the evolutionary—and revolutionary—changes in the business of real estate.

"In times of change, learners inherit the earth, while the learned find themselves beautifully equipped to deal with a world that no longer exists."

ERIC HOFFER, 1982 winner, Presidential Medal of Freedom

William Cruikshank's eponymous Cruikshank Company, founded in New York City in 1794, is considered the country's first real estate business. Cruikshank helped wealthy families like the Astors and Van Cortlandts move to larger homes outside the central city. Over the next 50 years, real estate practitioners emerged in areas where the choice of real estate became so complex and the turnover so intensive, said NAR historian Janet Pearl Davies, that large sellers and investors turned to "men with some specialized skill or knowledge" to help them buy and sell.[1]

In those days, there were no barriers to entry into the business, thus the inevitable cries against "sharks" and "curbstoners." A typical lure was a "free" lot in exchange for a small sum of money, perhaps $27.50 to $59.50. Unfortunately, there was a catch. The lot might be too small to accommodate a home—unless the buyer also purchased an adjoining lot at a higher price. Even if the buyer bought the adjoining lot, he might still not be able to build on it because it lacked water, sewers, light, gas, or other critical amenities.[2]

In his 1907 speech suggesting the creation of a national organization, Edward S. Judd (page 9) said the Association might address the need for a uniform system of license laws. The pros and cons of real estate licenses were hotly debated at the National Association's annual meetings beginning in 1912. Proponents of license laws put forth their value in protecting the public and honest brokers alike through the licensing process, educational exams, and a system of penalties for license violations. Those opposed to the idea believed the laws would be ineffective in excluding dishonest brokers and were simply unnecessary. "To have real estate men come out openly and demand they be licensed on these grounds is an admission of their own weakness," wrote St. Paul Real Estate Board Vice President J. J. Kenna in *The National Real Estate Journal* in early 1915, going on to suggest that peer pressure would be sufficient to keep incompetent brokers from joining the Association.

Eventually, Judd's camp won out. In 1916, NAR's Board of Directors—while holding up REALTORS® as the crème de la crème of the emerging profession—got behind the idea of at least minimum state requirements for all practitioners. License laws would offer a guarantee to legitimate real estate brokers, akin to a Good Housekeeping Seal of Approval, that they would not be subjected to "the unfair competition of the opportunist broker," according to Robert W. Semenow, author of *Questions and Answers on Real Estate* (Prentice Hall, 1978) and executive vice president of the Association of Real Estate License Law Officials from 1930 to 1977.

The first real estate license law was passed

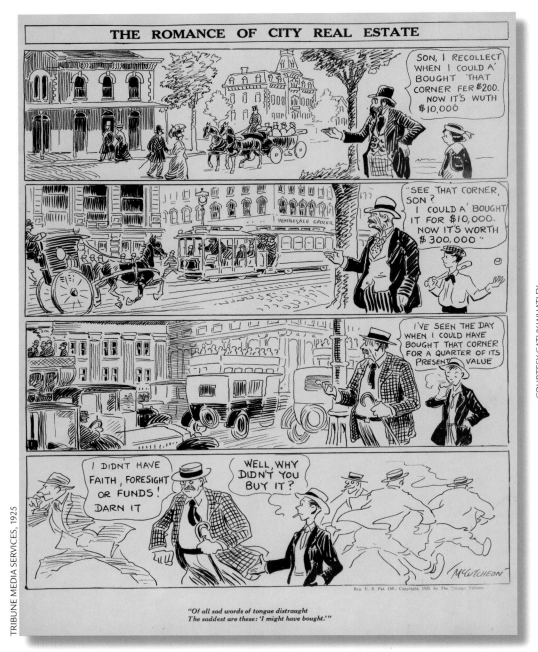

TRIBUNE MEDIA SERVICES, 1925

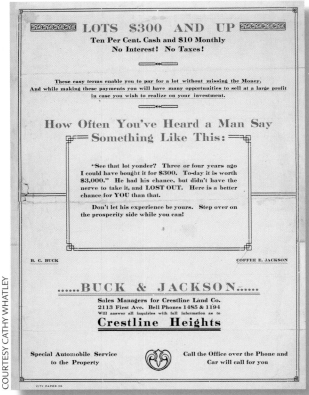

COURTESY CATHY WHATLEY

Rapid real estate appreciation enticed would-be investors in the years following NAR's founding. The need for honest, professional service was apparent, and NAR pushed for laws and industry standards that would safeguard consumers. One pioneering professional was B.C. Buck, a builder and founder of the Northeast (Florida) Builders Association. His son, James O. Buck, served as president of the Florida Association of REALTORS® in 1962, and his granddaughter, Cathy Whatley, was 2003 NAR president.

in California in 1917, but within a matter of months, the Supreme Court of California held it to be unconstitutional. A revised law, enacted in 1919, removed the prior difficulties, and in *Riley v. Chambers,* 185 P. 855 (1919), the California high court examined the law's requirement that licensees must possess certain character qualifications. The court ruled that the statute was not an invasion of personal rights and was therefore legal.

By 1922, 14 states had real estate license laws on the books. That year, the U.S. Supreme Court affirmed the validity of Tennessee's law, which had been challenged as unconstitutional under the Fourteenth Amendment. "The statute is drawn with care to details and their importance, importance to the business regulated and the persons who will desire to engage in it," declared Justice McKenna in the court's opinion.[3] Nathan William MacChesney—who as the Association's general counsel had drafted the first model law in 1913—prepared briefs and arguments that were presented before the court in *Bratton v. Chandler*.

Beyond the basic license requirements, California, Florida, and New York were the first states to require that license applicants pass a test to qualify. In Florida, the drive for minimum standards became urgent with the land boom of the early 1920s. Consumers were being lured to purchase worthless lands sight-unseen for very small down payments. The state began

requiring testing in 1924, but by 1926, land prices were dangerously inflated. The Great Miami Hurricane of that year helped bring the boom to an end, foreshadowing the Great Depression, which would hit the country three years later.

MacChesney revised his model law in 1927 after studying how the law operated in states where it had been enforced and its legality tested. In 1926, the Court of Appeals of New York decided in *Roman v. Lobe*, 243 N.Y. 51 (1926), 152 N.E. 461, that not only character qualifications but also educational qualifications were permissible. The case involved a practitio-

Photographs of REALTORS®' offices in *The National Real Estate Journal* made the connection between having an office and being a professional.

Entrance to offices of the Jemison Real Estate & Ins. Co., Birmingham, Ala.—Interior view

St. Joseph Valley Bank Building, Elkhart, and office of Realtor Kies—The only ground floor office in the new building

Interior and exterior views, offices of O. A. Vickey & Co., Los Angeles, Calif.

Exterior and interior views, offices of W. H. Shenners Co., Milwaukee

ner attempting to collect a commission for bro-kerage services, though at the time he performed them, he had let his broker's license lapse.

In 1929, Semenow and three other regula-tors—John N. Harkins, A. C. MacNulty, and A. S. Wechsler—got together to form the National Association of License Law Officials (today, the Association of Real Estate License Law Officials, www.arello.org). MacNulty was direc-tor of licenses in New York and was considered the "dean" of license law officials; Wechsler was his assistant director; and Harkins was chief examiner and investigator for the New Jersey Real Estate Commission. The group's first meet-ing was held during the NAR annual conven-tion in Toronto, and for many years after that the regulators met in conjunction with the NAR conventions. According to ARELLO history, NAR—particularly the Association's adminis-trator Lowell Baker—provided support to help the group get off the ground.

Today, all states have license laws that require prospective salespeople and brokers to pass a written exam; more than half of all states specify special education and experi-ence or some equivalent requirement to obtain a salesperson's or broker's license; and nearly every state requires real estate licensees to earn continuing education credits to maintain their real estate license.

THE GOLDEN THREAD

At the same time that the Association was advo-cating for license laws, NAR leaders were work-ing on creating higher standards for their mem-bers—the REALTORS® Code of Ethics. The code is often called the "golden thread" that ties the REALTOR® family together—a description coined in the mid-1970s by Chesley J. "Chet" Smith, then an NAR senior vice president.

William D. North, former executive vice president, called the Code the founders' "gift of vision." Others have described it as a "proud beacon," illuminating and guiding the journey to integrity and professionalism. REALTORS® and staff involved in teaching and enforcing the Code are often hailed as "keepers of the flame." Indeed, only those real estate professionals who voluntarily choose to embrace and live by the Code's principles, duties, and ideals may call themselves REALTORS®.

In May 1908, the *Chicago Tribune* editorial-ized: "The real estate dealer is no longer a mere speculator in land or buildings. His activities have increased until he is recognized among the influential forces in the community. His success is often gained by a knowledge of many mat-ters not at first counted as necessary parts of this business, [which] in recent years has attracted some of the best men in the community."[4]

The men gathered in Chicago that month for NAR's founding meeting recognized the growing importance of real estate brokerage in communities across the country—and the absence of any meaningful standards to guide its practitioners. Davies, in her 1958 book *Real Estate in American History*, recalled:

> *A code of ethics for the real estate business had been the national real estate organization's primary objec-tive. Its constitution had a mandatory provision for a committee on code of ethics. Its founders realized that one principal task must be to formulate in clear words the essentials of proper real estate business conduct. Those rules of conduct must be such that men in the business could agree upon them. They must be an expression of the group consciousness.[5]*

Edward A. Halsey, the National Association's first executive secretary, early on envisioned the concept that would become, in 1913, the Code of Ethics. Halsey, articulating things he believed the new Association needed to do, wrote: "Organize in some way that will give a rating of men who handle real estate, something similar to Dunn's and Bradstreet's, but a moral rating, not a financial rating."[6]

Frank Craven, 1911 chair of the Committee on Ethics, stated: "We cannot suggest a better starting point than the Golden Rule, 'Do unto others as ye would that others should do unto you.' " Craven also pointed out: "The real estate broker is depended upon by his client possibly more than any other [professional]. The average individual buys possibly one or two properties in a lifetime. He comes to you for information and advice."[7]

Judd was president during the 1913 convention in Winnipeg, Manitoba, and made the motion for adoption of the first Code of Ethics: "The motion is for the adoption of the rules for conduct . . . and that they be taken as the Code of Ethics of the National Association, and their adoption recommended everywhere as far as possible." Davies recalled: "A delegate rose to say, 'We have heard many important things here but nothing so important as the adoption of this resolution.'"[8]

Perhaps one of the most extraordinary aspects of the Code of Ethics is that it was developed and adopted by real estate brokers voluntarily, not driven by government forces or marketplace demands. As North noted in an August 1978 article "The REALTORS® Code of Ethics—A Gift of Vision," first published in

The first NAR Code of Ethics, the "golden thread" of the real estate profession.

BENJAMIN KENDE

The Executive Officer magazine and now part of the *Code of Ethics and Arbitration Manual*:

With the exception of a now defunct group of printers, the REALTORS® were the first business group outside the "learned professions of medicine, engineering, and law" to adopt a code of ethics. It was an uncommon event with uncommon men and women making an uncommon commitment to business integrity and fair dealing. It was not a commitment coerced by threat of government sanction but a commitment predicated on a need perceived by REALTORS® themselves. It was not a

"TO EDUCATE A MAN IN MIND AND NOT MORALS IS TO CREATE A MENACE TO SOCIETY."

Theodore Roosevelt

At the 1913 convention, where NAR passed its first Code of Ethics, the Committee on Credentials reported 595 members, 29 nonmembers, and 154 ladies in attendance.

commitment mandated by the marketplace because it involved the voluntary acceptance of liabilities and responsibilities, duties and costs, limitations and obligations, which the public did not even perceive as their due. It was, in sum, a commitment to the concept of service to the public as an article of faith in professionalism.[9]

The 1913 Code of Ethics consisted of 23 Articles, categorized as "Duties to Clients" and "Duties to Other Brokers." It obligated an Association member (who wouldn't be known as a REALTOR® until 1916) to "be absolutely honest, truthful, faithful, and efficient"; to "obtain sole agency in writing"; to "respect the listings of his brother agent, and to cooperate with him to sell"; to "advise an owner to renew a selling contract with some other agent, rather than solicit the agency"; to "always speak kindly of competitors"; to "always be loyal, square, frank, and earnest in matters that require the coopera- tion of other brokers"; to "advertise nothing but facts"; and to "give an honest opinion concern- ing a competitor's proposition when asked to do so by a prospective purchaser, even though such opinion will result in a sale by the competitor."

By the following year, the ongoing task of reviewing and refining the Code was already under way. Two categories of ethical duties became three, with a new category, "Duties

of the Broker to the Prospective Buyer," being added. The third edition, adopted in 1915, made "Suggestions to Owners and Investors" and added a "Duty to Organize."

The fourth edition of the Code, adopted in 1924, added a Preamble that included the Golden Rule. The 1924 Code also added "Suggestions to the Public," which defined the terms *client* and *customer* and incorporated Article IV from the National Association's by- laws. Article IV requires every member board to adopt the Code of Ethics; boards could now be expelled from NAR if they refused or failed

Etched in the lobby of NAR's Washington, D.C. building is the Preamble to the Code of Ethics, written in 1924. Ethical actions by REALTORS®, it reads, are "the instrumental- ity through which the land resource of the nation reaches its highest use and through which land ownership attains its widest distribution."

UNDER ALL IS THE LAND UPON ITS WISE UTILIZATION AND WIDELY ALLOCATED OWNERSHIP DEPEND THE SURVIVAL AND GROWTH OF FREE INSTITUTIONS AND OF OUR CIVILIZATION. THE REALTOR IS THE INSTRUMENTALITY THROUGH WHICH THE LAND RESOURCE OF THE NATION REACHES ITS HIGHEST USE AND THROUGH WHICH LAND OWNERSHIP ATTAINS ITS WIDEST DISTRIBUTION. ✷ HE IS A CREATOR OF HOMES, A BUILDER OF CITIES, A DEVELOPER OF INDUSTRIES AND PRODUCTIVE FARMS. SUCH FUNCTIONS IMPOSE OBLIGATIONS BEYOND THOSE OF ORDINARY COMMERCE. ✷ THEY IMPOSE GRAVE SOCIAL RESPONSIBILITY AND A PATRIOTIC DUTY TO WHICH THE REALTOR SHOULD DEDICATE HIMSELF, AND FOR WHICH HE SHOULD BE DILIGENT IN PREPARING HIMSELF. THE REALTOR, THEREFORE, IS ZEALOUS TO MAINTAIN AND IMPROVE THE STANDARDS OF HIS CALLING AND SHARES WITH HIS FELLOW REALTORS A COMMON RESPONSIBILITY FOR ITS INTEGRITY AND HONOR. ✷ IN THE INTERPRETATION OF HIS OBLIGATIONS, HE CAN TAKE NO SAFER GUIDE THAN THAT WHICH HAS BEEN HANDED DOWN THROUGH TWENTY CENTURIES, EMBODIED IN THE GOLDEN RULE: "WHATSOEVER YE WOULD THAT MEN SHOULD DO TO YOU, DO YE EVEN SO TO THEM."

ALLEN SLEDGE

An American Institute of Real Estate Appraisers class meeting in Chicago in 1936. Education was key to the professionalization of real estate.

CAPES PHOTO CHIC.

to enforce the Code with respect to the business activities of their members. The 1924 revision, however, also introduced an Article about the impact of race and ethnicity on property values; that provision was part of the Code for more than 25 years and served as tinder in the early years of the civil rights movement. (See Chapter 4, "Evolving Conscience," page 107, to learn about the struggle for equal opportunity.)

All told, the Code has been amended 31 times. REALTORS® serving on the Professional Standards Committee have labored long and hard to ensure that the Code is a living document that protects the sellers, buyers, landlords, tenants,

and others who place their trust in REALTORS®; that the Code's obligations are phrased in clear, objective, and unambiguous terms; and that the Code remains relevant and meaningful in the constantly changing real estate environment. In 1972, NAR leaders undertook an effort to ensure that REALTORS® would better understand how to model their conduct around the Code. Don Treadwell of Southgate, Michigan—who would go on to serve as NAR president in 1984— chaired a subcommittee that began the process of developing a series of explanatory Standards of Practice. Walter Scott of Decatur, Georgia, chaired the 1973 subcommittee that drafted the first 21 Standards of Practice. By 2007, there were 80 Standards of Practice in place.

In the early 1990s, NAR leaders responded to the perception of some members that the Code of Ethics was relevant only to the residential brokerage activities of REALTORS®. A study group, chaired by Bill Overacre of Lynchburg, Virginia, included representatives of each of the Association's affiliated institutes, societies, and councils, as well as REALTORS® with expertise in appraising, auctioneering, counseling, property management, syndication, and other real estate disciplines. The study group concluded that although the fundamental principles of the Code were applicable to all REALTORS® regardless of their areas of practice or expertise, the scope of the Code needed to expand to make it unmistakably clear that the activities of REALTORS® "in all fields of concentration or expertise" are governed by the Code of Ethics. The group's recommendations led to a drastically changed Code for 1995. The revisions also reintroduced the concept of "categories" of ethical duties— "Duties to Clients and Customers," "Duties to the Public," and "Duties to REALTORS®"—that had been part of the original 1913 Code.

In addition to the Standards of Practice, NAR's Professional Standards Committee has written 136 official case interpretations. Each of the case interpretations posits a set of real estate–related facts and then applies the relevant Articles and Standards of Practice to those facts to demonstrate appropriately ethical conduct or, alternatively, to show how the respondent failed to meet the Code's obligations. The Standards of Practice and the official case interpretations serve two purposes:

1. They help show REALTORS® and consumers exactly what conduct is required or prohibited by the respective Articles.

2. They provide guidance to hearing panels considering alleged violations.

HEADLINES

REAL ESTATE'S NEWS LETTER   **FOR TODAY AND TOMORROW**

| Vol. 16 • No. 29   July 18, 1949

PUBLISHED WEEKLY BY THE NATIONAL ASSOCIATION OF REAL ESTATE BOARDS
22 West Monroe Street, Chicago 3, Ill.   1737 K Street, N.W., Washington 6, D.C.

MEET THE TYPICAL REALTOR

Age 51   98% of Realtors are men

Married   41% of Realtors are veterans

Two children   26% served in World War I

One grandchild   17% served in World War II

Has "one man" office   2% served in both Wars

Employs two salesmen   ¼ of 1% served in Spanish American War

Has two other employees   61% of Realtors have college education

Earned $10,000 in 1948   19% have college degrees

     4% have graduate degrees

Rates establishment of ethical practice as most helpful activity of a real estate board   94% of Realtors are general brokers

     65% engage in insurance business

Rates state convention as most helpful activity of a state association   47% engage in property management

     46% engage in real estate appraisal

Wants to help NAREB in its fight against socialized housing   38% engage in real estate financing

     27% are farm brokers

Will support a national drive for more home ownership   23% are industrial property brokers

Believes NAREB should work closely with Labor on matters relating to building and federal legislation   43% of Realtors are in cities of over 100,000 population

     41% are in cities of 10,000 to 100,000 population

Favors an expanded public relations program so that more Americans may learn the dangers of socialized housing   16% are in cities of less than 10,000 population

Source: NAREB Survey in which more than 4,000 Realtors were polled.

Copyright 1949 by the National Association of Real Estate Boards, 22 W. Monroe St., Chicago, Ill. T. H. Maenner, president; H. Walter Graves, treasurer; Herbert U. Nelson, executive vice president. Subscription $10 per year—20c per issue. Entered as second class matter July 6, 1942, at the post office at Chicago, Ill., under the Act of March 3, 1879.

The profile of a typical REALTOR® in 1949.

In addition to keeping the Code vital and relevant, the Professional Standards Committee has two other charges: developing education for REALTORS® and developing enforcement procedures for local associations. To further the dual missions, 1997 NAR President Russ Booth of Midvale, Utah, and 1998 NAR President Layne Morrill of Kimberling, Missouri, appointed a Presidential Advisory Group on Code of Ethics Enforcement. The group was given the following charges:

- To determine whether the Code was being enforced vigorously and fairly
- To overcome obstacles to enforcement and to address real or perceived reluctance of local associations to receive and act on ethics complaints
- To ensure that the roles, rights, and responsibilities of associations engaged in Code enforcement activities were clearly and consistently articulated, communicated, managed, and understood
- To ensure that all member constituencies were cognizant of the fundamental principles of business ethics and conduct

The Presidential Advisory Group, chaired by Steve Hoover of Roanoke, Virginia, developed 16 recommendations, addressing such issues as public service, ethics awareness and education, and enforcement. The group's recommendations were discussed and debated nationwide before being adopted by the NAR Board of Directors. Perhaps the most remarkable change was a massive education initiative: Since 2000, every applicant for REALTOR® membership has been required to complete comprehensive Code of Ethics training as a condition of gaining membership. The companion "quadrennial ethics training" requires every REALTOR® to complete additional Code of Ethics training every four years.

Every local and state association of REALTORS® is required to adopt and enforce the Code. To ensure that the Code is enforced consistently, uniformly, and fairly from association to association nationwide, NAR adopted procedural policies, which are codified in the *Code of Ethics and Arbitration Manual*. Those procedures are critical to ensuring that both complainants and respondents are afforded due process at each step of the way. As North pointed out in his 1978 article:

There is no idea which cannot be misapplied; no faith which cannot be exploited; no concept which cannot be abused; and no principle which cannot be perverted. For this reason, the integrity of the Code and the value of its vision of the real estate industry depend ultimately upon its use.

If it is applied inconsistently, it becomes arbitrary and hence oppressive. If it is applied without understanding, it becomes unreasonable and hence dogmatic. If it is used in ignorance, it becomes meaningless; if it is used inappropriately, it becomes irrelevant; and if it is used without moderation, it becomes irrational.[10]

There is no question that the Code of Ethics has served the REALTOR® family and the real estate buying and selling public well for nearly a century, reminding REALTORS® that real estate is not just a service business; it is first and foremost a reputation business. Reputation requires honesty, loyalty, competency, cooperation, and compassion. It's REALTORS® putting their clients' and customers' interests ahead of their own. It's fair play and sharing experiences and expertise. It's keeping promises of professionalism and performance. It's a journey, not a destination. It's what being a REALTOR® is all about.

A MANDATE TO EDUCATE

Development of the Code of Ethics and licensing were important steps in turning a fledgling vocation into a profession. NAR also worked to elevate the profession through continuing education. Over the years, more than a dozen real estate organizations have spun off from the Association, many founded with the primary goal of providing specialty education to REALTORS®.

The National Real Estate Journal, launched in March 1910, provided members with verbatim accounts of convention proceedings and began the national discussion of industry best practices. *Headlines,* edited for many years by the Association's executive vice president, started as a weekly typed newsletter, similar in format to today's e-newsletters. In 1937, the Association introduced the pocket-sized *Freehold* magazine as a direct forum between members and NAR leaders. Many years later, NAR purchased the peer-reviewed *Real Estate Today* magazine from its affiliate, the National Institute of Real Estate Brokers. In 1996, that magazine merged with the twice-monthly *REALTOR®* News (successor to *Headlines*) to create *Today's REALTOR®* magazine and a sister Web site. "Today's" was dropped from the name three years later.

REALTOR® Magazine and its Web site operate as "the business tool for real estate professionals," while REALTOR.org serves as the official voice of the Association. Since its launch in 1997, however, REALTOR.org (briefly known as OneRealtorPlace) has also become a robust educational tool where members can access an online bookstore, a virtual library, and the Internet-based REALTOR® University.

Still, NAR's annual convention remains the premier learning opportunity for Association members. It has been held every year since 1908, with one exception: A wartime conflict forced its cancellation in 1944.

NAR journals, newsletters, newspapers, and magazines throughout the century.

Official records of NAR convention attendance go back to 1952; about 2,600 people attended that gathering in Miami Beach, Florida. Today, more than 20,000 people gather each year for the REALTORS® Conference & Expo. They're there to do the governance work of the Association, as well as to learn, network, and buy products on the trade exposition floor, which today exceeds 160,000 square feet. *Tradeshow Week* ranked it as one of the 200 largest trade shows in the country in 2005.

The conference is a far cry from the early convention days when a few hundred men would meet to hash out the business of the Association. In those days, delegations from various real estate boards would charter train cars to travel to the meetings—"each stop of the train added to the contingent of men," according to Jeffrey Hornstein, author of *A Nation of REALTORS®* (Duke University Press, 2005).[11] At the convention city, there would be opening pageants, local dignitaries, speech-making contests, and city tours. Member boards competed to host the events, Hornstein wrote, and attendees would be encouraged to prolong their visit to enjoy the host city.[12] Although much has changed about the business of real estate, the revelry of the conventions remains.

Over the years, San Francisco has hosted more NAR conventions than any other city— 11, beginning in 1922. Runners-up are Chicago and New Orleans, each with eight.

For many years, the Association also held governance meetings each spring at Chicago's Drake Hotel. Today, the Association's spring meetings are held in Washington, D.C., where REALTORS® can visit Capitol Hill and talk policy with their representatives in Congress.

The 2004 REALTORS®
Conference & Expo in Orlando, Florida.

Today, more than 20,000 people attend the REALTORS® Conference & Expo each year. Most go for the tremendous educational opportunities. Here, REALTORS® peruse the conference bookstore and get hands-on training in the Technology Learning Center.

NAR Convention Cities (1908—2007)

1908	Chicago	1923	Cleveland
1909	Detroit	1924	Washington, D.C.
1910	Minneapolis	1925	Detroit
1911	Denver	1926	Tulsa, Oklahoma
1912	Louisville, Kentucky	1927	Seattle
1913	Winnipeg, Manitoba	1928	Louisville, Kentucky
1914	Pittsburgh	1929	Boston
1915	Los Angeles	1930	Toronto
1916	New Orleans	1931	Baltimore
1917	Milwaukee	1932	Cincinnati
1918	St. Louis	1933	Chicago (held during the Chicago World's Fair, "A Century of Progress")
1919	Atlantic City, New Jersey		
1920	Kansas City, Missouri	1934	Minneapolis
1921	Chicago	1935	Atlantic City, New Jersey
1922	San Francisco	1936	New Orleans

1937	Pittsburgh	**1955**	New York
1938	Milwaukee	**1956**	St. Louis
1939	Los Angeles	**1957**	Chicago
1940	Philadelphia	**1958**	San Francisco
1941	Detroit	**1959**	Toronto
1942	St. Louis	**1960**	Dallas
1943	Cleveland	**1961**	Miami Beach, Florida
1944	*Canceled due to wartime conflict*	**1962**	Detroit
1945	French Lick, Indiana	**1963**	New York
1946	Atlantic City, New Jersey	**1964**	Los Angeles
1947	San Francisco	**1965**	Chicago
1948	New York	**1966**	Miami Beach, Florida
1949	Chicago	**1967**	Washington, D.C.
1950	Miami Beach, Florida	**1968**	New York
1951	Cincinnati	**1969**	San Francisco
1952	Miami Beach, Florida	**1970**	Chicago
1953	Los Angeles	**1971**	Miami Beach, Florida
1954	Cleveland	**1972**	Honolulu

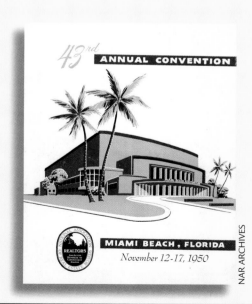

1973	Washington, D.C.	1990	New Orleans
1974	Las Vegas	1991	Las Vegas
1975	San Francisco	1992	Honolulu
1976	Houston	1993	Miami
1977	Miami Beach, Florida	1994	Anaheim, California
1978	Honolulu	1995	Atlanta
1979	New Orleans	1996	San Francisco
1980	Anaheim, California	1997	New Orleans
1981	Miami Beach, Florida	1998	Anaheim, California
1982	San Francisco	1999	Orlando, Florida
1983	Las Vegas (NAR's Diamond Jubilee, 75th Anniversary)	2000	San Francisco
		2001	Chicago
1984	Honolulu	2002	New Orleans
1985	New Orleans	2003	San Francisco
1986	New York	2004	Orlando, Florida
1987	Honolulu	2005	San Francisco
1988	San Francisco	2006	New Orleans
1989	Dallas	2007	Las Vegas

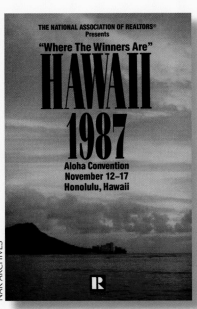

The Association Branches Out

Over the past century, NAR members have helped develop the methods and practices for a wide variety of specialties. In the process, REALTORS® have directly or indirectly launched more than a dozen real estate specialty organizations. Some today exist as affiliates or divisions of NAR. Others operate as independent organizations. REALTOR® family designations, earned through a course of specialty education, appear in italic type under the organization name.*

The Affiliates and Divisions of NAR

CCIM Institute *Certified Commercial Investment Member*	The CALIFORNIA ASSOCIATION OF REALTORS® established the first commercial designation, the Certified Property Exchanger, in 1954. Thirteen years later, in 1967, the CPE designation came under the administration of an NAR division, and in 1969 it was renamed CCIM (Certified Commercial Investment Member). It operated for several years as the Commercial Investment Real Estate Institute, part of the REALTORS® National Marketing Institute. The CCIM Institute was established in 1991. 
CIPS Network *Certified International Property Specialist*	The concept of the international REALTOR® member evolved over time, culminating in the launch of the CIPS Network in 1998. For the half century before, NAR had been involved in international real estate, first through the U.S. chapter of FIABCI, the international real estate organization headquartered in France, and later through its own International Policy Committee and later an International Section. In 2001, NAR was one of 23 national associations to found the **International Consortium of Real Estate Associations** (see page 262). 
Council of Real Estate Brokerage Managers *Certified Real Estate Brokerage Manager*	The Broker's Division of NAR was founded in 1923 and became the National Institute of Real Estate Brokers in 1942. In 1975, NIREB changed its name to the REALTORS® National Marketing Institute, and in 1984 RNMI decentralized into three councils—one for managers, one for commercial-investment specialists, and one for residential sales specialists. One year later, the Manager's Council was renamed the Real Estate Brokerage Managers Council. RNMI was dissolved in 2001, and in 2002, the name was changed to the Council of Real Estate Brokerage Managers. COUNCIL OF REAL ESTATE **BROKERAGE MANAGERS**
Council of Residential Specialists *Certified Residential Specialist*	Founded in 1976 as a council of the REALTORS® National Marketing Institute, the Council of Residential Specialists introduced the designation in 1977 and began operating autonomously in 2001 when RNMI was dissolved. 

*Note: In addition to the designations listed here, the Graduate, REALTOR Institute (GRI) designation is offered through state REALTOR® associations. And NAR offers specialty education leading to five certifications: At Home With Diversity, e-PRO, Real Estate Professional Assistant, Resort and Second Home Markets, and Transnational Referral.

CRE	**Counselors of Real Estate** *Counselor of Real Estate*	NAR members organized the Society of Real Estate Counselors a "by invitation only" group of high-level advisers, in 1953. Three years later, the name was changed to the American Society of Real Estate Counselors. The current name was adopted in 1996.
IREM	**Institute of Real Estate Management** *Certified Property Manager* *Accredited Commercial Manager* *Accredited Residential Manager* *Accredited Management Organization*	NAR organized a Property Management Division in 1923 for managers of nonoffice properties. (Office property managers were already represented by the independent Building Managers Association.) In 1933, the division became the Institute of Real Estate Management. The institute, by now open to managers of all property types, opened its first international chapter in Poland in 1998.
REBAC	**Real Estate Buyer's Agent Council** *Accredited Buyer's Representative* *Accredited Buyer's Representative Manager* *Seniors Real Estate Specialist*	In 1988, REBAC was founded as an independent entity by Barry Miller of Denver. It was purchased by the North American Consulting Group in 1990 and by NAR in 1996, becoming a wholly owned subsidiary. In 2007, REBAC began offering a designation for senior specialists. The Seniors Real Estate Specialist was developed 10 years earlier by California broker Tim Corliss.
REALTORS® LAND INSTITUTE	**REALTORS® Land Institute** *Accredited Land Consultant*	In 1920, NAR formed a Farm Land Committee, which in 1923 became the Farm Lands Division and in 1944 the Institute of Farm Brokers. The name was changed to the National Institute of Farm Brokers in 1953 and the National Institute of Farm and Land Brokers in 1963. Two more name changes followed: Farm and Land Institute in 1975 and REALTORS® Land Institute in 1986.
SIOR	**Society of Industrial and Office REALTORS®** *Society of Industrial and Office REALTORS® (granted in one of six specialty categories)*	NAR formed an Industrial Property Division in 1923. In 1941, it became the Society of Industrial REALTORS®, and in 1986, it changed its name to the Society of Industrial and Office REALTORS®.
Women's Council of REALTORS®	**Women's Council of REALTORS®** *Performance Management Network*	The council was founded at a meeting at NAR's convention in Milwaukee in 1938. In 1984, WCR established the Leadership Training Graduate designation. Later, in 1989, it established a Referral & Relocation certification, incorporated in 1994 into the LTG program. In 2003 WCR launched the Performance Management Network designation (see page 138.)

Independent Organizations

Appraisal Institute	In 1922, NAR formed an Appraisal Division, which in 1932 became the American Institute of Real Estate Appraisers. In 1991, AIREA broke off from NAR, merging with the independent Society of Real Estate Appraisers to become the Appraisal Institute. Subsequently, NAR formed its own appraisal competency, developing designations for general and residential appraisers.
Association of Real Estate License Law Officials	The National Association of License Law Officials held its first meeting in 1930 in conjunction with the NAR annual convention. The organization changed its name to the National Association of Real Estate License Law Officials in 1965 and the Association of Real Estate License Law Officials in 1993.
Worldwide ERC	1963 NAR President Daniel Sheehan Sr. formed an Employee Relocation Real Estate Advisory Committee, inviting representatives of corporations that transferred employees between cities. In November 1963, the Executive Committee recommended the formation of the Corporate Personnel Transfer Real Estate Advisor.
National Association of Home Builders	The Home Builders and Subdividers Division of NAR was established in 1925 and became the Land Developers and Home Builders Division in 1933. In 1942, division members merged with another builders organization, forming the independent National Association of Home Builders.
National Real Estate Fliers Association	In 1969, this association considered an affiliation with NAR; in 1977, it was merged into the Farm and Land Institute (today the REALTORS® Land Institute) as a specialty chapter.
Real Estate Securities and Syndications Institute	This specialty organization started as a committee of NAR and in 1973 was established as a separate institute. In 1975, RESSI was considered for council status within the REALTORS® National Marketing Institute, but the proposal was rejected. In 1990, four years after the Tax Reform Act of 1986 drove a stake in the syndication business, RESSI members voted to disaffiliate from NAR.
Urban Land Institute	NAR leaders established the National Real Estate Foundation in 1936 to undertake a study of urban real estate issues. In December 1939, the founders proposed a name change to Urban Land Institute. The name change was adopted in 1940, the same year ULI became an independent organization.

LEARNING TO SHARE

As the Association was growing in size and complexity, the listing exchanges that were the foundation of organized real estate were also growing up and gaining wider acceptance as a tool for cooperation among brokers.

These exchanges would become known as multiple listing bureaus and multiple listing services, or MLS. Over the years, the MLS has been called a win-win system, a legal road map for cooperation, an invasion of personal liberty, and protectionist. From a twenty-first-century perspective, it's hard to deny that the MLS—a system that enables real estate practitioners in a defined market area to share information about properties listed for sale and offer compensation to cooperating brokers—is one of the Association's most important contributions to organized real estate.

NAR's 1998 president, Layne Morrill of Kimberling, Missouri, remembering a time before formal MLS systems, called the MLS "one of the most fantastic systems developed. It's given us the ability to work together for a common goal and good."[13]

A cooperative selling system was a natural outgrowth of twentieth-century technological development. Early in the century, new modes of transportation were expanding the possibilities for real estate buyers—and adding complexity to the business of brokering sales. Train travel had already made it possible for people to live apart from where they worked. Soon the automobile would expand the picture even further. Working alone, a real estate practitioner couldn't possibly develop a detailed picture of the entire market.

Sharing listings in the days before NAR's founding typically meant an in-person gathering. At those gatherings, known as exchanges, practitioners would share information written on paper or cards. The first known real estate exchange opened at 111 Broadway in New York City in 1847. The effort was short-lived, but by the 1880s, exchanges operated in a dozen or so cities. Those organized exchanges were the forerunners of today's local associations of REALTORS®.

Exactly when and where the first MLS was founded is a matter of debate. Many sources credit the San Diego real estate exchange, which established a system in 1887, followed by exchanges in Cincinnati and Cleveland in 1892.[14] In a December 20, 1926, letter to NAR Executive Secretary Herbert U. Nelson, William A. Keadin said he originated the system in Cincinnati in 1907 and also coined the term. "I conceived the idea of establishing more friendly and honorable methods in the business between brokers by interchanging their listings through a central bureau, or clearinghouse, thereby creating more confidence between owners, agents, as well as the courts, and assuring owners under exclusive contracts the concerted action of the members of the bureau."

Keadin's mention of exclusive contracts is worth noting. Before the formation of the National Association, owners usually listed their property for sale on an open, or nonexclusive, basis with several brokers to gain the widest sales representation and highest price. Inevitably, there were times when several brokers showed a property to the same customer, and controversies arose about who was owed a commission. One of the first advances the Association made to the business of real estate was the exclusive listing contract. Having one practitioner hold an exclusive listing for a specified period of time protected owners—they no longer risked having to pay multiple commissions—and emphasized the need for cooperation.

By the early 1920s, practitioners in large cities such as Atlanta, Chicago, Philadelphia,

TELEPHONE CALEDONIA 0074

MANAGEMENT
SELLING
LEASING
APPRAISING
MORTGAGES

WM. A. KEADIN
REAL ESTATE
210 FIFTH AVENUE
BETWEEN 25TH AND 26TH STREETS
NEW YORK CITY

December 20th, 1926.

Mr. Herbert U. Nelson, Executive Secretary,
National Association of Real Estate Boards,
310 South Michigan Avenue,
Chicago, Ills.

Dear Sir:-

I was very gratified to read an article in the New York Times of Sunday, December 19th, by Mr. Frank H. Tyler, Chairman of the Board of Governors of the Multiple Listing Bureau, Brooklyn, N.Y., which stated that 235 cities are now using that system, as reported by your Association.

I wish to state that I had the honor of originating that system and of inaugurating the system in Cincinnati, Ohio, in October 1907, and that at the time the system proved quite a success in Cincinnati and from newspaper reports in many other cities throughout the United States, but never dreamed of the system being adopted so universally.

It was on my entering the real estate business in 1907, when the business was not looked upon very favorably for a beginning in life for an ambitious young man, and the brokers and agents were inclined to play fast and loose with prices, terms, commissions, etc., often among the more reputable offices, while the courts looked upon a real estate commission case with prejudice, that I conceived the idea of establishing more friendly and honorable methods in the business between brokers by interchanging their listings through a central bureau, or clearing house, thereby creating more confidence between owners, agents, as well as the courts, and assuring owners under exclusive contracts the concerted action of the members of the bureau..

I trust that you will keep up the good work of increasing the number of Real Estate Boards using the system until the business is put on the high plane that we hold our bankers.

With kindest regards and best wishes for continued success, I beg to remain

Yours very truly,

W. A. Keadin

NAR ARCHIVES

Irving B. Hiett, 1921 NAR President, appointed the first Multiple Listing Committee.

and San Francisco depended on the MLS. Irving B. Hiett of Toledo, Ohio, 1921 Association president, appointed the first Multiple Listing Committee, and in 1922, R. Emmett Morse of Houston copyrighted the *Manual of Multiple Listings*, which he sold for $1 each. It encouraged boards to operate MLSs and provided guidelines for participating REALTORS®. Keadin told Nelson that when he created the concept, he "never dreamed of the system being adopted so universally."

In fact, the MLS was far from universal at that time. Some found it objectionable. In July 1921, the Association convened a meeting of the REALTOR® secretaries (local board administrators, today typically known as executive officers). Nelson, at the time executive secretary of the Minneapolis Board, said, "We put in the multiple listing system and operated it for two years. . . . We gave it up." He said that the system came with "a lot of red tape" and that members tended to withhold "all the real bargains" that came along.[15]

A 1928 article by Jack Knabb, executive secretary of the Real Estate Board of Rochester, New York, said many brokers withheld information from the MLS to protect their clients' privacy. "They have clients that . . . would not disclose for the world that they want to sell their property. Consequently, multiple listing is a liability in their opinion. . . . There are other brokers who take the stand that multiple listing interferes with their personal liberty. They abhor any 'outside' control of their methods and habits."[16]

Another disadvantage was that files were cluttered with dead listings because of the failure of brokers to inspect properties and insist on salable prices, according to an article by L. L. Oreland of Madison, Wisconsin, in 1924.

Despite such objections, the idea of having a single clearinghouse for listings gained ground both with real estate professionals and

with buyers. There were good reasons. H. Jackson Pontius, NAR executive vice president from 1970 to 1978, wrote that the MLS saved buyers from having to visit every broker in town to see listings. It also enabled buyers to share their personal financial information with only one real estate practitioner. The MLS served sellers, Pontius said, by enabling them to work with just one broker, "who is specifically obligated to conscientiously devote adequate time and attention to the sale of the property."[17]

Early listing directories established important guidelines. According to a 1910 article in *The National Real Estate Journal*, exclusive agency contracts were for a minimum of three months. Listings were also to be published in a bulletin issued by the exchange weekly or semimonthly and mailed to all members of the exchange.[18]

Knabb—in the same article in which he voiced concerns—said that the public benefited from MLS listings and that the system made it easier for practitioners to exchange information. He said the MLS set in motion the greatest sales force with the least effort of any system or method that had been used in real estate until then. John A. Westrom, a REALTOR® from the Los Angeles area, wrote of the MLS: "In place of chaos, a wonderful feeling of comradeship and trust has developed among our members."[19]

In 1927, Association leaders established a Multiple Listing Section and scheduled an MLS conference for the Seattle convention that year. On December 7, 1929, the first Multiple Listing Bureau was formed in Jamaica, New York, according to a telegram that Grace E. Hamilton wired to NAR's Nelson.

Although Hiett had appointed a Multiple Listing Committee in 1921, it wasn't until 1956 that the Association appointed an offi-

When You Plan Selling or Buying *Start*

ON THE RIGHT FOOT FOR IMMEDIATE RESULTS

BY CALLING A MEMBER OF

THE MULTIPLE LISTING BUREAU

Over 700 Salesmen Working for the Price of One

What is THE MULTIPLE LISTING BUREAU?

The Multiple Listing Bureau is an organization composed of 118 real estate brokers. All are members of the Real Estate Board of Baltimore. These members cooperate with one another in the listing and selling of real estate. Although the owner only lists his property with one broker, he receives the combined efforts of over 700 salesmen in the sale of his home. When the home is sold, only one commission is paid for this concentrated and effective service.

THE MULTIPLE LISTING BUREAU

BALTIMORE, MARYLAND

Multiple Listing

PROGRESS REPORTS ON EVER-EXPANDING BOARD COOPERATIVE SYSTEMS

Members of the multiple listing division of the San Bernardino Real Estate board pose before a bus which they now charter to make their weekly tour of residential properties. Use of the bus, according to Chairman John Swing, provides better service to sellers as well as members of the division.

Multiple Service Used By Speculative Builder As Sales Outlet For New Homes

Members of the Martinez multiple listing association recently extended cooperation of their services to local speculative builder Crawford Builders of Martinez, the first in the area to take advantage of this invitation.

Good Luck.. MR. CRAWFORD!
WE REALTORS WANT
ALHAMBRA OAKS
TO BE A
SUCCESS

Martinez needs reasonably priced homes on terms that fit the family pocketbook.

New homes means the making of new community. As the areas and envelopes of much of the usable land around us now are the bigger of a bar to our growth. Your success will be ours.

AGAIN WE SAY . . . GOOD LUCK!

● WE APPRECIATE YOUR MULTIPLE LISTING

Martinez REALTORS, like most California REALTORS, believe in MULTIPLE LISTING. We feel that it is the easiest and most successful way to sell real estate. MULTIPLE LISTING helps everyone! It means every REALTOR in Martinez a booster for the home property owner but REALTOR has the right to sell a MULTIPLE LISTING under COOPERATION.

In permitting the REALTORS of Martinez to show and sell your new homes in Alhambra Oaks you demonstrate your faith in the benefits of multiple listing.

DAVE FOSTER, Realtor'   CAPPY RICKS, Realtor'
M. F. JEPPSEN, Realtor'   RAY TAYLOR, Realtor'
ERNEST MARCHI, Realtor'   RICHARD R. WELLS, Realtor'

REALTOR is a copyrighted term which can be used only by a real estate broker who is a member in good standing of a local real estate board which is affiliated with the National Association of Real Estate Boards and subscribes to the Code of Ethics adopted by the national board.

This is perhaps the first time that a speculative builder has used a multiple listing service as a sales organization for a selling outlet of homes erected in a tract.

Members of the Martinez Realty Board

and Multiple Listing Service sponsored promotional ads in which they lauded the builder for investing in their community. These advertisements, published in the Martinez Gazette, expressed appreciation for the construction of reasonably priced homes on terms that fit the average pocketbook. The public relations program served a dual purpose as principles of the multiple listing organization and the term "Realtor" were explained to the public. The ad also attracted the attention of prospective buyers.

Members of the Board who paid for the three-column, eight-inch ads, one of which is reproduced herewith, were listed as sponsors.

NATIONAL CITY-CHULA VISTA CELEBRATES FIRST BIRTHDAY

At the party given by the National City-Chula Vista board in February to celebrate the first birthday of its Multiple Listing Service, it was announced that sales totaling nearly $2,000,000 had been made during the first year of operation. This multiple group is one of many throughout the state which provides a bus (a city bus in this instance) to take its members on a weekly inspection tour of properties listed with the service the preceding week. But a unique feature of the National City-Chula Vista Thursday morning tours are the well attended coffee and donut get-togethers held each week at the office of some member.

INGLEWOOD REPORTS RESULTS

The Inglewood board's "cut" on multiple listing sales made during 1949 was $8600, according to Chairman Lee Madden.

AWARD MADE TO SOUTHWEST BRANCH

Southwest Branch of the Los Angeles Realty Board and LeRoy R. Egbert, one of its past chairmen, received unusual recognition at the recent Directors' Meeting of California Real Estate Association at Berkeley.

The recognition was in the form of special plaques, presented by the Oakland Real Estate Board to the Southwest Branch and to Egbert, for the help given to the Oakland Board by the Branch and Egbert at the time the Oakland group was organizing its Multiple Listing program.

When the Oakland Board decided to incorporate multiple listing it called upon the Southwest Branch for advice and help. At that time LeRoy R. Egbert, who was then Secretary of the Branch, made a special trip to the Oakland Board to talk to its members about the advantages of such a system and to assist the office personnel in the preparation of special forms, etc.

Because of the immediate success of Multiple Listing in Oakland as outlined to it by the Southwest Branch, members of the Oakland Group desired to express their appreciation and did so at the recent meeting in Berkeley by the presentation to the Board and to Egbert of the specially engraved plaques.

MULTIPLE LISTING SALES

	February, 1950			February, 1949		
	Sale Volume	Dollar Volume	Pct. Co-op Sales	Sales Volume	Dollar Volume	Pct. Co-op Sales
Berkeley Mart	63	$ 732,950	49.2%	30	$ 527,750	62.5%
E. Los Angeles—Montebello	66	545,625	55.0	34	282,406	56.0
Glendale	78	1,032,050	37.2	43	575,500	50.0
Long Beach	101	994,511	36.6	60	618,570	50.0
O. K. Multiple (North Hollywood)	144	1,600,927	55.0	70	828,125	49.0
San Bernardino	31	194,508	61.0	30	264,200	63.0
San Jose	89	918,849	67.2	51	434,325	67.0
Southwest Branch	117	1,052,097	46.6	97	824,497	31.1
United Multiple—(Venice)	37	368,175	49.0	29	343,250	51.0

CALIFORNIA REAL ESTATE MAGAZINE, APRIL, 1950   15

cial Committee on Multiple Listing Policy. Its main directives were to discourage high fees, allow all REALTORS® to participate, encourage cooperation with nonparticipants, and gather records for historical and statistical purposes.[20]

Despite the growing acceptance of the MLS during the 1950s—and even into the 1960s—many practitioners still relied on the old method of sharing information. The Association conducted MLS surveys in 1966 and 1970 that showed about half the local associations were operating an MLS. The surveys gave MLSs crucial benchmarking data, such as how listings were taken, updated, and dissemi-

A 1950 article touted the growth of multiple listing services in California. Meanwhile, local associations set about educating consumers on the benefits of working with a multiple listing service member.

From Hats to Houses

One practitioner who saw the evolution of the MLS from a simple cooperative to sophisticated, Web-based systems is Ebby Halliday, chairman of Ebby Halliday, REALTORS® in Dallas.

Halliday, 96, started her company in 1945, building it into one of the largest independent real estate companies in the country. Along the way, she attained iconic status, earning the title "First Lady of Real Estate." She also helped pave the way for the women in the ranks of the NATIONAL ASSOCIATION OF REALTORS® leadership.

Halliday was born in Arkansas and grew up on a wheat farm in Abilene, Kansas. Her father died when she was young, and she worked throughout high school in a department store to help support her family.

After graduating in 1929, she struck out on her own, relocating first to Kansas City, where she applied at a local department store. "The store wasn't hiring. Remember, this was the Depression. Banks were closing, and fellows were jumping from windows on Wall Street," Halliday said in a September 2006 conversation, "but I had good experience and a lot of enthusiasm. They sent me to the leased women's millinery department in the basement. My mission was to sell hats."

She stayed there four years and then transferred to a store in Omaha, Nebraska. In 1938, she moved to Dallas, where she managed the hat department in the old W.A. Green store. After parlaying $1,000 of her savings into $12,000—thanks to her dentist's advice to buy cotton futures—she opened her own hat boutique.

Before long, Halliday was approached by the husband of a customer. He asked her to sell his experimental cement houses, which he said would revolutionize housing. "He said, 'If you can sell my wife all those crazy hats, maybe you can sell houses, too,'" Halliday recalled later.

Ebby Halliday in 1997.

REALTOR® MAGAZINE

Indeed, the millinery business had served as a good training ground for real estate sales. "I learned that customers are always right—whether they are or aren't."

To attract buyers, she decorated one of the houses—a forerunner of today's model homes. Within nine months, she had sold 52 two- and three-bedroom houses for between $7,000 and $9,000 each. GIs returning from World War II were among her earliest customers.

In 1945, Halliday officially traded her hat inventory for houses and opened Ebby Halliday, REALTORS® in Dallas. Sixty-two years later, Halliday still works full-time and—with her longtime associate Mary Frances Burleson—operates the state's largest independent residential brokerage. With 28 sales offices and one corporate office, more than 1,600 sales associates and staff, and $4.7 billion in annual sales, Ebby Halliday, REALTORS®, was ranked the eighteenth-largest residential brokerage in the country, according to REALTOR® Magazine's 2006 ranking. Halliday has continued to follow the same work committees, she was a leader in the Women's Council of REALTORS®, serving as its national president in 1957. She was also active in the National Institute of Real Estate Brokers, the forerunner to today's Council of Real Estate Brokerage Managers, and served as the president of its Residential Division in the late 1960s; she was active in the Farm and Land Institute (today the REALTORS® Land Institute); and she served on the Association's Executive Committee in 1972 and 1973 under Presidents Fred Tucker and J. D. Sawyer. In 1979, the year NAR established its Distinguished Service Award, Halliday was a recipient. In 2006, she talked about her career and her work for NAR.

Q: What was it like conducting business when you started? Besides different methods of communication— no Internet, no cell phone, no handheld devices—what has changed?

A: Real estate was a slower process. The multiple listing service didn't come along until about 40 to 50 years ago. We sent a delegation to California to learn about how it worked, because we felt it rendered a better service for buyers and sellers and inspired cooperation. It revolutionized the industry. In those early days, we carried our listings around in our pockets and then on card files.

Q: When you opened your first office, what was it like to be a woman in what was predominantly a man's world?

A: It wasn't hard. I worked on a development all by myself in the beginning and didn't come in contact with a lot of men. The men I came in contact with were mostly buyers, so it didn't pose a problem that I was a woman. Because I helped found the Dallas chapter of the Women's Council in 1952, I was able to use that as my springboard to national

COURTESY EBBY HALLIDAY, REALTORS®

At age 20, Halliday was selling hats—and they remained her signature garb throughout much of her real estate career.

ethic that originally inspired her. "I worked like a dog but acted like a lady," she said.

Although Halliday was never NAR president, she has served the Association for more than half its 100-year history. Besides participating on a number of NAR

office. I'm sure there was some resistance to women, but I didn't realize it.

Q: *Were you an immediate success?*

A: Immediately. I was just thrilled with the idea of a larger product [than hats], but I think what I liked was the realization that home ownership was a basic strength of America. It was a wonderful feeling to get newly married couples into their first home. I don't take a lot of credit for my immediate success. The north Texas area was booming. We grew our company as the city grew. Part of my success was being involved in NAR. I joined shortly after opening my business, probably about 1946, and was one of the first female members of the local Dallas Board. The idea of RELO—a national network of companies offering relocation services—was born at a National Institute of Real Estate Brokers meeting at the Drake Hotel in Chicago in 1959. Every May, NAR officers and their committee people met at the Drake Hotel in smoke-filled rooms. Eventually, NAR established an office in Washington, D.C., and the May meetings were gradually changed. I was one of the founders of RELO [still headquartered in Chicago and now operated as Leading Real Estate Companies of the World]. Originally, we were a national organization, but then we went international.

Q: *Why was RELO so important?*

A: You need extraordinary service for people who are being uprooted and going to new jobs and neighborhoods and may be taking children to new schools. NAR spotted the need very, very early. It took the ball and ran with the idea. RELO was always separate from NAR, but it was an idea hatched by those of us who were active in the Association; it actually came out of an NAR-appointed committee that was studying the fact that relocation was needed as a service to corporations.

Q: *In those early days, local boards chartered Pullman train cars to take their members to the conventions. What was it like on the trains?*

A: It was a great way to travel and a lot of fun. The entire state delegation climbed on board the train, and there was a lot of partying. I recall a lot of good times going and coming. I think the first convention I attended was in Cleveland in 1954. Women were not officers or heads of committees back then. That took a few years to happen. Men were receptive to the idea of women officers once they realized the women were capable and didn't trade on their femininity. I learned from all the women I worked with, particularly Posie Willis. She was one of our early managers and one of the first women to work on national committees. [Florence "Posie" Willis received the Association's Distinguished Service Award in 1982, three years after Halliday.]

C. Armel Nutter, 1960 NAR president, recognized Halliday for her leadership in the Women's Council of REALTORS® (WCR). Halliday served as national president of WCR in 1957.

COURTESY EBBY HALLIDAY, REALTORS®

In 1963, Halliday became the first woman to be named REALTOR® of the Year by the Texas Association of REALTORS®.

Q: During your career, what have been NAR's greatest challenges?

A: To make the public understand the difference between a REALTOR® and a real estate practitioner and to make fellow practitioners understand the importance of having a watchdog for our industry.

Q: What were you most passionate about as an NAR leader?

A: The correct pronunciation of REALTOR®. So many people mispronounced it! I was also passionate about the importance of the Code of Ethics [In 1962, Halliday joined a speakers' bureau that traveled the country educating members about the Code.] and the Association in general. Discrimination was also one of the biggest issues facing the Association in my days as a national leader. NAR worked very hard to train everybody to not discriminate.

Q: Did you ever aspire to be NAR president?

A: No. I think that my life became so involved with the growth of our business and the creation of our technology department and our training. I was also in great demand as a speaker. At one time, I averaged one speech a week. That took up a lot of time, but it was also one of the reasons we [women] were accepted in the communities where we worked. It's so important to give back. I speak, sponsor sports teams, and organize stay-in-school programs. Our company gives the Ebby Rose of Distinction Award annually to non–real estate heroes in the community who do good work and improve the lives of others.

Q: Your own list of awards is very long. Which awards have meant the most to you?

A: There have been three. The Distinguished Service Award in 1979 was one. In 1963, I was the first woman to receive the Texas Association's REALTOR® of the Year Award. And in 2005, I was the first woman in real estate to receive the Horatio Alger Association of Distinguished Americans Award for overcoming adversity to achieve success.

Q: *How did you grow your company into one of the largest in the country?*

A: Our people are the biggest reason for our success. From the beginning, people came to us because we offered them a lot. We have excellent training. Associates are taught to

Halliday, right, with longtime associate Mary Frances Burleson.

cooperate, which I learned from the MLS. We offered computers early.

I learned a lot of my ideas by serving on National Association committees. In the late 1960s, I served on the Association's Special Committee on the Use of Computers. NAR formed a study group to consider the newfangled thing called a computer to see whether it would be useful to the industry. Out of that study group, or special committee, as we called it, came the interest to use computers. From another committee, of course, came the idea to form RELO.

I also served on the REALTORS® Legislative Committee, and I think political involvement has been good for our company's growth. We want our people to be involved in politics. We need to be watchdogs for legislation that affects our industry and give money to representatives who work for what we believe is right.

Q: *Besides listing and selling, your company has expanded into other services—leasing, property management, insurance, mortgages, and a counseling center to assist transferees and corporations. What's the most exciting change?*

A: The trend of topflight companies offering full service as a convenience to clients. We have mortgage officers assigned to every one of our sales offices. Clients can walk from their sales associate's office to the mortgage office. Like the MLS, technology revolutionized the industry. Our Web site [www.ebby.com] gets thousands of visits every day. It's such a wonderful service to clients, especially those who are relocating. There was a fear that the Internet would diminish the services of real estate professionals, but we haven't found that to be true.

Q: *What's the best part of growing the company?*

A: Helping develop people who do well. We've received so many notes from people who've been able to put their children through college. Before women came into the business

Actresses Lily Tomlin, left, **and Mary Kay Place**, right, visited Dallas in 2006, spending time at Halliday's company in preparation for upcoming television roles.

COURTESY EBBY HALLIDAY, REALTORS®

in large numbers, attorneys and banks around town would send me women who were newly widowed or divorced and ask me to counsel them and help them develop a career. A woman with five little boys came to me wanting to sell real estate. I told her I would help her learn the business. She sat across from me for 30 days and listened to me talk to clients and help associates learn to negotiate and list. I told her, "Never let the sun set without getting a contract signed on both ends." Well, she brought me her first contract and was so excited, but she had forgotten to get one signature. I said, "Dorothy, you're missing one signature." She said, "But it's dark outside." I said to her, "Dorothy, the sun is shining somewhere." She went back and got the other signature.

Q: You continue to operate an independent company. Why?

A: We've had many offers to sell, but we pride ourselves on being independent. One of our strengths has been our ability to judge what we want to do—and when we want to do it. We believe that being independent is an asset. We also believe it's a real obligation to the people who've helped build the business. I'm leaving the stock of the company to the people who built this company.

Q: Where do you see the company headed?

A: The company is sound enough to continue without me. We've brought on board a management team of 29 people. There's not a single person on that team who doesn't have someone else in mind as a replacement. We also have a senior management team. We have heads of departments who are all fabulous, and we've got Mary Frances [president since 1989] who has been with the company almost 50 years and is doing a magnificent job.

Q: You're 96 and work full-time. What's your secret?

A: I always say, "I inherited good genes, I don't smoke, I don't drink, and I don't retire!"

Q: What do you do when you're not working?

A: I'm involved in many community activities that keep me pretty busy. Yesterday, [Texas businessman] T. Boone Pickens was the speaker at an annual luncheon of the Texas Association of Business. The annual luncheon recognizes and honors a businessperson—I'm a former recipient of that award—and I composed a short musical piece as part of his introduction. Today, Lily Tomlin and Mary Kay Place spent the day with me because they are playing real estate practitioners in an HBO sitcom and wanted to see how we show property. That was a lot of fun.

Q: Would you care to guess whether NAR will still be around in another 100 years?

A: I think it will—it will be even more international in scope—because it will continue to have good leadership and uphold the ethics that were put in place by the founders.

nated; whether photos were used and, if so, whether black-and-white or color; and whether the group had a paid director.

In 1971, the Association adopted a policy that would become known as "the 14 points," and in 1972, the Association wrote its first

Handbook on Multiple Listing Policy, intended as a best-practices guide for board-operated MLSs. The 14-points policy, today known simply as MLS policy, ensures that MLSs owned by or affiliated with REALTOR® boards function in a manner consistent with the best interests of

A Phoenix MLS listing in 2006 and the same listing 40 years earlier.

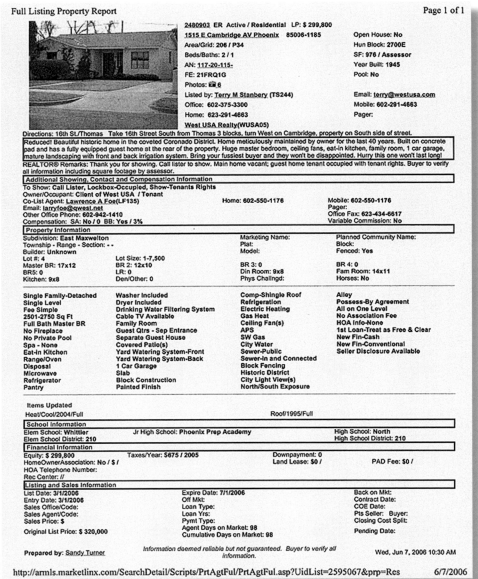

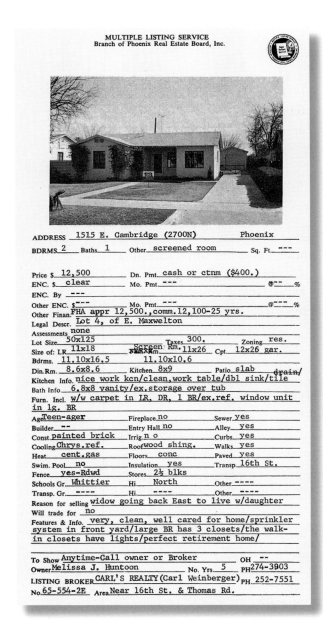

REALTORS®, their clients, and the public. Because the policy came in the midst of U.S. Justice Department allegations of price-fixing (discussed later in the chapter) there was a belief that the 14 points were a reaction to government intervention. The Association's general counsel at the time, William D. North, said that wasn't the case. Instead, the policies were designed to help MLS operators avoid rules that might restrict, limit, or interfere with members working with one another and their clients. For example, one point forbade MLSs from authorizing changes to listings without written permission of the listing broker. Nevertheless, the first point stated that MLSs "shall not fix, control, recommend, suggest, or maintain commission rates or fees. . . ." In the mid-1970s, the Association amended both its multiple listing policy and its Code of Ethics to remove all references to fees.

"As a result of NAR's [rule-making] efforts, what we have today is an orderly marketplace with consistent, enforceable listing procedures," said Richard Mendenhall of Columbia, Missouri, 2001 NAR president. "These rules and regulations are what make the MLS work for everyone."

Meanwhile, another big change was on the brink: the first viable computerized MLS. Computerization enabled practitioners to expand their geographic base, leading MLSs in California and other states to create regional MLSs. To facilitate regionalization—which promised reduced costs for members—a 1981 NAR task force produced several model plans for MLS cooperative agreements.

AN EXCLUSIVE CLUB?

As MLS coverage increased, debate ensued over whether nonmember licensees and home owners should have access to listing

data—without charge or for a fee. It was MLS policy that licensees had to be board members to have access to board-owned MLSs, and that policy was challenged repeatedly in court. In 1977, the case of *Glendale Board of REALTORS® v. Hounsell,* 72 Cal. App. 3d 210 (1977), upheld an earlier California ruling, *Marin County Board of REALTORS® v. Palsson* 16 Cal.3d 920 (1976), that the membership requirement violated the state's antitrust law, the Cartwright Act.

The *Palsson* decision paved the way for all nonmember licensees in the state to gain access to the MLS. However, because the decision was based on state law, courts in some other jurisdictions upheld the right to require board membership for MLS access. In 1988, however, three Atlanta real estate brokers affiliated with the National Association of Real Estate Brokers—Wendell White, E. Pearl Presley, and Fletcher L. Thompson—filed a lawsuit against the DeKalb County (Georgia) Board of REALTORS®. In *Thompson v. Metropolitan Multi,* 934 F. 2d 1566, 1579 (11th Cir. 1991), the plaintiffs charged that members-only access violated federal antitrust laws. The Eleventh U.S. Court of Appeals in 1991 reversed a lower court ruling, siding with the plaintiffs. The ruling local associations in Alabama, Florida, and Georgia develop policies and procedures to allow access by nonmember brokers.

In fact, as a result of the decision, NAR gave all local associations the option of dropping the membership requirement. At the time, there was some fear the change would result in an exodus of members, but that fear proved unfounded. Today, only about half the member associations that operate MLSs have a membership requirement. And recent federal court decisions—*Reifert v. S. Cent. Wis. MLS Corp.* No. 05-3601, 2006 WL 1585570 (7th Cir. June 12, 2006), *Buyer's Corner Realty, Inc., v. N. Ky. Association of REALTORS®,* 410

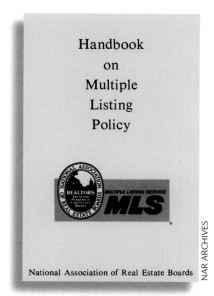

NAR ARCHIVES

The *Handbook on Multiple Listing Policy,* first published in 1972, was developed to help local associations operate MLSs in a manner that didn't restrict, limit, or interfere with members' businesses.

> "**As a result of NAR's efforts, what we have today is an orderly marketplace with consistent, enforceable listing procedures.**"
>
> —Richard Mendenhall

F.Supp.2d 574 (E.D. Ky. 2005), *aff'd*, No. 06-5100, 2006 WL 2827684 (6th Cir. Oct. 4, 2006), and *Prencipe v. Spokane Board of Realtors®*, No. CV-04-319-LRS, 2006 WL 1310402 (E.D. Wash. May 12, 2006)—have affirmed the right of local associations to limit access to members.

In the age of the Internet—where companies vie for control of lucrative information—the question of who can use MLS data continues to be contentious. Who owns the listing data? Who has the right to use it—and for what purpose? Many brokers believe they own the data and should therefore have some control over its use, and NAR agrees. However, a January 2005 survey showed that only about 6 percent of brokers nationwide copyrighted their listings. To help MLSs and brokers establish legal ownership rights to listing content, NAR's legal department developed sample documents to be used to create, confirm, and transfer rights to listing data.

The subject of how brokers can use MLS listing data on the Internet is at the heart of a legal battle the Association is waging with the U.S. Department of Justice. The Justice Department, in a 2005 suit filed against NAR, challenged a now-rescinded policy, created to govern the use of MLS data by brokers on the Internet. The department says both that policy and a new policy NAR created in response to Justice Department concerns operate anticompetitively by, among other things, impeding innovation in the business. The Association is vigorously defending both the MLS as a vehicle for broker-to-broker cooperation and the ability of brokers to control the use of their listings on the Internet by competitors.

The Association's stance does not mean it opposes widespread access to property sale information. Nor do NAR attorneys believe that NAR's proposed Internet Listing Display policy—if it's ever enacted—will result in brokers' pulling their listings off competitors' Web sites

en masse. Realtors® today are comfortable with widespread access to listing data online.

In fact, Realtors® themselves have agitated for structural changes to the MLS system that would make listing data more widely available. Currently, 200,000 real estate offices and branches use the more than 900 MLSs. Despite the consolidation that began in the 1980s, most MLSs remain local; only 100 are regional or statewide.

Because real estate is local business, the thought of 900 separate systems operating in distinct territories might seem quite logical. In the 1990s, however, the brokerage industry began its own wave of consolidation, leading to the creation of megabrokerages—including perennial No. 1, NRT Incorporated of Parsippany, N.J.—that operate in many MLS territories and, in some cases, many regions of the country. When their businesses cross MLS boundaries, brokers need to join multiple MLSs and deal with differing rules, systems, and local customs.

Could MLSs be made to keep up with the changing demands of a consolidating industry? That was the question on the mind of Vienna, Virginia, broker Thomas M. Stevens, 2006 NAR president, when he appointed an advisory committee, chaired by Gary Thomas of Aliso Viejo, California, to study the future of the MLS. Stevens had operated a large brokerage before selling it to NRT in 2002. He asked advisory committee members to start with a clean slate: How might the MLS look if it were started from scratch?

For the associations that operate MLSs and the vendors who serve them, it's a delicate question—one with no easy answers. On one point, however, all parties agree: Whatever change is on the horizon—be it further consolidation, creation of a national MLS, or something completely different—the system of cooperative selling that has served practitioners and the public so well over the past century must be preserved.

THE NEVER-ENDING STORY

The 2005 lawsuit is not the first time the U.S. Department of Justice has brought charges against REALTORS®. For more than 20 years, beginning in the 1940s, the Justice Department investigated the real estate industry—among others—on the grounds that it engaged in price-fixing. In those days, boards of REALTORS® published commission schedules for members, covering a wide range of real estate services. In the 1970s, after doing battle with the Justice Department, boards around the country entered into consent decrees with the department, and the Association undertook a major campaign to tell members, "Thou shalt not fix prices."

Thirty years later, however, some industry critics assert that "standard commissions" and "the 6 percent commission" are still alive, despite the Association's insistence that all commissions are negotiable. Since the consent decrees, the Association has remained pointedly silent on the subject. To avoid the impression of creating a benchmark commission, NAR does not survey its members on commission rates; in the absence of data, then, the myth of the standard commission lives on.

In the early days of the profession, the commission rate was typically based on the health of the local market, the overall economy, property location, and the length of the lease. But without a standardized compensation system, disagreements developed. In an 1890 issue of the *Real Estate and Building Journal,* a newspaper published by Hungerford & Smith in Chicago from 1866 to 1909, D. F. Crilly is mentioned as hiring Jas. A. Parish of a well-known real estate firm, Barnes & Parish, to settle a difficulty Crilly and his partner, a Mr. Blair, had over a joint property. Crilly advised Parish that "he would be well paid." When Parish asked for his commission, however, Crilly denied having engaged him and offered him $1,000, the equivalent of

a 2.5 percent commission. The judge decided on $3,125, not the $6,312.50 Parish sought.[21]

One of NAR's early objectives was to help ensure that members were reimbursed fairly for listing and selling a home. In 1910, Association secretary R. Bruce Douglas wrote in a booklet that a predetermined commission contributed to a broker's dignity, since he did not have to haggle over his rate of pay. Rates in 100 U.S. cities at the time varied from 1 percent to 5 percent for the same work, with minimum charges ranging from $15 to $50. The fluctuation typically depended on "a fair return for a good service," said Callistus S. Ennis, president of the Chicago Real Estate Board, who chaired the NAR Committee on Commissions, as well as its Broker's Division in the early 1920s.[22]

A schedule of rates also lessened the possibility of unethical practices. Brokers sometimes used a "net listing" agreement system, in which they set a price and kept the difference between the listing price and the sales price. NAR banned the practice in the early 1920s, when the newly formed Broker's Division recognized it as a conflict of interest. To pocket more of the sales proceeds, an unscrupulous broker could easily convince a naive client to list a property for much less than its actual market value.

By the early 1930s, *The National Real Estate Journal* was publishing an annual compilation of various boards' commission rates for sales, exchanges, leases, and appraisals. The compilation included U.S. and Canadian cities with a population of 100,000 or more. The first such digest was published as an experiment in the April 27, 1931, issue. The goal was twofold: to help brokers with out-of-town transactions and to help individual boards compare their rates with those of other cities.[23] The Association appointed a Committee on Rates, Rules, and Customs to work with its tax consultant, George P. Ellis, to decide whether it was feasible, or even desirable, to develop a standard schedule.

In this 1946 rate schedule, the Phoenix Association of REALTORS® recommended a minimum appraisal fee of $25 for properties up to $5,000 in value.

To ensure REALTORS® were paid for their services, this schedule of lease commission rates specified that "all lease commissions are due and payable when final leases are executed."

Phoenix Real Estate Board

Minimum Commission Rates Rules and Customs

(Revised to April, 1946)

As Formulated from Guide Established

by

National Association of Real Estate Boards

•

(This Schedule of Commissions shall be the minimum and shall apply to all activities; except where special circumstances require added fees by special arrangements with clients.)

•

DEAL WITH A REALTOR

He is Competent - Reliable - Established

THE TITLE REALTOR is a distinctive badge of responsibility. It can only be used by those licensed real estate brokers who are members in good standing of their Local Real Estate Board, The Arizona State Association of Boards of Realtors and National Association of Real Estate Boards and are bound by the Code of Ethics of these Boards.

COMMISSIONS AND CUSTOMS

ADVERTISING (Sales, Rentals, Exchanges)
A. Realtor may advertise at own expense.
B. Owner may advertise upon agreement with Broker.

Advisory Services:
A. By special arrangement.

Appraisal Fees:
A. No unconsidered opinions.
B. Appraisal fees on business, industrial, subdivision, and all properties outside City limits, by arrangements.
All necessary expense incurred in making appraisals to be added to the schedule of rates and where special services by architects, engineers, builders or others are required, an extra charge will be made.
Estimates of expenses furnished on request.
Special rates made on application for appraisals involving two or more properties of the same or different classification.
Residence Property: Valuations to and including $5,000—minimum fee, $25.00.
Over $5,000 to $100,000—$1.50 per $1,000 additional.
Over $100,000—$1.00 per $1,000 additional.
Business Property: Valuations to and including $10,000, minimum fee, $50.00.
Over $10,000 to $100,000—$1.50 per $1,000 additional.
Over $100,000—$1.00 per $1,000 additional.
Agricultural Lands: Valuations to and including $10,000—minimum fee, $50.00.
Over $10,000 to $100,000—$1.00 per $1,000 additional.
Over $100,000—75 cents per $1,000 additional.

Arbitration Fees:
A. Arbitration, division of estates, etc., same as for expert Testimony.

Auction Fees:
A. By agreement — not less than sales commission.

Building Restriction Adjustments:
A. For gathering facts, appearing before zoning or other commissions, not less than $50.00 per day.

Business Opportunities:
A. 5%, minimum $100.00.

Buying Real Estate:
A. Same as for sales.

Collections:
A. 5%, minimum fee $2.00. See Management.

Exchanges:
A. Same as for sales.

Expert Testimony:
A. Minimum $50.00 per day for each member testifying.

Inspection Fees:
A. Per advance agreement.

Leasing & Renting:
(All lease commissions due and payable when final leases are executed, or by special written agreement.)

A. **Business Property Leases To and Through 25 Years:** The following percentages, based on total amount of rental for number of years involved:
5% on total rental for one year lease.
3½% on total rental for two year lease.
3% on total rental for three year lease.
2⅝% on total rental for four year lease.
2.2% on total rental for five year lease.
Plus 1% total rental for each subsequent year through a maximum of 25 years.
(When computed under this schedule, all items involved such as taxes, insurance, assessments, any net ground rental, if separately involved, any loan amortization payments, whether paid directly or indirectly by lessee, shall constitute and be considered as the full rental.)
For options to extend—1% on total rental per year for each year of extension period, payable at time of executing extension.

B. **Long Term Business Property Leases, Over 25 Years:** For any regular commercial rentals over twenty-five years, the same commission shall apply as though an actual sale had been consummated, the total sales price to be determined as that amount upon which the average annual rental represents a return of twelve per cent gross. For example, an average annual rental of $6,000 ($500.00 per month) would represent a return of 12% on $50,000.00 — commission under this example at 5%, $2,500.00.

C. **Net Ground Leases, 20 Years or More:** For leases 20 years or more, the same commission shall apply as though an actual sale had been consummated, the total sales price to be determined as on that amount upon which the average annual rental represents a return of six per cent net. For example, an average rental of $6,000 ($500.00 per month) would represent a return of 6% net on $100,000.00, Commission under this example at 5%, $5,000.00.
Net Ground Leases Under 20 Years: For net ground leases under 20 years—Commission shall be 5% of the commission as above determined under Net Ground leases of 20 years or more, for each year of the Lease. For example, a net Ground Lease for: 5 years, 25% of above. 10 years, 50% of above. Other lease periods in proportion.

D. **House and Store Rentals:** When rented on month to month basis, 20 per cent on first month's rent; minimum $10.00.

E. **Resident and Apartment Leases:** 20% of first month's rent on leases less than 5 mos. 5% of total amount of lease for 5 months to one year. (Provided that 5 per cent of total amount of lease is not less than 20% of first month's rent.) 2½% of total amount of each subsequent year or fraction thereof.

F. **Renewal of Leases:** At regular rate based on current rates on date of lease, payable at time of renewal.

G. **Percentage Leases:** Based on minimum rental considered as straight rental as provided under Leasing and Rental Schedule.
On all amounts over minimum, 2½%.
When no minimum rental provided, then compute commission as though minimum rental were 75% of owner's asking price, or of fair straight rental.

Cancellation of Leases:
A. Regular leasing commission on unexpired balance.

Leasing Furnished Property:
A. Regular leasing commission on both building and contents. (Lessor to furnish inventory)

Sub Lease:
A. Same as regular leasing.

Agricultural Leases:
A. Cash Rental—5% of the total rent for first year of term lease;
2½% of each additional year.
B. Share Rental—$1.00 per acre; minimum $30.00.

Loan Commission:
A. First Mortgage Loans: 1 and 2%, subject to agreement.
B. Construction Loans: 2% of gross amount.
C. Renewals: Same as original loan commissions.
Minimum $25.00.

Management of Property:
A. Includes collections, keeping accounts, renting, leasing and operation of property.
B. Commission shall be regular commission for sales, rentals, leases, or renewals, PLUS:
On business property—5% of gross income.
On residential property—5% of gross income.
On agricultural property—5% of gross income.
C. Supervision of Repairs:
Up to $2,000—not less than 10%.
Over $2,000—by agreement for service rendered.

Option to Buy:
A. Where cash paid and option not exercised — 50% of consideration received but not more than sales commission would have been.
B. Where engaged by purchaser—By agreement.

Sales Commissions:
All commissions based on total sales price, and not on equities.
All properties—5% on total amount of sale including furniture, when involved in sale—Minimum $50.00.
Vacant Lots—By agreement.
Subdivision—By agreement.
Leaseholds: Same as for leases for unexpired term of original lease; plus 5% of any cash or other consideration paid for leasehold.
Earnest Money—Shall be approximately 10% of selling price—If forfeited, divide equally between broker and seller, but not more than sales commission would have been.
Net Price: Acceptance of net prices by Brokers prohibited except in options.
Commissions payable when transaction is completed.

Tax Adjustments
25% of first year's savings.

Sales commissions were "5% on total amount of sale including furniture . . . Minimum $50."

Local associations published rate schedules with recommended fees and commission rates for everything from appraisals to tax adjustments.

Although the rates were published as a guide rather than as a mandatory rule, the Justice Department, in the 1940s, began a grand jury investigation of NAR, Executive Vice President Herbert U. Nelson, and the Washington (D.C.) Real Estate Board. In an August 21, 1947, memo to the NAR Board of Directors, Nelson wrote, "Apparently, the effort will be made to show that we are endeavoring to establish prices through our commission schedules not only on a local basis but on a national basis."

NAR leaders were defiant. Morgan L. Fitch of Chicago, 1947 NAR president, said, "The National Association has spoken out in what it believes to be the public interest in the matter of housing, at times in opposition to the [Truman] administration." At the time, NAR was fiercely opposed to President Harry Truman's effort to expand public housing. "Apparently," Fitch said, "the time has come when a citizen of this country cannot speak out without being served notice that he does so at the peril of criminal prosecution."[24]

NAR held that commission schedules served members and the public. "We want to stir up this issue so that the public will realize its true significance," Nelson wrote in the Association's weekly *Headlines* on September 8, 1947. "The [administration's] purpose is to cripple trade associations, including NAREB. [From 1916 through 1972, NAR was known as the National Association of Real Estate Boards.] They are to become merely pleasant lunch clubs which never discuss anything that has to do with business in an important way."[25]

The case reached the U.S. Supreme Court in 1950 (*United States v. National Association of Real Estate Boards, et al.*, 339 U.S. 485), and the Court ruled against the Washington Board. Justice William O. Douglas delivered the majority opinion on May 8, 1950, writing, "Price-fixing is *per se* an unreasonable restraint

of trade. It is not for the courts to determine whether in particular settings price-fixing serves an honorable or worthy end. An agreement, shown either by adherence to a price schedule or by proof of consensual action fixing the uniform or minimum price, is itself illegal under the Sherman Act, no matter what end it was designed to serve." Douglas also said, "The fact that the business involves the sale of personal services rather than commodities does not take it out of the category of 'trade' within the meaning of Sec. 3 of the [Sherman Antitrust] Act."

The ruling reversed the judgment of the district court. However, the Supreme Court affirmed the lower court's ruling exonerating NAR and Nelson. Charges against NAR revolved around Article 9 of the Code of Ethics, which said, "An agent should always exact the regular real estate commission of the association of which he is a member, and always give his client to understand at the beginning that he is entitled to such and expects it."

Douglas stated, "We are left somewhat in doubt as to the extent if any to which the National Association and Nelson were architects of the fee-fixing conspiracy or participants in it. At best their relationship to it is, on this record, a somewhat attenuated one."

After the decision, though, Joseph B. Fleming, the Association's general counsel, wrote to NAR President Robert P. Gerholz of Flint, Michigan, saying it would be advisable to suspend Article 9, pending consideration by the Board of Directors at the annual meeting in the fall. The letter was dated June 14, 1950, and Fleming reiterated his opinion at an Executive Committee meeting at the Drake Hotel in Chicago in July. "By this action," he told committee members, "we would indicate our willingness to comply with the ruling of the Supreme Court and relieve ourselves of the possibility of the institution of further proceed-

When the Justice Department began investigating NAR's involvement in rate setting, Association leaders launched an attack on President Truman, charging that the inquiry was payback for REALTORS®' stance against public housing.

ings." Fleming also recommended that member boards analyze their bylaws having to do with commissions or rates to be sure they did not violate state antitrust laws.

At its November 16, 1950, convention in Miami Beach, Florida, the Board of Directors changed Article 9 to read: "The REALTOR® should charge for his services only such fees as are fair and reasonable in the light of the services rendered, the circumstances surrounding the individual transaction, and the local practice in

"It is . . . disappointing that this clearing of the good name of the REALTORS®' national organization does not appear to match in news the value of the charges of criminal conspiracy that brought such bold headlines when the Department of Justice secured its indictment against us."

The Association's *Headlines* newsletter in May 1950 carried news of NAR's victory in the U.S. Supreme Court on charges of price fixing.

similar transactions, all to the end that the client shall be charged no more than the real value of the services rendered by the REALTOR®."

Deciding on a fair commission rate in a changing market proved tough, however. In California from 1950 to 1956, the average selling price for residential properties increased an average of 19 percent, and the number of transactions involving brokers jumped 31 percent. At the same time, the number of new brokers increased 47 percent, and operating expenses climbed 24 percent. To be rewarded financially, NAR's Executive Officers Council reported, required "extraordinarily astute management and aggressive operations."[26]

Boards continued to publish commission schedules but emphasized their "advisory" role. And on May 9, 1961, NAR's Board of Directors adopted a bylaw change clarifying that commission schedules established a minimum rather than a prevailing rate.

In 1962, however, a California court prohibited the California Real Estate Association (today the CALIFORNIA ASSOCIATION OF REALTORS®) and 17 local realty boards from attempting to set minimum 6 percent commissions on property sales. The suit charged that the 6 percent minimum violated the state's antitrust laws. In a talk before the AFL-CIO, California Attorney General Stanley Mosk said, "This means that now the broker is free to let individual circumstances and general market conditions determine his fee, and the seller, at long last, has the opportunity to seek a better brokerage deal."

In the late 1960s and the 1970s, Richard W. McLaren, assistant U.S. attorney general for antitrust in the Justice Department, took a tough antitrust position, filing lawsuits against a range of service providers, including real estate professionals. "The stated objective of these suits was to assure competiti on in the development and delivery of personal services," according to *Antitrust and Real Estate*, published by NAR in 1982.

"IT IS EXPRESSLY STATED THAT [NAR] NEITHER RECOMMENDS NOR RECOGNIZES ANY AGREEMENT TO FIX OR IMPOSE UNIFORM RATES OF COMMISSION ON REAL ESTATE TRANSACTIONS."

–Rich Port

The Antitrust Division filed a suit on December 18, 1969, against REALTORS® in Prince George's County, Maryland, as well as against NAR. The Justice Department's position was that "advisory" commission schedules—and the phrase "but not less than 6 percent"—established a prima facie case of price-fixing.

Complaints were also filed against boards on Long Island, New York, and in Cleveland. McLaren wanted to stop boards from adopting, publishing, distributing, and suggesting any commission or fee schedule. In a January 23, 1970, letter to all local boards, NAR Executive Vice President Eugene P. Conser wrote, "Boards that want to avoid legal action should review their policies in detail and in collaboration with local counsel, eliminating wherever possible a potential cause for either federal or state action." He also advised:

Any documents relating to commission rates should be reviewed and modified if questionable. Any listing forms published or made available to members by the board [that] state a fixed rate of commission or contain a statement such as "board-approved rates" would be held to be a violation. Members must have the right to do business on the basis of rates independently established, and cooperating members may then determine individually whether they desire to cooperate on the basis of the rate as set forth in the listing.

NAR President Rich Port of LaGrange, Illinois, wrote, in a letter dated July 23, 1970, to all boards and state associations: "It is expressly stated that [NAR] neither recommends nor recognizes any agreement to fix or impose uniform rates of commission on real estate transactions." Port reiterated Conser's advice that boards eliminate published schedules, business forms in which a stated rate of commission was printed, and any references to board-approved schedules.

A number of boards entered into consent decrees with the U.S. Justice Department. In a separate action in 1971, REALTORS® in Chicago's northwest suburbs entered into a consent decree with state Attorney General William J. Scott. The decree enjoined the boards, the multiple listing service, and brokers from commission price-fixing and "other acts of illegal monopoly in restraint of trade which have affected the real estate market in 11 northwest suburban communities of Chicagoland."[27] Two years later, two real estate groups were charged with fixing commissions for the sale and management of cooperative apartments in New York City.

The Association developed a comprehensive legal action program to assist real estate boards and MLSs. Despite clear instructions from NAR, however, practitioners in many areas still seemed to act in unison, partly as a result of

A New Equation for Salespeople

During the decade that REALTORS® were settling price-fixing litigation, two Denver practitioners were launching a company that would radically change the balance of power between sales associates and brokers. They were Dave Liniger and Gail Main.

Liniger had been buying and selling houses while he was stationed with the U.S. Air Force in Phoenix. Seeing his investments pay off handsomely, he decided to earn his brokerage license to handle future sales. He worked for 100 percent commission and traditional brokerage companies, and from those experiences, he decided to create a hybrid operation—one with the compensation structure of a 100 percent company but the support services of a traditional broker.

With Main—first a business associate and later his wife—Liniger founded RE/MAX in Denver in 1973. The company's name is an acronym for "real estate maximums." Liniger and Main offered salespeople 100 percent commissions, support, and services but required them to share office expenses and management fees. Although theirs wasn't the first 100 percent company, they're widely credited with bringing the concept into the mainstream. Two years after founding the company, they began offering franchises. Today, RE/MAX International Inc. numbers 90,000 salespeople in the United States and 120,000 around the world in 63 countries.

Liniger, age 62, is still chairman of the board of RE/MAX and has been inducted into both the Council of Real Estate Brokerage Managers Hall of Leaders and the Real Estate Buyer's Agent Council Hall of Fame.

Q: You took your idea on the road to recruit people for company-owned offices. Why did you go that route but later switch to franchising?

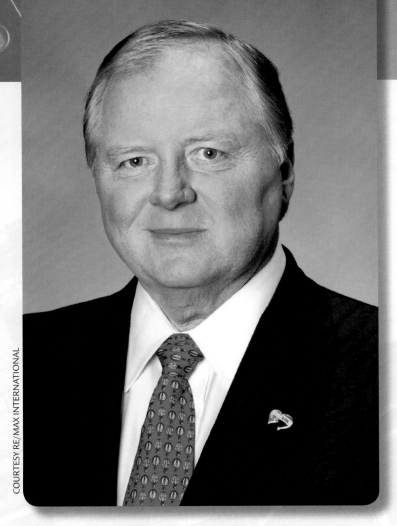

COURTESY RE/MAX INTERNATIONAL

Dave Liniger, RE/MAX chairman and cofounder.

A: We started with eight company-owned offices in Denver in 1973, thinking we'd be like other entrepreneurs and operate offices nationally and internationally. But I was young and naive. I quickly realized that the best way to expand on a huge scale was either through a major public company or through franchising. Franchising was the more logical route for us. You take your product or service and combine it with local ownership for what's basically a partnership. Other companies franchised before we did—ERA, Century 21, Red Carpet Realty, and Realty World. In 1975, we sold our first franchise in Kansas City and then a second one in Washington, D.C. We later sold all our offices in Denver to existing branch managers. By 1977, we were a full-time franchise company selling more than 100 franchises a year.

Q: What was the Association's reaction to franchising?

A: As a national trade association, it tried to be neutral and not take sides. But we had the feeling that NAR ignored us. None of us were invited to participate in NAR brainstorming, for example. It wasn't until 20 years ago that any franchisor or franchisee was president of NAR. When Bill Chee, who was president of NAR in 1993, came in and said "the lions are coming over the hill," he wasn't talking just about the Internet. He was being inclusive and including franchisors. He reached out and said everyone should be given an opportunity. He was a visionary and had a tremendous impact on our industry.

Q: In the book Everybody Wins: The Story and Lessons Behind RE/MAX, *authors Phil Harkins and Keith Hollihan say RE/MAX had a dream and a formula, not just an idea. What was in that dream and formula that made your concept stick, grow, and last?*

A: I worked for three real estate companies before I started RE/MAX—Ed Thirkhill Realty and Realty Executives in Arizona and Van Schaack in Denver. At Van Schaack, the average man—and there were only men working there—made $50,000 on the traditional 50-50 split. The company was incredibly successful and well managed and had a 40 percent market share. The sales associates were sophisticated and received outstanding training. I worked for the company nine months and was very impressed with the quality of its management. But I wanted to start a company that would allow a high commission [like Realty Executives] and also provide big-ticket items to enhance a career, such as formal training, sophisticated advertising, and relocation services. I tried to convince the [Van Schaack] owners to change their concept, but they wouldn't. They thought I had a screw loose.

Q: What other resistance did you face?

A: A lot of brokers objected to the concept at first because of the threat to their dollar. We felt ostracized. Some people thought our idea looked good but said, "When you're successful, we'll join you." When we first started, we tried to get an article about what we were doing published in *Real Estate Today®*. But it took until 1977 before we were successful enough for the publication to want to write a feature about us. And even then, the publisher was hesitant. The writer and her editor said that if the article wasn't published, they'd resign; the publisher backed down, and the article ran. [It included an editor's note stating that *"Real Estate Today®* does not espouse any opinion concerning the 100 percent commission concept. . . . Any broker interested in opening a 100 percent office or in converting his existing arrangement should take the precaution of consulting with his attorney and representatives of his state licensing commission."] The impact of the article was subtle credibility. It wasn't an endorsement, but it showed that we were a full-fledged member of the NAR club. I used to have that article on my wall.

Part of the reason for our slow start was the Code of Ethics. There was an Article of the Code at that time that said REALTORS® could not solicit one another's sales associates. We were threatened when we handed out brochures and cards. What we did to get good associates was to hire women, since most companies wouldn't. Our company was 75 percent female in the beginning. We're still more than 55 percent female.

Q: You and Gail started RE/MAX at the same time NAR was bringing salespeople into the fold with the REALTOR-ASSOCIATE® program. Fairly quickly, most local associations became "all REALTOR®" associations. Did

An early meeting of the RE/MAX management team with Dave Liniger, center, and Gail Main, second from right.

your concept help pave the way for salespeople to be full members, did NAR's movement help the RE/MAX concept gain success, or was the timing coincidental?

A: I don't know whether you can say we helped pave the way, but we were in favor of that change. We felt it was demeaning to have two classes—brokers who were REALTORS® and associates who weren't. It was a fabulous move on NAR's part, and I think NAR helped us tremendously.

Q: What's your stance toward involvement of RE/MAX associates and brokers in NAR? Do you believe it's important, and if so, why?

A: From the first day, we wanted to be part of the NAR club, not outsiders. We had a clause in our agreement with franchisees that said 100 percent of sales associates and brokers had to be members of NAR. We stressed to all our associates to get active in their local associations— not just to take but to give back. We publicized their

"When Bill Chee said 'the lions are coming over the hill,' he wasn't just talking about the Internet. He was including franchisors. . . . He was a visionary and had a tremendous impact on our industry."

accomplishments. Richard A. Mendenhall was one of the finest NAR presidents [in 2001], and he came from a RE/MAX background, which made us very proud. We also pushed for NAR designations. We endorsed the CRB [Certified Real Estate Brokerage Manager] designation program. When I was broke and had a hard time competing, I went to courses, took copious notes, and incorporated the information into RE/MAX. Gail was the first female CRB in Colorado. Then we said let's have more CRS® [Certified Residential Specialist] designees, and we pushed for that designation—then ABR® [Accredited Buyer Representative]. We've had great relationships with the various NAR councils.

Q: How has NAR helped the real estate industry?

A: What NAR did was professionalize an unprofessional trade. NAR's leadership upgraded the standards. It's made real estate a very honorable profession. It has also been a very effective lobbying organization for private home ownership in this country, which has had a profound effect on people's ability to accumulate wealth.

Q: What challenges do you see as very critical to the industry right now, and is NAR providing the leadership it should in those areas?

A: NAR is made up of 1.3 million people, and each one comes to the profession with ideas on how to succeed. If criticism can be made, I think it's that NAR has been slow to change and even fearful of change. It was fearful of RE/MAX, fearful of buyer agency. I think changes really started with Bill Chee, who wasn't afraid to make them.

As to the future, I think NAR needs to continue on its current course. It should focus on further enhancing REALTOR.com. It should also keep working to foster minority home ownership. NAR should also encourage states to toughen license laws. It's unfair to create artificial barriers to keep people from getting into the industry, but if it's too easy to get a license, it can be a disservice to consumers. We need better minimum standards. We have to be sure those who are licensed understand the business. [Real estate] is a much harder business today than it was.

material published outside NAR. In the *Real Estate Insider* newsletter of June 28, 1971, an article with the headline "8% Commission on the Horizon" stated: "Progressive Realtors [sic] will be raising commission rates to 8 percent before long because when we went from 6 percent to 7 percent, we did not catch up with inflation. . . . Those who have not yet raised rates to 7 percent are really hurting . . . they will soon have to go to 8 percent if they expect to provide the kind of service required to maintain a profitable operation."

Some individual companies found themselves in hot water. In 1977, six prominent real estate brokerages were convicted of conspiring to fix brokerage commissions at 7 percent in the Montgomery County, Maryland, area. A newspaper article at the time quoted an anonymous broker as saying most real estate brokerages were "walking on eggshells when it comes to fee schedules."

In 1980, yet another case reached the U.S. Supreme Court. In *McLain v. Real Estate Board of New Orleans*, 444 U.S. 232 (1980), the Court ruled that "alleged price-fixing by the brokers had a not insubstantial effect on interstate commerce" and thus violated federal antitrust law.

NAR decided it would avoid using any language regarding right or wrong real estate fees, compensation, or services provided. "Those decisions should be made by individual brokers on the basis of their assessment of their company and the competitive situation in which they find themselves."[28]

Indeed, with discounting taking hold in other realms—such as retailing—some NAR members began experimenting with lowering their rates on the basis of the services they provided or the listing price. They came to be known as *discount brokers;* their rationale was that a larger volume of business would compensate for their lower commissions. Others offered a sliding scale based on how quickly a house sold and how close to its listing price. Still others offered menu pricing. In regard to those models, the Association has walked a fine line, trying to help brokers prove their worth but at the same time making clear the Association does not dictate its members' business models.

Despite the hand-wringing going on at boards during the price-fixing investigations, the public seemed largely unaware of the alternative business models. In early 1989, Association President Ira Gribin of Sherman Oaks, California, caused something of a stir—including two articles in the *Washington Post*—with the simple statement, "Contrary to popular opinion, residential real estate sales commissions are negotiable."

More than a decade later, scrutiny of residential brokerage remained potent. The Consumer Federation of America released a report in 2006 saying the real estate industry stifled competition. The Association fired back, saying, "America's real estate industry is one of the most competitive business environments in the world, characterized by low barriers to entry, intense personal client service, and results-based compensation structure."

In 2006, the House Financial Services Subcommittee on Housing and Community Opportunity held a hearing on the issue at the behest of the Justice Department, the Federal Trade Commission, and others claiming a lack of competitiveness in residential real estate. Pat V. Combs, then NAR president-elect, represented the Association forcefully, saying that in 35 years in the business, she had never seen the industry more competitive. Members of Congress at the hearing weren't swayed by the Association's critics, saying they didn't see the need for Congress to intervene in the natural rough-and-tumble of a competitive industry.

The focus on commission rates was due, at least in part, to the housing boom, which saw home prices nationally rise an average of 55.53 percent between 2001 and 2006. As prices increased, critics figured, the fortunes of REALTORS® also went up. However, NAR surveys showed only modest increases in sales associates' income. With the Association membership jumping by more than 70 percent during the same five-year period, competition and the pressure to reduce commissions remained fierce.

A NEW AGE OF OPENNESS

At about the same time that local REALTOR® associations were settling price-fixing claims, the country was embarking on a new age of consumer advocacy, one that would make the residential real estate transaction both more transparent and more complex. The consumer movement, which had roots in the work of early twentieth century muckrakers, picked up steam in the 1960s with the work of Ralph Nader. His 1965 book *Unsafe at Any Speed: The Designed-In Dangers of the American Automobiles* helped speed passage of the National Traffic and Vehicle Safety Act in 1968, which set new automobile standards.

Perhaps the first manifestation of the movement in real estate came in 1974 with passage of the Real Estate Settlement Procedures Act. The law required that buyers receive information about all settlement costs associated with a real estate transaction and banned the payment of referral fees that might drive up the cost of the transaction.

RESPA's original provisions were so onerous that the Association immediately went to work seeking changes. "Even Carla Hills [President Gerald Ford's HUD secretary beginning in 1975] acknowledged it was a bad piece of legislation," Art Leitch, NAR's 1975 president, said in an unpublished 1982 interview with *Real Estate Today* magazine. Within a year, NAR had succeeded in getting major modifications to the law. "It's one of the best examples I know of

where REALTORS® were able to accomplish what we did because we were united in a common purpose," Leitch said.

For many years after that, NAR sought additional RESPA reforms that would make it easier for REALTORS® to offer convenient one-stop shopping for settlement services, such as mortgage and title, without excessive regulation. In 1996, after lobbying from NAR and other industry groups, HUD issued guidance on the operation of these affiliated business arrangements. But several years later NAR leaders balked at a reform proposal that seemed on the surface pro-consumer. It was introduced in 2002 by George W. Bush's HUD secretary, Mel Martinez. In testimony before the U.S. House Committee on Financial Services in late 2002, Martinez said, "This administration is committed to streamlining the process so consumers can shop for mortgages and better understand what will happen at the closing table."[29]

The proposed reforms removed regulatory barriers, something the Association had long sought, but in a way that pointedly favored banks in the delivery of settlement services. NAR and other groups argued that the proposal would be bad for consumers in the long run.

Martinez stepped down at the end of 2003 (he went on to represent Florida in the U.S. Senate), and his successor, Alphonso Jackson, withdrew the proposal in April 2004. Jackson said the Bush administration remained committed to reform but would undertake it with industry input. In the *2004 NAR Annual Report*, 2004 NAR President Walt McDonald of Riverside, California, declared Jackson's decision a major victory for NAR but added, "We support reforms that would maintain a level playing field for service providers and put consumers first."

Despite the fight over RESPA reforms, NAR has stood with HUD on enforcement of the existing law. During the same period it was calling for change in the RESPA law, the depart-

Carla Hills, secretary of Housing and Urban Development under President Gerald R. Ford. NAR lobbied Hills for changes to the new Real Estate Settlement Procedures Act in the year after the law's passage.

RANDY SANTOS

Alphonso Jackson, right, is greeted by NAR President Walt McDonald at a spring 2004 meeting. Jackson, at the time acting secretary of Housing and Urban Development (later he was confirmed for the post), drew cheers from REALTORS® for his withdrawal of a controversial RESPA reform proposal. He said HUD remained committed to reforming the 1974 law.

ment significantly stepped up its enforcement activities. Investigations since then have resulted in settlement agreements with dozens of real estate, mortgage, and title companies. In response, NAR introduced a series of educational tools to help its members navigate the complex law. "NAR takes RESPA very seriously and supports HUD's enforcement efforts," said NAR President Thomas M. Stevens in 2005. "Our RESPA Awareness Campaign helps REALTORS® understand the dos and don'ts of the law when it comes to their day-to-day business."

After the 1974 passage of RESPA came further transparency in residential real estate services. First came meaningful disclosure of agency relationships and, later, disclosure of property condition. NAR advocated both as a means of serving consumers and protecting REALTORS® from liability.

Of the two disclosure efforts, agency disclosure was by far the more complex and drawn out in its execution, probably because most real

estate practitioners were happily oblivious to the concept of agency. Until the 1980s, practitioners' relationships with seller clients were governed by the common law of agency. Under common law, agents owe six fiduciary duties to their clients: loyalty, accounting, disclosure, obedience, confidentiality, and diligence. NAR's founding fathers viewed their client relationships as a key element that differentiated them from those who didn't practice exclusive agency. They advocated for Association members to form exclusive agency relationships with sellers to avoid the confusion and potential harm caused by open listings.

But the system of cooperative selling meant that many practitioners were forming a relationship not with the seller but with the buyer. In 1983, the Federal Trade Commission issued a report, *The Residential Brokerage Industry.* Its main focus was on the FTC's continued concern over lack of price variation in residential brokerage services. But the report also looked at buyers' and sellers' understanding of their relationship with real estate practitioners. In cases where there was a cooperating broker involved in the transaction, 82 percent of sellers and 72 percent of buyers said they believed the cooperating broker was representing the buyer. At the time, however, that wasn't true. Most brokers worked either as the seller's agent or as the seller's subagent. Listings on the MLS constituted "blanket unilateral offers of subagency." Cooperating salespeople owed their agency duties to sellers and their agents, not to the buyers with whom they worked.

NAR's 1985 president, David D. Roberts Sr. of Mobile, Alabama, appointed a task force to clarify matters. The task force, chaired by Pall D. Spera of Vermont, acknowledged the confusion and said there was a "perceived increase in lawsuits against real estate brokers" alleging that they were breaching their fiduciary duties by acting as "undisclosed dual agents" of buyers and sellers. The report, issued in May 1986, encouraged state regulatory bodies or legislatures to pursue mandatory agency disclosure rules.[30]

Within the industry, debate was fierce over whether a brokerage could represent both the sellers and the buyers in a given transaction. Some practitioners said that brokerages had to choose—represent buyers or sellers, but not both. Barry Miller, a Denver practitioner who founded the Real Estate Buyer's Agent Council in 1988, called for exclusive buyer agency. NAR said that, as a practical matter, most companies could not survive representing just one side of transactions, nor should they have to, provided that brokers followed the law with regard to agency disclosure.

In 1990, Miller sold REBAC to the North American Consulting Group, an organization owned by Tom Dooley and Charles Dahlheimer. Under Dooley and Dahlheimer, REBAC broadened its mission, from recognizing exclusive buyer agency as the only acceptable form of buyer representation to endorsing buyer representation in all its legally recognized forms. That brought REBAC in line with NAR's position, but a vocal group of exclusive buyer's agents continued to protest NAR's stance.

At the recommendation of NAR's Professional Standards Committee, 1991 NAR President Harley Rouda of Columbus, Ohio, appointed a Presidential Advisory Group on Agency to look at the evolving agency issue. Sharon A. Millett of Maine headed the PAG. (Eight years later, she became Association president.) Millett's group made six recommendations; among them, that NAR change its MLS policy to recognize the growth in buyer representation, encourage written company policies on agency, and provide agency education to REALTORS®. The group also advocated that NAR members—and all other real estate licensees—provide consumers with timely, meaningful written disclosures of all possible

types of agency relationships. Such disclosure would give consumers the opportunity to make educated decisions about how they wanted to be represented. At the 1992 annual convention in Honolulu, Millett said, "NAR is going to make sure that all of our policies don't assume any longer that brokers represent the seller. Buyer agency is a legal, ethical, viable business practice for our members."[31] Eventual changes included revisions to the Code of Ethics to eliminate the emphasis on seller representation.

As the group had recommended, the Association undertook a massive education campaign to educate members on agency issues. It encouraged state regulators to make agency education a part of their continuing education requirements and affiliates to make agency part of the curriculum for earning a professional designation. It also called for reform in state laws. After Spera's task force report, 43 states and the District of Columbia had passed mandatory disclosure rules. "Many of these laws represent the first generation of agency reform," NAR general counsel Laurie Janik said at the release of Millett's report in 1992. "Now it's time to update them with second-generation, more effective disclosure requirements."[32]

A segment of brokers felt that the second-generation laws should do away with the concept of agency in real estate.

In 1992, the Association's first female president, Dorcas T. Helfant of Virginia Beach, Virginia, appointed a Presidential Advisory Group on the Facilitator/Non-Agency Concept to study the idea of practitioners working purely as facilitators and its potential implications for consumers and licensees. Earl Espeseth of Wisconsin chaired the group, and Millett served as vice chair. The group recommended that NAR not develop or promote the facilitator concept. Research had found that "consumers clearly want licensees to provide them with representation," it said, but added, "It is not

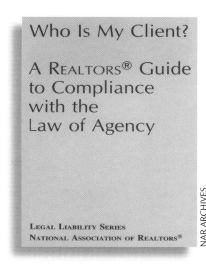

In 1986, NAR published *Who Is My Client? A REALTOR®'s Guide to Compliance with the Law of Agency.* The guide explained the role of cooperating brokers as subagents and helped spark interest in buyer representation. In 1988—the same year the Real Estate Buyer's Agent Council was founded—NAR introduced "MLS Plus," a policy that enabled listing brokers to make compensation offers both to buyer's agents and to subagents.

In the early 1990s, Sharon A. Millett led the drive to set clear agency policies and laws.

the intent of NAR to characterize the facilitator concept as unprofessional." The PAG recommended a legislative framework to clarify the law of agency as applied to real estate brokerage and made nine recommendations for state agency laws:

1. Include well-defined duties for each type of brokerage relationship.
2. Contain clear guidance on disclosed dual agency.
3. Clarify the common law of agency as applied to real estate brokerage relationships by creating a statutory agency relationship—with duties spelled out—and by creating a presumption that the relationship is one of statutory agency unless the licensee and the client enter into an agreement specifically providing for a different type of representation.
4. Provide for a broker in an in-company transaction to designate a licensee within the company to represent the seller and another licensee within the company to represent the buyer.
5. Eliminate consumers' vicarious liability for the actions of licensees.
6. Promulgate mandatory agency disclosure forms and rules providing for meaningful, timely, and mandatory written disclosure.
7. Specify how brokerage relationships end and describe the licensee's duties upon the termination of a client relationship.
8. Address the licensee's disclosure duties with respect to property condition and address broker liability issues.
9. Specifically abrogate the common law as applied to real estate brokerage relationships.

Later, the Association evolved recommendation No. 4, further developing the idea of *desig-*

nated agency as an alternative to disclosed dual agency for in-company sales. In 1993, the NAR Board of Directors endorsed the report, collectively recognizing that state laws clarifying agency roles would help address some of the potential liabilities that had spurred interest in the facilitator idea in the first place. Indeed, the PAG's recommendations became the basis for many states' second-generation agency laws. Several states, led by Illinois, passed laws saying licensees were presumed to represent the person with whom they were working unless the parties altered the arrangement with a written agreement.

While NAR was in the midst of changing its agency policies, the Consumer Federation of America and the American Association of Retired Persons released a brochure titled *Buying a Home: What Buyers and Sellers Need to Know about Real Estate Agents*. It said, "Buyer brokers will better represent the interests of buyers than will subagents. They are more likely, for example, to negotiate a lower sales price on a house." In a criticism CFA continues to launch on NAR, the 1992 brochure went on to state, "The one risk of working with a buyer broker is that they will be discriminated against by listing brokers, who would rather work with subagents."[33]

The criticism drew a slew of letters from practitioners on both sides of the issue. An article in *REALTOR® News* the week of August 3, 1992, reported that the topic of agency had generated more letters from members to the publication than any other subject.[34] As a result of the controversy, the Association commissioned a Gallup Poll in 1993, which showed that a greater percentage of buyers now better understood whom the broker represented in a transaction.[35]

Meanwhile, buyer agency was growing by leaps and bounds. REBAC's owners began publishing a newsletter and initiated the Accredited Buyer Representative (ABR®) designation. One of the preliminary qualifications for receiving the ABR® designation was membership in NAR. "We feel the name REALTOR® has a lot of credibility with the public," Tom Dooley said at the time.[36]

NAR purchased REBAC on November 11, 1996. "This is a watershed for our Association," said 1996 Association President Arthur "Art" L. Godi of Stockton, California. "It means we will now have the ability to fully serve REALTORS® who wish to practice buyer agency."

By 2005, REBAC membership had grown to more than 50,000. In 2006, REBAC bought the Seniors Real Estate Specialist program from Real Estate Business Services Inc., a wholly owned subsidiary of the CALIFORNIA ASSOCIATION OF REALTORS®, and began offering the SRES designation. In a REBAC publication celebrating its first ten years with NAR, CEO Dale Stinton called the REBAC purchase one of the best decisions NAR ever made.

After the REBAC purchase, there remained issues with how buyer agency was being practiced. Liability was on the rise. Buyer's agent duties were not well defined in state laws; as a result, courts were imposing divergent standards of care. So 1998 NAR President Layne Morrill of Kimberling, Missouri, appointed a new Presidential Advisory Group, headed by Maryann Bassett of Albuquerque, New Mexico. Among its recommendations was a call for states to define specific licensee duties for each type of brokerage relationship. The PAG also endorsed the concept of designated agency and said that once the concept was established in law, local and state REALTOR® associations should encourage its use. In addition, the PAG recommended that mediation be used to resolve disputes between practitioners and consumers—a practice the Association has strongly supported.

Although there's new complexity in real estate agency laws, agency relationships remain a cornerstone of business practices for REALTORS®.

With buyer agency gaining steam, The North American Consulting Group, headed by Tom Dooley and Charles Dahlheimer, purchased the Real Estate Buyer's Agent Council in 1990 and began publishing a newsletter, *The Buyers Rep*. The name was changed after NAR's 1996 purchase of REBAC.

On the heels of NAR's drive for agency disclosure was a push for property condition disclosure. But NAR had taken the first steps toward a better-informed buyer back in the 1970s, when it began promoting home inspections.

ALLOY PHOTOGRAPHY/VEER

EROSION OF CAVEAT EMPTOR

Caveat emptor, or "buyer beware," once formed the foundation of all real estate sales. Buyers relied on their own judgment or that of their agent (or the person they *thought* was their agent) to make a decision about a home purchase. In the 1970s, the home inspection and home warranty industries were born to offer buyers a level of assurance about their purchase. The consumer movement, accompanied by the country's growing litigiousness, played a role.

Builders were the first to experience increased liability. Still, concern materialized that risk for real estate practitioners selling existing homes was on the rise.

In 1977, the U.S. Department of Housing and Urban Development conducted a study of home inspection and warranty programs, which at the time represented a small but growing private industry for previously occupied houses. The first home warranty was the Home Owners Warranty Program, developed by the National Association of Home Builders (NAHB). NAR followed, crafting a home warranty program for existing homes under 1975 NAR President Art Leitch. "The importance of this program is seen in the fact that three existing homes are sold for each new one," said Leitch in an interview several years later. The program protected buyers against faults in the structural soundness of the home as well as failures in its major component systems.

In the 1980s, sellers' mind-sets began to change. The new catch phrase that took hold was "from buyer beware to seller take care." And sellers were not the only ones who had to take care. A landmark California decision in *Easton v. Strassburger*, 199 Cal. Rptr. 383 (Cal. App. 1 Dist.

1984), established a standard of care for real estate licensees. The court held that a real estate licensee had to conduct a reasonably competent and diligent inspection of residential property listed for sale and disclose to purchasers all facts affecting the value or desirability of the property. As a result, California passed the country's first property condition disclosure law, which became effective January 1, 1986. In Maine, property condition disclosure became mandatory through regulation. The rules, effective February 1, 1988, stated that real estate licensees had to ask for information on certain issues, such as a private water supply, in-

sulation, and known hazardous materials, and disclose that information to prospective purchasers.[37]

As Harley Rouda stepped into the NAR presidency, he saw that seller disclosure could be a way to add transparency to the transaction and reduce broker liability. Rouda, 1991 president, was focused on a statistic, widely quoted, that said 67 percent of lawsuits involving real estate transactions were based on misrepresentation. Disclosure, he reasoned, would leave a trail of evidence if buyers later wanted to file a lawsuit.

REAL ESTATE ROUNDUP

Mandatory Property Disclosure Forms: What's Your Opinion?

By Harley E. Rouda
President, National Association of
Realtors (NAR)

If you go shopping for a home, should the seller be required to tell you what they know about the property's known defects? People who think they have the right to know exactly what they're spending money on are writing their legislators to ask for buyers' protection through mandatory property condition disclosure forms. Such forms also offer important safeguards for sellers and real estate agents says NAR, which is urging state laws mandating that these forms be filled out for each residential sales transaction:

• They save the buyer a lot of grief and money by letting him or her know about such problems as environmental hazards—formaldehyde, radon, asbestos; structural additions, repairs or changes that may not comply with building codes or were done without the proper permits; neighborhood noise problems or other nuisances in the area; zoning violations; significant defects or malfunctions in the property's interior walls, ceilings, floors, insulation, roof, electrical systems, plumbing, etc. The disclosure forms are a handy checklist for buyers, so their concerns about the property's condition are addressed on the spot.

• They give the seller of a well-maintained house a market advantage over the competition. Buyers know you've had to make fairly detailed disclosures about the house and have pledged that you're telling everything, so you may be more likely to sell your home faster.

Rouda

• They may also lessen costly liability suits by purchasers against brokers charging they either knew of, or should have known about, defects in the home. Liability for failing to disclose a known defect is placed more squarely on the seller's shoulders, where it logically belongs.

Should filling out property disclosure forms be made mandatory for all property sellers? You can let your legislators know your views on this issue by writing your state legislature. For information on property condition disclosure forms and pending state legislation, as well as questions or comments, call or write State and Municipal Legislation Division, NAR, 777-14th St., N.W., Washington, D.C. 20005; (202) 383-1007, or the Office of the General Counsel, 430 N. Michigan Ave., Chicago, IL, 60611; (312) 329-8374.

After the state of California passed a law requiring sellers to disclose property condition information to prospective buyers, NAR President Harley Rouda sought state disclosure laws nationwide.

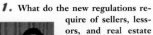

14 Things You Should Know about New Lead Paint Rules

New federal regulations requiring sellers or lessors of pre-1978 residential dwellings to disclose the presence of known lead-based paint in the property will go into effect Sept. 6, 1996, for owners of more than four residential dwellings, and Dec. 6, 1996, for owners of one to four residential dwellings.

For years, federal, state, and local governments have been attempting to limit the amount of human exposure to lead, a toxic metal that, when present in the human body, attacks the central nervous system. In 1978 the federal government banned the use of lead-based paint in residential buildings.

Existing lead-based paint in dwellings remains a source of environmental concern, say analysts for the NATIONAL ASSOCIATION OF REALTORS®. According

to the U.S. Department of Housing and Urban Development, more than one-half of the U.S. housing stock—and more than three-quarters of units built before 1978—contains some lead-based paint.

In 1992 the U.S. Congress passed the Residential Lead-Based Paint Hazard Reduction Act, which requires seller disclosure of lead-based paint and lead-based paint hazards in connection with the sale or lease of pre-1978 dwellings. The law directed the U.S. Environmental Protection Agency and HUD to issue regulations to implement those requirements. EPA and HUD issued the regulations on March 6.

Here are answers to some key questions about the regulations:

1. **What do the new regulations require of sellers, lessors, and real estate professionals?**
Before ratification of a contract for sale or lease
• Sellers and landlords must disclose known lead-based paint and lead-based paint hazards and provide available reports to buyers and tenants.
• Sellers and landlords must give buyers and renters a federal pamphlet titled *Protect Your Family From Lead in Your Home.*
• Homebuyers will get a 10-day period to conduct a lead-based

paint inspection or risk assessment at their own expense if desired. The number of days can be changed by mutual consent.
• Sellers and lessors must include certain language in sales contracts and leasing agreements to ensure that disclosure and notification actually take place. Sellers, lessors, and real estate professionals share responsibility for ensuring compliance.

2. **What are the specific responsibilities of real estate salespeople?**
Real estate salespeople must ensure that
• Sellers and landlords are aware of their obligations.
• Sellers and landlords disclose the proper information to buyers and tenants.
• Sellers give buyers the 10-day opportunity (or another mutually agreed-on period) to conduct an inspection.
• Lease and sales contracts include proper disclosure language and acknowledgments that all the required information was provided.

3. **What type of housing is covered?**
Most private housing, public housing, federally owned housing, and housing receiving federal assistance

4. **What housing is not covered?**
• Housing built after 1977
• Zero-bedroom units, such as efficiencies, lofts, and dormitories
• Housing with leases for less than 100 days, such as vacation houses or short-term rentals

NAR President Art Godi says that new federal lead-paint disclosure regulations make sense both for the public and for the real estate industry. "It's good business to let people know up front what they're buying," he said at the Washington, D.C., press conference announcing the new regulations. Godi is flanked by EPA Administrator Carol M. Browner and HUD Secretary Henry G. Cisneros.

16 Today's REALTOR®

The federal Lead-based Paint Disclosure Act of 1992 added another disclosure requirement in the sale and lease of homes built before 1978. During the rulemaking period, NAR worked with HUD to help clarify the role of real estate practitioners and then set about teaching REALTORS® about the rules, as in this 1996 *Today's REALTOR®* article.

Rouda formed a working group to examine and evaluate the essentials of property condition disclosure. He made an influential statement to the Association's Board of Directors in April 1991, encouraging state associations to develop and support legislation or regulation to mandate use of property condition disclosure forms. "Seller disclosure is in everyone's best interest," he said. "Sellers benefit because by focusing on the condition of their property, they are less likely to overlook a defect or material fact for which they could later be held liable. Also, this procedure serves as a checklist for buyers, so their concerns about the property's condition are addressed on the spot. And that may even help speed up the sale."[58]

Rouda won support, and NAR launched a nationwide campaign to encourage states to establish mandatory seller disclosure laws. The Association recommended the use of a standardized form that would inform buyers of the overall condition of the house they were purchasing and address specific problems, such as pests, water, radon, and lead. Remarkably, by the end of Rouda's term, seller disclosure laws were in place in more than 20 states. And that number has increased. A 2006 survey showed that more than 80 percent of surveyed jurisdictions had seller disclosure provisions, though the rules varied greatly. Nineteen percent required disclosure of airports in the area; five states required disclosure of noise sources. Only California and Oregon required disclosure of earthquake zones, but other states required disclosure of soil slippage, upheaval, or settling. The obligations of real estate licensees also varied. For example, more than 45 percent of jurisdictions required licensees to deliver or make available the seller's disclosure.

During Rouda's presidency, the hazards of lead-based paint for children were becoming known. Rouda felt the Association and its members were in a perfect position to educate the public. One day after a news conference by

Health and Human Services Secretary Louis W. Sullivan and the Alliance to End Childhood Lead Poisoning, Rouda released this statement: "In light of the new data released yesterday . . . indicating the increased risk of lead exposure in children, NAR is in full support of enhancing nationwide public health efforts."[39] Rouda said NAR supported lead testing to protect consumers, home values, and the stability of the marketplace. His statement went on to suggest that disclosure was the best way to stop childhood lead poisoning:

We strongly urge all home owners contemplating selling their homes to disclose to real estate brokers or agents, and to potential purchasers, lead hazards that present a significant risk to health. This is in accordance with Association policy, which advocates seller disclosure of all known material facts about a home. We are interested in working with Congress, and other groups, to develop incentives for states to expedite the process of adopting mandatory seller disclosure laws. The seller has the most intimate knowledge of his home, and is in the best position to disclose information about it.[38]

In 1992, Congress passed, and President George H. W. Bush signed, the federal Lead-based Paint Disclosure Act. The act applied to homes built before 1978, when manufacturers were banned from using lead in paint. It required that sellers and landlords (or their agents) provide prospective buyers and renters with information on lead-based paint. The law also required a written disclosure, which buyers and renters must sign. Buyers, the law said, had a right to perform lead testing but could waive that right.

During his 1996 NAR presidency, Art Godi helped resolve issues concerning HUD's regulations of lead-based paint rules. Godi also happened to be president during one of the most trying times in the Association's history. His leadership, and that of other NAR officers in those years, would prove pivotal as the Association grappled with how to serve its members in the age of the Internet.

To help NAR members integrate lead-based paint disclosure into their practices, *Today's REALTOR®* published this 1996 tale.

THE NATIONAL REAL ESTATE JOURNAL

Henry Ford built his first Model T, inset, in 1908. Within a few years, his cars were rolling off the assembly line. Growing auto use enabled NAR members to begin using signs to attract passing motorists. Right: A Cincinnati driver (circa 1917) sees a sign—one of a series—directing him "To the Knobs."

FROM THE COLLECTIONS OF THE HENRY FORD

COURTESY CATHY WHATLEY

THE TECHNOLOGY JUGGERNAUT

The Internet—with all the hype and promise that surround it—may be the newest technology to impact the real estate business, but it's hardly the first. In 1908, even as the ink was drying on the articles establishing the National Association of Real Estate Exchanges, scientists and engineers were building tools, inventing products, and perfecting processes that would change the world and the real estate industry: Henry Ford built the first Model T automobile. The first wireless message was sent from the Eiffel Tower. And electroluminescence, a phenomenon that would eventually help illuminate the computer screens of REALTORS®, was discovered.

Clearly, technological progress was driving the growth of the nation and the real estate industry would be a beneficiary. To exploit the explosion of scientific knowledge that began in the nineteenth century and accelerated in the twentieth century, the United States required laboratories, factories, warehouses, and offices. And, of course, employees needed housing.

The real estate industry was growing, and NAR's staff and its members readily adopted the tools that were becoming available to all businesses. By today's standards, of course, those devices could scarcely be called high-tech. From the beginning, manual typewriters clattered in Association offices and real estate agencies throughout the country—the first electric typewriters were decades away.

Dial telephones were introduced in 1919 and quickly began replacing telegraph messages

When NAR was founded, real estate practitioners were already using newspaper advertising and other print promotions to attract buyers.

The PLAN YOU HAVE HOPED FOR IS HERE

Mr. Successful Real Estate Man:

As I cannot call on you in person and tell you our story, I will try to explain it fully and briefly on this page. In the center insert you will find A WONDERFUL OFFER and an order blank---*Read it carefully, then act.* We know that our service will bring you back on a larger scale whenever your renewal date comes around.

Advertising on a Guaranteed Result Basis

As a successful real estate man you realize of course that advertising is a vital necessity yet you find it in most cases an uncertain proposition--no matter what paper you use. You are gambling; you may receive many live prospects at a low cost or your advertisement may not produce a single reply.

United Realty Associates Service

The United Realty Associates advertise each week in a selected list of the leading Sunday papers of America, with a combined circulation of several millions. All advertising is placed under our own name and is keyed, so that each paper must produce results or lose its place on our list in favor of another. This campaign goes into nearly every section of our great country, and locates a new live list of FARM PROSPECTS each week, people who are in the market for a farm, and who write us to that effect. *This service is given you in bulletin form.*

Advertising Under Your Own Name

In addition to the Weekly Buyers' Prospect Service, which is based on our National Sunday Paper Campaign, you will also receive full value for your investment in resultful advertising under your own name in the paper that carries more **farm lands for sale** advertising each Sunday than any [other?]. The *Joliet (Ill.) Herald-News.* *You could not buy this space cheaper.* ... *Herald-News* and secure

Cut Out The Hard Labor of Letter Writing

It's as easy as turning to a number in a telephone book. The Automatic Letter Writer solves the problem of handling correspondence economically and effectively.

It will reduce the cost of correspondence to a mere fraction of the time and labor you are now putting into it, and—more than that—it will keep your letters up to the highest level of *force, tact, effectiveness and clearness.*

Before The Automatic Letter Writer the day's mail melts away

There isn't a man living—no matter how efficient he is—who can dictate hundreds of letters, day after day, and make them all effective and forceful, and leave out nothing essential. The distractions of the office, the telephone, the wrong kind of luncheon—all sorts of interruptions put snarls and kinks into correspondence. Use The Automatic Letter Writer, and your letters will always be *smooth, courteous,* and with a *red-blooded grip* to them.

A Hundred Letters An Hour

The Automatic Letter Writer is a handsome, durable book—bound so it will open flat for stenographers' use—containing hundreds of numbered paragraphs, carefully written by trained and experienced correspondents, covering every business need. These paragraphs are tabbed and indexed for instant reference. ... collection of successful business letters in existence. The letters that have sold the most goods, collected the most money, settled the hardest complaints—are all in the three volumes of this practical library of letter writing. The Business Correspondence Library is a three years' course ...

YOUR ALLOTMENTS
And All Points of Interest In One Drawing

Let us submit a folder or circular to advertise your allotment.

We can submit you a proposition specially designed to meet your requirements which will make your sales come easier and quicker.

The above, a reproduction from one of our drawings gives an idea of the advantage gained by using such a drawing in your advertising and selling.

Aerial View Specialists
The Canton Engraving and Electrotype Co.
Canton Ohio

My dear Sirs:-

Sometime within the next couple weeks our aerial view artist will be in your city to make sketches and drawings preparatory to making birdseye views.

On your allotments it is possible for us to give you an illustration which will look like a photograph taken from a balloon. The picture would be made from a drawing which would show not only your allotment but associate it with the city and other interesting points near by. We can show in the illustration the natural contour of the land or make the drawing to show how the allotment will look when the improvements are completed.

Please do not confuse this with a draftsman's drawing as it is something entirely different. Our artists go all over the country making drawings of real estate allotments, factories and cities. The idea is to make a drawing that will not only show your allotment but to have an illustration that your prospective customer can see at a glance just how the land really looks and it association with other points of interest.

If you are interested our artist will call on you when he is in your city, at which time he would be pleased to show you samples and quote on the cost of the work and if you do not care to proceed further there will be absolutely no obligation in any way.

Do you want our artist to call ?

Awaiting your reply, we are

Most cordially yours,

THE CANTON ENGRAVING & ELECTROTYPE CO.

Write us to-day

Pres. & Treas.

The Canton Engraving and Electrotype Company

314 REX AVE., S. E.   CANTON, OHIO

Vendors capitalized on the growth of real estate as a profession, promising solutions to make marketing property easier.

Machines such as the manual typewriter, telephone, and adding machine were staples of the modern, professional real estate office.

THINKSTOCK

8 Column Machine
$125

Mechanical Accountant

Weight 12½ lbs.

This Machine Stops Profit Leaks

Because it is error-proof, preventing costly mistakes. It adds as quickly as the operator can read the figures. Just press the keys and glance at the result. Items are checked instantly, and can be corrected without going back over the work. There is no lever to pull—no extra operations—its speed is unlimited. The

Mechanical Accountant

will earn its cost many times the first year. Durable and simple in construction the Mechanical Accountant actually costs less than half the price of any other standard machine on the market. Let us put the Mechanical Accountant in your office for 30 days free trial. Each machine is guaranteed for two years. Made in five capacities from, $60.00 to $200.00. Write today for free booklet.

Prove Its Value at Our Expense.

MECHANICAL ACCOUNTANT COMPANY,   17 Warren Street   Providence, R. I.

RETROFILE/MEDIA BAKERY

By 1950, "cooperative selling" was the norm. Multiple listing service technology was rudimentary—local boards relied on lithograph machines to print MLS listings—but the use of computers and cameras was on the horizon. In 1954, Town and Country Homes Inc. of Boston, Massachusetts, introduced an electronic machine called The Home Finder. Built by the Underwood Corporation, The Home Finder used an electronic punch card tabulator to sort data so that prospects could quickly find the home to suit their needs. Prospects could then view applicable properties via Town and Country's Photoguide, a wall of photographs (top left of photo on right). The company used more than 50 Polaroid Land cameras to keep the Photoguide display up to the minute.

as the most convenient way to communicate. By the 1930s, automobiles had become both reliable and comfortable enough for REALTORS® to use to show homes. By the 1940s, ambitious real estate practitioners were reaching prospects by using Multigraphing, a printing process for mass-producing mailings.

Technology was advancing in other areas as well. In 1941, AT&T laid the first coaxial cable, a precursor to what Americans in the twenty-first century take for granted: broadband communications. In 1947, three AT&T scientists invented the transistor. That same year, the company announced it was working on something called "cellular telephony," a concept that would emerge 26 years later as a Motorola invention called the "cell phone."

In the 1950s, the first contact management solution, the rudimentary but reliable Rolodex, began showing up on desks across the country.

A French writing-instrument company named Bich dropped the *h* from its name, and soon real estate closing papers were being signed by ballpoints, which were cheaper than fountain pens and didn't leak. And in 1974, a 3M employee's discovery of a new way to mark pages in his hymnal led to the legendary Post-it note.

Of all the tools available to real estate practitioners in the middle of the twentieth century, however, those that generated the most interest involved the lifeblood of the industry: property listings. Their story begins much, much earlier.

Richard Mendenhall, 2001 NAR president, says the decision by brokers to share listings back in the 1880s was one of the most important real estate technology developments ever. "Their efforts led to the modern MLS, which has seen a steady evolution of technologies that have enabled the buying and selling of real estate to grow and become one of the most

For years, listings contained only printed information, but by the early 1960s, a Los Angeles company was boasting that "10,000 brokers and salespeople in 30 California real estate boards are now selling property with listings photographed and printed by the American Picture Co."

important components of our economy," says Mendenhall.

Listings have always been considered essential to the process of buying and selling real estate—and their evolution, by itself, provides considerable insight into the expanding role of technology in the industry. Initially, listings were simply brief descriptions of properties for sale and were often featured in newspaper ads placed by real estate professionals. Agencies also maintained additional listings for the communities they served. Those were usually available to consumers only after they had formed a client relationship with a sales associate or broker.

But beginning early in the twentieth century local REALTOR® associations determined it was valuable to compile databases of property listing information in the area serviced by their membership.

Keeping track of listings was strictly a manual process. "I remember how we used to sort listings," recalls William S. "Bill" Chee, 1993 NAR president from Honolulu. "The listings were on index cards, and you'd line them up with pins that looked like knitting needles."

As MLS systems grew, new methods for distributing information were being attempted. For many years, listing databases were bound into books and mailed or delivered by messenger to MLS participants, but local associations were tantalized by the promise of computerization.

The first business computer was UNIVAC, which cost a stunning amount at the time—$1 million—and was first used in 1951 to help with the U.S. census. Eventually, 46 UNIVACs were built for government and business purposes, including one for General Electric, which used it to compute its payroll.[40]

Soon the U.S. Patent Office was working overtime to keep up with computer-related innovations. In 1954, IBM unveiled FORTRAN, the first computer programming language. In

In the years before the personal computer, computers were vast, expensive machines used only by large companies, universities, and government agencies.

NATIONAL ARCHIVES/DEPARTMENT OF HOUSING AND URBAN DEVELOPMENT, 1965–1995/207-MPF-199

In the late 1960s, NAR formed a committee to explore computers' potential uses in real estate and local associations began the race to computerize their multiple listing databases. In 1974, the Long Island Board of REALTORS® became one of the first local associations to successfully computerize.

MLS Signs Contract for Computer

The Multiple Listing Service recently signed a contract with Realtronics Computer Systems for a sophisticated in house system featuring a Hewlett-Packard 21-MX computer. Signing are Realtronics President Bert Helfinstein [left] and MLS's Horace Bernstein. Standing from the left are Bennett Josephs and Rose Goldberg of MLS, and Richard Huggins of the computer firm. Expected to become operable in December, the system will provide a high-speed tool for selling homes, keeping track of customers, and appraising properties through the use of comparables.

In 1970, Ebby Halliday demonstrates the latest technology from national relocation network RELO, an acoustic coupler that transmits data via telephone lines.

1959 came the most influential development of all, the invention of the integrated circuit, which paved the way for more powerful and functional computers—from mainframes to laptops.[41]

In the late 1960s, real estate boards in Cleveland and Long Island, New York, tried to computerize their systems; a board in Detroit finally succeeded in early 1969. Almon "Bud" Smith, former NAR executive vice president, recalled in a 2006 interview that NAR purchased the program, REALTRON, from the Detroit board in 1973.

"NAR created RCS-MLS and tried to take it nationwide but was unsuccessful," said Smith.

Another distribution system used a device for sending and receiving listing information over the telephone. Bob Goldberg, NAR senior vice president for Marketing and Business Development, recalled that "it used an acoustic coupler, a kind of handset that you'd place in a cradle."

Transmission was agonizingly slow by today's standards. The data was transmitted as sound pulses, and listings printed out on thermal paper that spilled onto the floor.

By the 1970s, computers were becoming common in workplaces throughout the country. NAR installed its first computer in 1973, and by 1975, computerized MLSs were becoming a reality in many markets.

At the same time, telephone technology was evolving. For generations, U.S. telephones were like the Model T automobile: heavy and black. But in the 1960s, both the telephone and the telephone business began to change.

MULTIPLE LISTING SERVICE

CONFIDENTIAL

REALTOR'S MARKET INVENTORY

This Book Property of _____

NO. 16 — April 19-25, 1073   № 1205

ML SERVICE   GREATER BUFFALO BOARD OF REALTORS

NAR ARCHIVES

COURTESY NEW YORK STATE ASSOCIATION OF REALTORS®

Beginning in the mid-1970s, MLSs transitioned from bound books to computer. Early computer systems allowed brokers and salespeople to view current listings—but not update them.

In 1964, touch-tone handsets began to replace rotary dialing. In 1982, AT&T's hold on the telephone industry was shattered by the Justice Department, and a system of regional companies was created, which resulted in new service offerings and lower prices.

In 1973, Motorola announced the first cell phones, so named for the company's use of technology based not on hard wires but on wireless systems that allowed communication over small range-of-service areas, or cells. Clunky by today's standards, they were soon followed by a parade of ever-smaller devices with a growing array of features, including speakerphone, call-waiting, and eventually even a camera. Such innovations were welcomed by business professionals of all kinds, and REALTORS®, who spent large amounts of time away from their office, were among the early adopters. Even more important to the real estate industry was a phenomenon that would eventually alter the way the world communicates—the Internet.

In 1968, the U.S. Defense Department's Advanced Research Projects Agency announced it had perfected a system for linking computers worldwide. That groundbreaking achievement, called ARPANET, led to what became the Internet. For nearly a decade, however, that remarkable network of computers was used only by the military and academic communities. Eventually, the business world caught on to its promise.

In 1969, an Ohio insurance company founded a subsidiary called CompuServe Network Inc. to provide in-house computer processing support and generate additional income as a computer time-sharing business. In 1975, the company

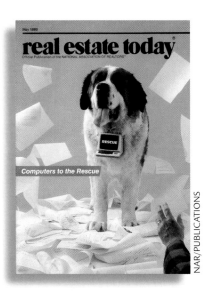

May 1985

real estate today
Official Publication of the NATIONAL ASSOCIATION OF REALTORS®

RESCUE

Computers to the Rescue

NAR/PUBLICATIONS

By 1985, *Real Estate Today* **magazine** was looking toward a paperless future.

Before cellular technology, it was a challenge to stay connected with the office while working in the field. One innovative practitioner in 1958 relied on a radio-telephone. By the 1990s, analog cell phones were essential mobile equipment for most real estate practitioners. Laptops and handheld computers, also known as personal digital assistants, were also gaining a following. Digital phones and wireless Internet access were still in the future.

NAR ARCHIVES/THE NATIONAL REAL ESTATE AND BUILDING JOURNAL

NAR/PUBLICATIONS

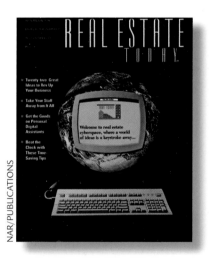

NAR/PUBLICATIONS

Whether you called it "cyberspace" or the "information superhighway," the Internet's transition from government and academic medium to business tool generated equal parts excitement and angst among real estate practitioners.

was spun off as CompuServe, which dominated the computer online business into the 1980s before its purchase by America Online, which was launched in 1985. AOL's monthly subscription pricing proved more popular than CompuServe's hourly rate approach.

CompuServe and AOL introduced the nation to online services, but the biggest breakthrough came a few years later. In 1989, a European engineer named Tim Berners-Lee made the Internet widely accessible by creating a graphical user interface, or GUI, which gave users access to the Internet with the click of a mouse. Berners-Lee called his invention the World Wide Web. Overnight it created a new industry: Internet service providers, or ISPs, which charged monthly fees to let users—including REALTORS®—access the Internet from their home or office computers. Still, AOL remained particularly popular with REALTORS® in those early Internet days. *Real Estate Today* magazine in 1995 took advantage of AOL's revolutionary instant messaging function to conduct an online technology roundtable.

The REALTOR® organization was steadily taking steps to transition from paper to pixels. The possibilities of instant exchange of data and digital storage of information were an exciting and increasingly practical idea—and some state associations jumped on the idea, creating online forums for their members. Executives who led those first efforts recall today that they felt like explorers. One was former NAR Executive Vice President Smith, who served from 1991 through 1997.

"None of us was thinking about the Internet," Smith recalled in 2006. "The advanced thinking was [that] there would be key players like AOL, and consumers would pay to enter their system to access information and send e-mail. We used computers internally as a way of giving everybody instant access to information, but in those days, nobody [thought] the Internet was something the average person would have access to. It was just a big mystery back then."

The Internet was indeed an enigma to most people. Even Microsoft's Bill Gates admitted in the mid-1990s that he had underestimated its power and influence. He announced he was belatedly authorizing development of new products that would help consumers "communicate, collaborate, and conduct electronic commerce" via the Web.

Within the real estate industry, the Internet was more than an enigma. It was considered by many to be a threat.

Goldberg remembers clearly the concern generated by the Internet. He had joined NAR in September 1995 to help bring the organization into the Internet age. "We realized we had to get REALTORS® on that information superhighway," recalls Goldberg. "We knew we had to stay a step ahead of consumers to show greater value. At the time, our message was considered heresy. When we told the world that our goal was to take all the listings out of a proprietary backroom system and make them available so [that] everyone could see all of our information, there were people out for our heads. Thanks to the vision of Bill Chee, we started taking steps in the right direction."

Chee, 1993 NAR president, had become impressed with how other businesses were beginning to explore the Internet as a way to better serve and thereby deepen their relationship with customers. He was also growing increasingly concerned that outside interests would win clients away from the MLS system unless the organization acted quickly and decisively.

Smith recalls a turning point that took place during NAR's Midyear Meetings in May 1993. Chee was preparing an address to NAR's Board of Directors, and he asked for Smith's advice. Smith recalls that he told his friend: "Bill, speak from your heart. They have to feel from you what the future holds for this industry. We're either going to lead the charge or become also-rans." The result has come to be one of the most important

documents in NAR's long history: the so-called "Lions Over the Hill" speech.

Chee chose to focus on what he believed were shortcomings in the MLS systems. He listed technology innovations available to competitors, who he said could threaten NAR members' hold on listings—innovations such as digital imaging systems, touch-screen kiosks, electronic classified ads, and even a "super MLS" controlled by major brokers. Warning that REALTORS® were in danger

RANDY SANTOS

Bill Chee of Honolulu issued a prescient warning to the Association's board of directors in 1993. Chee's "lions over the hill" speech urged NAR leaders to take immediate steps to avoid being marginalized by technology players and others with designs on the real estate consumer. He galvanized NAR leaders to start down a path that would lead to the creation of REALTOR.com. A video of his speech is posted at REALTOR.org.

By 1996, NAR's technology initiative—envisioned as a proprietary online system—was stumbling badly. NAR Executive Vice President Almon "Bud" Smith delivered the news to NAR's board of directors in May that more money would be needed to keep the initiative going. Two months later, Smith and 1996 President Art Godi, left, led an emergency meeting of the board. The July meeting was a turning point. NAR pulled the plug on the proprietary system and moved instead to create a publicly accessible Internet site—REALTOR.com.

of being what he called "disintermediated," or left out of the transaction, he continued:

> *Consumer trends are driving the market to provide more and more services and more and more access, while NAR's MLS systems are positioned at the opposite end of this trend by having outmoded technology. By making the MLS an exclusionary database, we are not only running counter to the habits and expectations of the consuming public, we are opening vast opportunities to emerging "lions." If you believe, as I do, that the hungry lion is coming over the hill, the big question is, What do we do?*

Chee answered his own question by contending that "we must consider some form of public access. We must become the lions by making

ourselves such a valuable resource that no one—no vendor, no buyer, and no seller—will see any benefit in bypassing the REALTOR® family."

Chee's remarks set in motion a series of decisions that would shape the Internet strategy of NAR as it approached the millennium. One of the first was to create an entity called the Federation. Goldberg was its chief marketing officer. "The idea behind the Federation was to find a way to join the strength of brokers, members, and the Association to keep outsiders from taking money out of this industry," he recalls. "The challenge was how to get REALTORS®' attention. We were trying to tell people they were going to be replaced technologically unless they developed the knowledge and the tools they needed to compete."

Convinced it must move quickly to get listings online, the Federation became the REALTORS® Information Network. In 1995, operating as a separate corporation with its own management and even its own board of directors, it undertook steps to launch a proprietary service but quickly ran out of money. According to Smith, RIN management "first asked NAR for $3 million, then $6 million more, and they still didn't have enough to go online. At NAR's Midyear Meetings in 1996, RIN was given an additional $3 million, and then, a few weeks later, we found it was still $4 million or $5 million away from getting anything done," recalled Smith.

Smith and 1996 NAR President Art Godi called a special meeting of NAR's Board of Directors to authorize an emergency bailout of the fledgling network. "The mood of the time was panic," recalled Godi several years later. "About 770 directors came to the special meeting in Chicago in July 1996. We had to lay it out to them. We said, 'Give us until November. Trust us.' Eighty percent voted to give us the go-ahead."

Martin Edwards Jr. was treasurer at the time—in 2002, he would serve as NAR president—and later said it was Smith and Godi's openness that unified the directors: "People from some of the states had questioned [the wisdom of] our continued financial commitment to RIN. Bud Smith did an unbelievable job that day. He and Art Godi stood up there and handled that meeting in such a controlled but open manner that everybody felt involved. You could see the mood change."

The decision was made to partner with a California company to help NAR reach its Internet objectives. The company's CEO, Stuart Wolff, had the requisite high-tech background and impressive resume. He'd been working on a venture that involved mall kiosks, but the Internet—and the power of REALTORS® information—captured his attention. "Although his experience was with kiosks, Wolff was a visionary who could see the Internet was the place to be," said Joe Hanauer, an NAR director at the time. A joint-venture company, RealSelect, was formed and began operating REALTOR.com for NAR. In 1999, RealSelect changed its name to Homestore.

Initially, many REALTORS® were concerned that REALTOR.com would hurt their business, but by March 2001, the REALTOR® population had increased, not declined, and Homestore's Wolff was able to tell *BusinessWeek:* "Our model was always to partner with our industry. It was our intent to use technology to help make REALTORS® more efficient, not put them out of business."[42]

The company went public in 1999 at the height of the dot-com boom, and the Association not only made up for earlier RIN losses but also realized a significant gain on the strategic sale of shares. The period brought excesses, however, including a financial scandal that resulted in the departure of most of Homestore's top executives. Over the next several years, Wolff and ten other employees were convicted on federal charges relating to a scheme to inflate company revenues.

Despite the setback, NAR remained determined. In January 2002, new management was installed at Homestore; in 2006, the company changed its name to Move Inc. REALTOR.com continued to be its flagship Web site. Today, Move.com and REALTOR.com continue to dominate the online real estate space, with more than 4 million listings and 7 million monthly visitors, but NAR and Move continue to confront "lions" seeking to supplant their No. 1 position.

Hanauer, who became chairman of the board of Move Inc. in 2002, said the financial scandals were trying. But he still looks back on the period of Homestore's growth as the most exciting time in the Association's history. Without NAR's early and decisive action to put listings online and to partner with RealSelect, he said, "real estate would [most] likely have been prey to nonindustry players, just as was the case with travel, employment, and many other service industries. REALTOR.com gave the industry an opportunity to drive a stake square in the middle of the real estate space and become competitive in the early stages."

RANDY SANTOS

Stuart Wolff was called a wunderkind when, at 33, he partnered with REALTORS® on the development of REALTOR.com. As chairman and CEO of Homestore, he helped NAR put millions of real estate listings online. But questionable accounting practices at the company forced Wolff and several other Homestore executives to resign in 2001 and 2002.

In 1996, NAR envisioned an organizational web site—part of *REALTOR.com* but accessible only to REALTORS®—that used building architecture as its model for categorizing content.

NAR's Internet strategy went well beyond making listings widely available to consumers:

- In 1997, it launched One Realtor Place®, a Web site that gave users around-the-clock access to information from throughout the REALTOR® organization.
- In 1998, NAR rolled out the National REALTORS® Database System, which enables local associations to post member records, thereby eliminating duplication, speeding service, and enabling REALTORS® to update their own records online.
- In 1999, NAR established the REALTOR® Electronic Commerce Network, which gives REALTORS® online access to products and services from the REALTOR® organization.
- In 2000, NAR added to its roster of training resources a course called e-PRO®, which leads to a professional certification in technology preparedness for REALTORS® and helps them develop the skills necessary to succeed in the competitive world of online real estate. The program is offered in partnership with Internet Crusade, whose partners—Mike Barnett, Saul Klein, and John Reilly—have strongly influenced the industry's adoption of new technology.
- In 2001, One Realtor Place® became REALTOR.org, which continues to provide NAR members with access to in-depth information about the

Today, *REALTOR.com* is the No. 1 consumer destination for real estate–related information, attracting more than 6.5 million unique users each month.

industry and now offers a multimedia experience, including streaming video and podcasting. At the site, REALTORS® can tap into REALTOR® University, developed in partnership with Learning Library, to study hundreds of industry-related courses online 24/7.

• In 2004, NAR created the Center for REALTOR® Technology to evaluate the impact of technology on the real estate industry and serve REALTORS®

and REALTOR® associations with technology expertise and counsel. That same year, the Association formed a partnership with an outside company to begin offering a new electronic lockbox technology, SentriLock, which is now being used by more than 100,000 REALTORS® around the country.

• In 2006, a survey by the Center for REALTOR® Technology revealed that

In 2001, One Realtor Place became the publicly accessible REALTOR.org. Today, the site is a multimedia platform with more than 700,000 registered users and 800,000 visitors per month.

During my 30 years as a real estate professional, I have seen the MLS go from paper pages to books and from books to computers. I have seen the advent of the fax machine, the personal computer, e-mail, voice mail, laser printers, color printers, software programs, electronic lockboxes, and, of course, the Internet—all tools that make our job easier and help us build better relationships with our clients. We have come a long, long way, and we have NAR to thank for much of it.

NAR leaders today look back on their Internet history with pride, saying the Association would not be where it is today—with a membership of more than 1.3 million—had it not been for their commitment to embracing technology.

"A decade ago, NAR leaders took a step into technology when the rest of the world was waiting to see the Internet's impact," said 2007 NAR President Pat V. Combs. "They took a leap when they formed RIN. It was not perfect, but in hindsight, the very step of doing something started us on the road to where we are now."

Dale Stinton, NAR CEO and executive vice president, said the Association's commitment to being a first mover on technological change is just as strong today as it was in 1993 when Chee delivered his "Lions" speech: "We believe the ability to use technology tools and solutions to build strong client relationships is key to success in the real estate industry today, and we are committed to provide our members with everything they need—training, tools, resources, and counsel—to build their businesses. Our goal has always been, and will continue to be, to maintain leadership in areas that are crucial to the best interests of our members and their clients."

the number of REALTORS® with Web sites had increased 129 percent over the previous five years. The survey also indicated that REALTORS® were making substantial investments in technology, responding quickly to Internet inquiries, and consider the Internet to be a major source of leads.

CRT's survey appears to confirm the observations by 2006 NAR President Thomas M. Stevens that "consumers are able to use information portals to look for homes to buy because REALTORS® have invested a huge amount of resources in technology to make accurate information available on secure sites, thus bringing added value to the transaction. All that information is available to consumers, free of charge, 24 hours a day."

From no computers in 1972 to a full-blown array of Internet resources, NAR had made a lot of progress in 35 years. In 2006, Patricia S. Fitzgerald, an NAR member from Jupiter, Florida, readily agreed:

Head for Business, Heart for Real Estate

Joe F. Hanauer in 2002

Many NAR leaders have contributed to making the Association a serious player in the real estate technology arena. But if one can be cited for his long-term commitment, business acumen, and moral leadership, it's Joe F. Hanauer of Laguna Beach, California.

Hanauer is a commercial practitioner who operates Combined Investments LP, which directs investments in companies primarily involved in real estate and financial services. He's also chairman of the board for Move Inc., the company that operates REALTOR.com.

He has helped guide the Association's Internet strategy from its earliest days—when REALTORS® were still smarting from the failure of their pre-Internet technology venture. At the time, Hanauer was a voice of reason—and his credentials ensured he'd be heard by everyone from the NAR Leadership Team to the rank-and-file member. He'd previously served as chairman of both Coldwell Banker Residential and the commercial firm, Grubb & Ellis, where he led a restructuring in 1994. Hanauer started his real estate career in Chicago as an associate with Thorsen, REALTORS®, a large brokerage that later was sold to Coldwell Banker. The sale precipitated his climb through Coldwell Banker's executive ranks.

During the startup of REALTOR.com, Hanauer provided crucial direction to NAR, urging industry executives to recognize the value of their intellectual property and adopt a unified Internet strategy. That strategy involved forming a partnership with a new entity called RealSelect that would run the Web site. RealSelect was later renamed Homestore, and, in 2006, Move.

In a 1998 article, Hanauer told fellow REALTORS® that the floodgates to real estate information were already open. If it was their information that traditionally made them the first point of contact, it would be their willingness to release that information directly to anyone who wanted it that would enable them to maintain that position in the age of the Internet. "Just make certain that the linkage between you and your data remains firmly in place," he said.

Preserving that linkage was the philosophy behind REALTOR.com.

Dennis R. Cronk of Roanoke, Virginia, who participated in the negotiations to form RealSelect, later called Hanauer "a key player in NAR's technological drive for excellence."

Just a year later, during a U.S. Justice Department investigation over fraudulent accounting activities at Homestore, Hanauer and the rest of the board were praised by investigators for being open and forthright about the company's financial situation. In the midst of the investigations, in January 2002, Hanauer was named chairman of the board. In addition to his continuing role with Move Inc., Hanauer is chairman of the International Real Property Foundation, a nonprofit organization created to teach U.S. real estate practices and promote private property rights worldwide; a trustee of Roosevelt University in Chicago; and Move's representative on the Policy Advisory Board for Harvard's Joint Center for Housing Studies, where he is a past chairman.

In 1996, he helped negotiate NAR's purchase of the Real Estate Buyer's Agent Council, which NAR executives have called one of the best business moves the Association ever made.

A World of Good

From the start, the most prominent members of the NATIONAL ASSOCIATION OF REALTORS® looked beyond U.S. borders. Samuel Skidmore Thorpe, the 1911 president, was in Berlin on August 1, 1914, the day Germany declared war on Russia. He managed to get out of the city and make his way safely to London.

In 1920, one year after his NAR presidency, William May Garland traveled to Switzerland to ask the International Olympic Committee to consider Los Angeles as a host city. Garland was successful. The games were held in Los Angeles in 1932, thanks largely to Garland's efforts to have a new stadium built in the city. (For more on Garland, see page 84.)

But it wasn't until after World War II, as the world fell under the shadow of the Cold War, that NAR leaders began to envision an inter-national role for the organization itself. Most REALTORS® at the time had limited interest in international real estate—understandable, given the small amount of international investment during the two or three decades following the war. But NAR leaders saw the Association as an important player in the struggle between democracy and communism. Which philosophy would gain traction globally—that of the Soviet Union, with its repudiation of private property rights, or that of the United States, with its principles of private ownership and free enterprise?

As authorities on how to conduct business in a "private property environment," Association leaders believed they had an obligation to share their experience and expertise beyond U.S. borders. The world economy would benefit, in their estimation, from adopting the principles of private ownership and free enterprise. REALTORS®, in turn, might eventually benefit from a global market.

Today, real estate is a global business, and the NATIONAL ASSOCIATION OF REALTORS® is a leader in the development of successful, ethical business practices.

WORLD WIDE WEB OF PARTNERSHIPS

Robert P. Gerholz, a builder from Flint, Michigan, was president of the National Association of Home Builders in 1944 and president of NAR in 1950. One of the highlights of his NAR presidency was a trip to Europe to address real estate practitioners there. His participation set the stage for NAR's earliest international involvement. The following year, NAR helped found a forum, headquartered in Paris; in 1952, it took the name International Real Estate Federation (going by its French acronym FIABCI). Since then, a number of NAR officers and members have served as world presidents and officers of FIABCI.

NAR encouraged REALTORS® to join FIABCI,

GLOBAL LEADERSHIP

NAR presidents frequently represent the Association on the international stage. Among those most active internationally:

Leonard P. Reaume (1930 NAR president) of Detroit, FIABCI world president, 1957–1959.

Philip C. Smaby (1976) of Bloomington, Minnesota, FIABCI world president, 1980–1981.

Ralph W. Pritchard (1980) of LaGrange, Illinois, FIABCI world president, 1985–1986.

David D. Roberts Sr. (1985) of Mobile, Alabama. Roberts actively supported NAR's international program and participated in two International Shelter Conferences organized by NAR.

Nestor R. Weigand Jr. (1988), FIABCI world president, 2001–2002, and president of the Leonard P. Reaume Memorial Foundation.*

Norman D. Flynn (1990) of Madison, Wisconsin. Flynn participated in the Third International Shelter Conference in Washington, D.C., and went on to help found the Eastern European Real Property Foundation, later the International Real Property Foundation. He began serving as IRPF's CEO in 2005. In addition, Flynn served as NAR's Regional Coordinator for Western Europe for more than ten years and currently serves as its Regional Coordinator for Eastern Europe.

William S. Chee (1993) of Honolulu helped expand NAR's outreach to Asia.

Arthur L. Godi (1996) of Stockton, California, did extensive fieldwork and teaching for the Eastern European Real Property Foundation and served a number of years as NAR's Regional Coordinator for Eastern Europe.

Russell K. Booth (1997) of Salt Lake City chaired the International Operations Committee before his presidency and had been named to cochair the International Consortium of Real Estate Associations, to succeed Sharon Millett, but resigned to lead a mission to Nigeria for the Mormon church.

Sharon A. Millett (1999) of Auburn, Maine, served as cochair of ICREA during its first two years.

Dennis R. Cronk (2000) of Roanoke, Virginia, helped develop NAR's bilateral relationship with the China Real Estate Association.

Richard A. Mendenhall (2001) of Columbia, Missouri, served as second cochair of ICREA.

*The Leonard P. Reaume Memorial Foundation was established in 1996 by Renee Reaume to honor her late husband (1930 NAR president) and, in particular, his commitment and contributions to the field of international real estate. The foundation supports a variety of international real estate efforts.

NAR's leaders were very active in FIABCI, the International Real Estate Federation, during its first 30 years and NAR remains a principal member of FIABCI today.

and on the strength of U.S. participation, a U.S. chapter was established in 1957, with NAR providing staffing. For many years, FIABCI and FIABCI-USA were the primary vehicles for REALTORS® interested in international business and practice. FIABCI-USA became NAR's de facto international committee; its members were behind the international real estate education that became the basis for the Certified International Property Specialist (CIPS) designation program that was established by FIABCI-USA in 1985.

But it wasn't long before NAR leaders recognized a need to extend their international presence beyond membership in FIABCI. In 1960, just three years after the founding of FIABCI-USA, NAR established an international affiliate program through which it negotiated bilateral agreements with foreign real estate organizations. The first such agreement was with the Philippine Association of Real Estate Boards. The agreements in the early years had limited objectives: to protect the REALTOR® trademark, then being used illegally in some countries; to promote adoption of a code of ethics by affiliate organizations; and to advance professionalism at home and abroad.

By the late 1970s, NAR leaders concluded that the relationship with FIABCI—though rewarding from a personal perspective—was not going to help NAR achieve its international goals. After delegates to a 1976 international housing conference published views in opposition to private property ownership, there was considerable concern that NAR needed an independent voice to strongly assert the importance of private property. "Until the Soviet Union started to break apart, those were very important issues," said Jack Howley, who joined NAR in 1985 as vice president of International Operations and today works as an independent adviser to the Association.

Philip C. Smaby of Bloomington, Minnesota, served as NAR president in 1976 and FIABCI world president in 1980–81. He later recalled discussing the issue while sitting in the InterContinental Hotel in Paris in 1980 with 1964 NAR President Ed Mendenhall of High Point, North Carolina, and 1980 NAR President Ralph W. Pritchard of LaGrange, Illinois. The three men determined that NAR needed a committee within its own structure to focus on international affairs. They went before the Executive Committee and got the go-ahead to form the International Policy Committee. Ed Mendenhall became its first chair in 1981. "At the first meetings, we had seven, eight, ten people attend," Smaby said. "Now we fill ballrooms, and hundreds of nations are involved in our activities. It's grown from that very humble beginning to what it is today."

For several years after forming the committee, NAR continued to operate the U.S. chapter of FIABCI as an affiliate. In 1991, however, the U.S. chapter established itself as a separate corporation and changed its name to FIABCI-USA. At about the same time, NAR created its own International Section. NAR continued its membership in FIABCI, however, and individual members of NAR are still active in the federation.

Meanwhile, the international affiliate program was humming along. By 1991, there were 13 bilateral agreements in place, and NAR leaders sought to strengthen the program, refashioning the agreements to promote business relationships between NAR members and members of international affiliate organizations. The program was also vastly expanded: Today, there are 70 affiliated real estate associations in 55 countries. The result is a vast network of practitioners around the world producing business opportunities—as well as social, cultural, and educational benefits—for Realtors®.

To bring the benefits of NAR's network closer to home, NAR also created the International Ambassador Association Program, which partners more than 35 local and state Realtor® associations directly with a foreign association. There are also

about 70 Local International Councils working to bring international investment to U.S. markets.

In the late 1980s, NAR launched an education program leading to the CIPS designation, and in 1998, the International Section was renamed the CIPS Network. Within a few years, the global market would grow dramatically in importance. From 1992 to 2004, foreign direct investment in the United States more than doubled, from less than $600 billion to $1.709 trillion. Foreign direct investment in U.S. real estate totaled $37.96 billion in 2004. Meanwhile, the 1990s saw a huge wave of immigrants coming to the United States, with an interest in setting down roots and becoming home owners.

As world attention on U.S. markets increased, global forums and education sessions became regular features of the Realtors® Conference & Expo, and in 1998, the International Networking Center was established as a feature of the conference. Today, the networking center has grown into

CIPS Network members receive a quarterly publication, *Global Perspectives in Real Estate,* and inclusion in the CIPS Network Directory, *Who's Who in International Real Estate.*

The International Networking Center at the REALTORS® Conference & Expo.

a hub for international practitioners and service providers seeking to reach this market segment. In 2006, NAR teamed up with SIMA, Europe's largest second-home/resort expo of worldwide properties, to launch the SIMA Showcase, where REALTORS® Expo attendees can learn about international real estate opportunities for themselves and their clients. In addition, NAR offers more than 150 real estate classes per year in markets around the world.

In 1999, NAR led an important global initiative: the development of international real estate standards. The initiative's aim was to advance practical business opportunities for U.S. and foreign practitioners. NAR and eight association partners laid the groundwork for establishment in 2001 of an international structure—the International Consortium of Real Estate Associations (ICREA)—to develop technology, business, and professional standards and carry

Real estate professionals in more than two dozen countries today form the International Consortium of Real Estate Associations. Here, the signers of the founding documents at a 2001 ceremony and scenes from an ICREA plenary session.

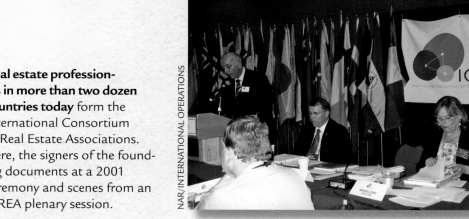

them into practice. Twenty-three national associations signed the founding agreement. Today, there are 28 national organization members, representing more than 2 million professionals worldwide. In 2003, ICREA launched WorldProperties.com, an international property Web site, which, by 2006, included nearly 3 million property listings, comparative real estate data, and a transnational referral system.

From modest beginnings, but with vision and leadership, NAR has created value for members, fostering a global market in which standards and practices of U.S. professionals are becoming widespread.

ACTIVISTS FOR PROPERTY RIGHTS

At the same time that NAR was opening doors for its members internationally, it was engaging in the public policy arena, working to spread its message about the value of private property ownership to a world audience.

The need for a strong voice became apparent in 1976, when the United Nations sponsored a Worldwide Conference on Human Settlements (Habitat I) in Vancouver, British Columbia. The conference shone a global spotlight on shelter needs, leading to the creation of the UN Centre for Human Settlements (UN-Habitat). However, delegates adopted positions unfavorable to private property rights. The preamble to the conference recommendations stated in part: "Land . . . cannot be treated as an ordinary asset, controlled by individuals and subject to the pressures and inefficiencies of the market. Private land ownership is . . . a principal instrument of accumulation and concentration of wealth and therefore contributes to social injustice; if unchecked, it may become a major obstacle in the planning and implementation of development schemes."[43]

NAR's executive vice president at the time, Jack Pontius, served with the U.S. delegation to the conference and prompted the Association to step up its efforts on behalf of property rights worldwide. Since the Vancouver meeting, NAR executives have served as delegates at a number of UN-Habitat meetings. Jack Carlson, who became NAR's chief executive following Pontius's retirement in 1978, was instrumental in bringing about a shift in UN policy. Carlson represented the Association at a 1983 conference in Helsinki, Finland, where he introduced an important NAR resolution on "security of tenure." It's a concept that refers to having legal, enforceable title to land—a fundamental indicator of whether low-income families in developing countries have a stake in society. Today, NAR holds and exercises Category II Consultative Status with the UN system and is called on for comment on policy affecting housing, land, and other real estate–related matters.

NAR followed up Helsinki with a series of three International Shelter Conferences, beginning in 1984. Jack Howley, a delegate at the Helsinki conference representing the U.S. Agency for International Development and later an NAR executive, said the shelter conferences were designed to explain the concepts of private ownership and security of tenure and promote their application throughout the world in a variety of social, economic, and political environments. NAR initiated the conferences and was their primary sponsor, but a number of cosponsors from the United States and around the world were involved, including the Canadian Real Estate Association, the Building Societies Association of England, FIABCI, the U.S. League of Savings Institutions, and the NAR affiliate Institute of Real Estate Management.

The Second International Shelter Conference, held in 1986 in Vienna, Austria, produced the Vienna Recommendations. In large part, those recommendations became the basis for the UN Global Strategy for Shelter, a policy blueprint for public-private cooperation in housing. The strat-

PROCEEDINGS OF THE
SECOND INTERNATIONAL SHELTER CONFERENCE
&
VIENNA RECOMMENDATIONS
ON SHELTER & URBAN DEVELOPMENT

I Y S H
1 9 8 7

*A Private Sector Contribution in Support of
the International Year of Shelter for the Homeless, 1987.*

Housing for All
Vivienda para todos · Un Logement pour tous

CONCLUSIONS AND RECOMMENDATIONS

THIRD INTERNATIONAL
SHELTER CONFERENCE

NAR was the principal sponsor of three global housing conferences between 1984 and 1990. The second conference laid the foundation for the United Nations policy on housing. The third conference was the catalyst for NAR's efforts to help establish private property markets in former communist nations.

egy was adopted by the UN General Assembly in December 1988.

Speaking in Vienna, 1985 NAR President David D. Roberts of Mobile, Alabama, said the shelter sector provides jobs and "generates considerable social benefit" for countries. He detailed the process of private property transfer in the United States and told delegates, "We would like to see those same processes established in the developing countries, and we offer our assistance wherever requested."[44]

Roberts's offer came just a few years before the Tiananmen Square protests in Beijing and the fall of the Berlin Wall, events that foreshadowed the collapse of Soviet communism—and the growth of NAR's role on the world stage.

AN OPENING TO CHINA

A year after Vienna, 1987 NAR President William M. Moore of Denver led a team of real estate professionals to the People's Republic of China (PRC). The contact opened a dialogue between NAR and the PRC Ministry of Construction. There were mutual expressions of future cooperation in the matter of housing reform.

In the ensuing years, the PRC's desire to privatize housing and real estate ownership and its need to learn the basic elements of modern real estate practice have been well documented. NAR's role has not been inconsiderable. Moore's initiative and the dialogue that followed led, more than a decade later, to a bilateral partnership with the China Real Estate Association, formed under the auspices of the Chinese Ministry of Construction. The partnership—negotiated by 2000 NAR President Dennis R. Cronk of Roanoke, Virginia—has enabled NAR to offer training programs throughout China on Western methods of buying, selling, owning, and developing real estate.

In 2003 testimony before Congress, James A. Dorn, vice president for academic affairs and China specialist with the libertarian Cato Institute, commented on the changes taking place in China: "Chinese citizens can now own their own businesses, buy shares of stock, travel widely, hold long-term land-use rights, own their homes, and work for nonstate firms. The depoliticization of economic life is far from complete, but the changes thus far have created new mind-sets and expanded individual choice."[45] Although Dorn's comments were not specific to NAR's role, they demonstrate the value that organizations like NAR have brought to China's democratization efforts.

And China wasn't the only communist country that would turn to NAR for guidance. In April 1990, three years after Moore's trip, the Third International Shelter Conference was held in Washington, D.C. The conference came just six months after the fall of the Berlin Wall and provided NAR an impetus to reach out to Eastern European nations. Nearly 400 attendees from 66 nations participated in the conference, taking up an effort initiated by NAR to develop a set of worldwide housing indicators. The Soviet Union not only sent a delegation but also presented a case study of Soviet real estate issues. The biggest challenge was the existing system: Virtually all housing was owned and maintained by the state, with no mechanism for private ownership.

After the conference, NAR was in communication with high-level Soviet housing officials, ultimately resulting in a conference in Moscow in September 1990 and further discussions about developing a private real estate market.

FOUNDATION FOR CHANGE

By 1991, Eastern Europeans were looking squarely to the United States for guidance on establishing real estate practices and professional real estate associations in their own countries. NAR played an active role, recommending priority areas for reform. However, having lived under communist rule for nearly 50 years, officials in Eastern Europe were not automatically thrilled with the alternative. In February, the U.S. Department of Labor sponsored a real estate symposium in Warsaw, Poland. Howley represented NAR, accompanied by New York practitioner David Michonski. Both

At a 2003 news conference in Beijing, NAR announces plans to sponsor a major international expo in China. Representing NAR were Colorado REALTOR® Gail Lyons and NAR staff Xiannian Ye and Miriam Lowe.

Howley and Michonski recalled a difficult atmosphere as they stood before their Polish guests and explained how free-market principles applied to housing.

"There were no property owners. There were no associations," Howley recalled, "only government bureaucrats who perceived that what was being said about property rights would affect their interests. There was a lot of tension in the hall. David confronted the issue head on and told them their prosperity depended on getting away from the system they were part of and respecting private enterprise and private property rights. Subsequently, our relationship with the Poles became very close."

Seven months later, in September 1991, the Russian deputy minister for Housing and Construction met in Scotland with representatives from the Counselors of Real Estate, an NAR

REALTORS® and their Polish counterparts gather at a conference in Cracow, Poland.

affiliate. The following month, another affiliate, the CCIM Institute, conducted an exchange visit in the United States. Among the visitors were the top managers of the most important housing and commercial construction conglomerate in Moscow.

One month before the dissolution of the Soviet Union, in November 1991, NAR was the prime sponsor of a weeklong conference in Moscow in collaboration with the Massachusetts Institute of Technology and UN-Habitat. The World Bank, the U.S. Department of Housing and Urban Development, and USAID participated as observers. The Urban Institute and the CCIM Institute were participating presenters. At the conference, a joint NAR-MIT team made recommendations for establishing a conceptual basis for private property law and helped frame legislation to put before the Russian parliament. In June 1992, NAR joined with USAID, UN-Habitat, MIT, and the Cracow Real Estate Institute to conduct a four-day seminar, "Housing Development and Marketing in Poland: Issues of Feasibility," in Cracow, Poland.

With the breakup of the Soviet Union, the U.S. government was interested in bringing about democratic reforms in Central and Eastern Europe, Howley said. "We saw an opportunity [with funding from Howley's former employer, USAID] to provide assistance in the privatization of real property." Thus, in 1992, NAR founded the Eastern European Real Property Foundation (EERPF). Its goal was to assist in the transition from centrally planned to market-driven economies in the newly independent countries and, in particular, to assist in the creation of real estate associations and markets.

"There were a lot of people who I think had been hoping that moment would arrive, when private initiative could be turned loose," Howley said. "Being able to buy and sell and speculate in property could be better and more equitable than the rigidity of the Soviet system. I think NAR saw a business opportunity, but at the same time, it had a kind of moral crusade." In fact, the founding of the EERPF was tied to the Association's philosophical anchor—expressed in the preamble to its Code of Ethics—that widely allocated ownership is critical to a free and democratic society.

On October 8, 1992, USAID signed an agreement to provide $3.5 million to help the EERPF establish and promote private markets in Bulgaria, the Czech Republic, Hungary, Poland, Romania, and the Slovak Republic. In 1993, the foundation received an additional USAID grant of $1.5 million to provide assistance in Russia and Ukraine. All told, USAID provided about $10 million for programs in 11 countries in Eastern and Central Europe and for establishment of an umbrella group, the Central European Real Estate Associations Network (CEREAN). With that aid, the EERPF assisted in the development of more than 60 real estate associations, representing more than 50,000 real estate professionals. The EERPF helped those associations develop, become financially independent, build membership, and play an active role in public policy debates.

Today, there are active private real estate markets functioning in all 11 targeted countries. Legal reforms have been uneven, with the most progress in the Czech Republic, Hungary, Poland, and Russia. But all the countries now have laws to protect private property, and the professions of real estate broker, appraiser, and property manager are well established. For its work, the EERPF was named USAID Domestic Partner of the Year for 1997 and was singled out by J. Brian Atwood, administrator of USAID under President Bill Clinton, as an outstanding example of a successful vehicle to deliver public development assistance of lasting value.

Two factors were key to the EERPF's success. One was support from local associations—including the Northern Virginia Association of REALTORS®, the Chicago Association of REALTORS®,

WEEK OF OCTOBER 19, 1992

Norman D. Flynn, vice president of Eastern Europe Real Property Foundation and former NAR president, addresses remarks to participants of the Oct. 8 signing ceremony for an agreement committing the first installment of a total $3.5 million from the U.S. Agency for International Development to the foundation to allow American real estate experts to aid privatization of real estate markets in Eastern European countries. Carol Adelman, USAID assistant administrator for Europe, and Peter Kimm, USAID director of housing, also participated in the ceremony, which took place in the Treaty Room of the U.S. State Department in Washington, D.C.

U.S. real estate experts set to aid Eastern Europe

A public-private partnership agreement finalized this month between representatives of the U.S. real estate industry and a federal government

REALTORS® will be established to work on Eastern European programs, said Flynn.
Foundation officials noted that

COURTESY NORMAN FLYNN

In 1992, REALTOR® News reported on NAR's plans to provide real estate expertise to the nations of Eastern Europe.

Attending the 1995 CEREAN Conference were, from left, Valentin Stobetsky of the Russian Guild of REALTORS®; Norman D. Flynn, 1990 NAR president; Al Van Huyck, first executive vice president of the Eastern Europe Real Property Foundation; and Konstantin Aprelov, who served for four years as the president of the Russian Guild.

At a news conference in Prague, the Czech Republic, held during the Central European Real Estate Associations Network (CEREAN) Conference in 2000, Ivan Zikesh of the Czech Republic answers questions with his NAR counterparts: Vice President of International Operations Jack Howley, 1990 NAR President Norman Flynn, and 2000 NAR President Dennis Cronk.

and several Florida associations—that believed the opening of global markets would be of interest to their members. The other was the decision to provide countries with a business model and basic operating capital to fund and train a core staff. "If the foundation had had to wait until those countries could collect the rather modest capital needed to form an association, it wouldn't have been as effective," Howley said. (In fact, the decision by NAR's own founders to hire a professional staff from the start was one of the main differences between NAR and earlier national real estate organizations that faltered.) Many individual REALTORS® also contributed to the EERPF's success, volunteering their time to teach courses on brokerage, appraisal, property management, and commercial property analysis.

Over time, the foundation's geographic interests extended to other parts of the developing world. In 2001, the EERPF was renamed the International Real Property Foundation. In partnership with NAR, it continues to seek financing to provide assistance in Eastern Europe, Latin America, the Caribbean, Asia, and Africa. NAR members remain directly involved in the Latin and Asian markets, teaching and providing association-management advice and counsel.

LEADERS OF THE FREE WORLD

Meanwhile, NAR has continued to participate in influencing global housing policy. The Association helped plan for the 1996 UN-Habitat World Conference in Istanbul, Turkey, and cofounded the Coalition for Sustainable Cities in 1997 to foster development of public-private partnerships in the effort to enhance the quality of urban environments around the world. As an outgrowth of its international public sector work, NAR joined with Habitat for Humanity International and the Canadian Real Estate Association in 2006 to create the International Housing Coalition.

The IHC is a nonprofit advocacy organization dedicated to raising the priority of housing on the international development agenda. It supports the basic principles of private property rights, secure tenure, effective title systems, and efficient and equitable housing finance systems—all essential elements to economic growth, civic stability, and democratic values.

When NAR leaders in the post–World War II era were getting their feet wet in the international arena, they could hardly have imagined the central role their Association would play with the fall of Communism, growth of the European Union into a potential economic powerhouse, and emergence of China and India. Especially noteworthy have been NAR's advocacy of secure tenure as a desired worldwide norm, development of techniques for measuring housing conditions around the world, and participation in reform of the former Soviet bloc countries. The face of NAR abroad is that of an organization and system of ethical and productive practice, professionalism, and private- and public-sector power. NAR and the U.S. business system are frequently put forth as models to be emulated.

Said Howley, "You only have to look at the number of international practitioners and the business that's being done to see that the vision [for becoming involved internationally] was the right thing to do."

The Executive Suite

Edward Halsey

Bruce Douglas

In 2004, the management firm of Booz Allen Hamilton asked a group of business school professors to select the world's most enduring institutions. On their list of ten were such disparate entities as the Salvation Army, the Rolling Stones, and the modern Olympic Games.[46] What those seemingly dissimilar organizations share, according to the study's director, is the same quality that has enabled the NATIONAL ASSOCIATION OF REALTORS® to celebrate a century of success: enduring leadership.

In 100 years, NAR has had just 11 executive vice presidents, including one (Herbert U. Nelson) who served for 33 years and another (Eugene P. Conser) who served for 15. How that group of Association professionals shepherded NAR from infancy to its status today as the world's largest professional business group is a fascinating story.

It begins with Edward A. Halsey, who in 1908 was asked to serve as president of the fledgling National Association of Real Estate Exchanges. Halsey, who had worked with Edward Judd to organize the Association's first convention at Chicago's YMCA, declined the offer, insisting that the role of president should be filled by a qualified real estate professional elected each year by the membership. The job he would take part-time, said Halsey, was that of executive secretary. It was a decision that would shape the operation of the Association for the next 100 years.

In 1909, Halsey was succeeded by R. Bruce Douglas, who had been serving as president of the Milwaukee Real Estate Board. His vision for a national real estate association was an organization that could bring ethical behavior to a marketplace he believed had become corrupt.

CHIEF EXECUTIVES OVER THE YEARS

The NATIONAL ASSOCIATION OF REALTORS® has had 11 chief executives in its 100-year history. From 1908 to 1937, the chief executives of the Association used the title Executive Secretary; from 1937 to 2001, the title was Executive Vice President. In November 2001, CEO was added to the title.

Dale A. Stinton	Nov. 1, 2005–
Terrence (Terry) M. McDermott	1997–2005
Dr. Almon R. "Bud" Smith	1991–1997
William D. North	1986–1991
Dr. Jack Carlson	1979–1986
H. Jackson Pontius	1970–1978
Eugene P. Conser	1955–1970
Herbert U. Nelson*	1922–1955
Tom S. Ingersoll	1911–1922
R. Bruce Douglas	1909–1911
Edward A. Halsey	1908–1909

*From 1922 to 1937, Nelson's title also included General Manager.

"[It] is easier to become a real estate man and handle thousands of dollars' worth of property and money than to become a barber charging ten cents for a shave," Douglas fumed. "A barber must go before the investigating board, and if he is not a good barber, they don't give him a license. A real estate man has no preliminary examination to meet. He is not questioned as to his mental training, education, honor, or anything of the kind."[47]

Douglas began the work on a code of ethics that was adopted by NAREE in 1913. He also worked to expand membership in what, by today's measure, was a tiny organization. When he left his position in 1911, NAREE had grown to include 42 boards.

By then it was apparent that the organization needed a full-time executive secretary, and it found a good one: Thomas S. Ingersoll, a diligent and congenial presence known to NAREE members as "Our Tom." Recognizing that a larger organization would result in more and better resources for all members, Ingersoll worked hard to grow the organization, crisscrossing the country to visit local association leaders. He was so successful that by the time he left in 1922 to become executive secretary of the Los Angeles Realty Board, NAREE membership had expanded nearly tenfold to include more than 400 local boards.

Ingersoll was succeeded by one of the most influential figures in the Association's history. A Minnesotan, Herbert Undeen Nelson had worked as a young man in lumber camps in the Pacific Northwest, where he first encountered members of the left-leaning Industrial Workers of the World, also known as Wobblies. Later, Nelson would recall that "the Wobblies were communists, and what they said they would do to private property rights if they ever got the chance put fear in my heart." From the beginning of his service as NAR executive secretary and general manager, Nelson worked hard to promote legislation that would protect property rights. He also expanded the Association's member education and public relations efforts.

In Washington, D.C., Nelson came to be regarded as a leading expert on housing, taxation, and finance. He wrote the first draft of the Home Owners Loan Act, which refinanced existing mortgages and provided emergency relief for distressed home owners during the Depression, when U.S. home ownership actually dropped to 44 percent. He was also a strong advocate of the formation of the Federal Home Loan Bank System and the Federal Housing Administration.

During Nelson's tenure, the position was renamed executive vice president. At his retirement in 1955, Association membership had risen to more than 1,200 local boards and 56,000 members, and U.S. home ownership had climbed to more than 55 percent. In addition to his activities on behalf of the Association, Nelson was a great archivist of important Association documents. In 1960, the Association established and dedicated the Herbert U. Nelson Memorial Library in its Chicago headquarters.

Finding a worthy successor to Nelson was a challenge, but the search committee of five former Association presidents succeeded when it recruited Eugene P. Conser from his post as executive secretary of the California Real Estate Association. A former real estate professional himself, Conser had also worked as a financial journalist, taught real estate courses at the University of California at Los Angeles, and been secretary-manager of the Apartment Association of Los Angeles County.

Conser drew upon his considerable experience to nearly double the size of NAR by emphasizing education, upgrading real estate license laws, and enforcing the REALTOR® Code of Ethics. His first objective, however, was to deal with the fact that the organization had just $45,000 in reserves. "NAREB (as the Association was known until 1973) was nearly 50 years old and still trying to make do with annual dues of just $10," he would recall. Conser won approval for a small dues increase and then moved to address another problem.

Tom Ingersoll

NAR ARCHIVES

Herbert U. Nelson

NAR ARCHIVES

"NAREB needed to establish a public identity," he said.

At the time, NAR was headquartered in cramped offices above the Schubert Theatre in Chicago. It was one of several Chicago locations the Association would occupy before its present headquarters—the 12-story REALTOR® Building at 430 N. Michigan Avenue—was purchased in 1975. To build visibility for the Association, Conser created a field organization of Association representatives who traveled the country to set up local associations and conduct seminars. Out of his efforts came the Graduate, REALTOR® Institute, or GRI, designation, still flourishing more than 50 years later.

In 1970, Conser was succeeded by H. Jackson Pontius, who had been recruited from his post as executive vice president of the California Real Estate Association. Although born and raised in Fort Dodge, Iowa, and educated at Iowa State University in Ames, Pontius had migrated after graduation to California.

During World War II, he worked as a manager for Douglas Aircraft Company. In 1948, he joined CREA as education director and assistant state secretary. During his years with the state association, he served on the University of California President's Real Estate Adviser Committee, the Commission on Real Estate Education and Research, and former Governor Ronald Reagan's Building and Construction Industry Task Force.

During his eight years with the National Association, Pontius emphasized member services and political activity, noting, "I believe that the real estate industry has increasingly begun to realize the strength, both politically and professionally, that comes from unity." Membership in NAR grew from 93,000 to more than 660,000, a leap aided by the decision in 1972 to add the new membership category of REALTOR-ASSOCIATE®. That change took place in 1973 and was accompanied by the name change to NATIONAL ASSOCIATION OF REALTORS®.

In Washington, D.C., Pontius worked with NAR leaders and NAR General Counsel William D. North to create the Voluntary Affirmative Marketing Agreement, an agreement with the U.S. Department of Housing and Urban Development whereby boards and members could participate in fair housing–related activities. Pontius also helped initiate programs to protect NAR and its members facing litigation. His efforts with 1975 NAR President Arthur Leitch led to the errors and omissions insurance now available to REALTORS®.

In 1978, with Pontius planning to retire, a search committee chose NAR Senior Vice President Bill Magel as his successor. Magel was known throughout the REALTOR® organization for his collaborative approach to Association strategy, building strong relationships with the local and state REALTOR® associations and NAR's affiliate organizations. As senior vice president,

A holiday greeting from the Nelson family.

1926

A Family Album is such fun
To proudly show a friend,
And so to you this glimpse of us
In twenty-six we send.

1935

We can't believe the years are only
Nine the pictures span,
And that the babe and child and boy
Are boy and youth and man.

he had moved quickly to launch the REALTOR-ASSOCIATE® program and was instrumental in the organization's name change. On July 19, 1978, Magel had just signed his contract when he was struck down by a fatal heart attack at the age of 43. Magel's untimely death forced the leadership to conduct its second national search for an executive vice president in less than a year. Their choice was a candidate with exceptional credentials.

Jack Carlson held a master's degree in public administration and a Ph.D. in economics, both from Harvard University. He had served as an assistant to the secretaries of defense and the air force, been an assistant secretary of the interior for energy and minerals, run unsuccessfully against Sen. Orrin G. Hatch in a Republican primary in Utah, and served for three years as senior vice president and chief economist for the U.S. Chamber of Commerce.

The challenges confronting Carlson were summarized in the May 1983 issue of the Association's magazine, then known as *Real Estate Today:* "An economic recession and the worst housing depression since the 1930s have compelled NAR to take a more aggressive role on behalf of its members and the property owners they serve. These financially troubled times have called for solid management, a reordering of priorities, and a marshaling of monetary and staff resources."

Carlson worked hard to give NAR a strong voice in Washington, D.C. He created a weekly publication, *REALTOR® News,* to further communicate NAR's key messages and developed the Association's housing affordability index, still used by the media as an economic indicator. He recognized the growing importance of information technology and was instrumental in NAR's early efforts to make high-tech tools and solutions available to members. Carlson also had a keen eye for leadership ability: In 1980 he recruited longtime NAR

Executive vice presidents Eugene Conser, Jack Carlson, and Jack Pontius.

counsel William D. North from the law firm of Kirkland and Ellis to join the Association's senior management team as senior vice president and general counsel.

North had earned his law degree from Harvard. Before working in private practice, he had served with the U.S. Office of Naval Intelligence. When Carlson left NAR, North succeeded him, first as acting executive vice president and then as the REALTORS®' executive vice president of choice from among 80 applicants. As NAR's general counsel, North had helped the Association negotiate an agreement with the U.S. Department of Housing and Urban Development and later wrote a book, *Passwords and Prejudice,* providing guidance to real estate practitioners on their fair housing obligations.

As the new executive vice president, North was immediately confronted with the specter of what the *Chicago Sun-Times* called "the most anti–real estate tax legislation in history," the notorious Packwood tax proposals to revise Internal Revenue Service rules concerning the

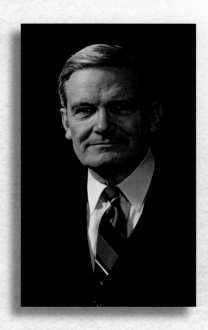

Bill North

Five of the past six executive vice presidents of NAR, stretching from 1955 to 1997: Eugene Conser, Jack Pontius, Almon "Bud" Smith, William North, and Terry McDermott.

depreciation of real property. In May 1986, North told the newspaper, "If this law passes, who is going to invest in real estate again?"

The reforms passed, however, with devastating consequences for some commercial practitioners. North is credited with working diligently to present the industry's position. As he reminded legislators in 1986, "The real estate industry has consistently led the nation into good times and should not be so penalized by tax legislation that it cannot fulfill that role again."

Along with his efforts in Washington, D.C., North introduced management efficiencies that helped reduce the Association's operating costs. He also worked hard to build relationships within the REALTOR® organization, noting, "The strength of this Association is the local affiliations we have. No single part of us can do it alone." When he announced his plans to retire in 1991 after 21 years of service, 1988 NAR President Nestor R. Weigand of Wichita,

Kansas, said, "Bill North was a pillar of integrity when we needed it most."

By 1991, NAR and the real estate industry were on the threshold of the information age. The man chosen to replace North, from a field of nearly 100 candidates, understood the challenges that lay ahead. "As the needs of our members change," he said, "NAR must be flexible enough to meet them. It's my responsibility to see that NAR stays ahead of the times." Almon "Bud" Smith later said his efforts to meet the technology needs of the Association's members were among the most challenging of his career.

Smith had served as executive vice president of local associations in Cincinnati and Cleveland. From 1978 to 1991, he was CEO of the OHIO ASSOCIATION OF REALTORS®. In November 1991, he took over NAR's top staff job at the Association's convention in Las Vegas.

He soon discovered that because of a flat real estate market and stagnant membership growth, the Association was on course to exhaust its reserves in 18 months. Smith concluded that NAR had become a victim of the "silo" phenomenon that often infects business organizations.

"Almost every department focused on itself to the exclusion of others, which led to duplication of spending," he recalled in 2006. To remedy the situation, Smith made staff cuts and introduced team-building training. To get staff out of their silos, he encouraged them to visit brokers, MLS offices, and local and state REALTOR® associations. "As a result, we started working together with better integration of our efforts. We came together as a whole."

At the same time, Smith was dealing with rapid changes in technology. When he arrived, NAR had enough computers for only half the staff, and the machines were "operating on three different platforms that couldn't communicate with one another. We made some major changes in the area of equipment and training, which opened up whole new vistas of cooperation and integration," he told an interviewer in 2006.

Even more daunting was the Association-wide effort to bring REALTORS® into the Internet age by creating the REALTORS® Information Network. After serious financial challenges, that effort paved the way for the launching of REALTOR.com, which continues to be the Web's most visited site for information about homes for sale.

By 1997, Smith had reached the end of his six-year contract. After an intensive search, Terrence M. "Terry" McDermott was named to replace Smith. The 54-year-old Chicagoan had risen to become president and chief operating officer of Cahners Publishing Company, the nation's largest publisher of business and special interest magazines. Following his long career in publishing, McDermott had served as executive vice president of the American Institute of Architects. His combination of experience in the for-profit and not-for-profit fields led him to tell an interviewer in 1997, "Associations today are becoming more like for-profit businesses. To be successful, they have to have the same disciplines as for-profit organizations. Members expect the staff of NAR to live in the same world as they do and respond to the same financial pressures and opportunities."

Chief among the financial pressures and opportunities experienced by NAR during McDermott's service were the Association's continuing efforts to establish a major presence on the Internet, an effort McDermott saw as essential in the increasingly competitive and Web-oriented world of U.S. real estate.

McDermott helped grow NAR's membership to more than 1.2 million members and oversaw the purchase and development of a new Association building in Washington, D.C. (The main headquarters remains in Chicago.) It was the first newly constructed environmentally friendly (green) building in the nation's capital, and McDermott saw it as a venue from which NAR's million-plus members could advocate for their communities: "A million REALTORS® focused on improving the quality of life in the communities they serve are one of the greatest assets property owners have in the public policy arena."[48]

During his tenure McDermott added "chief executive officer" to his title. On his retirement in 2005, NAR's Board of Directors ended a nine-month search by turning to a longtime staff member, Dale A. Stinton.

Equipped with an MBA from DePaul University, Stinton had joined NAR's Finance Department in 1981. He was named chief financial officer in 1991 and chief information officer in 1998 and served briefly as acting executive vice president in 1996.

As CEO and executive vice president, Stinton stepped into a number of major challenges, including the multiyear battle NAR has waged with banking regulators to keep big banks out of real estate. In 2006, he told an interviewer that his role is to support and guide the key staff and REALTORS® who lead the Association. "When it's needed, I will be a strong spokesperson for NAR on the Hill or anywhere else," he says, "but really, I refer to that as sacred ground for the Leadership Team. It's always best for the REALTORS® to be speaking to the public on the issues."[49]

Stinton also said that as CEO he will place high value on innovation, teamwork, and continuous learning. "The search for creativity is a part of building a company that is a true learning organization," he said.

His comment holds much promise for NAR. Teamwork, creativity, and continuous learning are among the qualities the 2004 Booz Allen Hamilton study concluded are shared by institutions that endure.

Dale Stinton was named executive vice president and CEO in 2005.

Presidents of NAR (1909–2009)

Richard F. Gaylord of Long Beach, California, is the 100th president of NAR. Two anomalies in the count balance each other. William May Garland served back-to-back terms, in 1918 and 1919. But 1933 saw two presidents: one, Canadian William H. Gardner, was named honorary president by the board after an illness forced him to withdraw from membership.

    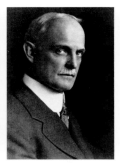  

1909	1910	1911	1912	1913	1914	1915
William W. Hannan	Alexander S. Taylor	Samuel S. Thorpe	Edward S. Judd	Charles L. Simpson	Thomas Shallcross Jr.	Walter C. Piper
Detroit, MI	Cleveland, OH	Minneapolis, MN	Chicago, IL	Kansas City, MO	Merion Station, PA	Detroit, MI

1906
After the Great San Francisco Earthquake, Colbert Coldwell founds Tucker, Lynch and Coldwell, later renamed Coldwell Banker.

1908
The National Association of Real Estate Exchanges is founded in Chicago. Dues are $1 per year, with a one-time membership fee of $50.

1911
The Association has its first headquarters, a room in the Minneapolis real estate office of NAR President Samuel Skidmore Thorpe.

1912
Three members of the Winnipeg Real Estate Exchange perish in the sinking of the RMS *Titanic* on its maiden voyage from England to New York.

1913
At its annual convention in Winnipeg, Manitoba, the Code of Ethics is adopted, with the Golden Rule as its theme.

No 54 A Typical Bread line in the early stages of relief distribution

THE LATE THOMAS BEATTIE.   THE LATE JOHN HUGO ROSS.   THE LATE MARK FORTUNE.

1916
Henry P. Haas
Pittsburgh, PA

1917–1918
William M. Garland
Los Angeles, CA

1919
John L. Weaver
Washington, D.C.

1920
Federick E. Taylor
Portland, OR

1921
Irving B. Hiett
Toledo, OH

1922
Nathaniel J. Upham
Duluth, MN

1923
Louis F. Eppich
Denver, CO

1914
War erupts in Europe. *The National Real Estate Journal* says, "The European war will act as a tremendous stimulus for American trade."

1916
The Association's name is changed to the National Association of Real Estate Boards and the term REALTOR® is adopted.

1917
The United States enters World War I. NAR offers the U.S. War Department the Association's service free of charge in securing sites for mobilization camps.

1918
On November 11, Germany signs the armistice ending World War I.

1920
The nineteenth amendment is ratified, giving women in the United States the right to vote.

NAR's headquarters move to Chicago and the city's Drake Hotel (pictured in 1920) is established as a regular meeting place.

Presidents of NAR (1909–2009)

1924
Hugh R. Ennis
Kansas City, MO

1925
Charles G. Edwards
New York, NY

1926
Robert Jemison Jr.
Birmingham, AL

1927
Clarence C. Hieatt
Louisville, KY

1928
Henry G. Zander
Chicago, IL

1929
Harry H. Culver
Balboa, CA

1930
Leonard P. Reaume
Detroit, MI

1923
The National Association of Real Estate Boards emblem is adopted.

1924
NAR establishes a legal department and a real estate library. Dues are increased to $5.

1927
State secretaries (later known as association executives) meet for the first time, forming their own specialty institute.

1928
NAR's three-way agreement is born, with NAR entering into agreements with state associations in California and Colorado.

1929
October's stock market crash marks the beginning of the Great Depression.

1931
Harry S. Kissell
Springfield, OH

1932
Lawrence T. Stevenson
Pittsburgh, PA

1933
William C. Miller
Washington, D.C.

1933
William H. Gardner
honorary
Winnipeg, Manitoba

1934
Hugh Potter
Houston, TX

1935
Walter S. Schmidt
Cincinnati, OH

1936
Walter W. Rose
Orlando, FL

1930
NAR moves to 59 E. Van Buren in Chicago.

Boards around the country organize divisions to work for fairer taxes. The following year NAR organizes a National Property Owners' Division and sponsors research on state and local taxes.

1932
Architect Frank Lloyd Wright, speaking at the NAR annual convention in Cincinnati, promotes manufactured housing.

1933
Franklin Delano Roosevelt, in his first inaugural address, tells Americans that "action needs to be taken to prevent the tragedy of the growing loss, through foreclosure of our small homes and our farms." His program to help farmers, home owners, and the unemployed is dubbed "The New Deal."

1934
Under the National Housing Act, the NAR-backed Federal Housing Administration is created.

Presidents of NAR (1909–2009)

1937
Paul E. Stark
Madison, WI

1938
Joseph W. Catharine
Brooklyn, NY

1939
Edgar L. Ostendorf
Cleveland, OH

1940
Newton C. Farr
Chicago, IL

1941
Philip W. Kniskern
Swarthmore, PA

1942
David B. Simpson
Portland, OR

1943
Cyrus C. Willmore
St. Louis, MO

1938

Amendments to the 1934 Housing Act pave the way for the creation of the Federal National Mortgage Association, now known as Fannie Mae, marking the realization of a long-held goal of REALTORS®—a steady flow of funds for mortgage lending.

1941

Following the bombing of Pearl Harbor in December, the United States declares war on Japan. Within days, Germany declares war on the United States.

1942

NAR leaders establish the REALTORS® Washington Committee "to do our share in the war effort, to keep our members informed, and to assist them to adjust their businesses to war conditions." NAR President Phillip W. Kniskern (1941) wires President Roosevelt saying, "The REALTORS® of America pledge their full support to you and to the government in defense of the country. . . . We stand at your command."

1944

NAR cancels its convention in support of the war effort.

1944	1945	1946	1947	1948	1949	1950
John W. Galbreath	Van Holt Garrett	Boyd T. Barnard	Morgan L. Fitch	Hobart C. Brady	Theodore H. Maenner	Robert P. Gerholz
Columbus, OH	Denver, CO	Philadelphia, PA	Chicago, IL	Wichita, KS	Omaha, NE	Flint, MI

1944

REALTORS® hail the GI Bill of Rights, which provides low-interest loans to returning veterans for the purchase of homes, farms, and businesses. *The National Real Estate Journal* predicts the bill will "be a big stimulus to postwar home building."

1945

Germany and Japan surrender, ending World War II. Of more than 15,000 REALTORS® in the United States at the start of the war, 1,143 served in the armed forces and 19 died while in military service.

1947

Jackie Robinson becomes the first African American major league baseball player.

1948

In *Shelley v. Kraemer,* the U.S. Supreme Court says states cannot enforce racially restricted covenants.

1949–1950

The Patent and Trademark Office approves NAR's registration of the terms REALTORS® and REALTOR®, respectively.

DODGERS CLUB HOUSE KEEP OUT

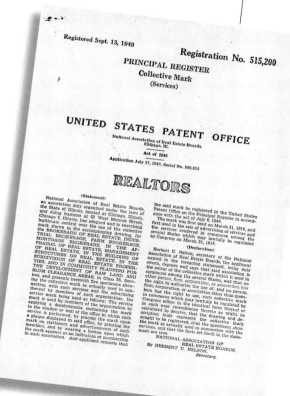

Presidents of NAR (1909–2009)

1951
Alexander Summer
Teaneck, NJ

1952
Joseph W. Lund
Boston, MA

1953
Charles B. Shattuck
Los Angeles, CA

1954
Ronald J. Chinnock
Chicago, IL

1955
Henry G. Waltemade
New York, NY

1956
Clarence M. Turley Sr.
St. Louis, MO

1957
Kenneth S. Keyes
Apopka, FL

1950
The Korean War sets off tension over the spread of communism and heightens Americans' fear of nuclear war.

1952
NAR establishes "Build America Better," a program to help cities revitalize blighted areas.

1953
Ronald J. Chinnock of Chicago organizes an NAR committee to prepare cities for the hydrogen bomb. Meanwhile, thousands of Americans are building underground bomb shelters.

1954
In *Brown v. [Topeka] Board of Education,* the U.S. Supreme Court strikes down the "separate but equal" doctrine, paving the way for the Civil Rights Movement.

1956
NAR establishes REALTOR® Week.

1958
H. Walter Graves
Philadelphia, PA

1959
James M. Udall.
Los Angeles, CA

1960
C. Armel Nutter
Moorestown, NJ

1961
O.G. (Bill) Powell
Des Moines, IA

1962
Arthur P. Wilcox
Boston, MA

1963
Daniel F. Sheehan Sr.
St. Louis, MO

1964
Ed Mendenhall
High Point, NC

1958
NAR celebrates its fiftieth anniversary with the publication of *Real Estate in American History,* by Pearl Janet Davies.

Pearl Janet Davies

1959
Lorraine Hansberry's "A Raisin in the Sun"—the story of a black family trying to move into a white neighborhood— debuts on Broadway.

1960
President Dwight D. Eisenhower meets with NAR leaders (to his left is 1959 President James Udall).

The Herbert U. Nelson Memorial Library and Information Center is established in NAR's Chicago office.

1961
The Soviet Union clashes with France, Great Britain, and the United States over the fate of West Berlin. With the construction of the Berlin Wall and mobilization of U.S. troops, NAR asks its 70,000 members to bombard the government with letters "that can help our president act in confidence to 'break down the wall.'"

1962
NAR launches its first national advertising and public relations campaign. The first full-page ad in the program appeared in *U.S. News & World Report* in October 1962.

1963
In November, President John F. Kennedy is assassinated.

Presidents of NAR (1909–2009)

1965
Maurice Read
Berkeley, CA

1966
Jack Justice
Miami Beach, FL

1967
Richard B. Morris
Buffalo, NY

1968
Lyn E. Davis
Dallas, TX

1969
John Cotton
San Diego, CA

1970
Rich Port
LaGrange, IL

1971
Bill N. Brown
Albuquerque, NM

1965
NAR President Maurice Read speaks about the beginnings of urban sprawl. "The new dynamics of urban expansion are shifting from the steady spread of a central mass to the formation of satellite cities. . . ."

1968
Civil rights leader Martin Luther King Jr. is assassinated

President Lyndon Johnson signs the Fair Housing Act, banning discrimination in public and private housing on the basis of race, color, religion, or national origin.

1969
Apollo 11 astronauts Neil Armstrong, Michael Collins, and Edwin E. "Buzz" Aldrin Jr. land on the moon.

NAR President John Cotton calls for affirmative action to provide jobs for minorities.

1970
Vietnam War protestors burn their draft cards and chant "Flower Power." But protests reach a crescendo in May, when four students are killed and nine wounded by National Guardsmen at Kent State University in Kent, Ohio.

EQUAL HOUSING OPPORTUNITY

PUBLIC RELATIONS and the BOARD OF REALTORS

1972
Fred C. Tucker Jr.
Indianapolis, IN

1973
J.D. Sawyer
Middletown, OH

1974
Joseph B. Doherty
Andover, MA

1975
Art S. Leitch
Bonsall, CA

1976
Philip C. Smaby
Bloomington, MN

1977
Harry C. Elmstrom
Ballston Spa, NY

1978
Tom Grant Jr.
Tulsa, OK

1972
The Association's name is changed to NATIONAL ASSOCIATION OF REALTORS® and membership is opened to sales associates.

ERA is founded.

1973
NAR establishes the "block R" logo, replacing the emblem adopted in 1923.

An Arab oil embargo results in national gasoline shortages and talk of gas rationing. President Joseph Doherty appoints a Blue Ribbon Committee on Energy, chaired by Donald Hovde.

RE/MAX is founded.

1974
NAR acquires its current headquarters building—430 N. Michigan Avenue in Chicago—for $6.5 million.

The oil embargo ends but gas prices continue to rise.

Richard M. Nixon resigns.

1976
In honor of the U.S. bicentennial, NAR leaders present an original painting of "Uncle Sam" to President Gerald Ford for exhibit at the Smithsonian.

1977
NAR launches an energy conservation program in response to Jimmy Carter's call for citizens to combat the national energy crisis.

Presidents of NAR (1909–2009)

1979
Donald I Hovde
Madison, WI

1980
Ralph W Pritchard
LaGrange, IL

1981
John R Wood
Naples, FL

1982
Julio S Laguarta
Houston, TX

1983
Harley W Snyder
Valparaiso, IN

1984
Donald H Treadwell
Southgate, MI

1985
David D Roberts
Mobile, AL

1979
In Iran, university students take 66 American hostages to protest U.S. support of the former Shah. The hostages are freed 444 days later.

1980
With inflation running at 13 percent and an unemployment rate near 8 percent, single-family sales plunge by 22 percent from a year earlier. NAR leaders call for a balanced federal budget to control inflation.

1981
To combat inflation, Fed Chairman Paul Volcker (with President Reagan) drives interest rates to an all-time high.

Mortgage rates surpass 18 percent, ending the year at around 17 percent. The Association calls for a constitutional amendment to balance the federal budget and introduces the Housing Affordability Index.

1982
NAR launches the Real Estate Information Network, a computer network that allows subscribers to exchange information on properties and buyers.

President Ronald Reagan hails the work of his Commission on Housing, saying "no segment of our economy has suffered more from the twin afflictions of inflation and high interest rates."

1983
Keller Williams is founded.

1984
The first Macintosh computer is released.

1986
Clark W. Wallace
Moraga, CA

1987
William M. Moore
Denver, CO

1988
Nestor R. Weigand
Wichita, KS

1989
Ira Gribin
Sherman Oaks, CA

1990
Norman D. Flynn
Madison, WI

1991
Harley E. Rouda
Columbus, OH

1992
Dorcas T. Helfant
Virginia Beach, VA

1987

NAR initiates a REALTOR® Pride campaign, urging members to identify themselves as REALTORS® on their business cards, signs, and letterhead.

A 32 percent decline in stock values exceeds the magnitude of the 1929 stock market crash.

Prudential enters residential real estate.

1989

The NAR board of directors approves "The Voice for Real Estate®" as NAR's unifying theme.

The failure of hundreds of savings and loan associations leads to passage of major reforms in the thrift industry and creation of the Resolution Trust Corporation. The act sets forth state licensing and certification requirements for appraisers.

1989

One day after Germans breach the Berlin Wall, U.S. President George H.W. Bush addresses REALTORS® at their convention in Dallas. "I was moved as you were by the pictures of Berliners from East and West standing atop the wall." Calling the 1980s "the decade of renewal," Bush predicts the 1990s will be "the decade of democracy."

1991

Mortgage interest rates dip below 10 percent for the first time in 12 years.

1992

Dorcas Helfant becomes the first woman president of NAR.

NATIONAL ASSOCIATION OF REALTORS®

The Voice for Real Estate

Presidents of NAR (1909–2009)

1993
William S. Chee
Honolulu, HI

1994
Robert H. (Bob) Elrod
Orlando, FL

1995
Edmund (Gill) Woods
Holyoke, MA

1996
Art Godi
Stockton, CA

1997
Russell K. Booth
Salt Lake City, UT

1998
R. Layne Morrill
Kimberling City, MO

1999
Sharon A. Millett
Auburn, ME

1993
NAR President Bill Chee makes his "lions over the hill" speech to NAR leaders in April, warning that emerging technologies could result in a loss of MLS. Chee's speech galvanizes NAR leaders to embark on a technology initiative. In 1996, that initiative is launched as the Web site REALTOR.com.

1995
President Bill Clinton unveils a National Homeownership Strategy aimed at raising the nation's home ownership rate to 67.5 percent by 2000. U.S. Census data shows the goal is reached.

Internet fever takes hold, with an estimated 8 million U.S. adults accessing the Internet.

1996
With partner RealSelect, NAR launches REALTOR .com. By year's end, the site has more than 1 million property listings.

NAR announces plans to launch its first organizational Web site, One REALTOR® Place.

1998
Microsoft launches its long-anticipated HomeAdvisor real estate Web site. To many in real estate, Bill Gates—Microsoft's CEO (later chairman)—epitomizes the "lion over the hill" Chee referred to in 1993, though Chee's remarks were more broadly targeted.

A national public awareness campaign is launched with the aim of increasing consumer awareness of the value of real estate practitioners. The tagline: "We're REALTORS®. Real Estate Is Our Life."

1999
"Within These Walls . . . ," a permanent exhibition at the Smithsonian Institution's National Museum of American History opens in May with NAR as the sole sponsor.

2000
Dennis R. Cronk
Roanoke, VA

2001
Richard A. Mendenhall
Columbia, MO

2002
Martin Edwards Jr.
Memphis, TN

2003
Catherine B. Whatley
Jacksonville, FL

2004
Walt McDonald
Riverside, CA

2005
Al Mansell
Midvale, UT

2006
Thomas M. Stevens
Vienna, VA

2000

Stocks plunge in March, signaling the end of the first dot-com boom.

2001

The International Consortium of Real Estate Associations is founded.

NAR kicks off its partnership with Habitat for Humanity International, building a home in NAR's 2001 convention city, Chicago.

2001

Within 48 hours of the September 11 terrorist attacks, NAR leaders establish the REALTORS® Housing Relief Fund, which raises more than $8 million to pay housing costs for families of victims.

2001

NAR and its partners kick off the first HOPE Awards gala in Washington, D.C., in October.

A wave of corporate accounting scandals leads Americans to look toward real estate as a place to invest.

2002

NAR launches a fight—deemed "the battle of the century"—to keep large banking conglomerates from entering real estate.

The Association also launches a REALTOR® Pride campaign, encouraging members to wear their pin and to tell consumers they're REALTORS®.

The U.S. launches a military drive to unseat the Taliban in Afghanistan. NAR leaders waive dues for members called to active duty and for those whose spouses are called.

REALTORS®
Housing Relief Fund

Presidents of NAR (1909–2009)

2007
Pat V. Combs
Grand Rapids, MI

2008
Richard F. Gaylord
Long Beach, CA

2009
Charles McMillan
Fort Worth, TX

2003

In March, the United States invades Iraq, ousting President Saddam Hussein but setting off a prolonged conflict.

Residential mortgage interest rates dip below 6 percent in January—the lowest level since the early 1960s.

2004

NAR membership breaks the 1 million mark.

The Association's new Washington, D.C., building opens in the fall and becomes the capital's first newly-constructed LEED-certified building.

NAR wins a major trademark case before the U.S. Trademark Trial and Appeal Board, retaining the right to the membership marks REALTOR® and REALTORS®.

2005

President Al Mansell launches two major fund-raising drives, raising millions of dollars in aid for victims of the December 2004 South Asian tsunami and August 2005 Hurricane Katrina in the U.S. Gulf Coast.

Duke University Press publishes *A Nation of REALTORS®* by Jeffrey M. Hornstein.

2006

Fifteen months after Hurricane Katrina, REALTORS® hold a historic annual conference in New Orleans, and thousands participate in rebuilding and rehabilitation projects.

2007

NAR's board of directors elects Charles McMillan president-elect for 2008. McMillan becomes the first African American in line for the NAR presidency.

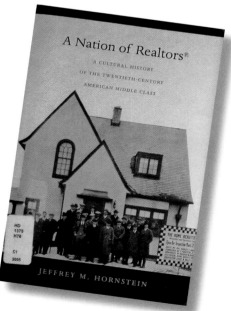

Notes

CHAPTER 1

1. Reports on Peter van Vlissingen's arrest appeared in the *Chicago Tribune*, November 20, 1908, and *New York Times*, November 17, 1908.
2. Pearl Janet Davies, *Real Estate in American History* (Washington, D.C.: Public Affairs Press, 1958), 4–8.
3. Ibid., 50–52, and "Realty Men Band to Kill 'Sharks'; Delegates from Scores of Cities Form National Organization to Fight Cheats," *Chicago Tribune*, May 13, 1908, 14.
4. Davies, 21–23.
5. "Real Estate Men; They Assemble in Large Numbers at Nashville, Tenn.," *Davenport Daily Leader*, February 18, 1892.
6. "The Real Estate Men," *Chicago Tribune*, May 10, 1908, 14.
7. Charles Chadbourn, Executive Committee Meeting Minutes (NAR Archives), March 27, 1916, 6.
8. Davies, 110–111.
9. Jeffrey M. Hornstein, *A Nation of REALTORS®: A Cultural History of Twentieth-Century American Middle Class* (Durham: Duke University Press, 2005), 77.
10. Nathan William MacChesney, letter to Lloyd Lewis (NAR Archives), February 17, 1947.
11. Thomas Scully, letter to P.B. Gove, G. & C. Merriam Company (NAR Archives), December 3, 1965.
12. William D. North, *Membership Marks Manual* (Chicago: NAR, 1984), vii–viii.
13. *Brief and Argument for Protection of Term REALTOR®*, explanatory note, 8. On September 13, 1920, the district court in Hennepin County, Minnesota, ruled that the defendant "be enjoined from placing opposite the name of any of the defendants . . . in the body of its telephone directory the word REALTOR® and from placing the name of any of said defendants hereinafter named, in its classified list under the heading 'REALTORS®.' "
14. News item in *REALTOR® Headlines*, April 1, 1957. "The Peninsula association was organized in 1955 in the area in which San Francisco and nearby cities are located. It refused to heed warnings of local boards and [NAR] that its use of "Realter" and a symbol similar to that employed by [NAR] constituted infringements on the rights of [NAR] and its constituent local boards." The 1956 Board of Directors minutes includes a letter from Executive Vice President Eugene P. Conser stating that "boards in that area protested . . . the infringement. It is their contention that prosecution is [NAR]'s responsibility and should be taken immediately. President Turley met with representatives of the board on his visit to California early in March and agreed."
15. *Jacob Zimmerman v. NATIONAL ASSOCIATION OF REALTORS®*, March 31, 2004, 16–20.
16. "CBS nicks 'REALTOR®' from CSI," Inman News Features (www.inman.com), December 13, 2002.

17. In the years since salespeople became members, most local associations have become "all REALTOR®" boards. Thus, few members call themselves REALTOR®-ASSOCIATE® today.
18. Public Relations Committee Resolution, Board of Directors Meeting Minutes, NAR Archives, January 1961, 100.
19. Nathan William MacChesney, letter (NAR Archives), September 30, 1940.

Chapter 2

1. Calvin Coolidge, "Better Homes," *Better Homes in America Plan Book for Demonstration Week, October 9–14, 1922* (New York: *The Delineator,* 1922), 4. Coolidge was vice president of the United States in 1922 and headed the Better Homes Advisory Council. (Accessed through the Library of Congress Web site. At http://memory.loc.gov/ammem /coolhtml/coolhome.html, click on Guide to People, Organizations, and Topics in *Prosperity and Thrift,* and then on Better Homes Movement.) Accessed 11/29/06.
2. Davies, 1–2.
3. Ibid., 1.
4. Ibid., 2.
5. Randall Johnston Pozdena, *The Modern Economics of Housing: A Guide to Theory and Policy for Finance and Real Estate Professionals* (Westport: Quorum Books, 1988), 6.
6. Davies, 49.
7. "Historical Census of Housing Tables: Homeownership." U.S. Census Bureau. http://www.census.gov/hhes/www /housing/census/historic/owner.html. Accessed 8/31/07.
8. Eric Belsky and Joel Prakken, *Housing's Impact on Wealth Accumulation, Wealth Distribution, and Consumer Spending* (Belsky of the Joint Center for Housing Studies at Harvard University and Prakken of Macroeconomic Advisers LLC conducted the study, which was commissioned by NAR Research), November 2004, 2, 6.
9. Hornstein, 120.
10. Davies, 93.
11. Ibid., 95.
12. Ibid., 133.
13. Clifton Daniel, editor in chief, *Chronicle of the 20th Century* (New York: Dorling Kindersley Publishing Inc., 1995), 248, 259.
14. Davies, 138.
15. Ibid.
16. Ibid., 139–140.
17. Ibid., 141.
18. Herbert Hoover, The Memoirs of Herbert Hoover: The Cabinet and the Presidency, 1920–1933 (New York: The Macmillan Company, 1952).
19. Ibid., 94.
20. Davies, 143.
21. Herbert U. Nelson, "Attempt to Standardize Home Shows," letter to Franklin D. Roosevelt, September 12, 1923.
22. "Consumerism and the Home," Coolidge-Consumerism Collection, Library of Congress, http://lcweb2.loc.gov:8081 /ammem/amrlhtml/inhome.html. Accessed 11/29/06.
23. "House and Yard: The Design of the Suburban Home," National Register Bureau, U.S. Department of the Interior, www.cr.nps.gov/nr/publications/bulletins/suburbs/part3.htm. Accessed 1/24/07.

24. Davies, 149.
25. Phillip Longman, "The Mortgaged Generation: Why the Young Can't Afford a House," *Washington Monthly*, April 1986.
26. Eleanor S. Herman, "A History of Real Estate," *Real Estate Today*, May 1983, 10.
27. Hornstein, 147.
28. "The Real Estate Industry Lobby and Public Housing in the 1930s," Historymatters.gmu.edu (George Mason University), http://historymatters.gmu.edu/d/5106. Accessed 8/31/07.
29. Herbert U. Nelson, "Public Housing," *Headlines*, September 5, 1942, 1.
30. Herman, 9.
31. Davies, 176, and "Nelson Traces 10 Decades of Real Estate Achievement," NAR Archives, November 14, 1952, 4.
32. Franklin D. Roosevelt, "Outlining the New Deal Program," Radio broadcast on NBC and CBS, May 7, 1933. Transcript published by the Franklin and Eleanor Roosevelt Institute, www.feri. Org/common/news/details .cfm?QID=2068&clientid=11005. Accessed 1/7/07.
33. Davies, 177.
34. Ibid., 179, and "Where We've Been," *Real Estate Today*, May 1983, 16.
35. Paul Stark, "Rebuilding Our Cities," *The National Real Estate Journal*, May 1937, 37.
36. "Where We've Been," 17.
37. Ibid., 13.
38. Herbert U. Nelson, "GI Opportunities," *Headlines*, June 19, 1944, 2.
39. "Extent of Federal Influence on 'Urban Sprawl' Is Unclear," U.S. General Accounting Office, April 1999, 1.
40. "Taxing Times for Housing," document in NAR Archives, 74. The home ownership rate declined from 65.6 percent in 1980 to 64.5 percent in 1984.
41. Ravi Kamath, "The NAR's Housing Affordability Index," *Real Estate Review*, Winter 1988, 101.
42. John Burchard and Albert Bush-Brown, The Architecture of America—A Social and Cultural History (Boston: Little, Brown & Company, 1961), 355.
43. Wayne Grover, "Condo or Co-op? What's the Difference?" Bankrate.com, July 21, 2003, www.bankrate.com/brm /news/real-estate/condos1.asp. Accessed 2/12/07.
44. Simon Riveles, Esq., "Condominium vs. Cooperative Ownership: A Primer," 2004, http://www.wrlawfirm.com /Articles/wrm.article.Condo.Versus.Coop.Primer.html. Accessed 2/12/07.
45. Willem van Vliet, editor, *Encyclopedia of Housing* (London: Sage Publications, 1998), 76.
46. Ibid.
47. Ibid., 77.
48. F. John Devaney, *Tracking the American Dream: Fifty Years of Housing Change*, U.S. Department of Commerce, Bureau of the Census, 1994, 31.
49. Dell Upton, Architecture in the United States (New York: Oxford University Press, 1998), 38
50. Upton, 38–39.
51. Leland M. Roth, American Architecture: A History (Boulder: Westview Press, 2001), 232.
52. Ibid., 231
53. Clifford Edward Clark, *The American Family Home, 1800–1960* (Chapel Hill: University of North Carolina Press, 1986), 183.
54. "House and Yard" (See Note 23).
55. Marcus Field and Mark Irving, *Lofts* (London: Calman & King, 1999), 5.

Chapter 3

1. Davies, 129.
2. Hornstein, 133.
3. Ibid., 148.
4. NAREB News Service Release. No. 93. NAR Archives, 1944–1945 bound volume.
5. "Remove Obstructions on Building: Statement by Van Holt Garrett." NAREB News Service Release, 1944–1945 bound volume.
6. Rep. Paul Kanjorski speech made at the REALTORS® Midyear Legislative Meetings in 2003, the year he became lead sponsor of the Community Choice in Real Estate bill, legislation that would prevent large banking conglomerates from owning real estate brokerage and management companies.

Chapter 4

1. Richard Wright, Native Son (New York: HarperCollins, Harper Perennial Modern Classics, 2005), 248–249. Original hardcover published by Harper & Brothers, 1940.
2. Hornstein, 2.
3. Douglas S. Massey and Nancy A. Denton, *American Apartheid: Segregation and the Making of the Underclass* (Cambridge and London: Harvard University Press, 1993).
4. Ibid., 25.
5. Hornstein, 30.
6. Massey and Denton, 29.
7. Ibid., 20.
8. Hornstein, 101, 105.
9. Ibid., 108.
10. Ibid, 107.
11. William D. North, *Passwords and Prejudice: A REALTORS® Guide to Fair Housing Compliance.* (Chicago: National Association of Realtors®, 1986), 7.
12. Ibid.
13. Massey and Denton, 37.
14. Alexander von Hoffman, "Like Fleas or Tigers? A Brief History of the Open Housing Movement." Joint Center for Housing Studies, Harvard University, 1998, 8.
15. Ibid., 3.
16. Ibid., 21.
17. North, 7–8.
18. Ibid., 118.
19. William Brown, "Access to Housing: The Role of the Real Estate Industry," Economic Geography, 48(1), January 1972, 69–70.
20. A.M. Slaughter, "Testimony before the U.S. Commission on Civil Rights," Oakland California, May 12, 1964. Quoted in Brown, 70.
21. Brown, 70.
22. Massey and Denton, 55, 47.

23. Peter Dreier, "Labor's Love Lost? Rebuilding Unions' Involvement in Federal Housing Policy," *Housing Policy Debate*, 11(2), Fannie Mae Foundation, 2000, 333.

24. von Hoffman, 27.

25. Rose Helper, Racial Practices and Policies of Real Estate Brokers (Minneapolis: University of Minneapolis Press, 1969), 35.

26. Ibid., 35.

27. Ibid., 33.

28. Ibid., 23.

29. Ibid., 273.

30. von Hoffmann, 29.

31. 1961 U.S. Commission on Civil Rights Report Book 4: Housing (Washington, D.C.: United States Commission on Civil Rights, 1961), 1, 17.

32. Ibid., 81.

33. Ibid., 140.

34. von Hoffman, 33.

35. Ibid., 38–39.

36. Ibid., 39.

37. "Luring Blacks, Keeping Whites," *Time*, October 31, 1977. At www.time.com/time/magazine/article/0,9171,945794,00.html. Accessed 12/29/06.

38. von Hoffmann, 45.

39. North, 12.

40. Diane Wedner, "Arthur Leitch: REALTOR® Led Fair-Housing Push," Los Angeles Times, July 19, 2001, Sec. 2, 13.

41. Lucien Salvant, "30th Anniversary of the Fair Housing Act: Part 1." *Today's REALTOR®*, April 1998, 23.

42. Daniel Lauber, *Ending American Apartheid: How Cities Achieve and Maintain Racial Diversity* (River Forest, IL: Planning/Communications, 1989), http://www.planningcommunications.com/Ending%20American%20Apartheid%202005.pdf. Accessed 10/13/06.

43. Salvant, 24.

44. Ibid.

45. Ibid., 26.

46. Ibid., 27.

47. Ibid.

48. von Hoffman, 27.

49. Sheryll Cashin, *The Failures of Integration: How Class and Race Are Undermining the American Dream* (New York: Public Affairs, 2004), 12.

50. "Why a Diversity Program? Racial and Ethnic Diversity," NATIONAL ASSOCIATION OF REALTORS®, undated, http://www.realtor.org/divweb.nsf/pages/toolkitwhy?OpenDocument. Accessed 12/29/06.

51. "Homeownership Rates by Race and Ethnicity of Householder," U.S. Census Bureau, http://www.census.gov/hhes/www/housing/hvs/annual 05/ann05t20.html. Accessed 12/29/06.

52. "HOPE Awards Celebrate Minority Homeownership," NATIONAL ASSOCIATION OF REALTORS®, May 12, 2005, http://www.realtor.org/realtororg.nsf/pages/2005MYMHOPEAwards?OpenDocument. Accessed 12/19/06.

53. Sally Ross Chapralis, *Progress of Women in Real Estate: 50th Anniversary, Women's Council of REALTORS®* (Chicago: Women's Council of REALTORS®, 1988), 4.

54. Davies, 5.

55. Deborah Ahrens, "Women's Place Is in the Home—Selling It," Missouri REALTOR®, July/August 1992, 12.

56. "Ladies Welcome," *Headlines*, March 13, 1950, 4.

57. Ahrens, 12.

58. Chapralis, 37.

59. Ahrens, 12.

60. Examples include Rene Syler interview with Vera Gibbons, "Single Women Plunge Into Real Estate," CBS News: "The Early Show," March 6, 2006, and Garry Boulard, "Women Homebuyers Represent Growing Market Segment," New Mexico Business Weekly, June 9, 2006.

61. Paul Bishop and Harika "Anna" Barlett, "Single Women Home Buyers: A Market Worth Watching," Real Estate Insights, National Association of Realtors®, March 2007, http://www.realtor.org/reinsights.nsf/pages/archives?OpenDocument. Accessed 8/31/07.

62. *Women in the Labor Force: A Databook*, U.S. Department of Labor, Report 996, September 2006, 1. Accessed at http://www.bls.gov/cps/wlf-databook-2006.pdf. Accessed 8/31/07.

Chapter 5

1. Hornstein, 50.

2. "South Florida Region: Resident Population Estimates and Projections, 1920–2030," South Florida Regional Planning Council, http://www.sfrpc.com/ftp/pub/census/PopProj_SF3.pdf. Accessed 8/31/07.

3. NAR case study.

4. Sam Staley and Leonard C. Gilroy, "Smart Growth and Housing Affordability: Evidence from Statewide Planning Laws," Policy Study No. 287, Reason Foundation, December 2001. Accessed at http://www.reason.org/ps287.pdf. Accessed 8/31/07.

5. NAR case study.

6. NAR case study.

7. NAR case study.

8. Marc A. Weiss, The Rise of the Community Builders (New York: Columbia University Press, 1987), 19.

9. Ibid., 40–41.

10. Ibid., 19.

11. Ibid., 46.

12. Ibid., 68.

13. Ibid.

14. Ibid., 3.

15. Ibid., 56.

16. Hornstein, 62.

17. Ibid., 21.

18. Weiss, 65.

19. Ibid., 76, 86.

20. Hornstein, 140.

21. Weiss, 144.

22. Ibid., 152.

23. NAR case study.

24. Robert Fogelson, *Downtown: Its Rise and Fall 1880–1950* (New Haven, Conn.: Yale University Press, 2003), 114.
25. Davies, 39.
26. Fogelson, 169.
27. Fogelson.
28. Davies, 72.
29. Robert McElvaine. *The Great Depression* (New York: Times Books, a division of Random House. 1993), 75.
30. Davies, 192–194.
31. Ibid., 193.
32. Jane Jacobs. *The Death and Life of Great American Cities.* New York: Random House, 1961, 7.
33. Joseph W. Lund, "Build America Better." Address to the National Association of Real Estate Boards, 1952, 5–6.
34. "Flight to the Suburbs," *Time*, March 22, 1954.
35. Joan Didion, *The White Album.* (New York: Simon & Schuster, 1979), 180.
36. News article announcing selection of William D. North as NAR executive vice president, *Chicago Sun-Times*, May 27, 1986.
37. Clark Wallace, interview with G.M. Filisko, November 2006.
38. Davies, 228.

Chapter 6

1. Davies, 18.
2. Robert W. Semenow, *Survey of Real Estate Brokers License Laws* (prepared for the National Association of Real Estate Boards and the National Association of License Law Officials), December 1936, 16–17.
3. *Bratton v. Chandler*, 260 U.S. 110 (1922).
4. "The Real Estate Men," Chicago Tribune, May 10, 1908, 14.
5. Davies, 97.
6. Ibid., 63.
7. Ibid., 97.
8. Ibid., 99.
9. William D. North, "The REALTORS® Code of Ethics: A Gift of Vision." *The Executive Officer*, August 1978, 18–19.
10. Ibid., 19.
11. Hornstein, 35.
12. Ibid., 41.
13. Layne Morrill, interview with G.M. Filisko, November 2006.
14. "It Started in San Diego—or Was it Cincinnati?" *Real Estate Today, Anniversary Edition*, 1988, 58.
15. Herbert U. Nelson, statement excerpted from the minutes of a conference of the National Association of REALTOR® Secretaries, NAR Archives, July 13, 1921.
16. "Benefits of Multiple Listing to the Board and the Individual REALTOR®," *Real Estate Practice*, June 1928, 4.
17. Pontius, H. Jackson. *Operation of Multiple Listing Services.* (Chicago: NAR, date unknown), 8.
18. *The National Real Estate Journal*, 1910.
19. "Benefits of Multiple Listing to the Board and the Individual REALTOR®," 4.
20. *Brief history of the Committee on Multiple Listing Policy*, NAR Archives, date unknown.
21. "Mr. Parish Wins His Suit," *The Real-Estate and Building Journal.* July 26, 1890.

22. Callistus S. Ennis, "Bases for Establishing Commission Rates," *NAREB Annuals*, July 1, 1923, 15.

23. "Board Commission Rates in Cities of Over 100,000," *The National Real Estate Journal*, April 27, 1931, 35.

24. Morgan Fitch, *Headlines*, September 1, 1947, 1.

25. Herbert U. Nelson, "The Real Issue," *Headlines*, September 8, 1947, 2.

26. *The Real Estate Commission Rate*, Bulletin No. 12, Executive Officers Council. Chicago: NAR, pp. 2–3.

27. "Antitrust ban on brokers," *Chicagoland's Real Estate Advertiser*, July 9, 1971, 1, 15.

28. Gabriella Filisko, "Antitrust Laws Dictate the Association's Position," *Real Estate Today*, August 1989,14.

29. Statement by The Honorable Mel Martinez before the United States House Committee on Financial Services. October 3, 2002. http://www.hud.gov/offices/cir/test100302mm.cfm. Accessed 7/6/07.

30. William D. North, Forward to *Agency and Real Estate, Legal Liability Series*. (Chicago: NAR, November 1986.)

31. Sharon Millett, quoted in "Board recognized greater buyer broker participation," *REALTOR® NEWS*, December 7, 1992, 1.

32. Laurie Janik, quoted in "Update: Changes to NAR agency policies under way," *REALTOR® NEWS*, August 3, 1992, 10.

33. "Groups urge purchasers to use buyer brokers," *REALTOR® News*, Aug. 3, 1992, p. 11.

34. "States' agency disclosure laws vary," *REALTOR® News*, August 3, 1992, p. 10.

35. "REBAC signs pact with RE/MAX," *Agency Law Quarterly*, Winter 1994, p. 13.

36. "NAR formally brings buyer brokerage council into the fold," NAR news release, April 29, 1996.

37. *Property Condition Disclosure*. NAR Archives, 1991, p. 2.

38. "Property Disclosure by Seller Helps Everyone, NAR Says." NAR news release, June 24, 1991.

39. NAR news release, October 8, 1991.

40. Burton Grad. *"The First Commercial Univac I Installation." Computer History Museum, 1997*. http://www.softwarehistory.org /history/Grad1.html. Accessed July 21, 2007.

41. Mary Bellis, "Fortran: The First Successful High-Level Programming Language, Invented by John Backus and IBM," *About.com*. http://inventors.about.com/library/weekly/aa072198.htm. Accessed July 21, 2007.

42. "Q&A with Homestore.com's Stuart Wolff," *Business Week*, March 26, 2001. http://www.businessweek.com/magazine/content /01_13/b3725037.htm. Accessed July 18, 2007.

43. Henry Lamb, "The UN and Property Rights." *Sovereignty.net*, 1997. http://www.sovereignty.net/p/land/unproprts.htm. Accessed July 21, 2007.

44. *Proceedings of the Second International Conference and Vienna Recommendations*, 1986, 41–42.

45. James Dorn, "Ownership with Chinese Characteristics: Private Property Rights and Land Reform in the PRC," Statement before the Congressional-Executive Commission on China Issues, February 3, 2003.

46. Holstein, William J. "Office Space: Armchair MBA; Innovation, Leadership, and Still No Satisfaction." *New York Times*. December 19, 2004. http://select.nytimes.com/search/restricted/article?res=FA0716FA3E540C7A8DDDAB0994DC404482. Accessed July 18, 2007.

47. "The Association EVPs—Extremely Valuable People," *Real Estate Today*, May 1983, 30–32.

48. Frederik Heller, "The Power of One Million," *REALTOR® Magazine*, May 2004, 41.

49. Hwang, Haley and Stacey Moncrieff, "CEO Dale A. Stinton: A New Era." *REALTOR® Magazine*. December 2005, 42.

Bibliography

"$700,000 Forger Quickly Punished: Peter van Vlissingen, Chicago Real Estate Dealer, Confesses to 20 Years of Fraud," *Chicago Tribune*, November 17, 1908, p. 1.

"A. H. Frederick Indicted: Successful St. Louis Politician Must Answer Charge of Forgery, *New York Times*, April 14, 1915, p. 22.

Adams, James Truslow. *The Epic of America*. Boston: Little, Brown & Company, 1931.

Agency and Real Estate, Legal Liability Series. Foreword by William D. North. NAR, November 1986.

Albro, Walt. "They Say They're Buyer's Reps, But They Act Like Subagents." *Today's REALTOR®*, February 1997.

Albro, Walt. "Who Is Terry McDermott?" *Today's REALTOR®*, May 1997.

Anderson, Archie E., Director for the Committee on Multiple Listing Policy. "Multiple Listing Survey—1970. Department of Board Services, National Association of Real Estate Boards, September 1970.

Anderson Productions Ltd. *Community Builder: The Life & Legacy of J.C. Nichols*. Steven C.F. Anderson, Executive Producer, Kansas City Public Television, 2006.

Announcement of Jack Carlson's death. NAR Archives. Dec. 8, 1992.

"Annual Report of President J.D. Sawyer, 1973." Chicago: NAR, 1973.

Arthur, Beth. "Background History of the NAR Three-Way Agreement." NAR Archives, April 2, 2002.

"The Association EVPs—Extremely Valuable People," *Real Estate Today*, May 1983.

Bancroft, Hubert Howe. *The Book of the Fair*. San Francisco: The Bancroft Company, 1893.

Bellis, Mary, "Fortran: The First Successful High-Level Programming Language, Invented by John Backus and IBM." About.com. http://inventors.about.com/library/weekly/aa072198.htm (accessed July 21, 2007).

———, "Twentieth Century Inventions 1900–1925," About.com. http://inventors.about.com/library/weekly/aa121599a.htm (accessed July 18, 2007).

Belsky, Eric, and Joel Prakken. *Housing's Impact on Wealth Accumulation, Wealth Distribution, and Consumer Spending*, Joint Center for Housing Studies. Cambridge: Harvard University, December 2004.

"Benefits of Multiple Listing to the Board and the Individual Realtor®." *Real Estate Practice*. Chicago: National Association of Real Estate Boards, 1928.

Birnbaum, Jeffrey. "Realtors® Wield the Power of Intimidating Views." *Washington Post*, Monday, October 4, 2004, p. E1.

Bleasdale, Julie A. "The Great Debate." *Real Estate Today*. April 1993, p. 17.

"Board Commission Rates in Cities of Over 100,000." *The National Real Estate Journal*. April 27, 1931, p. 35.

"Board OKs Affirmative Marketing Agreement," *REALTOR's Headlines*, December 1, 1975, p. 1.

"Board recognized greater buyer broker participation," *REALTOR® News*. December 7, 1992, p. 1.

"Board-related multiple listing systems face challenge from non-Realtor® licensees." *REAL Trends*, January 1992, Vol. VI, p. 1.

Bopp, Richard E., and Linda C. Smith. *Reference and Information Services: An Introduction*, second edition, 1995.

"Brief History of the Committee on Multiple Listing Policy," NAR archives.

Brinkley, Douglas. *Wheels for the World*. New York: Penguin Group, 2003.

Brittain, Joseph K. "Summary of Real Estate License Legislation, 1924–1925." National Association of Real Estate Boards.

Broberg, Brad. "Heading Toward Diversity: Smart Growth Addresses Race and Class Issues." *On Common Ground*, Winter, 2007.

"Brochure adds to debate on agency, commissions." *REALTOR® News*, August 3, 1992, p. 1.

Brown, William. "Access to Housing: The Role of the Real Estate Industry." *Economic Geography*. 48(1), January 1972, pp. 66–78.

"Build America Better." Address of Joseph W. Lund, president, National Association of Real Estate Boards, 1952.

Burchard, John, and Albert Bush-Brown. *The Architecture of America—A Social and Cultural History*. New York: Little, Brown & Co., 1966.

California Real Estate Magazine, "William May Garland," October 1948, p. 12.

Cashin, Sheryll. *The Failures of Integration: How Class and Race Are Undermining the American Dream*. New York: PublicAffairs, 2004.

Chicago Tribune, "Chicagoan Made Realty Leader: E.S. Judd, President of National Association of Real Estate Exchanges," June 22, 1912, p. 16.

———, "The Real Estate Men," May 10, 1908, p. 14.

———, "Realty Men Band to 'Kill' Sharks: Delegates from Scores of Cities Form National Organization to Fight Cheats," May 13, 1908, p. 14.

———, "What Is a 'REALTOR®'?" Editorial of the day. December 18, 1916, p. 8.

Clarifying Agency: Real Estate Professionals, Consumers, and Disclosure, a Reference Manual. Chicago: NAR, 1993.

Clark, Clifford Edward. *The American Family Home, 1800–1960*. Chapel Hill, NC: University of North Carolina Press, 1986.

"CompuServe." Wikipedia. http://en.wikipedia.org/wiki/CompuServe (accessed July 18, 2007).

Cooper, James C., *et al. Competition in the Real Estate Brokerage Industry, A Report by the Federal Trade Commission and U.S. Department of Justice*. April 2007. www.usdoj.gov/atr/public/reports/223094.htm (accessed July 20, 2007).

Cumbow, Robert C. "Trademark Basics: A Brief Overview of the Fundamentals of Trademark Law," May 14, 2004. Available as a PDF at www.grahamdunn.com (accessed September 5, 2007).

Daniel, Clifton, ed. *Chronicle of the 20th Century*. New York: Dorling Kindersley Publishing Inc., 1995.

Davenport Daily Leader, "Real Estate Men: They Assemble in Large Numbers at Nashville, Tenn.," February 18, 1892.

Davies, Pearl Janet. "Real Estate Achievement in the United States." Unpublished manuscript, 1957.

———. *Real Estate in American History*. Washington, DC: Public Affairs Press, 1958.

Devaney, F. John. U.S. Bureau of the Census. *Tracking the American Dream: 50 Years of Housing History from the Census Bureau: 1940 to 1990.* Current Housing Reports, Series H121/94-1. Washington: Government Printing Office, 1994.

Didion, Joan. *The White Album.* New York: Simon and Schuster, 1979.

Dreier, Peter. "Labor's Love Lost? Rebuilding Unions' Involvement in Federal Housing Policy." *Housing Policy Debate,* Vol. 11, Issue 2, 2000. Fannie Mae Foundation.

Dwyre, Bill. "L.A. and the Olympics Were a Golden Match." *Los Angeles Times,* March 30, 2006.

"Each-for-All-and-All-for-Each Real Estate Selling Plan." *The National Real Estate Journal,* 1927

"End of the Great Convention," *National Real Estate Journal,* September 1917, pp. 242–243.

Ennis, Callistus S. "Bases for Establishing Commission Rates." National Association of Real Estate Boards Annals, Chicago: NAR, July 1, 1923.

Eskew, Garnett Laidlaw, assisted by John R. MacDonald. *Of Land and Men: The Birth and Growth of an Idea.* Urban Land Institute, 1959.

Evans, Mariwyn. "What's Next for the MLS?" *REALTOR® Magazine,* June 2006, p. 56.

Ethics of the Real Estate Profession. National Association of Real Estate Exchanges, 1913.

The "Facilitator" as an Alternative to Agency. NAR, 1993.

Field, Marcus, and Mark Irving. *Lofts.* London: Calman & King, 1999.

Filisko, Gabriella. "Money Isn't the Only Lure . . . or Is It?" *Real Estate Today,* Aug. 1989, p. 14.

————. "Bill Chee: A Quiet General." *Real Estate Today,* January/February 1993.

Filisko, G.M. "Keeping Pace." *REALTOR® Magazine,* July 2006.

Fogelson, Robert M. *Downtown: Its Rise and Fall, 1850–1950.* New Haven: Yale University Press, 2001.

For the Record: Key Issue Summaries. NAR, Summer 2003.

"Former Executive Found Guilty of Insider Trading." *New York Times.* June 23, 2006. http://select.nytimes.com /search/restricted/article?res=FB0C16F734550C708EDDAF0894DE404482 (accessed July 18, 2007).

Garland, William. "To the Individual Members of the National Association of Real Estate Boards." *The National Real Estate Journal,* August 1918.

"A Word from President Garland." *The National Real Estate Journal,* October 1918.

Geffner, Marcie. "MLS: Back to the Future." *California Real Estate,* May 1995, p. 32.

"Glossary of [Agency] Terms," *REALTOR® News,* Aug. 3, 1992.

Grad, Burton. *"The First Commercial Univac I Installation." Computer History Museum, 1997.* http://www .softwarehistory.org/history/Grad1.html (accessed July 21, 2007).

"The Great War and the Shaping of the 20th Century." Community Television of Southern California, 1996–2004. http://www.pbs.org/greatwar (accessed February 12, 2007).

"Groups urge purchasers to use buyer brokers," *REALTOR® News,* Aug. 3, 1992, p. 11.

Grover, Wayne. "Condo or Co-op? What's the Difference?" Bankrate.com, http://www.bankrate.com/brm/news /real-estate/condos1.asp, July 1, 2003 (accessed February 12, 2007).

"H. Jackson Pontius, His Legacy of Growth and Achievement," *REALTORS® Review,* November 1978.

Handbook on Multiple Listing Policy, Chicago: NAR, 1972 (with subsequent revisions).

Harkins, Phil and Keith Hollihan. *Everybody Wins: The Story and Lessons Behind RE/MAX.* Hoboken, N.J.: John Wiley & Sons, Inc., 2005.

Harney, Kenneth R. "Realty Case Aftermath." *The Washington Post.* Oct. 15, 1977.

Heller, Frederik. "The Construction of NAR's New Washington Building." http://www.realtor.org/vlibrary.nsf /pages/newdc (accessed February 15, 2007).

———. "Field Guide to the History of the NATIONAL ASSOCIATION OF REALTORS®." NAR. www.realtor.org /libweb.nsf/pages/fg002#topich. (accessed July 18, 2007).

———. "The Power of One Million." *REALTOR® Magazine.* May 2004.

Helper, Rose. *Racial Practices and Policies of Real Estate Brokers.* Minneapolis: University of Minnesota Press, 1969.

Herman, Eleanor S. "A History of Real Estate." *Real Estate Today,* May 1983, pp. 6–12.

Historical Census of Housing Tables: Homeownership. U.S. Census Bureau. Housing and Household Economic Statistics Division. Revised: December 2, 2004. http://www.census.gov/hhes/www/housing/census/historic/owner.html (accessed July 18, 2007).

"A History of Leadership." AOL corporate Web site. http://www.corp.aol.com/whoweare/history (accessed July 18, 2007).

Holstein, William J. "Office Space: Armchair MBA; Innovation, Leadership, and Still No Satisfaction." *New York Times.* December 19, 2004. http://select.nytimes.com/search/restricted/article?res=FA0716FA3E540C7A8DDDA B0994DC404482 (accessed July 18, 2007).

"Home Buyer & Seller Survey Shows Rising Use of Internet, Reliance on Agents." Washington: NAR news release, Jan. 17, 2006.

"Homeownership Rates by Race and Ethnicity of Householder." www.census.gov/hhes/www/housing/hvs /annual05/ann05t20.html (accessed December 29, 2006).

"Homestore, as Move.com, Tries a New Beginning" *New York Times.* May 1, 2006. http://select.nytimes.com /search/restricted/article?res=F30A17FF3A5B0C728CDDAC0894DE404482 (accessed July 18, 2007).

"Homestore Fights for Life as Bad News Piles Up." *New York Times.* January 27, 2002. http://select.nytimes.com /search/restricted/article?res=F70713FC3C5E0C748EDDA80894DA404482 (accessed July 18, 2007).

Hoover, Herbert. *The Memoirs of Herbert Hoover: The Cabinet and the Presidency, 1920–1933.* New York: The Macmillan Company, 1952.

Hornstein, Jeffrey M. *A Nation of REALTORS®: A Cultural History of the Twentieth-Century American Middle Class.* Durham, NC: Duke University Press, 2005.

Horstman, Barry M. "Golden Age of Architecture." *Cincinnati Post,* November 21, 1998.

Housing for All: Conclusions and Recommendations of the Third International Shelter Conference. NAR, 1990.

"HUD's Agreements with National Housing Industry Groups," HUDclips. www.hudclips.org/sub_nonhud/cgi /nph-brs.cgi?d=FHEH&s1=@docn=+000000106&SECT1=NAVOFFHL&SECT5=CLIP&p=1&r=0&f=S (accessed September 4, 2007).

Hwang, Haley and Stacey Moncrieff. "CEO Dale A. Stinton: A New Era." *REALTOR® Magazine.* December 2005.

"Inventors and Inventions from 1901 to 1950: The First Half of the Twentieth Century." Enchanted Learning. http:// www.enchantedlearning.com/inventors/1900a.shtml (accessed July 18, 2007).

"Is Public Housing a Panacea for Ridding Our Cities of Disease and Crime?" *Headlines.* Chicago: National Association of Real Estate Boards, September 5, 1942.

"It Started in San Diego—or Was It Cincinnati?" *Real Estate Today*, Anniversary Issue, 1988.

Jacobs, Jane. *The Death and Life of Great American Cities.* New York: Vintage Books, 1992.

Kamath, Ravi. "The NAR's Housing Affordability Index." *Real Estate Review*, Winter 1988.

Keadin, William A. Letter to Herbert U. Nelson, NAR Archives, Dec. 20, 1926.

Kentlands: The Official Kentlands Community Web Site. http://kentlandsusa.com/kentlands/community.php
    (accessed May 14, 2007).

Klein, Saul D., John W. Reilly, and Mike Barnett. *Real Estate Technology Guide.* Chicago: Dearborn Real Estate
    Education, 2004.

Kotkin, Joel. "The Evolution of the Commercial Real Estate Industry," Coldwell Banker Commercial White
    Paper, 2006.

Lang, Robert E., and Rebecca R. Sohmer. "Legacy of the Housing Act of 1949: The Past, Present, and Future of
    Federal Housing and Urban Policy." *Housing Policy Debate*, Vol. 11, Issue 2, 2000. Fannie Mae Foundation.

Lamb, Henry. "The UN and Property Rights." Sovereignty.net, 1997. http://www.sovereignty.net/p/land/unproprts
    .htm (accessed July 21, 2007).

Lauber, Daniel. *Ending American Apartheid: How Cities Achieve and Maintain Racial Diversity* (River Forest, IL:
    Planning/Communications, 1989). www.planningcommunications.com/Ending%20American%20Apartheid%202
    005.pdf (accessed October 13, 2006).

Legal Research Center Inc., *Real Estate Agency Annual Report for 2003,* prepared for NAR Government Affairs.

Leong, Evan and Kari Leong. Interview with Bill Chee. Greater Good Radio. December 23, 2006. http://www
    .greatergoodradio.com/?p=255 (accessed July 18, 2007).

"Light in the Frightening Corners." *Time*, July 28, 1967.

Longman, Phillip. "The Mortgaged Generation: Why the Young Can't Afford a House." *Washington Monthly*,
    April 1986.

MacChesney, Nathan William. "Brief and Argument for Protection of Term REALTOR®," circa 1924.

———. "MacChesney Act for a State Real Estate License Law, 1927 Revised Act," Publisher and date unknown.

Manning, Jason. "Ma Bell Breaks Up." The Eighties Club. http://eightiesclub.tripod.com/id310.htm (accessed
    July 18, 2007).

Marples, Gareth. "The History of Home Mortgages—A 'Dead Pledge.' " The-history-of.net. http://www.thehistoryof
.net/history-of-home-mortgages.html (accessed July 18, 2007).

"Martinez Moves to Protect Homebuyers; Calls for Simplified Mortgage Process." U.S. Department of Housing and
Urban Development, October 15, 2001.

Massey, Douglas S., and Nancy A. Denton, *American Apartheid: Segregation and the Making of the Underclass.*
Cambridge and London: Harvard University Press, 1993.

Meloney, Marie M., ed. *Better Homes in America Plan Book for Demonstration Week, October 9–14, 1922.* New York:
Bureau of Information, *The Delineator,* 1922. Accessed at *Prosperity and Thrift: The Coolidge Era and the
Consumer Economy 1921–1929.* Library of Congress Web site: http://memory.loc.gov (accessed June 22, 2007).

Membership Marks Manual, Policy Reference File 109. Chicago: NAR, 1984.

McCrea, Bridget. "Jesperson, Games, Rouda Offer Homestore's New Management Some Advice," Inman News
Features. February 5, 2002.

McDonald, Walt. "Letter from the President." *NATIONAL ASSOCIATION OF REALTORS® 2004 Annual Report.* Chicago: NAR,
2004.

McElvaine, Robert S. *The Great Depression.* New York: Times Books, a division of Random House, 1984 and 1993.

"Milestones in AT&T History." AT&T corporate Web site. http://www.att.com/history/milestones.html (accessed
July 18, 2007).

"Milestones in Residential Real Estate: 1900–1999," *REALTOR® Magazine Online.* December 1999. http://www
.realtor.org/rmomag.NSF/pages/MilestonesChrArchive1999Dec (accessed July 18, 2007).

Milligan, Kevin. White paper entitled "NAR's Federated Structure Explained." July 2000.

Minneapolis Morning Tribune, "Charles N. Chadbourn, REALTOR®, Dies at 83," December 15, 1942.

Mize, Richard. "REALTORS® Win Fight to Protect Their Good Name." Knight Ridder/Tribune Business News.
Washington: April 10, 2004, p. 1.

"MLS and the Cleveland Board." *Cleveland REALTOR®,* September/October 1992, p. 12.

Moncrieff, Stacey. "The Guiding Light?" *Real Estate Today,* March 1993, p. 12.

Moncrieff, Stacey. "In Memory of Arthur Leitch: Fair Housing Giant." *REALTOR Magazine,* March 2002,
p. 18.

"Mr. Parish Wins His Suit." *The Real-Estate and Building Journal.* Chicago: Hungerford & Smith, July 26, 1890.

"Multiple Listing Service," Wikipedia. http://en.wikipedia.org/wiki/Multiple_Listing_Service (accessed July 18, 2007).

NAR. "Art S. Leitch, President, 1975." NATIONAL ASSOCIATION OF REALTORS® Archives.

———. "At Home with Diversity Homepage." Chicago: NAR. http://www.realtor.org/divweb.nsf (accessed December 29, 2006).

———. "Attempt to Standardize Home Shows." NAR Archives, 1923.

———. "HOPE Awards Celebrate Minority Homeownership." http://www.realtor.org/realtororg.nsf/pages /2005MYMHOPEAwards?OpenDocument (accessed December 29, 2006).

———. "Identifying Logo Fits New Image," *REALTOR® Headlines.* NAR, April 16, 1973. p. 1.

———. News release announcing the death of H. Jackson Pontius. Undated.

———. News release announcing the selection of H. Jackson Pontius as NAR executive vice president. Feb. 5, 1970.

———. News release expressing NAR's support of lead-based paint hazards disclosure. October 8, 1991.

———. "Report of the Presidential Advisory Group on the Facilitator/Non-Agency Concept," November 1993.

———. "Structure, Conduct, and Performance of the Real Estate Brokerage Industry," November 2005.

———. "Taxing Times for Housing." Proceedings of a Conference on Tax Reform and How Tax Reform May Affect Savings, Investment, and Homeownership. NAR, 1985. Chicago: NAR Archives.

———. "Three-Way Agreement: Who Originated the Idea?" NAR Archives, circa 1948.

———. "Why a Diversity Program? Racial and Ethnic Diversity." http://www.realtor.org/divweb.nsf/Pages /divhallmark?OpenDocument (accessed December 29, 2006).

———. NAR Board of Directors Minutes. November 11–12, 1975.

"NAR formally brings buyer brokerage council into the fold," NAR news release, April 29, 1996.

"NAR plans to encourage state laws on agency duty." *REALTOR® News,* December 6, 1993, p. 13.

"NAR responds to court decision on MLS access." *REALTOR® News,* October 7, 1991, p. 1.

Nathan William MacChesney Biography. Northwestern University Archives. http://www.library.northwestern.edu /archives/findingaids/nathan_william_macchesney.pdf (accessed August 11, 2006).

National Association of Real Estate Boards, "William May Garland." *Headlines,* October 4, 1948, p. 1.

National Association of Real Estate Boards. "Nelson Traces 10 Decades of Real Estate Achievement." *The National Real Estate Journal.* November 14, 1952.

"National Association of Real Estate Boards Reports." *The National Real Estate Journal.* April 25, 1927.

————, "The Lessons of a Lifetime of Developing," February 1939, p. 30.

————, "Los Angeles Honors New National President," October 1917, pp. 368–370.

————, "Nichols' Notes on Selling," February 1939, p. 56.

————, "Portrait of a Salesman: Jesse Clyde Nichols," February 1939.

————, "The President's Report," August 1919.

————, Remarks by William M. Garland at the July 1919 Convention, August 1919, p. 8.

————, "Subdivisions . . ." August 15, 1912, pp. 461–462.

Nelson, Herbert U., ed. "G.I. Opportunities." *Headlines,* June 19, 1944, p. 2.

————. "The Real Estate Issue," *Headlines.* September 8, 1947, p. 2.

————. "Nathan William MacChesney's *Headlines,* October 4, 1954, p. 2.

News Article announcing the selection of William D. North as NAR executive vice president. *Chicago Sun-Times,* May 27, 1986.

North, William D. "Firming the Foundation." *Membership Policy and Board Jurisdiction Manual,* Appendix R, Chicago: NAR 1996. (Originally published in the 1980 manual.)

————. "The Fourteen Points—In Search of a Rationale," *The Executive Officer,* December 1974, p. 5. (Revised August 1976)

————. "The Realtors® Code of Ethics: A Gift of Vision." *The Executive Officer,* August 1978, pp. 18–19.

————. *Passwords and Prejudice: A Realtor®'s Guide to Fair Housing Compliance.* Chicago: National Association of Realtors®, 1986.

North, William D., preface to *Who Is My Client? A Realtors® Guide to Compliance with the Law of Agency, Legal Liability Series,* Chicago: NAR, November 1986.

"Official Proceedings of the Ninth Annual Convention, National Association of Real Estate Exchanges. Held in New Orleans, Louisiana, March 27–31, 1916." *National Real Estate Journal,* April 1916, pp. 173–261.

Okrent, Daniel. *Great Fortune: The Epic of Rockefeller Center.* New York: Penguin Group, 2003.

"The Origins of the MLS." Trend MLS. www.trendmls.com/Guest/AboutUs/History.aspx. Accessed July 18, 2007.

Pacyga, Dominic A. and Charles Shanabruch, eds. *The Chicago Bungalow: Chicago Architecture Foundation.* Mount Pleasant: Arcadia Publishing, 2001.

Parry, David. "The Development of Organized Real Estate in San Francisco," *The Argonaut.* Journal of the San Francisco Museum and Historical Society. Volume 15, No. 2.

Pasadena Tournament of Roses. Tournament of Roses History. www.tournamentofroses.com/history /grandmarshalpast.asp (accessed December 13, 2006).

Pearson, "Subdivisions and the Best Manner of Handling Them," *The National Real Estate Journal,* August 15, 1912, p. 460.

Pearson, Robert, and Brad Pearson, *The J.C. Nichols Chronicle: The Authorized Story of the Man, His Company, and His Legacy, 1880–1994,* Lawrence: University Press of Kansas. 1994.

Pfeiffer, William and June Babiracki Barlow. "Best Sellers." *California Real Estate,* July/August 1991, p. 27.

The Political Graveyard. Index to Politicians: Garland. http://politicalgraveyard.com/bio/garland.html (accessed December 13, 2006).

Pontius, H. Jackson. *Operation of Multiple Listing Services.* National Association of Real Estate Boards. Date unknown.

Poppeliers, John C. *What Style Is It? A Guide to American Architecture.* Hoboken: John Wiley & Sons, 2003.

Pozdena, Randall Johnston. *The Modern Economics of Housing: A Guide to Theory and Policy for Finance and Real Estate Professional.* Westport: Quorum Books, 1988.

Proceedings of the Second International Conference and Vienna Recommendations on Shelter and Urban Development. Washington: NAR, 1987.

"Profile: Art Leitch," unpublished interview conducted for the 75th anniversary of NAR by the editors of *Real Estate Today.*

"*Property Condition Disclosure,*" Chicago: NAR, 1991.

"Property Disclosure by Seller Helps Everyone, NAR Says." NAR News Release, June 24, 1991.

"Q&A with Homestore.com's Stuart Wolff." *Business Week,* March 26, 2001. http://www.businessweek.com/magazine /content/01_13/b3725037.htm (accessed July 18, 2007).

Real Estate Board Operation Manual. Compiled by the Executive Officers Council of the National Association of Real Estate Boards, December 1960 (revised 1967), Public Relations and Publicity chapter.

The Real Estate Commission Rate, Bulletin #12, Executive Officers Council, pp. 2–3.

"The Real Estate Industry Lobby and Public Housing in the 1930s." *History Matters,* http://historymatters.gmu.edu /d/5106 (accessed January 29, 2007).

————. *Real Estate License Laws: Their Development and Results.* National Association of Real Estate Boards. Chicago: NAR, 1928.

The REALTOR® *Tradition in Minneapolis: 1887–1987.* Minneapolis: Greater Minneapolis Area Board of REALTORS®, 1985.

The REALTOR®: Weekly Bulletin of the Minneapolis Real Estate Board, August 8, 1939, p. 1.

REALTOR.org. "About NAR's Three-Way Agreement." http://www.realtor.org/aesubs.nsf/pages/threewayagreement (accessed June 22, 2007).

"REBAC signs pact with RE/MAX," *Agency Law Quarterly,* Winter 1994, p. 13.

"REITs 101: The History of REITs." http://www.reitnet.com/reits101/history.phtml, April 2005 (accessed June 22, 2007).

Report of the Multiple Listing Committee. Chicago: National Association of Real Estate Boards. March 6–8, 1921.

Report of the Presidential Advisory Group on the Facilitator/Non-Agency Concept. NATIONAL ASSOCIATION OF REALTORS®, November 1993.

Riveles, Simon, Esq. "Condominium vs. Cooperative Ownership: A Primer." http://www.wrlawfirm.com/Articles /wrm.article.Condo.Versus.Coop.Primer.stml, 2004 (accessed February 12, 2007).

Roark, Paul, Tom Papageorge, *et. al. The Residential Real Estate Brokerage Industry, A Federal Trade Commission Staff Report,* December 1983. http://www.ftc.gov/bc/realestate/workshop/index.htm (accessed July 20, 2007).

Robbins, Roy M. *Our Landed Heritage: The Public Domain, 1776–1936.* Princeton: Princeton University Press, 1942.

Roosevelt Institute. Franklin Roosevelt broadcast. "Outlining the New Deal Program," radio broadcast on NBC and CBS, May 7, 1933. Transcript published by the Franklin and Eleanor Roosevelt institute. www.feri.org/common /news/details.cfm?QID=2068&clientid=11005 (accessed January 7, 2007).

Roth, Leland M. *American Architecture: A History*. Boulder: Westview Press, 2001.

Saavedra, Raul Jr. "History of the Real Estate Industry." Excerpted from *Vault Guide to Real Estate Careers,* by Saavedra. April 2003. http://www.vault.com/articles/History-of-the-Real-Estate-Industry-18187121.html. Accessed July 18, 2007.

Salvant, Lucien. "30th Anniversary of the Fair Housing Act, Part 1." *Today's REALTOR®*. April 1998, pp. 23–27.

Sawyer, J. D. "J.D. Sawyer Biographical Sketch." NAR Archives, March 23, 1979.

Schmidt, Walter S. "The President's Page." *The National Real Estate Journal,* May 1935, June 1935, December 1935, and January 1936.

Selleck, John. "The New Global Standard for the Transmission of All MLS Data." *The Real Estate Professional,* March/April 1995, p. 27.

Semenow, Robert W. *Survey of Real Estate Brokers License Laws,* Chicago: National Association of Real Estate Boards, 1936.

Semenow, Robert W. "Review of the License Law Structure," date unknown.

Sharoff, Robert. "New Building, Greater Presence." *REALTOR® Magazine,* May 2004.

Slaughter, A. M. "Testimony before the U.S. Commission on Civil Rights." Oakland, California, May 12, 1964. Quoted in Brown, "Access to Housing."

Staley, Sam, and Leonard C. Gilroy. "Smart Growth and Housing Affordability: Evidence from Statewide Planning Laws." Policy Study No. 287, Reason Foundation, December 2001.

Stark, Paul. "Rebuilding Our Cities." *The National Real Estate Journal,* May 1937.

"States' agency disclosure laws vary." *REALTOR® NEWS,* August 3, 1992, p. 10.

Statement by Herbert U. Nelson. Conference of the National Association of REALTOR® Secretaries, July 13, 1921.

Statement by The Honorable Mel Martinez before the United States House Committee on Financial Services. October 3, 2002. http://www.hud.gov/offices/cir/test100302mm.cfm (accessed July 6, 2007).

"Strong and Weak Points of Multiple Listing." *The National Real Estate Journal*, January 28, 1924.

"A Study of Home Inspection and Warranty Programs," Vol. 1, U.S. Department of Housing and Urban Development, June 1977.

"Sun City: 40 Years of Success." Sun City Visitors Center (Web site). http://www.suncityaz.org/History /sun_city%20-%2040%20years.htm (accessed May 14, 2007).

Sumber, Edward L. "Attorney explains MLS: REALTOR® Multiple Listing Service Is Discussed." *Real Estate Weekly*, April 9, 2003. http://www.findarticles.com/p/articles/mi_m3601/is_36_49/ai_100243488. Accessed July 18, 2007. Copyright 2003 Hagedorn Publication and Copyright 2003 Gale Group.

Susanka, Sarah. *The Not So Big House*, Newtown: The Taunton Press, 2001.

Taxpayer, "Charles Nathaniel Chadbourn, 1859–1942," February 1943.

"Technology Timeline: 1752–1990." PBS Online/WGBH, 2000. http://www.pbs.org/wgbh/amex/telephone/ timeline/timeline_text.html (accessed July 18, 2007).

Theobald, A.D. "Real Estate License Laws in Theory and Practice." Publisher unknown. 1931.

Tedeschi, Bob. "E-Commerce Report: Providing Free Real Estate Listings from a Broader Market." *New York Times*, May 1, 2006. http://select.nytimes.com/search/restricted/article?res=F10711FE3A5B0C728CDDAC0894DE404482 (accessed July 18, 2007).

Time, "Luring Blacks, Keeping Whites," October 31, 1977. http://www.time.com/time/magazine/article /0,9171,945794,00.html (accessed December 29, 2006).

"Proposition 14," *Time*. September 25, 1964. http://www.time.com/time/magazine/article/0,9171,876158,00.html (accessed December 29, 2006).

"Timeline." The Virtual Typewriter Library. www.typewritermuseum.org/collection/timeline/index.html (accessed July 18, 2007).

"Timeline 1908–1909." Timelines of History. http://timelines.ws/20thcent/1908_1909.html (accessed July 18, 2007).

United Realty 1908. Chicago: National Association of Real Estate Exchanges, June 26, 1908.

"Update: Changes to NAR agency policies under way." *REALTOR® News*, Aug. 3, 1992, p. 10.

Upton, Dell. *Architecture in the United States*. New York: Oxford University Press, 1998.

U.S. Bureau of the Census. Census of Housing, 1940, Vol. 2, General Characteristics, Part 1, United States Summary, Introduction, Table 3.

U.S. Department of Housing and Urban Development. "Executive Order 11063." hud.gov. www.hud.gov/offices /fheo/FHLaws/EXO11063.cfm (accessed December 29, 2006).

U.S. Department of Justice. "Fair Housing Act." www.usdoj.gov/crt/housing/title8.htm (accessed December 29, 2006).

U.S. Department of the Interior, National Park Service National Register. "House and Yard: The Design of the Suburban Home." www.cr.nps.gov/nr/publications/bulletins/suburbs/part3.htm (accessed February 12, 2007).

U.S. General Accounting Office. "Extent of Federal Influence on 'Urban Sprawl' Is Unclear," Washington: GAO. April 1999.

U.S. Patent and Trademark Office, Trademark Trial and Appeal Board: *Jacob Zimmerman v. National Association of Realtors®*, March 31, 2004.

"Valuation of the Realtor® Brand from the Perspective of Benefits Attributable to Members." Prepared by absolute-BRAND, July 2005.

VanGiezen, Robert, and Albert E. Schwenk. "Compensation from before World War I through the Great Depression." *Compensation and Working Conditions*, Fall 2001.

Van Vliet, Willem, editor. *The Encyclopedia of Housing*. Thousand Oaks: Sage Publications, 1998.

Von Hoffman, Alexander. "Like Fleas on a Tiger? A Brief History of the Open Housing Movement." Joint Center for Housing Studies, Harvard University, 1998.

———, "A Study in Contradictions: The Origins and Legacy of the Housing Act of 1949." Housing Policy Debate, Vol. 11, Issue 2, 2000. Fannie Mae Foundation.

Waldron, Stacey A. "The MLS Withstands the Test of Time." *Real Estate Today*, August 1989, p. 26.

Wedner, Diane. "Arthur Leitch; Realtor Led Fair-Housing Push." *Los Angeles Times*, July 19, 2001.

Weiss, Marc A. *The Rise of the Community Builders: The American Real Estate Industry and Urban Land Planning*. New York: Columbia University Press, 1987.

Welfeld, Irving. *Where We Live: A Social History of American Housing*. New York: Simon & Schuster, 1988.

"Where We've Been," *Real Estate Today*. May 1983, pp. 13–17.

Williams, Jack. "REALTOR® Arthur Leitch: Fair Housing Pioneer." *San Diego Union-Tribune*, July 17, 2001, p. B-7.

Worley, William S. *J.C. Nichols and the Shaping of Kansas City: Innovation in Planned Residential Communities.* Columbia: University of Missouri Press, 1990.

Wright, Richard. *Native Son.* New York: HarperCollins Harper Perennial Modern Classics, 2005. (Original hardcover: Harper & Brothers, 1940.)

"Today in History: September 4," Library of Congress. http://memory.loc.gov/ammem/today/sep04.html (accessed May 24, 2007).

"The Plan of Chicago." Chicago History Museum. The Electronic Encyclopedia of Chicago. Chicago Historical Society. 2005 (accessed May 24, 2007).

INTERVIEWS

Bowman, Gloria. Interviewed by Robert Sharoff, December 2006.

Chee, William S. Interviewed by Jim Hatfield, October 2006.

Conser, Eugene. Interviewed by *Real Estate Today* magazine staff, May 16, 1983. NAR Archives.

Edwards, Martin. Interviewed by G.M. Filisko, December 2006.

Everson, Paul. Interviewed by Stacey Moncrieff, February 15, 2007.

Fitzgerald, Patricia. E-mail correspondence with Jim Hatfield, October 2006.

Garner, Keith. E-mail correspondence with Jim Hatfield, October 2006.

Godi, Art. Interviewed by Stacey Moncrieff, November 2003.

Goldberg, Bob. Interviewed by Jim Hatfield, October 2006.

Hanauer, Joseph. Interviewed by Jim Hatfield, October 2006.

Kline, Tim. Interviewed by Robert Sharoff, December 2006.

Lee, Eve. Interviewed by David Mahfouda, September 26, 2006.

Lewis, Hazel. Interviewed by David Mahfouda, October 20, 2006.

Mendenhall, Richard. E-mail correspondence with Jim Hatfield, October 2006.

Milligan, Kevin. Interviewed by Robert Sharoff, December 2006.

Mini, Mike. Interviewed by Robert Sharoff, December 2006.

Myles, Ron. Interviewed by Brad Broberg, November 2006, and Robert Sharoff, December 2006.

Niersbach, Cliff. Interviewed by Barbara Ballinger, August 2006.

North, William. Interviewed by Damian Da Costa, November 27, 2006.

North, William D. Interviewed by *NAR Staff Lines,* September 1986.

Okamoto, Allen. Interviewed by David Mahfouda, October 20, 2006.

Peters, Sharon. Interviewed by Robert Sharoff, December 2006.

Roth, Leland M. Interviewed by Barbara Ballinger, January 2005.

Saliga, Pat. Interviewed by Barbara Ballinger, January 2006.

Sawyer, John. Interviewed by Stacey Moncrieff, February 9, 2007.

Schwemm, Robert. Interviewed by David Mahfouda, September 27, 2006.

Sherman, Malcolm. Interviewed by Damian Da Costa, October 12, 2006.

Smith, Almon R. "Bud." Interview and e-mail correspondence with Jim Hatfield, October–December 2006.

Stinton, Dale. E-mail correspondence with Jim Hatfield, October 2006.

Underwood, Fred. Interviewed by Damian Da Costa, December 14, 2006.

Wallace, Clark. Interviewed by G.M. Filisko, November 2006.

U.S. SUPREME COURT DECISIONS

Bratton v. Chandler, 260 U.S. 110 (1922).

Brown v. Board of Education of Topeka, 347 U.S. 483 (1954).

Hurd v. Hodge, 334 U.S. 24 (1948).

Jones v. Alfred H. Mayer Co., 392 U.S. 409 (1968).

McLain v. Real Estate Board of New Orleans, 444 U.S. 232 (1980).

Plessy v. Ferguson, 163 U.S. 537 (1896).

Reitman v. Mulkey, 387 U.S. 369 (1967).

Shelley v. Kraemer, 334 U.S. 1 (1948).

The United States of America v. National Association of Real Estate Boards, et al., 339 U.S. 485 (1950).

Index

A

Abrahams, Albert, 92
Accredited Buyer Representative
    (ABR®), 240–241
Advocacy
    approach to, 103
    effectiveness of, 101
    NAR, 89–95
Affirmative Marketing Agreement, 125
Affordability measures, 165–166
African Americans, equal housing
    opportunities for, 106–137
Agency, 238–241
    buyer, 241–242
    designated, 241
    laws, 240
Ahrens, Deborah, 143
American culture, home ownership
    in, 35
"American Dream," 35
    attaining, 41–47
American Home Week, 64
American Institute of Real Estate
    Appraisers, 202
Anderson, Geoff, 166
Anderson, Mo, 144, 145
Annual conventions, National
    Association of Real Estate
    Exchanges, 11
Apartments, owned, 70–73
Appraisal information, 42
Appraisal Institute, 18, 213
Appraisal of Real Estate, The
    (Babcock), 110
Architectural Record, The, 55
Architecture in the United States
    (Upton), 73
*Architecture of America, The—A Social
    and Cultural History* (Burchard &
    Bush-Brown), 70

Armstrong, Robert, 86
Asian Real Estate Association of
    America (AREAA), 134
Association of Real Estate License Law
    Officials, 213
Atwood, J. Brian, 271
Automobile, rise of, 170–172

B

Babcock, Frederick M., 110, 111
Baltimore Board of Real Estate
    Brokers and Property Agents, 4
Barnard, Boyd T., 285
Belgium, condominiums in, 71
Berge, Palmer, 95
Better Homes in America Inc., 46
Birnbaum, Jeffrey, 104
Black Belt, 107
Blockbusting, 112, 114–115
Booth, Russell K., 204, 263, 292
Brady, Hobart C., 285
Bratton v. Chandler, 197
Brokerage industry, 226
Brooklyn, New York, first co-op
    apartments in, 70
Brown, William N., 112, 288
Brown v. Topeka Board of Education,
    115
Buck, B. C., 196
Buck, James O., 196
Buffalo Real Estate Board, 49
Build America Better Committee,
    54–58
"Build America Better" program, 156–
    164, 165, 174, 176, 177, 178
Bungalows, 73
Burchard, John, 70
Burchard Houses, changes in, 70–77
Burleson, Mary Frances, 218, 222
Burnham, Daniel Hudson, 9
Bush, George Herbert Walker, 99
Bush, George Walker, 66, 92, 99
Bush-Brown, Albert, 70

Business models, alternative, 236
"Buy a Home" campaign of 1914,
    42, 43
Buyer agency, 241–242
"Buyer beware," erosion of, 242–245
Buyers Rep, The, 241

C

California Association of REALTORS®,
    63, 126, 133
California Real Estate Association,
    154, 275, 276
    Women's Division, 142
Canadian Real Estate Association, 10
Candidate support, 102
Capitol Hill, greening of, 105
Carew Tower, 56, 57
Carlborg, Herbert A., 29
Carlson, Jack, 267, 277
Case interpretations, 203
Catharine, Joseph W., 284
CBS, misuse of REALTOR® mark by, 29
Center for REALTOR® Technology,
    259–260
Central European Real Estate
    Associations Network
    (CEREAN), 271
Certificate of Change of Name, 26
Certified Commercial Investment
    Member (CCIM) Institute, 211,
    270
Certified International Property
    Specialist (CIPS), 264, 265
    Network, 211, 265
Certified Real Estate Brokerage
    Manager (CRB), 235
Certified Residential Specialist
    (CRS®), 235
Chadbourn, Charles Nathaniel, 14,
    18, 20–21, 32
    Chicago REALTOR® article by, 31
    legacy of, 21
    on the term REALTOR®, 24–25

Chapman, Lucile N., 138
Chappell, Sally A. Kitt, 170
Chee, William S. (Bill), 233, 235,
    250, 255–256, 260, 263, 292
Chicago, importance in the real estate
    world, 7–8
Chicago Association of REALTORS®, 7
Chicago Freedom Movement, 120
Chicago Real Estate Board, 23, 111
    offices, 11
China Real Estate Association,
    268–269
Cincinnati Real Estate Board, 56
CIPS Network. *See* Certified
    International Property Specialist
    (CIPS)
Cities
    decline of, 172
    growth of, 40, 41, 168–176
    makeovers of, 179
    post-war, 172–176
City, The: A Global History (Kotkin),
    169
City Beautiful movement, 9
City Planning Committee, NAR, 154
Civil rights movement, 111–113
Clinton, Hillary Rodham, 99
Clinton, William Jefferson, 99
Coalition for Sustainable Cities, 272
Code of Ethics. *See also* Ethical
    standards
    ethical duties under, 200–202, 203
    NAR, 109, 110, 112, 198–204
    National Association of Real Estate
        Exchanges, 14
    training related to, 204
    value of, 204
Code of Ethics and Arbitration Manual,
    204
Columbian Exposition of 1893, 7,
    8, 40
    international real estate congress
        at, 6

Combined Investments LP, 261
Combs, Pat Vredevoogd, 102, 128, 144, 185, 236, 260, 294
Commercial districts, zoning of, 169–170
Commercial real estate, 173–174
CommercialSource online convention, 181
Commission rates, 227–229, 230
Commissions, 100 percent, 232
Commission schedules, 230, 231
Committee on Multiple Listing Policy, 217
Common law of agency, 238
Communications, advances in, 246
Communities, growth management for, 149–189
Community Builder: The Life and Legacy of J. C. Nichols, 163
Community builders, 154
Community Builders Handbook, 163
Community Choice in Real Estate Act, 103
Community Development Block Grant program, 92, 93, 164
Community planning, NAR roles in, 147, 165
Community service, NAR, 182–186
CompuServ, 253–254
Computerization, 250–252
Computerized MLS, 225
Computers, linking, 253–255
Condominiums, 70–73
Conser, Eugene P., 31, 231, 275
Construction funding, 42
Consumer movement, 237
Contra Costa (California) Real Estate Board, 90
Conventions, NAR, 205–207
Coolidge, Calvin, 36
Cooperative (co-op) apartments, 70
"Cooperative selling," 249

Cotton, John, 288
Council of Real Estate Brokerage Managers, 211
Council of Residential Specialists, 211
Counselors of Real Estate, 212
Country Club District, 152, 154, 158
Country Club Plaza, 160–161, 163
Craven, Frank, 199
Credit scores, 133
Cronk, Dennis R., 261, 263, 269, 293
Cruikshank Company, 195
Culver, Harry H., 156, 157, 282
"Curbstoners," 4, 8, 24

D

Dahlheimer, Charles, 239
Davies, Pearl Janet, 9, 25, 40, 138, 172–173, 181, 195, 198, 199
Davis, Lyn E., 288
Deed restrictions, 155
Demonstration homes, 46–47
Designated agency, 240, 241
Developers, tax reform and, 179–180. *See also* Urban development
Discount brokers, 236
Discrimination, 109. *See also* Diversity; Minority entries; Segregation
Distinguished Service Award Winners, 190–191
Diversity, as a NAR goal, 136–137
Doherty, Joseph B., 289
"Dollar men," 86
Dooley, Tom, 239
Dorn, James A., 269
Douglas, R. Bruce, 227, 274–275
Downtown: Its Rise and Fall 1880–1950 (Fogelson), 169
Driesler, Stephen, 83
Dues, NAR, 17

E

Eastern Europe, democratic reforms in, 270–272. *See also* Poland

Eastern European Real Property Foundation (EERPF), 270–272
Easton v. Strassburger, 242–243
Ebby Halliday, REALTORS®, 218
Economy, real estate business impact on, 193
Edge cities, 179
Education, continuing, 205–207
Edwards, Charles G., 282
Edwards, Martin, Jr. 16, 66, 187, 256–257, 293
Eisenhower, Dwight David, 80
Elmstrom, Harry C., 289
Elrod, Roben H. (Bob), 292
e-Neighborhoods, 189
Ennis, Callistus S., 227
Ennis, Hugh Robert, 32, 282
Eppich, Louis F, 281
e-PRO®, 258
Equal Opportunity Committee, 130, 131
Equal Opportunity—Cultural Diversity Committee, 134
Equal opportunity housing, 106–137, 162
Equitable Building, 170
Espeseth, Earl, 239
Ethical standards, 5. *See also* Code of Ethics entries
Everybody Wins: The Story and Lessons Behind RE/MAX (Harkins & Hollihan), 233
Exclusive listing contract, 214
Executive Order 11065, 115–119
Existing-Home Sales (EHS) Series, 60–61, 71

F

Fair housing, NAR role in, 137
Fair Housing Act of 1968, 96, 122–125
Fair Housing Amendments Act of 1988, 91, 132

Fair Housing Partnership, 132
Farmers Home Admin (FmHA), 91
Farr, Newton C., 284
"Father REALTOR®," 20–21, 32
Federal Fair Housing Act of 1968, 91
Federal Home Loan Bank Act of 1932, 49, 87
Federal Home Loan Mortgage Corporation (Freddie Mac), 51
Federal Housing Administration (FHA), 51, 52, 55, 87, 155–156. *See also* "FHA Minimum House" home ownership and, 35 *Underwriting Manual* of, 111
Federal housing programs, 93
Federal mortgage discount bank, 55
Federal National Mortgage Association (Fannie Mae), 51, 55
Federal political coordinators (FPCs), 100
Federal Reserve Act of 1915, 41
Federal Reserve Board, 60
Federal tax credit, 63–65
Ferro, Fred, 167
"FHA Minimum House," 73. *See also* Federal Housing Administration (FHA)
FIABCI-USA, 264. *See also* International Real Estate Federation (FIABCI)
"Firming the Foundation" (North), 17
Fitch, Morgan L., 229, 285
Fitzgerald, Patricia S., 260
Flagler, Henry Morrison, 149
Flat tax, 81
Fleming, Joseph B., 229–230
Florida, growth of, 149–150
Florida Association of REALTORS'®, Smart Growth Council, 151
Flynn, Norman D., 263, 291
Forbes, Steve, 81
Ford, George, 152
Ford, Gerald Rudolph, Jr., 93, 164

Ford, Henry, 73, 246
Ford Motor Company River Rouge
    plant, 170
Foreign investment, 179
Fort Collins Association of
    REALTORS®, 66
FORTRAN, 250
Fort Wayne REALTORS®' Girls Club,
    141
Foster, Cora Bacon, 138
"14 points" policy, 224
Fraud, 3, 14
Frederick, August H., 10–11, 14–18
Freehold, 205
Freeway construction projects, 174
Frist, Bill, 16

G

Galbreath, John W., 285
Gardner, William H., 283
Garland, William May, 42, 44, 57,
    84–85, 86, 262, 281
Garrett, Van Holt, 88–89, 285
Gated communities, 75
Gaylord, Dick, 294
"Gentlemen's agreement," 116
Gerholz, Robert P., 262, 285
GI Bill, 53
Gingrich, Newt, 99
Giovaniello, Jerry, 91, 103
*Glendale Board of REALTORS® v.
    Hounsell*, 225
Global housing policy, 272–273
Godi, Arthur L., 81, 83, 241, 245,
    256, 263, 292
Goldberg, Bob, 252, 256
Goldberger, Paul, 163
"Golden R" program, 97
"Golden thread," 198, 199
Goldstein, Sandra, 151
Good Neighbor Awards program,
    187–189
    winners in, 188–189

Gove, Philip Babcock, 31
Government, relationship of
    REALTORS® with, 78–105
Government Appraisal Committees,
    84–85
Government housing, 48–49
Graduate REALTOR® Institute (GRI),
    276
Gramercy Park, 70
Grant, Tom, Jr., 289
Graves, H. Walter, 287
Great Chicago Fire of 1871, 7. *See also*
    Chicago entries
Great Depression, 47–54, 55, 172
Greater Baltimore Board of
    REALTORS®, 1, 187
Green movement, 77
Gribin, Ira, 99, 127, 236, 291
Groskin, Horace, 169
Growth management, 149–189
    laws governing, 149–151
    measures of, 165
"Guiding Principles for REALTORS®
    and Smart Growth," 166

H

Haas, Henry P., 84, 86, 281
Habitat for Humanity International,
    183–185
Halliday, Ebby, 143, 218–223, 252
Halsey, Edward A., 8, 10, 11, 12,
    198–199, 274
Hanauer, Joe F., 257, 261
Handbook on Multiple Listing Policy,
    224. *See also* Multiple listing
    services (MLS)
Hannan, William W., 17, 18, 147,
    280
Harding, Warren Gamaliel, 43
Harkins, John N., 198
Headlines, 205
Helfant, Dorcas T., 129, 143–144,
    145, 239, 291

Helper, Rose, 115
Hemingway, George R., 45
Hieatt, Clarence C., 282
Hiett, Irving B., 216, 281
Highway Act of l956, 176
Highway development, 176
Historic homes, 75, 76
Hoffer, Eric, 194
"Home at Work" program, 67
Home building, 73
    expositions for, 46
Home Finder, 249
Home loan discount banks, 87
"Home of the Month" (*McCall's*
    magazine), 51, 73
Home ownership, 34–7
    decline in, 54
    factors working against, 47
    growth in, 40–41, 65–66
    in presidential campaigns, 99
    promoting, 43–477
Home Ownership Participation for
    Everyone (HOPE) awards, 65,
    66, 135, 136
Home Owners Loan Act, 275
Home Owners' Loan Corporation
    (HOLC), 50–51, 113
Home Owners Warranty Program,
    242
Homestead Act of 1862, 37–40
Homestore, 257
Hoover, Herbert Clark, 42–43, 46,
    87, 155, 156
Hornstein, Jeffrey M., 25, 35, 110,
    141, 154, 206
*House Detective: Finding History in
    Your Home*, 68
Housing
    affordable, 66–67
    federal presence in, 87–89
    postwar demand for, 88–89
Housing Act of 1938, 51
Housing Act of 1940, 91

Housing Act of 1949, 114
Housing Act of 1961, 164
Housing Affordability Index, 63
Housing and Community Development
    Act of 1974, 92, 93
Housing boom, post-World War II, 54
Housing construction, 47
"Housing ladder," 63–65
Housing market, statistics on, 60–61
Housing Opportunities Made Easier
    (HOME), 167
Housing Opportunity Program,
    66–67, 137, 167
Housing policy, 43
Housing production, federal role
    in, 87
Housing shortages, 42, 46, 54
Hovde, Donald I., 290
Howley, Jack, 264, 269–270, 272,
    273
HUD/NAR partnership, 125, 128–
    132. *See also* National Association
    of REALTORS® (NAR); U.S.
    Department of Housing and
    Urban Development (HUD)
Hurricane Katrina, 183–185
Hurricane relief, 183–185

I

Income tax system, 41, 83
Index of dissimilarity, 114
Inflation, 63
Ingalls, Bertha W., 39
Ingersoll, Thomas S., 13, 160, 275
Institute of Real Estate Management,
    173, 212
Integration, 115–122. *See also*
    Segregation
    in housing, 120
Interest rates, 63
    congressional action on, 62
International Ambassador Association
    Program, 265

International Consortium of Real Estate Associations (ICREA), 266–267
International Housing Coalition (IHC), 272–273
International Policy Committee, 265
International Real Estate Federation (FIABCI), 262–265
International real estate standards, 266
International Real Property Foundation, 261
International Shelter Conferences, 267–268
Internet, 253–260
    MLS data on, 226
Internet Crusade, 258
Ipswich House, 68–69
Isakson, Johnny, 102, 103
Issues Mobilization Committee, 101

J

Jacobs, Jane, 174
Jacobsen, Hugh Newell, 148
Janik, Laurie, 27–28
J. C. Nichols and the Shaping of Kansas City (Worley), 161
J. C. Nichols Company, 158, 163
Jefferson, Thomas, 71, 73
Jemison, Robert, Jr., 282
Johnson, Lyndon Baines, 121, 122, 123
Johnson, Reverdy, 70
Jones v. Alfred H. Mayer Co., 123
Judd, Edward Sanderson, 7, 9, 12, 18, 41, 195, 199, 280
Justice, Jack, 288
Justice Department investigations, 227, 229, 230–231

K

Kabati, Pamela Geurds, 187
Kaplan, Pat G., 144, 145
Keadin, William A., 214, 215

Keenan, Laurie, 145
Kelly, Margaret M., 145
Kemp, Jack, 129, 131
Kenna, J. J., 19
Kennedy, John Fitzgerald, 115, 116
Kentlands, 77
Kerfoot, William D., 7
Kerner Report, 122–122
Keyes, Kenneth S., 286
King, H. C., 17
King, Martin Luther, Jr., 120, 121, 123
Kissell, Harry S., 49, 50, 283
Knabb, Jack, 216
Kniskern, Philip W., 284
Krysler, Gary, 138–141

L

Laguarta, Julio S., 98, 290
Land
    demand for, 3
    owning, 37–41
    policy toward, 37
    prices of, 76
    surveys of, 37–38
Land development, for middle-income home buyers, 162
Land use research, 57
Lanham Act, 26
Law of Real Estate Brokerage, The (MacChesney), 23
Lead-based Paint Disclosure Act of 1992, 244–245
Leadership Council, 120, 125
Lee, Eve, 120, 122, 125
Legal action program, NAR, 231
Leitch, Arthur S. (Art), 125, 126–127, 237, 242, 289
Lewis-Wiltz, Hazel W., 128, 130–131, 137
Licensing laws, uniform system of, 18–19
Liniger, Dave, 232–235

Liniger, Gail, 145
"Lions Over the Hill" speech, 255–256, 260
Listing directories, 216
Listings, 250. *See also* Multiple listing services (MLS)
Local boards, 17
Local real estate organizations, 4
Lofts, 75–76
Lund, Joseph W., 54, 174–176, 286

M

MacChesney, Nathan William, 12, 17, 23, 26, 32, 197
    legal defense by, 27
MacChesney Act, 19
MacDougall, Edward A., 57
Mackey, John, 116
MacNulty, A. C., 198
Maenner, Theodore H., 285
Magel, Bill, 276–277
Main, Gail, 232–235
"Make America Better" program, 164–165
Malls, 178
Mansell, Al, 101, 183, 184, 293
Manual of Multiple Listings, 216
Marin County Board of REALTORS® v. Palsson, 225
Marshall, Thurgood, 123
Martinez, Mel, 92
Maryland Association of REALTORS® Life Achievement Award, 117
McCully, Marshall, 39
McDermott, Terrence M., 279
McDonald, Walt, 16, 100, 237, 238, 293
McElvaine, Robert S., 172
McLain v. Real Estate Board of New Orleans, 236
McMillan, Charles, 294
Membership Marks Manual, 31
Mendenhall, Ed, 287

Mendenhall, Richard A., 65, 66, 68, 182, 225, 235, 249, 263, 265, 293
Merrion, Joseph, 90
Michonski, David, 269–270
Middle class, home ownership by, 35
Midwestern real estate boards meeting, 7
Midyear Legislative Meetings, 103
Miller, Barry, 239
Miller, William C., 283
Millett, Sharon A., 144, 145, 166, 239, 263, 292
Milligan, Kevin, 17
Milwaukee Real Estate Board, 274
Minneapolis Real Estate Board, 14, 27
Minority communities, outreach to, 133. *See also* Segregation
Minority markets, 134, 135–136
Mission Hills subdivision, 159
Mitchell, Clarence, Jr., 123
Mitchell, Fred B., 84
MLS policy, 224, 225. *See also* Multiple listing services (MLS)
MLS surveys, 217–224
Modern-housing movement, 88
Molinaro, Joe, 166, 167
Monticello, 71–72, 73
Moore, William M., 268, 291
Morrill, R. Layne, 204, 214, 241, 292
Morris, Richard B., 31, 288
Morse, R. Emmett, 216
Mortgage discount bank system, 49–54
Mortgage finance system, 87
Mortgage financing, 47
Mortgage interest deduction (MID), 81–83
Mortgage lending, 43–46
Mortgage revenue bonds, 65
Mortgages
    FHA, 51
    interest on, 42

Moscow conference, 270

Move.com, 257

"Mr. Blandings" model, 161, 162

Mrs. Murphy's Exemption, 123, 124

Multiple Listing Bureau, 216

Multiple Listing Committee, 216

Multiple listing services (MLS), 214–226, 249–252. *See also* MLS entries

  membership requirement, 225–226

Musicians Village, 185

Myles, Ron, 165, 166, 167, 180

N

NAR Action Center, 102. *See also* National Association of Realtors® (NAR)

NAR Convention Cities (1908-2007), 208–210

NAREB v. the Peninsula Real Estate Association, 27. *See also* National Association of Real Estate Brokers, Inc. (NAREB)

NAR meetings, presidential hopefuls at, 99

NAR Midyear Legislative Meetings, 103

Nashville Real Estate Board, 4

National Association of Home Builders (NAHB), 51, 74, 156, 213, 242

National Association of License Law Officials, 18, 198

National Association of Real Estate Boards, 19

  home ownership and, 35

National Association of Real Estate Brokers, Inc. (NAREB), 18, 24, 113, 130–131, 225, 275–276

National Association of Real Estate Exchanges, 41

  boards participating in 1908 organizing meeting, 10

  Code of Ethics of, 14

early priorities of, 11–18

federated structure of, 11–13

founding of, 1

members of, 15

National Association of Realtors® (NAR), 10. *See also* NAR entries

affiliates/divisions of, 211–213

African Americans and, 107

chief executives of, 274–279

City Planning Committee of, 164

civic duty of, 84–85

Code of Ethics of, 109, 110, 112, 198–204

commercial division of, 180

community planning roles of, 147, 165

community service by, 182–186

disaster-relief efforts of, 16

fair housing and, 136–137

favorable real estate tax treatment lobbied by, 79

first organizing meeting of, 3

founding of, 1

growth of, 16, 18

home ownership and, 35

international role of, 262–273

Internet strategy of, 256–260, 261

Land Developers and Home Builders Division of, 73, 74

leadership of, 235

legal action program of, 231

Licensing Committee of, 19

membership growth of, 65

membership in, 54

new capital building of, 104–105

1961 Philadelphia meeting, 31

in presidential campaigns, 99

progression of, 192–279

Research Department studies, 60

role in economy, 41

Smart Growth Program of, 166–167

strengthening of the real estate market and, 22

strength of, 102–103

Washington presence of, 83–103

National Committee Against Discrimination in Housing, 112

National Historic Preservation Act, 75

National Home Show Advisory Bureau, 55

National Housing Act of 1934, 51

National mortgage bank system, 41

National mortgage discount bank, 87

National Museum of American History, 68

National organizations

  early attempts at, 4–5

  early enthusiasm for, 6–7

  primary duties of, 8

National Real Estate Association, 4–6

  collapse of, 6

  1892 Nashville meeting of, 5

National Real Estate Fliers Association, 213

National Real Estate Foundation for Practical Research and Education, 57

National Real Estate Journal, The, 13, 19, 26, 53, 55–56, 197, 205

National Realtors® Database System, 258

Nation of Realtors, A: A Cultural History of the Twentieth-Century American Middle Class (Hornstein), 25, 35, 154, 141

Nelson, Herbert Undeen, 17, 49, 50, 53, 89, 90, 156, 216, 229, 275

"Net listing" agreement system, 227

New Deal program, 50

New Orleans Metropolitan Association of Realtors®, 44

New Orleans Real Estate Board, 44

Newspaper advertising, 246

New Urbanism movement, 76–77

New York, zoning in, 170

New York Real Estate Exchange, 4

Nichols, Jesse Clyde, 57, 152, 154, 155, 156, 158–163

  as a "new urbanist" pioneer, 163

Nixon, Richard Milhous, 93, 164

North, William D., 17, 27, 112, 122–123, 124, 179, 198, 199, 204, 224, 277–278

Northwest Ordinance of 1787, 37. *See also* Ordinance of 1785

Nutter, C. Armel, 287

O

Oak Park Housing Center, 124

Ohio Association of Realtors®, 97

Okamoto, Allen, 134

On Common Ground, 167

One Realtor Place®, 258

Open housing movement, 133–135

"Operation Home Delivery," 185, 186

Ordinance of 1785, 37. *See also* Northwest Ordinance of 1787

Ostendorf, Edgar L., 284

Overacre, Bill, 203

"Own a Home" campaign, 85

"Own Your Home" campaign, 44–45

P

Panic of 1837, 37

Panic of 1893, 6, 40

Panic of 1907, 40

"Paralysis in Government" (PING) campaign, 98

Partnerships, World Wide Web of, 262–267

Passwords and Prejudice (North), 124

Patent Office Trademark Trial and Appeal Board, 28

Pending Home Sales Index, 61, 67

Perego, Grace, 141, 142

Permanence, planning for, 159–163

Philadelphia Real Estate Board, 169

Philippine Association of Real Estate Boards, 264

Piper, Walter C., 280

Planned communities, 75

Planning
language and methods of, 151–164
reform of, 149

"Planning for permanence," 159–163

Planning Small Houses, 73

Plessy v. Ferguson, 107, 115

Poland, real estate symposium in, 269–270

Political Action Committees (PACs), 91–102
REALTORS® involved in, 79

Political objectives, achieving, 85

Politics, REALTORS® and, 78–105

Pontius, H. Jackson (Jack), 216, 267, 276

Portland (Maine) Real Estate Association, 7

Port, Rich, 95, 191, 231, 288

Potter, Hugh, 52, 57, 283

Powell, O. G. (Bill), 287

Prairie-style homes, 72, 73

Preemption Act of 1841, 37

Presidential Advisory Group on Agency (PAG), 239, 240, 241

Presidential Advisory Group on Code of Ethics Enforcement, 204

Presidential Advisory Group on the Facilitator/ Non-Agency Concept, 239–240

Price-fixing, 227–237

Princess Park Florida subdivision, 153

Principles of Real Estate Law (MacChesney), 23

Pritchard, Ralph W., 263, 265, 290

Private Property Week, 63, 64

Professional Standards Committee, 202, 203, 204

Progress of Women in Real Estate: 50th Anniversary, Women's Council of REALTORS® (Chapralis), 143

Property condition disclosure law, 243–245

Property listings, 249. *See also* Multiple listing services (MLS)

Property Owners' Bill of Rights, 118

Property rights, 95
activists for, 267–268

Proposition 14, 122, 125, 126

Public Awareness Campaign, 67

Public housing, 90, 114, 164

Public Works Administration, 172

Q

"Quadrennial ethics training," 204

Questions and Answers on Real Estate (Semenow), 195

R

Racial Policies and Practices of Real Estate Brokers (Helper), 115

Racial turnover, 115

Racism. *See* Segregation

Ranch homes, 73–75

Rate schedules, 227–229

RCA Report, 181

RCS-MLS, 252. *See also* Multiple listing services (MLS)

Read, Maurice, 288

Reagan, Ronald Wilson, 63, 98, 132

Real estate
exchanges, 214
fraud in, 14
specialization in, 18
women in, 138–145

Real Estate Achievement in the United States (Davies), 9

Real Estate Association of New York State, 6

Real Estate Board Operation Manual, 33

Real estate brokers, black, 113

Real estate business/industry
economic impact of, 193

evolution/progression of, 18–21, 192–279
technological progress in, 246–260

Real Estate Buyer's Agent Council (REBAC), 212, 240–241, 239, 261

Real estate dealers, unscrupulous, 3, 4

Real estate firms, testing of, 128

Real Estate in American History (Davies), 25, 40, 181, 198

Real Estate Insider, 231–236

Real estate investment trusts (REITs), 180–181

Real estate licensees, standard of care for, 243

Real estate license legislation, 23, 195–198

Real estate market index, 60

Real estate ownership, benefits of, 41

Real Estate Political Education Committee (REPEC), 91, 97

Real estate practitioners. *See also* REALTOR® entries
as leaders, 9
local organizations of, 4

Real Estate Securities and Syndications Institute, 213

Real estate services, transparency in, 238

Real Estate Settlement Procedures Act (RESPA), 92, 127, 237–238

Real estate "sharks," 3, 8

Real Estate Today, 205, 254

Real estate transactions, laws and regulations governing, 4

"Realology," 154

Realtists, 130–131

REALTOR-ASSOCIATE®, 16, 30

REALTOR® Certificate, 26

REALTOR.com, 257, 261

"REALTOR® confederacy" model, 16

REALTOR® Electronic Commerce Network, 258

REALTOR: Its Meaning and Use, 27, 32

REALTOR® logo, 94–95. *See also* REALTOR® trademark
rules for, 30

REALTOR® Magazine, 16, 205

REALTOR® marks, misuse of, 28–30. *See also* REALTOR® trademark

REALTOR.org, 29, 205, 258–259

REALTORS®
favorable real estate tax treatment lobbied by, 79
as good neighbors, 187–189
government relations among, 78–105
political clout of, 79, 81–83
as real estate professionals, 16

REALTORS® Association of New Mexico, 167

REALTORS® Commercial Alliance (RCA), 181

REALTORS® Conference & Expo, 206, 207, 265

REALTORS® Housing Relief Fund, 182–183, 187

REALTORS® Information Network (RIN), 256

REALTORS® Land Institute, 212

REALTORS® Political Action Committee (RPAC), 16, 94, 96–97
contributions to, 102
fund-raising by, 100

REALTORS'® Washington Committee, 89, 95

REALTORS® Week, 58–63

REALTOR® trademark. *See also* REALTOR® logo
coining of, 14, 20, 21
correct use in dictionaries, 30–31
court challenges to, 27–28
defense of, 25–28
dollar value of, 33
guidance for use of, 29–30

history of, 24–33
on Internet social networking sites, 31–32
pronunciation of, 32
registration of, 27
as a term of distinction, 24–33
Realtrix, 29
Reason Public Policy Institute report, 149–151
Reaume, Leonard P., 49, 263, 282
"Redlining," 111, 113
Reece, J. D., 163
RELO network, 220–221
RE/MAX, 232–235
Residential Brokerage Industry report, 238
Residential landscape, early-twentieth-century, 109
"Restrictive covenants," 111–113, 162–163
Retirement communities, 75, 76
Rich, Jill, 187
Righeimer, Jim, 99
Riley v. Chambers, 196
Rise of the Community Builders, The (Weiss), 151–152
Roberts, David D., Sr., 238, 264, 268, 290
Robinson, Frank, 116
Rockhill Park subdivision, 158
Roman v. Lobe, 197
Roosevelt, Franklin Delano, 35, 45, 46, 49–50
Roosevelt, Theodore, 11
Rosenthal, Richard, 104
Rosenwald, Julius, 47
Rose, Walter W., 17, 283
Roth, Leland, 73, 76
Rouda, Harley E., 239, 243–245, 291

S

Salt Lake City Board, 29
San Antonio Real Estate Exchange, 17

San Diego Real Estate Exchange, 214
Savings and loan crisis, 180
Sawyer, John D., 93, 94–95, 289
Schmidt, Walter S., 54–57, 283
Schwemm, Bob, 125
Scott, Walter, 202
Scully, Thomas, 27, 31
Segregation, housing, 91, 106–137
Self-testing, 128–129
Seller disclosure laws, 244–245
Semenow, Robert W., 195, 198
Seniors Real Estate Specialist (SRES) program, 241
SentriLock lockbox technology, 259
September 11, 2001 terrorist attacks, 182–183
Servicemen's Readjustment Act of 1944, 53
Shallcross, Thomas, Jr., 280
Sharkey, Marilyn, 142
Shattuck, Charles B., 286
Sheehan, Daniel F., Sr., 287
Shelley v. Kraemer, 112, 113
Sherman, Malcolm, 116–117
Shopping centers, 178
Sibley, Frank J., 99, 187
Siegel, Stuart, 189
SIMA Showcase, 266
Simpson, Charles L., 280
Simpson, David B., 284
Single-family homes, 73–77
6 percent commission, 230
Skyscrapers, 169
Slum clearance programs, 174
Slums, growth of, 113–114
Smaby, Philip C., 263, 264–265, 289
Smart-growth movement, 147, 151
principles of, 166–167
Smart Growth Network, 166, 167
Smart Growth Presidential Advisory Group, 166
Smart Growth Program, 137
NAR, 166–167

Smith, Almon, 252, 255, 256, 278–279
Smith, Chesley J., 198
Smith, Nancy Wilson, 125
Snyder, Harley W., 290
Socialism, threat of, 42
Society of Industrial REALTORS®, 94, 173
Society of Industrial and Office REALTORS®, 212
South Asian tsunami, 183, 184
Southern Pine Association, 44
Spera, Pall D., 238
Split-level house, 75
Standards of Practice, 205
Stark, Paul E., 51, 284
Staro, Chuck, 99
Stevens, Thomas M., 185, 226, 238, 260, 293
Stevenson, Lawrence T., 283
Stinton, Dale A., 95, 104, 279
Stoll, Edwin L., 29, 31
St. Paul Real Estate Board, 19
"Strike forces," political, 83
Subdividers, 152, 154–155
Subdivisions, 155
Suburbs, 73. *See also* Urban entries
development of, 59, 178–179
as the new frontier, 172
Summer, Alexander, 286
Sun City active adult retirement community, 75, 76
Sunset Park, 70
Supreme Court, 107
Survey panels, NAR, 60

T

Taxation, REALTORS® and, 79. *See also* Federal tax credit; Flat tax; Income tax
Tax issue tool kits, 83
Tax Reform Act of 1986, 179, 180–181

Tax relief, 98
Taylor, Alexander S., 280
Taylor, Durand (Duke), 28–29
Taylor, Frederick Earle, 46, 281
Taylor, John, 162–163
Taylor, Zachary, 70
Teardown trend, 76
Telephone technology, 252–253
Terrorist attacks, 182–183
"Testing," 128
Thompson v. Metropolitan Multi, 225
Thorpe, Samuel Skidmore, 13, 17, 262, 280
"Three-way agreement," 13, 16–17
Today's REALTOR®, 205, 245
Town houses/homes, 71, 79
Trademark Act of 1946, 26
Traditional Neighborhood Design, 76–77
Treadwell, Donald H., 202, 290
Tsunami, 183, 184
Tucker, Fred C. (Bud), Jr., 94, 289
Turley, Clarence M., Sr., 286

U

Udall, James M., 287
UN Centre for Human Settlements (UN-Habitat), 267. *See also* UN-Habitat World Conference
Underwood, Fred, 128, 129, 134
Underwriting Manual (FHA), 111, 156
UN-Habitat World Conference, 272. *See also* UN Centre for Human Settlements (UN-Habitat)
United States. *See* American entries; Federal entries; Government entries; National entries; Presidential entries; U.S. entries; White House Minority Homeownership Initiative
United States v. National Association of Real Estate Boards, et al., 229

UNIVAC, 250

Upham, Nathaniel J., 17, 281

Upton, Dell, 73

Urban areas, growth of, 168–176

Urban decay, solutions to, 164–165

Urban Land Institute (ULI), 18, 57, 156, 163, 172, 213

Urban redevelopment, 156–164

Urban renewal programs, 174, 179

USAID, 270, 271

U.S. cities, growth of, 5. *See also* Urban entries

U.S. Commission on Civil Rights, 119

U.S. Declaration of Independence, 108

U.S. Department of Housing and Urban Development (HUD), 92, 125, 124, 126. *See also* HUD/ NAR partnership

U.S. Department of Justice. *See* Justice Department investigations

U.S. Housing Authority, 88

U.S. Supreme Court, 107

V

van Vlissingen, Peter, 3

Ventura County Coastal Association of Realtors®, 167

Vienna Recommendations, 267–268

Voice for Real Estate®, 101

Voluntary Affirmative Marketing Agreement (VAMA), 125–128, 132, 276

von Hoffman, Alexander, 114, 124, 133

W

Wallace, Clark W., 179, 291

Waltemade, Henry G., 286

Warranty programs, 242

Washington operations, reforms to, 92

Weaver, John Lowrie, 85, 281

Webb, Del, 75, 76

Wechsler, A. S., 198

Weigand, Nestor R., Jr., 263, 278, 291

Weil, Benjamin M., 169

Weiss, Marc A., 151–152

Westrom, John A., 216

Whatley, Catherine B. (Cathy), 35, 67, 100, 144, 196, 293

What Women Realtors® Are Doing, 142

"White City" exposition complex, 7

White House Minority Homeownership Initiative, 66

Wiktionary.org, 32

Wilcox, Arthur P., 287

Willaman, Glenn, 17

Willis, Florence (Posie), 221

Willmore, Cyrus C., 284

Wilson, Woodrow, 79, 86

"Within These Walls…" exhibition, 68–69

Wolff, Stuart, 257

Woman Realtor, The, 138

Women in real estate, 138–145 influence in the home buying market, 144–145

Women's Council of Realtors®, 138–139, 141, 142, 212

Wood, John R., 98, 290

Woods, Edmund, Jr., 81, 83

Woods, Gill, 292

WorldProperties.com, 267

World War I, 84–85 real estate market after, 42, 44, 79 war property effort during, 83–86

World War II, homebuilding during, 51–55

Worldwide ERC, 213

World Wide Web, 254

Worley, William S., 161

Wright, Cora Ella, 140, 142

Wright, Frank Lloyd, 72, 73

Wright, Richard, 107

Wright, Thomas T., 4

Z

Zander, Henry G, 282

Zimmerman, Jacob, 28

Zimmerman, Shea, 103

Zimmerman v. NAR, 28

Zoning, 43, 155 of commercial districts, 169–170